Belief Functions in Business Decisions

Studies in Fuzziness and Soft Computing

Editor-in-chief
Prof. Janusz Kacprzyk
Systems Research Institute
Polish Academy of Sciences
ul. Newelska 6
01-447 Warsaw, Poland
E-mail: kacprzyk@ibspan.waw.pl
http://www.springer.de/cgi-bin/search_book.pl?series=2941

Further volumes of this series can be found at our homepage.

Vol. 66. R.J. Howlett and L.C. Jain (Eds.)
Radial Basis Function Networks 1, 2001
ISBN 3-7908-1367-2

Vol. 67. R.J. Howlett and L.C. Jain (Eds.)
Radial Basis Function Networks 2, 2001
ISBN 3-7908-1368-0

Vol. 68. A. Kandel, M. Last and H. Bunke (Eds.)
Data Mining and Computational Intelligence, 2001
ISBN 3-7908-1371-0

Vol. 69. A. Piegat
Fuzzy Modeling and Control, 2001
ISBN 3-7908-1385-0

Vol. 70. W. Pedrycz (Ed.)
Granular Computing, 2001
ISBN 3-7908-1387-7

Vol. 71. K. Leiviskä (Ed.)
Industrial Applications of Soft Computing, 2001
ISBN 3-7908-1388-5

Vol. 72. M. Mareš
Fuzzy Cooperative Games, 2001
ISBN 3-7908-1392-3

Vol. 73. Y. Yoshida (Ed.)
Dynamical Aspects in Fuzzy Decision, 2001
ISBN 3-7908-1397-4

Vol. 74. H.-N. Teodorescu, L.C. Jain and A. Kandel (Eds.)
Hardware Implementation of Intelligent Systems, 2001
ISBN 3-7908-1399-0

Vol. 75. V. Loia and S. Sessa (Eds.)
Soft Computing Agents, 2001
ISBN 3-7908-1404-0

Vol. 76. D. Ruan, J. Kacprzyk and M. Fedrizzi (Eds.)
Soft Computing for Risk Evaluation and Management, 2001
ISBN 3-7908-1406-7

Vol. 77. W. Liu
Propositional, Probabilistic and Evidential Reasoning, 2001
ISBN 3-7908-1414-8

Vol. 78. U. Seiffert and L.C. Jain (Eds.)
Self-Organizing Neural Networks, 2002
ISBN 3-7908-1417-2

Vol. 79. A. Osyczka
Evolutionary Algorithms for Single and Multicriteria Design Optimization, 2002
ISBN 3-7908-1418-0

Vol. 80. P. Wong, F. Aminzadeh and M. Nikravesh (Eds.)
Soft Computing for Reservoir Characterization and Modeling, 2002
ISBN 3-7908-1421-0

Vol. 81. V. Dimitrov and V. Korotkich (Eds.)
Fuzzy Logic, 2002
ISBN 3-7908-1425-3

Vol. 82. Ch. Carlsson and R. Fullér
Fuzzy Reasoning in Decision Making and Optimization, 2002
ISBN 3-7908-1428-8

Vol. 83. S. Barro and R. Marín (Eds.)
Fuzzy Logic in Medicine, 2002
ISBN 3-7908-1429-6

Vol. 84. L.C. Jain and J. Kacprzyk (Eds.)
New Learning Paradigms in Soft Computing, 2002
ISBN 3-7908-1436-9

Vol. 85. D. Rutkowska
Neuro-Fuzzy Architectures and Hybrid Learning, 2002
ISBN 3-7908-1438-5

Vol. 86. M.B. Gorzałczany
Computational Intelligence Systems and Applications, 2002
ISBN 3-7908-1439-3

Vol. 87. C. Bertoluzza, M.Á. Gil and D.A. Ralescu (Eds.)
Statistical Modeling, Analysis and Management of Fuzzy Data, 2002
ISBN 3-7908-1440-7

Rajendra P. Srivastava
Theodore J. Mock
Editors

Belief Functions in Business Decisions

With 23 Figures
and 57 Tables

Springer-Verlag Berlin Heidelberg GmbH

Professor Rajendra P. Srivastava
Ernst & Young Professor and Director
Ernst & Young Center for Auditing Research and Advanced Technology
The University of Kansas
School of Business
1300 Sunnyside Avenue
Lawrence, KS 66045
USA
rsrivastava@ku.edu

Professor Theodore J. Mock
Arthur Andersen Alumni Professor
University of Southern California
Laventhal School of Accounting
Los Angeles, CA 90089
USA
tmock@marshall.usc.edu

ISSN 1434-9922

DOI 10.1007/978-3-7908-1798-0

Cataloging-in-Publication Data applied for
Die Deutsche Bibliothek – CIP-Einheitsaufnahme
Belief functions in business decisions: with 57 tables / Rajendra P. Srivastava; Theodore J. Mock, ed. – Heidelberg; New York: Physica-Verl., 2002
(Studies in fuzziness and soft computing; Vol. 88)

Originally published by Physica-Verlag Heidelberg in 2002
MyCopy version of the original edition 2002

Hardcover Design: Erich Kirchner, Heidelberg
www.springer.com/mycopy

Preface

We are pleased to edit the book "Belief Functions in Business Decisions." The purpose of this book is to compile research being conducted in the area of business decisions using belief functions. The book is published as a volume under the series "Studies in Fuzziness and Soft Computing" by Physica-Verlag (A Springer-Verlag Company). We wish to thank the publisher, and in particular Professor J. Kacprzyk, Consulting Editor, for his encouragement and support.

We were very fortunate to have an enthusiastic response to our call for papers for this volume and sincerely thank our authors for their contributions. This book would not have become a reality if it were not for their contributions.

The diverse nature of belief functions applications to business decisions posed a challenge for us to find reviewer's for the contributed articles. We sincerely appreciate the efforts by the reviewers in providing constructive and timely criticism of the papers. In particular, we would like to thank and acknowledge the valuable help provided by the following reviewers: Keith Harrison, J-Y. Jaffray, Juerg Kohlas, Philippe Smets, and Prakash Shenoy. Finally, we would like to thank our families, in particular our wives, Madhuri Srivastava and Mary Jo Mock, for their understanding and support during the compilation process.

This book is divided into three parts. The first part deals with the foundations of belief functions and contains three chapters. The first chapter discusses the basics of belief functions and is contributed by the editors. The main objective of this chapter is to introduce the intuitive and conceptual aspects of belief functions. It also provides examples of applications of belief functions in the auditing domain. One important observation is that uncertainty encountered in audit evidence is modeled more conveniently in belief functions than in the probability framework. This chapter complements the paper by Philippe Smets presented in Chapter 2. Smets has done a superb job in providing a comprehensive treatment of belief functions from its historical developments to its various interpretations. He also discusses how one can make decisions under the belief-function framework in the traditional sense of maximizing utilities. He illustrates this process for two interpretations of belief functions: the transferable belief function model (TBM) and upper and lower probabilities. The third chapter "Empirical Models for the Dempster-Shafer Theory" by M. A. Klopotek, S. T. Wierzchon investigates three different interpretations of belief functions: the marginally correct approximation, the qualitative model, and the quantitative model. Another unique feature of their presentation is that they use rough set theory and structured query language (SQL) to express the semantics of belief functions. This chapter will be especially useful if one is interested in managing uncertainties in databases.

Part 2 on "Systems and Auditing Applications" contains four chapters. The first chapter on "The Descriptive Ability of Models of Audit Risk" is contributed by G. Monroe and J. Ng. The audit risk model is used by the AICPA (American Institute of Certified Public Accountants) in the United States of America and by accounting professionals in other countries to plan the audit of the financial statements of a company. In this chapter the authors discuss their empirical findings where auditors are asked to make judgment about audit risk using their intuition and compare this with the value generated by various models. Interestingly, their findings indicate that there is no statistical difference between the auditor's intuitive assessments and the values generated by the belief function model.

The second chapter compares the effectiveness and efficiency of audit procedures using three different approaches. Here, M. K. P. Jung and H. E. Fink report the results of simulation experiments of determining audit risk in complex situations. They find that the "belief based audit is always more efficient than a simple one and can be less efficient than the traditional approach." They also contend that the belief-based approach is the most effective among the three models used.

K. Harrison, R. Srivastava, and D. Plumlee contribute the third chapter, which deals with auditors' assessment of the strength of audit evidence. Importantly, they find that a statistically significant percentage of the auditors represented their estimates in ways that were consistent with belief functions and were inconsistent with Bayesian probabilities.

Peter Gillett contributes chapter 4 of this part. His paper deals with concepts of conflict and nonspecificity under belief functions. He contends, "assessing this conflict can be important for the strategic choices of whether to seek additional evidence or to discount or retract existing evidence, and which beliefs to retract." He further contends: "it is important to consider not just the external conflict between beliefs, but the internal conflict within belief functions arising from masses assigned to non-intersecting focal elements." He discusses six measures of conflict: two that apply only to separable belief functions, and that require the canonical decomposition to be found, and four based on extensions of the entropy concept. Finally, he discusses a method for using conflict to decide which of a set of beliefs to retract (or discount). He uses a missile defense context to illustrate the concepts.

The third part of the book deals with application of belief functions to operations management, finance and economics. This part has five chapters. The first chapter illustrates an example of evidential reasoning in a merger and acquisition decision when uncertainties are represented in terms of belief functions. In the paper, Srivastava and Datta take an expert system approach of evidential reasoning where the network of evidence, variables, and their interrelationships are obtained from an expert. This is the first application of belief functions in the area of mergers and acquisitions. R. Jirousek, J. Vejnarova, and J. Gemela describe a new way of defining possibilistic belief networks as a sequence of low-dimensional distributions connected by operators of composition. In order to make this approach more comprehensible, they introduce an extended motivation part explaining the basic notions through a simple example. They conclude the paper by providing a detailed example of an application of the apparatus for financial analysis of engineering enterprises. The third chapter by P. McBurney and S. Parsons deals with using belief functions to forecast demand for mobile satellite services. They contend that forecasting demand for a new product or service is always difficult and it is even more difficult when the product category itself is new and unfamiliar to potential consumers. Also, the unknown nature of the impact of technology on product quality and service quality makes it even more difficult to forecast demand. They find that belief functions provide a means of representing and combining varied beliefs for forecasting demand, which is more expressive than traditional point probability estimates.

Chapter 4 of Part 3 on "Modeling Financial Portfolios Using belief Functions" is contributed by C. Shenoy and S. Shenoy. The main objective of their paper is to demonstrate how the theory of belief functions can be used to model financial portfolios. In particular, they show how to model portfolio changes as new information becomes available about different factors that influence individual stocks or a portfolio. Finally, Don Lien provides an application of belief functions in economics. He discusses the relationship between Knightian uncertainty and belief functions and provides an illustration of a futures hedging decision under Knightian uncertainty.

Rajendra Srivastava, Lawrence, Kansas

Theodore J. Mock, Rancho Palos Verdes, California

Contents

Introduction to Belief Functions[1]

Rajendra P. Srivastava* and Theodore J. Mock**

*University of Kansas, **University of Southern California

1. Introduction

The refusal to choose is a form of choice; Disbelief is a form of belief. -Frank Barron

This chapter introduces a theoretical perspective that may be used in business research and practice when confronting decision tasks that involve uncertainly. The main body of the chapter is an introduction to Belief Functions. The introduction includes a discussion of the fundamental constructs and then illustrates the use of belief functions in a business (audit) setting.

Human decision-making is a complex process, especially in situations where significant ambiguity exists. Ambiguity and uncertainty are inherent characteristics of tasks in all disciplines whether it is accounting, auditing, business, law, or medicine. The primary objective of this chapter is to introduce some important aspects of belief formulation within a business decision context.

There are two major issues when it comes to dealing with belief formulation under ambiguity and uncertainty. In general, uncertainty deals with situations where one is not sure about the outcome of an event. For example, consider an urn with 100 balls, 50 red and 50 black. If one is considering the event of drawing a ball from the urn, the outcome of whether the color would be red or black is uncertain (not sure).

The first issue deals with the framework that can be used to express or measure uncertainty and ambiguity present in such task settings. Shafer and Tversky (1985) and Shafer and Srivastava (1990) describe this process of choosing a framework as a process of choosing a "formal language" or "semantics" to express the uncertainties in analyzing a task. They argue that the context and the domain of

---

[1] Based on Srivastava and Mock 2000. Belief Functions in Accounting Behavioral Research. *Advances in Accounting Behavioral Research*, Vol. 3: 225-242.

the problem determine what language is appropriate. This chapter introduces one language and set of notation that is appropriate.

The second issue deals with the calculus or "syntax" (Shafer and Tversky 1985) through which information is combined to make a judgment or decision. There are many frameworks and formal languages that can be used to represent uncertainties such as those based on probability theory, fuzzy logic, possibility theory (Zadeh 1978, 1979), belief functions (Shafer 1976, Smets 1990a, 1990b, 1998, Yager et. al 1994), and epistemic belief functions (Spohn 1990, 1998). These frameworks have different characteristics and thus seem to "work better" in certain problem domains rather than in other domains.

As illustrated in this book, belief functions provide a flexible and adaptable way to combine evidence from a variety of sources. One aspect of this flexibility is that the belief function framework reduces to the Bayesian framework under a special condition (Shafer and Srivastava 1990).

Importantly, belief functions provide a superior way of mapping uncertainty judgments and for incorporating ambiguity within the decision-making process (Srivastava 1997a)[2]. For example, suppose an auditor has obtained and assessed audit risk factors (*inherent factors*) for a client such as its business environment, its economic condition, and the CEO's honesty and integrity. Assume that all of these factors provide positive evidence to the auditor that the financial statements are fairly stated. Based on this, the auditor could attribute a low level of support, say 0.2 on a scale of 0-1, that the financial statements are fairly stated, a zero level of support that the financial statements are materially misstated, and a 0.8 level of uncommitted support. Such a representation of uncertainty is difficult under the probability framework, as it is unclear as to how the uncommitted support (the ambiguity) should be treated.

Thus an advantage of using belief functions in business is that it provides a more natural and logical way to model ambiguity compared to the Classical probability framework. To further illustrate this point, let us consider the urn example introduced earlier. Consider a situation with two urns. Urn One has 100 balls, 50 red and 50 black. The outcome of whether the color of a ball drawn from Urn One is red or black is uncertain, but quantifiable. Given only two possible outcomes (red or black) with equal likelihood (50 red and 50 black balls), one can make a judgment that each outcome has a 50-50 chance of occurring.

Ambiguity deals with those situations of uncertainty where one is not able to quantify a judgment about the chance of each outcome occurring. For example,

---

[2] See chapter 2.4: "Auditors' Evaluation of Uncertain Audit Evidence" and also Harrison 1999.

suppose you have a second urn (Urn Two) with 100 balls of red or black color, but the proportion of red and black balls is not known. It may be in any proportion, from all being red to all being black. Einhorn and Hogarth (1986) call the situation of Urn One a situation of complete knowledge and the situation of Urn Two a situation of complete ambiguity.

Under the probability framework, one often assumes uniform priors in situations of ambiguity such as Urn Two. Thus in either situation, using the probability framework, one would assign 0.5 that a drawn ball would be red or black. This feature of the probability framework of not being able to distinguish between the two urns has led Einhorn and Hogarth (1986, p. S228) to a paradoxical conclusion based on observed behaviors of subjects:

> ... either urn 2 has complementary probabilities that sum to more than one, or urn 1 has complementary probabilities that sum to less than one. As we will show, the nonadditivity of complementary probabilities is central to judgments under ambiguity.

Srivastava (1997a) has shown that *no such super- or sub-additivity is needed to explain the decision maker's behavior* if belief functions are used to treat ambiguity.

Thus the main purposes of this chapter are to introduce belief functions and then to consider their application to decision-making in an auditing task. We first introduce belief functions and discuss how belief functions help to overcome certain problems inherent in the use of probabilities.

2. Introduction To Belief Functions

The belief-function formalism has its origin in the seventeenth century work of George Hooper and James Bernoulli (Shafer 1976, Gabbay and Smets 1998, Shafer and Srivastava 1990, Smets 1998, 1990a, 1990b, and Yager et. al 1994). It is based on the mathematical theory of probability and it reduces to the Bayesian formalism under a special condition, as discussed later. There are three basic functions that are important to understand the use of belief functions in a decision-making process: *basic belief mass functions* or m-values, *belief functions,* and *plausibility functions*.

Basic Belief Mass Function (m-values)

The *basic belief mass*[3] function (or m-values) is similar to the probability function. Consider an example to illustrate the properties of this function. Consider a decision problem with ***n*** possible elements or states of nature forming a mutually exclusive and exhaustive set represented by $\{a_1, a_2, a_3, \ldots a_n\}$. Call this set a *frame* and represent it by the symbol Θ. Under the probability framework, probabilities are assigned to each state of nature and these probabilities must add to one. More specifically, the probability mass assigned to each state of nature, a_i, is $P(a_i) \geq 0$ where $i = 1, 2, \ldots n$ and the sum of all these probabilities is equal to one, i.e.,

$$\sum_{i=1}^{n} P(a_i) \quad .$$

Under the belief function framework, basic belief masses or m-values are assigned not only to each state of nature but also to all possible combinations of these states of nature. For example, m-values are assigned to all the single elements, to all the subsets consisting two elements, three elements, and so on, and to the entire frame Θ. Similar to probabilities, these m-values add to one, i.e., $\sum_{A \subseteq \Theta} m(A)$, where A represents all the subsets of the frame. We will consider Shafer's belief-function framework where the basic belief mass assigned to the empty set is zero by definition[4].

Consider an auditing example to help us understand the basic concepts of m-values. Suppose an auditor has performed certain ratio and trend analyses pertinent to the stated accounts receivable balance and has decided that the analyses provide a positive but low level of belief, say 0.2 on a scale of 0 - 1, that the account balance is fairly stated. If the state that the accounts receivables balance is fairly stated is represented by 'a' and the state that the account balance is materially misstated by '~a' then, based on the evidence obtained, we have the following *basic belief masses*, i.e., m-values: m(a) = 0.2, m(~a) = 0, and m({a, ~a}) = 0.8, and the sum is one.

In an audit context, one can interpret these m-values as the level of support directly obtained from the evidence for the argument of the m-value function. For the above example, we have direct ratio and trend analysis evidence that the account is fairly stated with 0.2 level of belief, no belief that the account is materially misstated, and 0.8 belief still uncommitted. This 0.8 is assigned to the

---

[3] Shafer calls this function the *basic probability assignment* function.

[4] Under Transferable Belief Functions of Smets (1990a, 1998), one can assign a non-zero mass to the empty set.

entire frame Θ = {a, ~a}. Note that in this example, the evidence is "positive" in that it supports the hypothesis that the accounts receivable is fairly stated.

A negative piece of evidence is represented by a finite (non-zero) belief mass assigned to '~a' that the account is materially misstated. Suppose that the ratio and trend analyses signal that the account balance may be materially misstated but with a low level of support, say 0.1, for ~a and no evidence that the account balance is fairly stated. This situation can be written as: m(a) = 0, m(~a) = 0.1, and m({a, ~a}) = 0.9.

Mixed audit evidence can be expressed by assigning some basic belief mass to 'a', some to '~a', and some to the entire frame Θ = {a, ~a}. An example of mixed evidence is where part of the support, say 0.2, is for 'a', 0.1 for '~a', and the remaining, 0.7 is assigned to {a, ~a}. In terms of m-values, one can express this evidence as: m(a) = 0.2, m(~a) = 0.1, and m({a, ~a}) = 0.7. This kind of evidence is not easy to model under the probability framework.

There are two ways one can assess these basic belief masses or m-values. The first is through the decision maker's subjective judgment as illustrated above. This judgment could be based on experience or on other knowledge. The second approach is based on an assumed *compatibility relationship* between two frames (see Figure 1).

Figure 1: Assumed Compatibility Relationships Between Two Frames, {t, ~t} and {c, ~c} (Srivastava and Mock 2000. p 230).

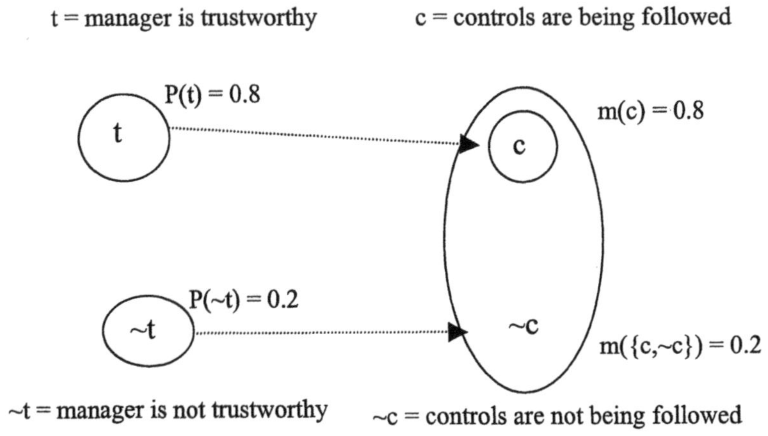

Belief Function

Belief on a set of elements, say, A of a frame Θ is defined as the total belief on A. This represents the sum of all the basic belief masses assigned to the elements contained in A plus the basic belief mass assigned to A. Mathematically this can be written as: $Bel(A) = \sum_{B \subseteq A} m(B$, where B is any subset of A.

Consider the example discussed earlier where the auditor has performed analytical procedures in testing the accounts receivable balance. Based on the audit findings, assume that the auditor concludes that the evidence provides a low level of support, say 0.2, that accounts receivable balance is fairly stated, no support for the account to be materially misstated, with 0.8 level of belief uncommitted. In terms of basic belief masses, one can write the auditor's judgment as: m(a) = 0.2, m(~a) = 0, and m({a, ~a}) = 0.8.

Using the definition of belief functions as described above, the belief that the accounts receivable is fairly stated is 0.2, belief that the account is materially misstated is 0, i.e., Bel(a) = 0.2, and Bel(~a) = 0. Also, we have a belief of one in the entire frame, i.e., Bel({a, ~a}) = 1.0. This value is obtained as follows. According to the definition, the belief in a set A, say A = {a, ~a}, is the sum of the basic belief masses on all the subsets contained in A, and the belief mass on the entire set A. In our example, this definition implies that the belief on {a, ~a}, Bel({a,~a}), is the sum of the basic belief masses on 'a', '~a', and {a, ~a}, i.e., the sum of m(a) = 0.2, m(~a) = 0, and m({a, ~a}) = 0.8, which is one in the present example.

Plausibility Function

The plausibility of an element or a set of elements, say A, of a frame, Θ, is defined to be the maximum possible belief that could be assigned to A if all future evidence were in support of A. Mathematically one can write plausibility as Pl(A) $= \sum_{A \cap B \neq \emptyset} m(B)$ Also, one can show that the plausibility function is related to the belief function through the following relationship: Pl(A) = 1- Bel(~A).

Consider the above example of analytical procedures with the basic belief masses: m(a) = 0.2, m(~a) = 0, and m({a, ~a}) = 0.8. This evidence provides a belief of 0.2 that the account is fairly presented. However, 0.8 level of belief which is assigned to the entire frame, {a, ~a}, is in principle uncommitted. In the best possible scenario, if new pieces of evidence provided only positive support, then all of this uncommitted belief could be assigned to 'a'. This provides the following value for plausibility of 'a': Pl(a) = 0.2 + 0.8 = 1.0. Similarly, in the other extreme case, if new pieces of evidence provided support to only '~a' then the uncommitted belief of 0.8 could be assigned to '~a' yielding a 0.8 level of plausibility for '~a', i.e., Pl(~a) = 0.8.

Ambiguity Function

In belief functions, the ambiguity in a state A is defined as the difference between the plausibility of A and the belief in A, i.e.,

$$\text{Ambiguity in A} = \text{Pl(A)} - \text{Bel(A)}$$

In the above example, the belief that the account is fairly stated in 0.2 and its plausibility is 1.0. Therefore, the ambiguity in 'a' that the account is fairly presented is 0.8 (Ambiguity in 'a' = Pl(a) – Bel(a) = 1.0 – 0.2 = 0.8). Similarly, the ambiguity in ~a is 0.8.

Consider also the example of two urns discussed earlier. Urn Two (Ambiguous) is the urn with 100 balls of black and red color with no knowledge of the proportion of red and black balls. Urn One is the urn with complete knowledge that it contains 100 balls of 50 red and 50 black colors. The belief mass that a red ball is picked from Urn Two is zero and similarly a belief mass that a black ball is picked is zero, i.e., m_2(red ball) = 0, and m_2(black ball) = 0 where the subscript represents the urn number. These values suggest that we have no direct evidence whether the ball picked will be of red or black color. The plausibility of picking a red ball would be one and similarly the plausibility of picking a black would be one. Thus, the ambiguity that the ball would be of red color is one (completely ambiguous) and so is the ambiguity that the ball would be of black color.

However, in the case of Urn One, the belief masses are: m_1(red ball) = 0.5, and m_1(black ball) = 0.5, and the corresponding beliefs and plausibilities are: Bel(red ball) = Bel(black ball) = 0.5, and Pl(red ball) = Pl(black ball) = 0.5. In this case the ambiguity that a red ball is picked is zero and the ambiguity that a black ball is picked is also zero. Under the belief-function framework we see that the two urns are represented very differently.

3. Illustration of the Use of Belief Functions in Auditing

In business studies, research that considers uncertainly is rarely useful unless it can be applied to specific tasks. In this section we discuss two audit applications. The applications deal with the planning and evaluation of an audit as discussed by Srivastava and Shafer (1992) and Srivastava et. al (1996).

The audit risk model of SAS 47 (AICPA 1983) has been proposed to be a framework that can be used for planning an audit. The audit risk model introduced in SAS 47 is AR = IR×CR×DR, where AR is the risk that the auditor gives an opinion that the financial statements are fairly stated, but the financial statements may contain material misstatements. IR, CR, and DR are respectively inherent risk, control risk and detection risk. SAS 47 suggests that if the auditor does not want to depend on the environmental factors, then he should set IR to one and plan the audit based on the assessed control risk and planned detection risk. Under the probability framework, IR = 1 implies that the auditor is assuming that there are material errors in the financial statement for sure, but that may not be what the auditor's thinking when he sets IR = 1. Under belief functions, setting IR = 1 during initial audit planning implies that plausibility of material errors present in the financial statements is one, however, there is no evidence in support or against the financial statements being fairly stated.

The audit risk model has been criticized on a number of grounds, including Srivastava and Shafer (1992) who argue that the risks in the model really imply plausibility of material misstatements instead of probability of material misstatements. They argue that the plausibility interpretation of the risks in the audit risk model makes intuitive sense. Our first example of the use of belief functions in auditing reviews this idea.

The external auditor plans the audit to be able to reach an opinion considering the possibility of existence of material errors in the financial statements. If no material misstatements are found and the evidence supports the opinion that the financial statements are fairly stated with a high level of confidence, say 0.95, then the auditor issues a *clean opinion*[5]. Given the earlier definition of plausibility, this implies that the plausibility of material misstatement is 0.05. This plausibility can be interpreted, as the maximum possible risk the auditor is willing to take that the financial statements might be materially misstated without giving a *qualified opinion*[6]. Note that this interpretation does not imply that there is any evidence in support of material misstatements.

The audit process is a process of collecting, evaluating, and aggregating evidence. Srivastava and Shafer (1992) have shown analytically how one can combine positive items of evidence accumulated with respect to various accounts within the balance sheet. Srivastava et. al (1996, see also Srivastava 1995a, 1995b) have

---

[5] The auditor can issue a number of possible opinions including a *clean opinion* meaning that the financial statements do not contain material misstatements.

[6] The auditor gives a *qualified opinion* when the evidence suggests that there is a material misstatement in one of the accounts of the financial statements but this misstatement is not so severe that it impacts the entire financial statements. In such a case the auditor would give an *adverse opinion*.

discussed the aggregation of evidence in a complex network of variables, where the variables are the balance sheet, the balance sheet accounts, and the audit objectives or the management assertions concerning the accounts. A network structure arises when one piece of evidence supports more than one audit objective or more than one account. For example, confirmations of accounts receivable provide evidence relevant to both the existence and valuation objectives of the account. We will demonstrate below through a simple example how two items of positive evidence can be combined in the belief-function framework.

Suppose that the auditor assesses a low level of belief, say 0.1 on a scale of 0–1, that the financial statements are fairly stated based on evidence concerning environmental factors, such as the economic conditions under which the client operates, the administrative style of the CEO, and the CEO's integrity. Assume there is no reason to believe that the financial statements are materially misstated given current economic conditions and a trustworthy CEO with integrity. Assume also that these inherent factors (IF) yield the following m-values: $m_{IF}(f) = 0.1$, $m_{IF}(\sim f) = 0$, and $m_{IF}(\{f,\sim f\}) = 0.9$, where 'f = financial statements are fairly stated', and '~f = financial statements are not fairly stated'.

Suppose the auditor collects additional evidence by performing analytical procedures, such as comparing this year's financial statement balances with last year's balances and computing various ratios. Assume that the auditor again assesses a low, but positive, level of support, say 0.2 on a scale of 0–1, that the financial statements are fairly stated based on this evidence. Assume also that the analytical procedures provide no reasons to believe that there is material misstatement in the financial statements. This judgment about analytical procedures (AP) may be expressed in terms of the following basic belief masses or m-values as: $m_{AP}(f) = 0.2$, $m_{AP}(\sim f) = 0$, and $m_{AP}(\{f, \sim f\}) = 0.8$.

We have the following beliefs for 'f' and '~f' from the first piece of evidence, the inherent factors: $Bel_{IF}(f) = 0.1$, $Bel_{IF}(\sim f) = 0$. The corresponding plausibilities are: $Pl_{IF}(f) = 1.0$, and $Pl_{IF}(\sim f) = 0.9$. The plausibility of material misstatement based on the inherent factors is 0.9, although there is no belief that the financial statements are materially misstated.

Srivastava and Shafer (1992) showed analytically that the plausibility of material misstatements in the financial statements based on inherent factors is equivalent to inherent risk (IR). Thus, in the current example IR = 0.9. Conceptually, this is equivalent to saying that the auditor has 0.1 level of support from environmental factors that the financial statements are fairly stated and 0.9 level of maximum possible support that the financial statements could be materially misstated, even though there is no evidence that they are materially misstated.

Similarly, the beliefs and plausibilities for 'f' and '~f' based on the analytical procedures are: $Bel_{AP}(f) = 0.2$, $Bel_{AP}(\sim f) = 0$, $Pl_{AP}(f) = 1.0$, and $Pl_{AP}(\sim f) = 0.8$. This means that the auditor has direct evidence from analytical procedures that the financial statements are fairly stated with 0.2 degree of belief, no evidence and thus zero belief for material misstatement, and 0.8 level of plausibility that material misstatement could exist (even though there is no direct evidence of misstatement). Similar to the prior case, a plausibility of 0.8 that the financial statements are materially misstated represents the risk associated to analytical procedures as considered in SAS 47.

One of the difficulties in actual audits is the combination of various items of evidence, such as those discussed above. Using belief functions, one would use Dempster's rule of combination. Dempster's rule is similar to Bayes' rule. In fact, Dempster's rule reduces to Bayes' rule under the condition where the basic belief masses, i.e., m-values, are assigned to only singletons of the frame (Shafer 1976).

In the above example, we have two items of evidence with the following m-values:

$$m_{IF}(f) = 0.1,\ m_{IF}(\sim f) = 0,\ m_{IF}(\{f,\sim f\}) = 0.9,$$

$$m_{AP}(f) = 0.2,\ m_{AP}(\sim f) = 0,\ m_{AP}(\{f, \sim f\}) = 0.8.$$

According to Dempster's rule, we cross multiply all the m-values and assign the resulting masses to the intersection of the arguments. In situations where the intersection is empty with a finite belief mass ("conflict situations"), we need to renormalize the remaining masses (Shafer and Srivastava 1990). In the above case, we do not have any conflict. Thus the following are the combined m-values as a result of cross multiplication of the two sets of m-values:

$$m_T(f) = m_{IF}(f)m_{AP}(f) + m_{IF}(f)m_{AP}(\{f,\sim f\}) + m_{IF}(\{f,\sim f\})m_{AP}(f)$$

$$= 0.1\text{x}0.2 + 0.1\text{x}0.8 + 0.9\text{x}0.2 = 0.28,$$

$$m_T(\sim f) = m_{IF}(\sim f)m_{AP}(\sim f) + m_{IF}(\sim f)m_{AP}(\{f,\sim f\}) + m_{IF}(\{f,\sim f\})m_{AP}(\sim f)$$

$$= 0 + 0\text{x}0.8 + 0.9\text{x}0 = 0,$$

$$m_T(\{f,\sim f\}) = m_{IF}(\{f,\sim f\})m_{AP}(\{f,\sim f\}) = 0.9\text{x}0.8 = 0.72.$$

The beliefs and plausibilities are: $Bel_T(f) = 0.28$, $Bel_T(\sim f) = 0$, $Pl_T(f) = 1.0$, and $Pl_T(\sim f) = 0.72$. Thus, based on the inherent factors and analytical procedures the auditor has 0.28 degree of belief that the financial statements are fairly presented. But there is still 0.72 degree of plausibility that material misstatements may be present.

Usually, the auditor will need to collect more evidence to increase the belief that the financial statements are fairly stated to a threshold level, say 0.95, or reduce the plausibility of material misstatement to 0.05, i.e., reduce the overall audit risk to 0.05 in order to give a clean opinion[7].

The analytical model proposed by Srivastava and Shafer (1992) for combining various items of evidence at different levels of the balance sheet is for planning purposes. One can also use their model for evaluation purposes, provided all the pieces of evidence gathered are positive in nature. This is not the case in general. In fact, in general, the auditor may encounter some positive evidence, some negative evidence, and some mixed items of evidence. In order to combine evidence from various sources at different level of the financial statement, Srivastava et. al (1996) used computer software called "Auditor's Assistant" developed by Shafer et. al (1988). This software allows the user to draw the evidential network for audit planning and evaluation decisions and also calculates the beliefs for the specified network.

Srivastava et al (1996, see also, Wright et. al 1998) applied the belief function approach for planning and evaluation of an audit of a healthcare unit. They showed how one could develop a network of variables with accounts and audit objectives and connect various items of evidence to pertinent variables (i.e., audit objectives of an account, the accounts on the balance sheet, and the balance sheet as whole).

The inputs to such a network are the auditor's judgments about the planned (or achieved) level belief to be obtained (or obtained) from various items of evidence. The Auditor's Assistant program aggregates all the evidence and provides the overall beliefs. If the overall belief obtained at the variable of interest, say the financial statement, is below a specified threshold level, say 0.95, the auditor would (1) collect more evidence to increase the overall belief to the threshold level and issue an unqualified opinion, (2) either issue a qualified opinion or an adverse opinion if the overall belief that the financial statements are materially misstated is more than a threshold value, 0.05 in the present example, or (3) issue a disclaimer if the auditor is not able to collect further evidence. If the overall belief that the financial statements are fairly stated is equal to or more than the threshold value then the auditor would not collect any further evidence and would issue an unqualified opinion.

---

7 See Shafer and Srivastava (1990) for an example of the use of Dempster's rule with conflicting pieces of evidence.

Other Studies

There are a number of other studies the interested reader can consult to see further illustrations of the use of belief functions in behavioral auditing and accounting research. Many of these are listed in our references and are referenced in the following chapters. For example, Krishnamoorty, Mock and Washington (1999) utilized the belief-function framework in a cascaded inference context and Srivastava and Mock (1999) used an evidential reasoning approach based on the belief-function framework for WebTrust assurance services (AICPA 1997a, 1997b). They also applied a decision theoretical approach to estimate a minimum acceptable audit fee based on the costs associated with various risks.

Srivastava (1996) has used belief functions in value judgments and has analyzed the impact of framing of evidence on decision-making. As discussed earlier, Srivastava (1997a) has also used belief functions to model ambiguity and demonstrated its benefits in decision making behavior.

4. Conclusion

Ambiguity and uncertainty are common in business settings. However, probability theory does not have a natural, logical way of dealing with ambiguity. One common way of dealing with ambiguity in probability is to assign uniform priors. This leads to some illogical implications, as illustrated in an audit context. An important advantage of a formalism based on belief functions is that it does explicitly and logically deal with ambiguity. As shown, this approach can be applied to auditing and leads to more logical interpretations of audit risk and evidence. Belief functions tend to have the following advantages over the probability framework in these contexts

1. If the audit risk model (see SAS 47) is viewed as a plausibility model (Srivastava and Shafer 1992) with a belief function interpretation of its components, this interpretation makes more intuitive sense than alternative frameworks.

2. There is some evidence that a judgment about the basic assessment of the strength of evidence using a belief function framework is more intuitive to decision makers (Harrison 1999, and Curly and Golden 1994).

3. Representation of positive, negative, and mixed items of evidence is more convenient. For example, positive evidence in support of an audit objective 'o' can be expressed in terms of a non-zero m-value, say 0.2, for 'o' and zero

value for '~o', i.e., $m(o) = 0.2$, $m(\sim o) = 0$, $m(\{o, \sim o\}) = 0.8$. A negative item of evidence would be represented by a non-zero m-value for '~o', say 0.1, a zero value for 'o', i.e., $m(o) = 0$, $m(\sim o) = 0.1$, and $(\{o, \sim o\}) = 0.9$. A mixed item of evidence can be expressed by assigning a non-zero m-value for both 'o' and '~o', i.e., $m(o) \neq 0$, and $m(\sim o) \neq 0$. As an illustration, we can express a mixed item of evidence as $m(o) = 0.3$, $m(\sim o) = 0.1$, and $m(\{o, \sim o\}) = 0.6$.

4. Representation of different levels of assurance coming from the same item of evidence for two different audit objectives is expressed more conveniently. For example, in the case of a confirmation test, assume that the auditor finds that all the respondents have said that they owe money to the company, but some of them have made comments that their account balance is overstated. Based on this information the auditor's judgment is that a high level of support, say 0.8, is obtained for 'existence' objective (e) and a medium level of support, say 0.6, is obtained for 'valuation' objective (v). This can be expressed in terms of m-values as: $m(e) = 0.8$, $m(\sim e) = 0$, $m\{(e, \sim e\}) = 0.2$, and $m(v) = 0.6$, $m(\sim v) = 0$, $m(\{v, \sim v\}) = 0.4$.

Belief functions also have potential use and research implications for business problems in general as is illustrated in the following chapters of this book. As noted, uncertainty and ambiguity exist and should be formally dealt with in many business contexts.

A number of research opportunities arise with respect to belief functions, especially in behavioral research. For example, it would be interesting to see whether decision makers tend to think of uncertainty as depicted in the belief-function framework. Also, given that some research has shown that judgments about the level of belief in support of a given assertion is more natural when beliefs function are used, the basic measurement (calibration) issue of the level belief obtained from various types of audit evidence is an important area for future research. A related issue is whether decision makers are able to combine items of evidence according to Dempster's rule of combination. Lastly, there are a number of issues concerning the efficiency and effectiveness of the belief-function framework as compared to other approaches of dealing with uncertainty and ambiguity[8].

---

[8] See, for example, Chapter 2.2: "The Descriptive Ability of Models of Audit Risk" by Monroe and Ng.

References

American Institute of Certified Public Accountants. 1983. *Statement on Auditing Standards, No, 47: Audit Risk and Materiality in Conducting an Audit.* New York: AICPA.

American Institute of Certified Public Accountants. 1997a. *AICPA/CICA WebTrust Principles and Criteria for Business-to-Consumer Electronic Commerce.* http://www.aicpa.org/webtrust/princrit/htm.

American Institute of Certified Public Accountants. 1997b. Report of the Special Committee on Assurance Services. www.aicpa.org.

Curley, S. P., and Golden, J.I. 1994. Using belief functions to represent degrees of belief. *Organization Behavior and Human Decision Processes*: 271 – 303.

Einhorn, H. J., and Hogarth, R. M. 1986. Decision Making under Ambiguity. *The Journal of Business,* 59(4), Pt. 2 (October), S225-S250.

Gabbay, D. M., and P. Smets. 1998. *Handbook of Defeasible Reasoning and Uncertainty Management Systems.* Kluwer Academic Publishers.

Harrison, K. 1999. Evaluation and Aggregation of Audit Evidence under Uncertainty: An Empirical Study of Belief Functions. Ph.D. Dissertation, School of Business, University of Kansas.

Krishnamoorthy, G., T.J. Mock, and M. Washington. 1999. A Comparative Evaluation of Belief Revision Models in Auditing. *Auditing: A Journal of Practice and Theory,* Vol. 18, pp. 104-126.

Monroe, G and J. Ng. 2001. *The Descriptive Ability of Models of Audit Risk. Belief-Functions in Business Decisions.* R. Srivastava and T. Mock (Eds).

Shafer, G. 1976. *A Mathematical Theory of Evidence.* Princeton University Press.

Shafer, G., and A. Tversky. 1985. Languages and Designs for Probability Judgment. *Cognitive Science,* vol. 9, pp. 309-339.

Shafer, G., P.P. Shenoy, and R. P. Srivastava. 1988. Auditor's Assistant: A knowledge engineering tool for audit decisions. *Proceedings of the 1988 Touche Ross/University of Kansas Symposium on Auditing Problems.* Lawrence, KS: School of Business, University of Kansas, pp. 61-84.

Shafer, G., and R.P. Srivastava. 1990. The bayesian and belief-function formalisms: A general perspective for auditing. *Auditing: A Journal of Practice and Theory* 9 (Supplement), pp. 110-48.

Smets, P. 1990a. The Combination of Evidence in the Transferable Belief Model. *IEEE Transactions on Pattern Analysis and Machine Intelligence,* 12, 5 (May).

Smets, P. 1990b. Constructing the Pignistic Probability Function in a Context of Uncertainty. *Uncertainty in Artificial Intelligence 5.* ed. by Henrion, M., Shachter, R.D., Kanal, L.N., and Lemmer, J.F. North-Holland: Elsevier Science Publishers B.V.

Smets, P. 1998. The Transferable Belief Model For Quantified Belief Representation. *Quantified Representation for Uncertainty and Imprecision,* Vol. 1. Edited by P. Smets. Kluwer Academic Publishers

Spohn, W. 1998. Ordinal Conditional functions: A Dynamic Theory of Epistemic States. Causation. *Decision, Belief Changes, and Statistics,* II, edited by W. L. Harper and B. Skyrms. D. Reidel.

Spohn, W. 1990. A General Non-Probabilistic Theory of Inductive Reasoning, *Uncertainty in Artificial Intelligence.* Elsvier Science Publications: 149-158.

Srivastava, R. P. 1995a. A General Scheme for Aggregating Evidence in Auditing: Propagation of Beliefs in Networks. *Artificial Intelligence in Accounting and Auditing,* Vol. 3, Miklos A. Vasarhelyi, editor, Markus Wiener Publishers, Princeton: 55-99.

Srivastava, R. P. 1995b. The Belief-Function Approach to Aggregating Audit Evidence" *International Journal of Intelligent Systems* (March): 329-356.

Srivastava, R. P. 1996. Value Judgments using Belief Functions. *Research in Accounting Ethics*, Vol. 2, pp. 109-130.

Srivastava, R. P. 1997a. Decision Making Under Ambiguity: A Belief-Function Perspective. *Archives of Control Sciences,* Vol. 6 (XLII): 5-27.

Srivastava, R. P. 1997b. Integrating Statistical and Non-Statistical Evidence Using Belief Functions. *Encyclopedia of Computer Science and Technology*, Vol. 37, edited by Allen Kent, James G. Williams, and Carolyn M. Hall, published by Marcel Dekker, Inc., New York (Supplement 22), pp. 157-174.

Srivastava, R. P. and G. Shafer. 1992. Belief-Function Formulas for Audit Risk. *The Accounting Review,* Vol. 67, No. 2 (April): 249-283.

Srivastava, R. P., and G. Shafer. 1994. Integrating Statistical and Non-Statistical Audit Evidence Using Belief Functions: A Case of Variable Sampling. *International Journal of Intelligent Systems,* Vol. 9: 519-539.

Srivastava, R. P., S. Dutta, and R. Johns. 1996. An Expert System Approach to Audit Planning and Evaluation in the Belief-Function Framework. *International Journal of Intelligent Systems in Accounting, Finance and Management*, Vol. 5, No. 3: 165-183.

Srivastava, R. P., and T. J. Mock. 1999. Evidential Reasoning for WebTrust Assurance Services. *Journal of Management Information Systems*. Winter 1999-2000, Vol.16, No. 3, pp. 11 – 32.

Srivastava, R. P. and T. J. Mock. 2000. Belief Functions in Accounting Behavioral Research, *Advances in Accounting Behavioral Research*, Vol. 3: 225-242.

Wright, A., T. J. Mock, and R. P. Srivastava. 1998. Audit Program Planning using A Belief Function Framework. *Proceedings of the 1998 Deloitte & Touche University of Kansas Symposium on Auditing Problems*, Lawrence, KS: School of Business, University of Kansas, pp. 115-142.

Zadeh, L. A. 1978. Fuzzy sets as a Basis for a Theory of Probability. *Fuzzy Sets and Systems,* 1: 3-28.

Zadeh, L. A. 1979. A Theory of Approximate Reasoning. *Machine Intelligence,* edited by J. E. Ayes, D. Mitchie andn L. I. Mikulich. Chichester, UK: Ellis Horwood.

Decision Making in a Context where Uncertainty is Represented by Belief Functions

Philippe Smets
IRIDIA
Université Libre de Bruxelles
50 av. Roosevelt, CP 194-6, 1050 Bruxelles, Belgium
psmets@ulb.ac.be
http://iridia.ulb.ac.be/~psmets

January 10, 2001

Abstract

A quantified model to represent uncertainty is incomplete if its use in a decision environment is not explained. When belief functions were first introduced to represent quantified uncertainty, no associated decision model was proposed. Since then, it became clear that the belief functions meaning is multiple. The models based on belief functions could be understood as an upper and lower probabilities model, as the hint model, as the transferable belief model and as a probability model extended to modal propositions. These models are mathematically identical at the static level, their behaviors diverge at their dynamic level (under conditioning and/or revision). For decision making, some authors defend that decisions must be based on expected utilities, in which case a probability function must be determined. When uncertainty is represented by belief functions, the choice of the appropriate probability function must be explained and justified. This probability function does not represent a state of belief, it is just the additive measure needed to compute the expected utilities. Other models of decision making when beliefs are represented by belief functions have also been suggested, some of which are discussed here.

1 Introduction

Uncertainty induces beliefs, i.e. graded dispositions that guide our behavior. Translated within a normative approach, this leads usually to the construction of a model to represent quantified beliefs that is linked directly to 'rational' agent behavior described within decision contexts (DeGroot, 1970). It has been argued that decisions are 'rational' only if we use a probability measure over the various possible states of the nature and compute with it the expected utility of each possible act, the optimal act being the one that maximizes these expected utilities (DeGroot, 1970; Savage, 1954). Accordingly, whenever a decision must be made, the decider's beliefs must induce a probability function on the set of possible outcomes. Nevertheless the fact that beliefs can only be observed through our decisions does not necessarily mean that beliefs cannot be entertained without any revealing behavior manifestations (Smith & Jones, 1986 p.147). The idea that entertained beliefs and beliefs in a decision context can be distinguished is defended in the transferable belief model (Smets & Kennes, 1994). When these two types of beliefs are distinguished the classical justification for the use of probability functions to represent quantified beliefs does not apply for what concerns the entertained beliefs. Of course it still applies for what concerns decisions themselves.

New normative models to represent quantified belief have been proposed recently, in particular those based on belief functions. These models are often criticized for supposedly not providing a method for rational decision making. This paper reviews solutions proposed in some of the models where uncertainty is represented by belief functions. Four types of such models have been described.

1. Some authors consider that the belief function is the lower envelope of a family of probability functions (section 4.1). Some of them assume the existence of some underlying but imprecisely known probability function (Walley, 1987; Giles, 1982). Others just assume that beliefs are represented by the family of probability functions itself, not explicitly assuming some underlying partially unknown probability function (Kyburg, 1987b; Levi, 1980; Smith, 1961; Voorbraak, 1993). In both cases, a set of expected utilities can be computed for each decision, but these sets usually do not induce an unambiguous order among the set of possible acts. To resolve that ambiguity, Schmeidler (1989) proposes the use of the lower expectation to make decisions. A generalization of it can be found in Jaffray (1988)) and Strat (1990b, 1990a) who, inspired by Hurwicz (Luce & Raiffa, 1957), advocate the use of a weighted average of the upper and the lower expectations (Section 6).

2. In the transferable belief model (Smets & Kennes, 1994) (section 4.3), we have proposed and justified the use of the so-called pignistic probabilities as the appropriate probability function to be used when decision is required (Smets, 1990; Smets & Kennes, 1994; Smets, 1993c) (section 5). In a similar framework, Appriou suggested another solution based on the most plausible singletons (Appriou, 1991) (section 5.9).

3. In Dempster's original work (Dempster, 1967) and in the hint model of Kohlas and Monney (Kohlas & Monney, 1995) (section 4.2) the problem of decision making is not essential, and no particular solution seems to have been defended. Nevertheless (Schaller, 1991) studies the use of the hint models for multiple criteria decision making. The same remark applies to the models where a belief is understood as the probability of knowing (Ruspini, 1986, 1987)) or of proving (Pearl, 1988) (section 4.4).

In this paper, we review some of the solutions proposed for decision making when the uncertainty is represented by a belief function. We consider the case of one decider and one criteria. Before proceeding to decision making itself, we present the mathematical background on belief functions (Section 2) and probability theory (Section 3) useful in this paper and some of the models that lead to a belief function (Section 4). It is essential that these models are not confused. They might look similar. Indeed when considering just the static representation of uncertainty, they all end up with a belief function. But once the dynamic of the model is considered, the differences show up.

Sections 5 and 6 present some of the solutions proposed to make rational decisions in the transferable belief model and in the upper and lower probabilities frameworks, respectively. We focus on the theoretical aspects of decision making under uncertainty represented by belief functions. Applications can be found in the other papers published in this monograph.

2 Mathematical background on belief functions

In this section, we summarize the mathematical knowledge about belief functions needed for this presentation. Details can be found in (Shafer, 1976a; Smets, 1988, 1998b).

2.1 Belief functions

Let Ω be a finite space, called the frame of discernment. The elements of the set Ω are called 'worlds'. One world corresponds to the actual world; it is denoted hereafter ω_0. There is an agent, denoted You (De Finetti, 1974), who does not know which world is the actual world and who can only express the strength of his/her opinion (called degree of belief) that the actual world belongs to this or that subset of Ω.

That ω_0 belongs to Ω is assumed under the so-called 'closed world assumption', whereas under the 'open world assumption' ω_0 might not be an element of Ω (Smets, 1988, 1998b). The closed world assumption is assumed in probability theory and it justifies the axiom $P(\Omega) = 1$. In the transferable belief model, we acknowledge that You may have built Ω so that ω_0 does not belong to Ω.

On Ω, we define a function $bel : 2^\Omega \rightarrow [0, 1]$ called a 'belief function' (Shafer, 1976a). For $A \subseteq \Omega$, $bel(A)$ denotes the strength of Your belief that $\omega_0 \in A$. Mathematically, *bel* is a Choquet capacity monotone of infinite order. It satisfies the following inequalities:

$$
\begin{aligned}
&1)\ bel(\emptyset) = 0 \\
&2)\ \forall n \geq 1, \forall A_1, A_2, ...A_n \subseteq \Omega \\
bel(A_1 \cup A_2 \cup ...A_n) \ &\geq \ \sum_i bel(A_i) - \sum_{i>j} bel(A_i \cap A_j) \\
&\quad .... - (-1)^n bel(A_1 \cap A_2 \cap ...A_n).
\end{aligned}
$$

Under the closed world assumption, one adds $bel(\Omega) = 1$. Under the open world assumption, one adds only $bel(\Omega) \leq 1$.

Other useful functions have been defined, like the basic belief assignment m, the plausibility function pl, the implicability functions b, the commonality function q, the weight function w ... (Smets, 1998b). Their usefulness depends on the context. They are in one-to-one relations with bel.

The basic belief assignment (bba) related to a belief function bel is the function $m : 2^{\Omega} \rightarrow [0,1]$ defined as:

$$\begin{aligned} m(A) &= \sum_{B \subseteq A} (-1)^{|A|-|B|} bel(B), \quad \forall A \subseteq \Omega, A \neq \emptyset, \\ m(\emptyset) &= 1 - bel(\Omega). \end{aligned}$$

Mathematically, m is the Möbius transform of bel. The value $m(A)$ for $A \subseteq \Omega$ is called the basic belief mass (bbm) given to A. It may happen that $m(\emptyset) > 0$. It reflects either that we are working under an open world assumption or that there exists some kind of contradiction in the belief state (Smets, 1992b).

The relation from m to bel is given by:

$$bel(A) = \sum_{\emptyset \neq B \subseteq A} m(B), \quad \forall A \subseteq \Omega.$$

The plausibility function $pl : 2^{\Omega} \rightarrow [0,1]$ is defined as:

$$pl(A) = bel(\Omega) - bel(\overline{A}), \quad \forall A \subseteq \Omega.$$

Shafer (1976a) accepts the closed world assumption, what can be expressed by saying that bel is 'normalized'. In that case, $bel(\Omega) = 1$, $pl(\Omega) = 1$ and $m(\emptyset) = 0$. In the transferable belief model, we do not require such a normalization (Smets, 1992b). We use the notation bel and pl, whereas Shafer uses the notation Bel and Pl. The difference should enhance that the functions bel and pl are not necessarily normalized.

The meaning of bel and of the other functions varies according to the meaning the authors give to $bel(A)$. In this presentation, we will discuss the upper and lower probabilities model, the hint model, the transferable belief model and the probability model extended to modal propositions (section 4).

2.2 Notation

In order to homogenize the notation, we use the next conventions that we have found convenient, even though it might seems cumbersome in some cases. The full notation for bel and its related functions is:

$$bel_{Y,t}^{\Omega,\Re}[EC_{Y,t}](\omega_0 \in A) = x.$$

It denotes that the degree of belief held by the agent Y (shortcut for You) at time t that the actual world ω_0 belongs to the set A of worlds is equal to

x, where A is a subset of the frame of discernment Ω and $A \in \Re$ where $\Re$ is a Boolean algebra of subsets of Ω. The belief is based on the evidential corpus $EC_{Y,t}$ held by Y at t, where $EC_{Y,t}$ represents all what agent Y knows at t. In practice many indices can be omitted for simplicity sake. Usually $\Re$ is 2^Ω, the power set of Ω. When $\Re$ is not explicitly stated, it means that *bel* is defined on 2^Ω. '$\omega_0 \in A$' is often denoted as 'A'. Y, t and/or Ω are omitted when the values of the missing elements are clearly defined from the context. So $bel^\Omega[E](A)$ or even $bel(A)$ are often used.

Note that $bel_{Y,t}^{\Omega,\Re}[EC_{Y,t}]$ (and its simplified forms) denotes the belief function, and can be understood as a finite vector of length $|\Re|$, which components are the values of $bel_{Y,t}^{\Omega,\Re}[EC_{Y,t}](A)$ for every $A \in \Re$.

In the above notation, *bel* can be replaced by any of m, pl, q, b, etc... The indices should made it clear what the links are. So $m_{Y,t}^{\Omega,\Re}[EC_{Y,t}]$ and $pl_{Y,t}^{\Omega,\Re}[EC_{Y,t}]$ are the bba and the plausibility function related to $bel_{Y,t}^{\Omega,\Re}[EC_{Y,t}]$.

2.3 Set of probability functions compatible with a belief function

Given any normalized belief function bel^Ω on Ω, one can always define a family $\Pi(bel^\Omega)$ of probability functions P^Ω on Ω that satisfy any of the next three definitions:

$$\begin{aligned}
\Pi(bel^\Omega) &= \{P^\Omega : bel^\Omega(A) \leq P^\Omega(A),\ \forall A \subseteq \Omega\} \\
\Pi(bel^\Omega) &= \{P^\Omega : P^\Omega(A) \leq pl^\Omega(A),\ \forall A \subseteq \Omega\} \\
\Pi(bel^\Omega) &= \{P^\Omega : bel^\Omega(A) \leq P^\Omega(A) \leq pl^\Omega(A),\ \forall A \subseteq \Omega\}
\end{aligned}$$

The three definitions are equivalent. $\Pi(bel^\Omega)$ and bel^Ω are in one-to-one correspondence. We call $\Pi(bel^\Omega)$ the set of probability functions compatible with bel^Ω.

2.4 The belief function kinematic

Let Ω be a frame of discernment and bel^Ω be a belief function on Ω. For $E \subseteq \Omega$, let Ev_E be the evidence that states that the actual world is not in $\overline{E}$. Suppose You learn Ev_E for sure. You must then revise Your beliefs accordingly. This is achieved by Dempster's rule of conditioning, i.e.:

$$bel^\Omega[Ev_E](A) = bel^\Omega(A \cup \overline{E}) - bel^\Omega(\overline{E}) \tag{1}$$

We use the strange expression 'the actual world is not in $\overline{E}$' instead of the more classical one 'the actual world is in E' as far as we don't assume initially that the actual world is an element of Ω (see the open world assumption, (section 2.1)).

Suppose now that we have two pieces of evidence Ev_1 and Ev_2 that bear on Ω. Let $bel^\Omega[Ev_1]$ and $bel^\Omega[Ev_2]$ be the belief functions derived from each piece of evidence taken individually. If these pieces of evidence are 'distinct', than we can compute the belief $bel^{\Omega}[Ev_1, Ev_2]$ induced by their conjunction on Ω. Its related bba satisfies:

$$m^{\Omega}[Ev_1, Ev_2](A) = \sum_{B,C:B\cap C=A} m^{\Omega}[Ev_1](B)m^{\Omega}[Ev_2](C).$$

This rule can also be written as:

$$m^{\Omega}[Ev_1, Ev_2](A) = \sum_{B,C\subseteq\overline{A}:B\cap C=\emptyset} m^{\Omega}[Ev_1](A\cup B)m^{\Omega}[Ev_2](A\cup C).$$

Another very useful rewriting of the same equation is:

$$f^{\Omega}[Ev_1, Ev_2](A) = \sum_{B\subseteq\Omega} f^{\Omega}[Ev_1, Ev_B](A)m^{\Omega}[Ev_2](B),$$

where $f \in \{m, b, bel, pl, q\}$ and $bel^{\Omega}[Ev_1, Ev_B]$ is the belief function obtained by the application to $bel^{\Omega}[Ev_1]$ of Dempster's rule of conditioning on Ev_B (relation 1).

The definition of 'distinctness' is detailed in (Smets, 1992a, 1998b). It translates the fact that the sources who produce the two belief functions based on Ev_1 and Ev_2 , respectively, are 'distinct', 'unrelated', 'independent'. No precise definition of these terms are presented here, as they will hardly be needed in this paper.

3 Mathematical background on probability theory.

3.1 An operational definition of P.

The classical definition of a subjective probability is based on an analysis of rational betting behavior. The (subjective) probability of a proposition is usually characterized as the value of the opportunity to gain a unit value if the proposition is true (Ramsey, 1964). More formally, one variant of the operational definition of a subjective probability is the following:

Definition 3.1 ***Operational definition of subjective probabilities.*** *Consider a finite space Ω, a game on the betting frame Ω, a player and a banker. We have '$P^{\Omega}_{You,t}(A) = x$' iff You consider at time t and for any $M > 0$ that the player must pay \$$xM$ to the banker to enter a game where the player wins \$M from the banker if the actual world belongs to A and \$0 otherwise, and You are ready to be any of the player or the banker.*

We insist on the fact that You are not allowed to 'run away' from the game. You must accept to be either the banker or the player, this being settled after You have assessed the value of x. The present definition is based on 'forced bets'. The case where You could 'run away' is analyzed in the upper and lower probabilities framework (section 6).

3.2 The assessment of P

In order to assess the value of a subjective probability, one can consider the following method. Let a finite space Ω and $A \subseteq \Omega$. Consider two bets. In bet 1, You bet on A versus $\overline{A}$ where You gain \$$x$ if A is true, and \$0 otherwise (with \$$x$ being any reasonable prize like \$100). In bet 2, You have an urn with a proportion p of Black balls. You bet on Black versus not-Black where You gain \$$x$ if the randomly selected ball (where every ball has the same chance to be selected) is Black, and \$0 otherwise. Which bet do You prefer?

- If You prefer bet 1, it means that $P(A) > p$.
- If You prefer bet 2, it means that $P(A) < p$.
- If You are indifferent between the two bets, it means that $P(A) = p$.

By varying p, one can (in theory) always find a state of indifference between the two bets. So one can assess the value of $P(A)$.

In practice, this method is not good to assess probabilities and more elaborated methods have been developed by psychometricians. Nevertheless many of the methods they developed are ingenious variants of the one we just described.

3.3 Decision making

Suppose a decision maker wants to select an optimal act among an exhaustive set of possible acts, denoted A. The outcome of each act depends on the exact value of the actual world ω_0. Let Ω denote the set of possible worlds, the actual one being assumed to belong to Ω (the closed world assumption is assumed). Savage (1954) has proposed a set of rationality axioms that justify the use of an additive measure $P^{\Omega} : 2^{\Omega} \to [0, 1]$ and a utility function $u : A \times \Omega \to \text{Reals}$. The optimal act is the one that maximizes the expected utility $\overline{u}(a)$ where:

$$\overline{u}(a) = \sum_{\omega \in \Omega} u(a, \omega) P^{\Omega}(\omega).$$

The naturalness of this set of axioms, even though often criticized (Rivett, 1975), has nevertheless stood the test of time. We will accept them hereafter.

That the additive measure P^{Ω} represents *stricto sensu* Your beliefs is not required in Savage's approach. In fact, Savage only proves the existence of the additive measure, its interpretation being left aside. Nevertheless most authors take it for granted that this additive measure represents Your beliefs. This is one of the major assumptions relaxed in the transferable belief model.

3.4 Dutch books

The reason why beliefs must be represented by a probability function is often based on the Dutch book argument. A Dutch book is a set of bets that would lead to a sure loss whatever is the value of the actual world. The only way to avoid being vulnerable to a Dutch book, i.e., to be certain to always avoid facing sure loss, consists in representing Your beliefs by a probability function. In that case, Your beliefs are said to be 'coherent'.

Just to illustrate how the rule $P(\overline{A}) = 1 - P(A)$ is derived, consider the next two bets on A versus $\overline{A}$. In bet 1, player wins if A, and the prize You propose to enter the game is \$.3. In bet 2, player wins if $\overline{A}$, and the prize You propose to enter the game is \$.6. Then I decide that You will be the banker in both bets. In that case the player will pay You \$.9 to enter the two games. Whatever occurs, A or $\overline{A}$, the banker, thus You, will have to pay \$1 to the player. So You are doomed to loose \$.1 whatever occurs, a behavior normally considered as irrational. If the sum of the prizes proposed to enter the game is larger than \$1, then You will be the player, and doomed to loose money whatever occurs. The only way to avoid such sure losses is achieved by using prizes that add to \$1, hence the corresponding axiom in probability theory.

Similar bets can be organized to derive the additivity axioms of probability measures.

Bayes rule of conditioning, i.e., $P(A|B) = \frac{P(A \cap B)}{P(B)}$, is derived through the consideration of bets where the player wins \$1 if $A \cap B$ occurs, \$0 if $\overline{A} \cap B$ occurs, and the bet is canceled (the player gets back the money paid to enter the game) if $\overline{B}$ occurs.

It is essential to realize that the Dutch book argument does not tell what the values of these probabilities must be. It only states that if You bet at .7 on Heads in a coin tossing experiment, than You must bet at .3 on Tails to avoid to be victim of a Dutch book. The Dutch book argument does not require that the probability of Heads is .5 (or any other value). The latter is a problem of reasonableness that has nothing to do with the Dutch book argument (Kyburg, 1988)). One can be widely unreasonable without sinning against either logic or probability. This might seem surprising and even unpalatable to some probabilists, but no rationality arguments can be proposed that force You to bet at .5 on Heads.

Note that Savage's approach and the Dutch book argument consider only forced bets. You are not allowed to refuse the proposed bets. A more general approach that cope with unforced bets has been considered in (Smith, 1961; Giles, 1982; Walley, 1991). They concern the upper and lower probability theory (see Section 6).

3.5 A note on conditioning and belief revision

In probability theory, the changes in belief that result from conditioning and belief revision are usually not distinguished. Nevertheless, Hacking (1988) uses these two forms of changes in belief to distinguish between personalist and Bayesian probabilists, the latter being a special case of the former.

A personalist probabilist considers that $Prob^H[f](h)$, what is classically denoted by $Prob_f(h)$, is the number representing Your personal probability for $h \subseteq H$, when You know f. Note furthermore that one assumes not only that fact f is true, but also that You know that fact f is true.

Probability given facts, denoted $P[f]$ is not to be confused with conditional probability, denoted $P(.|e)$ where e is the conditioning event. Using our full notation, conditional probability is defined as,

$$Prob^H[f](h|e) = \frac{Prob^H[f](he)}{Prob^H[f](e)}$$

for positive denominators, where f is the background facts known to You and e is the conditioning event. Conditional probabilities indicate how confident You would be, knowing only f, if You knew e as well.

When it comes to the problem of avoiding a Dutch Book, the fact f cannot be reconsidered. It is fixed and known, so no bet is to be considered if f were not the case. For what concerns e, the situation is different. We are considering bets where You could win or loose when e is the case, and bet is canceled if e is not the case. So when e is concerned, we must be careful on how the probabilities are allocated, as if they do not satisfy probability theory, then a Dutch Book could be built against the bettor. Therefore, conditioning must be performed according to the Bayesian rule. But as described, conditioning consist in considering 'hypothetical events', i.e., events that have not yet occurred but might.

The distinction between probability given facts (factual revision) and conditional probabilities (hypothetical conditioning) is usually not made. In the TBM, such a distinction is made.

Note: As an example consider the Peter, Paul and Marry Saga (see section 5.5.1, we suggest to the reader who is not familiar with the Saga to skip this note and to come back to this note once he/she has reached the section presenting the Saga). Let f denote Your knowledge about the killer before learning about Peter's alibi, and let $P[f]$ be Your pignistic probability on {Peter, Paul, Marry}. In the Saga, we have $P[f]$(Peter) = 1/4, $P[f]$(Paul) = 1/4, $P[f]$(Marry) = 1/2. Suppose You want to bet on Paul versus Marry given the hypothetical (conditioning) event that Peter is not the killer. Probabilities would be $P[f]$(Paul|not Peter) = 1/3, $P[f]$(Marry|not Peter) = 2/3. You must use these probabilities in order to avoid a Dutch Book. Indeed, You must be ready to face bets that are canceled if Peter is the killer or if Peter is not the killer, as well as bets that are canceled if Paul is or is not the killer, etc... Once You learn about Peter's alibi, the bets that would be canceled if Peter is the killer cannot be considered anymore. In that case the arguments based on cancellable bets that lead to Bayes' rule do not apply anymore when it comes to the fact 'Peter is not the killer'. You 'revise' Your probabilities and get $P[f,\text{not Peter}]$(Paul) = 1/2, what is different from the previous $P[f]$(Paul|not Peter). In the TBM, revision and conditioning are different. Revision is performed by Dempster's rule of conditioning whereas conditioning is done by Bayes rule applied to the pignistic probabilities. Too bad the word 'conditioning' was used to describe Dempster's rule, but the tradition is very strong. It would have been better to call it 'Dempster's rule of revision'.□

Suppose Your beliefs on H are represented by the probability function P^H. We propose the next definition:

1. the 'factual revision on f' is the process that transforms P^H into $P^H[f]$,
2. the 'hypothetical conditioning on e' is the process that transforms P^H into $P^H(.|e)$.

They correspond to the 'given facts' and the 'conditioning' processes, respectively. The value of $P^H(.|e)$ is obtained by Bayes' rule of conditioning. The value of $P^H[f]$, as such, is still to be defined. For that purpose and staying within the probability context, Hacking introduces the next assumption, called the 'dynamic assumption':

$$Prob^H[f,e](h) = Prob^H[f](h|e) = \frac{Prob^H[f](he)}{Prob^H[f](e)}$$

i.e., You equate Your conditional probabilities to Your probabilities given facts.

A Bayesian probabilist is then defined as a personalist probabilist who accepts the dynamic assumption. For a Bayesian, the distinction between hypothetical conditioning and factual revision is not important. Jeffrey (1988) and Teller (1976) produce arguments based on so-called dynamic Dutch books in order to justify the adequacy of the dynamic assumption.

In the TBM, the dynamic assumption is not assumed, therefore revisions and conditioning are not identical. Nevertheless the TBM resists to the dynamic Dutch books as shown in (Smets, 1993c) (see also section 5.8).

4 Various interpretations attached to a belief function

The expression 'Dempster-Shafer theory' is confusing because it covers several models. Usually the expression 'Dempster-Shafer theory' concerns mathematical models dealing with uncertainty. It corresponds to a 'package' made of at least three components: a belief function and two rules called Dempster's rule of conditioning and Dempster's rule of combination. Unfortunately often authors omit to state exactly what the belief function is supposed to quantify, and most confusion encountered in the literature about belief functions results from the fact people shift between definitions.

4.1 The upper and lower probability model

The strength of the agent's opinion is quantified by a probability function P defined on Ω. This function P is only known to belong to a family of probability functions defined on Ω. This family is denoted Π. Then P_* is defined as the lower envelope and P^* as the upper envelope of Π.

$$\begin{aligned} P_*(A) &= \min\{P(A) : P \in \Pi\}, \\ P^*(A) &= \max\{P(A) : P \in \Pi\}. \end{aligned}$$

The lower envelope does not always characterizes the Π family. We will restrain ourselves to the classical case where $P_*(A) = \inf\{P(A) : P \in \Pi\}$. In that case, there is a one-to-one correspondence between P_* and Π, where Π is then equal to the set of probability functions compatible with P_* (section 2.3):

$$\Pi = \{P : P_*(A) \leq P(A) \leq P^*(A),\ \forall A \subseteq \Omega\}.$$

The constraints on P^* are in fact redundant as $P^*(A) = P_*(\Omega) - P_*(\overline{A})$. They can thus be neglected.

In general, the lower envelope P_* of a convex family of probability functions is not a belief function (not even capacities monotone of order 2). Nevertheless, for some convex families, the lower envelope happens to be a belief function, and this is the kind of families considered by those using the interpretation of *bel* as a lower probability.

In that model, for every $A \subseteq \Omega$, there exists a value $P(A)$ that quantifies the strength of the opinions held by the agent that the actual world belongs to A. But the function P is not known, and we only know that the function P belongs to a convex family Π the lower envelope of which is a (normalized) belief function.

In this context, the dynamic assumption is accepted (section 3.5). So conditioning and revision become synonymous. The appropriate rule to represent conditioning is the natural extension rule ((Walley, 1991; Jaffray, 1992; Fagin & Halpern, 1991). Suppose the conditioning event is A, i.e., You know for sure that $\omega_0 \in A$. Each P in Π is conditioned on A by Bayes rule. This conditioning procedure induces a new family of (conditional) probability functions, denoted Π_A, where:

$$\Pi_A = \{P[A] : P[A](X) = P(X \cap A)/P(A), \forall X \subseteq \Omega, P \in \Pi\}.$$

This family is convex. When the lower envelope of Π is a belief function, then the lower envelope of Π_A, denoted $bel[A]$, is also a belief function (Jaffray, 1992; Fagin & Halpern, 1991). It satisfies:

$$bel[A](X) = \frac{bel(X \cap A)}{bel(X \cap A) + pl(\overline{B} \cap A)}.$$

Jaffray (1992) presents the relation between the basic belief assignment related to *bel* and the basic belief assignment related to $bel[A]$.

In that upper and lower probability context, Dempster's rule of conditioning can be derived in very special cases (Moral & de Campos, 1990; Gilboa & Schmeidler, 1992)). Suppose the conditioning event is A, and we apply Bayes conditioning rule only to the probability functions in Π that satisfy $P(A) = pl(A)$. Then the lower envelope of the family Π^*_A of conditional probability functions so built is equal to the belief function obtained by applying Dempster's rule of conditioning to *bel*, the lower envelope of Π.

$$\Pi^*_A = \{P[A] : P[A] \in \Pi_A, P(A) = \max\{P'(A) : P' \in \Pi\}\},$$

$$\min\{P[A](X) : P[A] \in \Pi_A^*\} = bel(X \cup \overline{A}) - bel(\overline{A}),$$

where

$$bel(X) = \min\{P(X) : P \in \Pi\}.$$

Nevertheless, this restricted conditioning process hardly fits with the general idea of conditioning and that it would be the adequate way to condition in the upper and lower probability context is still an open question. In fact, Kyburg (1987a) and Voorbraak (1991) both criticize Dempster-Shafer theory as inadequate because Dempster's rule of conditioning leads to incorrect results for conditioning. But their implicit interpretation of belief functions was the upper and lower probabilities model, a context where indeed Dempster's rule of conditioning should not be applied (or at least its use should then be clearly justified).

In the upper and lower probability context, Dempster's rule of combination is not used as it does not seem to correspond to any realistic process.

In fact Kyburg and Voorbraak do not consider the explicit existence of some unknown probability function. They just assume that a family Π of probability functions characterizes the agent beliefs and they defend that the conditioning process be defined by the natural extension rule.

That *bel*, defined as the lower envelope of Π, represents 'degrees of belief', as admitted by these authors, cannot be answered as the concept of a 'degree of belief' is hardly uniquely defined.

4.2 Dempster's model and the hint model of Kohlas and Monney

Dempster (1967, 1968, 1972) studied belief functions while trying to solve the problem of fiducial inference. Dempster's approach assumes two finite spaces X and Y, a probability measure P^X on X, and a one-to-many mapping $\Gamma : X \rightarrow 2^Y$ from X to the power set of Y. So P^X induces 'random sets' on Y, and all that can be stated about the probability $P^Y(y_0 \in A)$ that the actual (but unknown) value y_0 of Y is in $A \subseteq Y$ is that

$$P^Y(y_0 \in A) \in [bel^Y(A), pl^Y(A)]$$

where

$$\begin{aligned} bel^Y(A) &= \sum_{\Gamma(x)\subseteq A} P^X(x), \\ pl^Y(A) &= \sum_{\Gamma(x)\cap A\neq\emptyset} P^X(x). \end{aligned}$$

It is mathematically true that for any belief function bel^Y on Y, one can describe a space X, a probability measure P^X on X and a mapping $\Gamma : X \rightarrow 2^Y$ that together generate the belief function bel^Y. If the X domain, the P^X and the Γ mapping have a meaningful interpretation, then the model can be appropriate.

It can be shown that the model can be reduced to the previous upper and lower probability model. Suppose we knew the values of the conditional probability functions $P^Y[x]$ defined on Y for every $x \in X$. Then:

$$P^Y(A) = \sum_{x \in X} P^Y[x](A) P^X(x).$$

The conditional probability functions happen to be unknown, except for the constraint that $P^Y[x](y) = 0$ if $y \notin \Gamma(x)$. Let Π be the family of all conditional probability functions on Y that satisfy the last constraints. Then:

$$bel^Y(A) = \min\{P^Y(A) = \sum_{x \in X} P^Y[x](A) P^X(x) : P^Y[x] \in \Pi\}$$

So in a certain sense, there is a mathematical link between Dempster's model and the upper and lower probability model. That this link corresponds to some reality depends on the application to which the model is applied.

The hint model of Kohlas and Monney (1994) is a full-grown example of Dempster's model. The x's are assumptions, P^X is a probability measure that expresses the agent's beliefs about which assumption x holds, and Y is a space of hypotheses. The Γ mapping expresses the fact that assumption x is a support for the set of hypotheses $\Gamma(x)$.

Kohlas and Monney assume Dempster's original structure (X, P^X, Γ, Y) where X, Y, P^X and Γ are as defined above. They assume the existence of a question whose answer is unknown. The set Y is the set of possible answers to the question. One and only one element of Y is the correct answer to the question. The goal is to make assertions about the answer in the light of the available information. We assume that this information allows for several different interpretations, depending on some unknown circumstances. These interpretations are regrouped into the set X and there is exactly one correct interpretation. Not all interpretations are equally likely and the known probability measure P^X on X reflects our information in that respect. Furthermore, if the interpretation x∈X is the correct one, then the answer is known to be in the subset $\Gamma(x) \subseteq Y$. The structure (X, P^X, Γ, Y) is called a hint. An interpretation $x \in X$ supports the hypothesis $H \subseteq Y$ if $\Gamma(x) \subseteq H$ because in that case the answer is necessarily in H. The degree of support of H, denoted $sp(H)$, is defined as the probability of all supporting interpretations of H (Kohlas & Monney, 1994, page vi), with a few adaptations). The *sp* function is the bel function studied in this paper.

The hint theory corresponds to Dempster's original approach. They call their measure a degree of support, instead of belief, to avoid personal, subjective connotation, but degrees of support and degrees of belief are mathematically equivalent and conceptually very close. In the hint theory, the primitive concept is the hint from which degrees of supports are deduced, whereas, in the transferable belief model, the primitive concept is the degree of belief.

Conditioning in the hint model must be handled with care (Smets, 1993b). One can:

1. condition on the fact that the actual value x_0 of X is in $A \subseteq X$, in which case P^X is conditioned on A according to Bayes' rule. Then:

$$bel^Y[x_0 \in A](H) = \frac{bel^Y(\Gamma(A) \cap H)}{bel^Y(\Gamma(A))}, \ \forall H \subseteq Y.$$

This rule is known as the geometrical rule of conditioning (Shafer, 1976b; Suppes & Zanotti, 1977).

2. condition on the fact that the actual value y_0 of Y is in $H' \subseteq Y$. Then:

$$pl^Y[H'](H) = \frac{pl^Y(H \cap H')}{pl^Y(H')},$$

i.e., Dempster's rule of conditioning.

Decision process in the hint model is not an essential element of the theory which is more focussed on reasoning under uncertainty than deciding. Apparently no specific solutions seems to have been advanced in such a context, except for the work of Schaller (1991). It is not obvious which, if any, of the pignistic transformation or the upper and lower expectation solution is applicable. We will not further study how decision should be made in that model. We refer to Schaller (1991).

4.3 The transferable belief model of Smets

The TBM (for transferable belief model) provides a model for the representation of quantified beliefs. The value $bel(A)$ represents the agent's belief that the actual world belongs to $A \subseteq \Omega$. No concept of probability measure underlies the description of the TBM. A study of the rationality properties that should be satisfied by a function which purpose is to quantify someone's beliefs leads to the use of belief functions (Smets, 1997, 1993d). These axiomatic studies lead also to the derivation of Dempster's rule of conditioning. From this construction, we have derived (and often justified) many other concepts like the conjunctive combination rule (that is essentially equal to Dempster's rule of combination), the disjunctive rule of combination, the specialization concept, the least commitment principle, the cautious combination rule, the measure of information content, the concept of doxastic independence, ...

The core of the TBM is essentially inspired by what is described in Shafer's book (note that some of Shafer's later papers enhance other interpretations).

The TBM is a model to represent quantified beliefs free from any probability connotation. It is based on the assumption that beliefs manifest themselves at two mental levels: the credal level where beliefs are entertained and the pignistic level where beliefs are used to make decisions.

Usually these two levels are not distinguished and probability functions are used to quantify beliefs at both levels. The justification for the use of probability functions is usually linked to "rational" behavior to be held by an ideal agent involved in some decision contexts (Ramsey, 1964; Savage, 1954; DeGroot, 1970).

This result is accepted here, except that these probability functions quantify the uncertainty only when a decision is really involved.

In the TBM, we assume that the pignistic and the credal levels are distinct which implies that the justification for using probability functions at the credal level does not hold anymore (Dubois, Prade, & Smets, 1996). At the credal level, beliefs are represented by a belief function; at the pignistic level, this belief function induces a probability function that is used to make decision. This probability function should not be understood as representing Your beliefs, it is nothing but the additive measure needed to make decision, i.e., to compute the expected utilities. Of course this probability function is directly induced by the belief function representing Your belief at the credal level. The link between the two levels is achieved by the pignistic transformation that transforms a belief function into a probability function. Its nature and justification is detailed in section 5.

In the TBM, the basic belief assignment receives a natural interpretation. For $A \subseteq \Omega$, $m(A)$ is that part of Your belief that supports A, i.e., that the actual world ω_0 belongs to A, and that, due to lack of information, does not support any strict subset of A.

If some further pieces of evidence become available to You and You accept them as valid, and if their only impact bearing on Ω is that they imply that the actual world ω_0 does not belong to $\overline{B}$, then the mass $m(A)$ initially allocated to A is transferred to $A \cap B$. Indeed, some of Your belief (quantified by $m(A)$) was allocated to A, and now You accept that $\omega_0 \notin \overline{B}$, so that mass $m(A)$ is transferred to $A \cap B$ (hence the name of the model). The resulting new basic belief assignment is the one obtained by the application of Dempster's rule of conditioning .

The degree of belief $bel(A)$ quantifies the total amount of justified specific support given to A. It is obtained by summing all basic belief masses given to subsets $X \subseteq \Omega$ with $X \subseteq A$ (and $X \neq \emptyset$). Indeed a part of belief that supports that the actual world ω_0 is in B also supports that ω_0 is in A whenever $B \subseteq A$. So for all $A \subseteq \Omega$,

$$bel(A) = \sum_{\emptyset \neq B \subseteq A} m(B)$$

We say justified because we include in $bel(A)$ only the basic belief masses given to subsets of A. For instance, consider two distinct elements x and y of Ω. The basic belief mass $m(\{x, y\})$ given to $\{x, y\}$ could support x if further information indicates this. However given the available information the basic belief mass can only be given to $\{x, y\}$. We say specific because the basic belief mass $m(\emptyset)$ is not included in $bel(A)$ as it is given to the subset $\emptyset$ that supports not only A but also $\overline{A}$.

The degree of plausibility $pl(A)$ for $A \subseteq \Omega$ quantifies the maximum amount of potential specific support that could be given to A. It is obtained by adding all the basic belief masses given to subsets X compatible with A, i.e., such that $X \cap A \neq \emptyset$:

$$pl(A) = \sum_{B \cap A \neq \emptyset} m(B) = bel(\Omega) - bel(\overline{A}).$$

We say potential because the basic belief masses included in $pl(A)$ could be transferred to non-empty subsets of A if new information could justify such a transfer. It would be the case if we learn that $\overline{A}$ is impossible.

The plausibility function *pl* is just another way of representing the information contained in *bel* and could be as well forgotten, except it often provides a mathematically convenient alternative representation of the beliefs.

4.4 Probability functions extended to modal propositions

Ruspini (1986, 1987) has proposed to consider $bel^{\Omega}_{Y,t}(A)$ as the probability that the agent Y knows at time t that A holds. Pearl (1988) proposed to understand it as the probability that A is provable. In both cases, we assume a set of worlds to which probabilities are attached. We can write

$$bel^{\Omega}(A) = P(\Box A) = P(\{w : w \in \Omega, w \models \Box A\}).$$

where the $\Box$ operator denotes the modal operator which meaning, here, can be seen as 'knowing' or 'proving'.

The static analysis of the $P(\Box A)$ function where A is a non-modal proposition shows that it is indeed a belief function over the set of non-modal propositions (see also Tsiporkova *et al.* (1999b, 1999, 1999a, ?)). The dynamic analysis allows to derive both the geometrical rule of conditioning and Dempster's rule of conditioning, the first after conditioning on a subsets of worlds that entail a given proposition, the second by a minimal chance of the accessibility relation described in Kripke semantic for modal logic. We are not aware of any particular solution proposed within such frameworks to make decisions. They will not be further studied in this paper.

5 Decision making in the TBM framework

5.1 The origin of the pignistic probability function

Let Ω be a finite set of worlds, and ω_0 denote the actual world. Let bel^{Ω} denote Your belief about the actual value of ω_0. When a decision must be made that depends on ω_0, You construct a probability function P^{Ω} on Ω in order to select the optimal decision, i.e., the one that maximizes the expected utility. We assume that P^{Ω} is a function of the belief function bel^{Ω}. It translates the saying that beliefs guide our actions. Hence one must transform bel^{Ω} into a probability function that will be used for selecting the best decision.

Let F be the betting frame, i.e., the frame on which decisions must be made. It is the set of alternatives in Ω on which we must build the probability function.

Here, the betting frame F will be equal to Ω, but later on (section 5.4), we will see that F and Ω can be different.

Let $BetP^F$ denote the probability function on F needed for selecting the optimal decision (*Bet* is for betting and P for probability). The transformation between bel^Ω and $BetP^F$ that we will derive will be called the pignistic transformation. It is denoted by Γ_F. So

$$BetP^F = \Gamma_F(bel^\Omega).$$

We call $BetP^F$ a pignistic probability to insist on the fact that it is only a probability measure used to make decisions and not a probability function that represents Your beliefs. Of course $BetP^F$ is mathematically a classical probability measure on F.

The structure of the pignistic transformation is derived from the rationality requirement that underlies the following scenario.

Example 5.1. Buying Your friend's drink. Suppose You have two friends, Glen (G) and Judea (J). You know they will toss a fair coin and the winner will visit You tonight. You want to buy the drink Your friend would like to have tonight: coke, wine or beer. You can only buy one drink. Let $D = \{\text{coke, wine, beer}\}$ and $F = D$.

Let $bel^D[G]$ quantify Your belief about the drink Glen will ask for, should he come. Given $bel^D[G]$, You build the pignistic probability $BetP^D[G]$ about the drink Glen will ask by applying the (still to be defined) pignistic transformation. You build in the same way the pignistic probability $BetP^D[J]$ based on $bel^D[J]$, Your belief about the drink Judea will ask for, should he come. The two pignistic probability distributions $BetP^D[G]$ and $BetP^D[J]$ are the conditional probability distributions about the drink that will be asked for given Glen or Judea comes. The pignistic probability distributions $BetP^D$ about the drink that Your visitor will ask for is then:

$$BetP^D(d) = .5BetP^D[G](d) + .5BetP^D[J](d), \ \forall d \in D.$$

You will use the pignistic probability function $BetP^D$ to decide which drink to buy.

But You might as well reconsider the whole problem and first compute Your belief bel^D about the drink Your visitor (V) would like to have. We have shown (Smets, 1997) that bel^D is given by:

$$bel^D(d) = .5bel^D[G](d) + .5bel^D[J](d), \ \forall d \subseteq D.$$

Given bel^D, You could then build the pignistic probability $BetP^D$ You should use to decide which drink to buy. It seems reasonable to assume that both solutions must be equal. This requirement is called the linearity assumption and formally defined below. In such a case, the pignistic transformation is uniquely defined. □

5.2 Deriving the pignistic transformation

Formally, we require that the pignistic transformation satisfies the following assumptions.

Proposition 5.1 ***Credal-Pignistic Link.*** *Let F be a finite set and let bel^F be a belief function defined on F. Let $BetP^F$ be a probability function on F. For all $\omega \in F$,*

$$BetP^F(\omega) = \Gamma_F(bel^\Omega)(\omega).$$

Axiom 5.1 translates the idea that our beliefs guide our behaviors. The function Γ_F is called the pignistic transformation. Evaluation of $BetP^F(A)$ for $A \subseteq F$ is obtained by adding the probabilities $BetP^F(\omega)$ for $\omega \in A$.

Proposition 5.2 ***Linearity.*** *Let bel_1 and bel_2 be two belief functions on the frame of discernment F. Let Γ_F be the pignistic transformation that transforms a belief function over F into a probability function $BetP^F$ over F. Then Γ_F satisfies, for any $\alpha \in [0,1]$,*

$$\Gamma_F(\alpha bel_1 + (1-\alpha)bel_2) = \alpha\Gamma_F(bel_1) + (1-\alpha)\Gamma_F(bel_2)$$

The origin of the linearity requirement was explained in section 5.1. Technical assumptions must be added that are hardly arguable:

Proposition 5.3 ***Efficiency.*** $BetP^F(\Omega) = 1$.

Proposition 5.4 ***Anonymity.*** *Let R be a permutation function from F to F. The pignistic probability given to the image of $A \subseteq F$ after permutation of the elements of F is the same as the pignistic probability given to A before applying the permutation:*

$$BetP^{F*}(R(A)) = BetP^F(A),\ \forall A \subseteq F,$$

where $BetP^{F*}$ is the pignistic probability function on $F*$ after applying the permutation function.

Proposition 5.5 ***Impossible Event.*** *The pignistic probability of an impossible event is zero.*

Proposition 5.6 ***Projectivity.*** *If bel^F happens to be a probability function P defined on F, then $\Gamma_F(P) = P$.*

Proposition 5.3 tells that the pignistic probabilities given to the elements of F add to one. Proposition 5.4 states that renaming the elements of Ω does not change the pignistic probabilities. Proposition 5.5 tells that the pignistic probabilities given to a subset is not changed when one adds to it any element known to be impossible. Proposition 5.6 recognizes that if someone's belief is already described by a probability function, then the pignistic probabilities and the degrees of belief are numerically equal.

Under these assumptions, it is possible to derive uniquely Γ_F. The proof can be found in Shapley (1953).

Theorem 5.1 ***Pignistic Transformation Theorem.*** *Let bel^F be a belief function on space F and m^F its related bba. Let $BetP^F = \Gamma_F(bel^F)$. The only solution $BetP^F$ that satisfies propositions 5.1 to 5.6 is:*

$$BetP^F(\omega) = \sum_{A \subseteq F, \omega \in A} \frac{1}{|A|} \frac{m^F(A)}{(1 - m^F(\emptyset))}, \ \forall \omega \in F, \tag{2}$$

where $|A|$ is the number of elements of Ω in A, and

$$BetP^F(A) = \sum_{\omega \in A} BetP^F(w), \ \forall A \subseteq F.$$

It is easy to show that the function $BetP^F$ obtained from (2) is indeed a probability function.

Relation (2) can be also expressed as a function of bel^F instead of m^F. It becomes:

$$BetP^F(\omega) = \sum_{A \subseteq \overline{\omega}} \frac{|A|! \ (|\Omega| - |A| - 1)!}{|\Omega|!} \ \frac{bel^F(w \cup A) - bel^F(A)}{bel^F(\Omega)}.$$

As such, this equation is hardly useful but it enhances that the pignistic transformation produces a probability function whenever bel^F is monotone for inclusion (hence a capacity monotone of order 1).

Example 5.2. A pignistic transformation. Let $F = \{a, b, c\}$, and $m^F(\{a\}) = .3$, $m^F(\{a, b\}) = .2$, $m^F(\{b, c\}) = .2$, and $m^F(\{a, b, c\}) = .3$. Then $BetP^F(a) = .3 + .2/2 + .3/3 = .5$, $BetP^F(b) = .2/2 + .2/2 + .3/3 = .3$ and $BetP^F(c) = .2/2 + .3/3 = .2$. We also have, a.o., $BetP^F(\{a, b\}) = .5 + .3 = .8$. □

The pignistic probability so derived fits with common sense. It consists in distributing every basic belief mass equally among the elements that belong to its focal element. In (Smets & Kennes, 1994), we had called this property the generalized insufficient reason principle. It was a very unfortunate name as some readers thought that the pignistic transformation is *justified* by a generalization of the insufficient reason principle. It is not the case. The insufficient reason principle, as such, is not an acceptable rationality principle as it is responsible for most contradictions encountered in probability theory. The reason why the TBM escapes from these contradictions is that the betting frame F is established before applying the transformation. All contradictions encountered when applying the insufficient reason principle result from the fact the betting frame (or its equivalent) can vary, what leads to contradictions. Had it been fixed, the insufficient reason principle would not be prone to contradictions and would become a quite valid principle.

5.2.1 Historical notes

1. In a context similar to ours, Shapley (1953) derived the same relation (2). The model he derived was later called the 'transferable utility model' (Roth, 1988) whereas, unaware of it but amazingly, we called our model the 'transferable belief model'.

2. The solution derived from the pignistic transformation was already proposed in (Dubois & Pradre, 1982; Williams, 1982) as 'natural' solutions but without justification.

5.3 The case of two independent frames

Let bel^{Ω} be a belief function on a frame of discernment Ω. Let Ω' be a coarsening of Ω, i.e., the elements of Ω' are the elements of a partition of Ω. Let $bel^{\Omega\downarrow\Omega'}$ denote the belief function defined on Ω' such that:

$$bel^{\Omega\downarrow\Omega'}(A) = bel^{\Omega}(A),\ \forall A \subseteq \Omega'.$$

Marginalization is a special case of coarsening: for example let $\Omega = X \times Y$ and $\Omega' = X$.

Suppose a belief function $bel^{X\times Y}$ on the frame of discernment $X \times Y$ which bba $m^{X\times Y}$ satisfies:

$$\begin{aligned} m^{X\times Y}(w) &= m^{X\times Y\downarrow X}(x)m^{X\times Y\downarrow Y}(y), \text{ if } w = x \times y \text{ for } x \subseteq X, y \subseteq Y, \\ &= 0, \text{otherwise.} \end{aligned}$$

In that case, X and Y are said to be non-interactive under $bel^{X\times Y}$. In probability theory, non-interactivity and stochastic independence are equivalent. In the TBM, this equivalence is more delicate (Ben Yaghlane, Smets, & Mellouli, 2000).

Consider the pignistic probabilities on the spaces $X \times Y$, and those on X and on Y. They will be related as if the two variables were stochastically independent.

Theorem 5.2 *Let X and Y be two non-interactive variables under $bel^{X\times Y}$. Then, $\forall x \in X, \forall y \in Y$:*

$$\Gamma_{X\times Y}(bel^{X\times Y})(x,y) = \Gamma_X(bel^{X\times Y\downarrow X})(x)\Gamma_Y(bel^{X\times Y\downarrow Y})(y),$$

or equivalently:

$$BetP^{X\times Y}(x,y) = BetP^{X}(x)BetP(^{Y}(y).$$

This theorem states that the pignistic probabilities computed on the elements of the $X \times Y$ space are equal to the product of the pignistic probabilities computed on their marginals. This is of course a rephrasing of the major property encountered in probability theory under stochastic independence. This result is important, as its absence would have raised serious doubts about the validity of the pignistic transformation.

It was hoped that this constraint would be only satisfied by the pignistic transformation, in which case we would have obtained a second justification for its use. But this is not the case. Indeed, if the probability needed at the pignistic level was defined on the elements of F as proportional to the plausibility given to these elements, then the last relation of theorem 5.2 would be also satisfied.

5.4 The betting frame

The pignistic transformation depends on the structure of the frame on which the decision must be made. One must first define the 'betting frame' F, i.e., the set of atoms on which stakes will be allocated. The granularity of this frame F is defined so that a stake could be given to each element of F independently of the stakes given to the other elements of F. Suppose one starts with a belief function bel^{Ω} on a frame Ω. If the stakes given to elements A and B of Ω must necessarily be always equal, both A and B belong to the same granule of the betting frame F. For instance, suppose You want to bet on the fact that Michel lives in Paris or in Brussels. Let M = 'Michel lives in Paris' and T = 'it rains now in Tokyo'. Let $\Omega = \{M\&T,\ M\&\neg T,\ \neg M\&T,\ \neg M\&\neg T\}$. There are this four worlds in Ω. Nevertheless, the stakes put on the worlds $M\&T$ and $M\&\neg T$ are by 'necessity' equal as we bet only on Michel's home town. So $M\&T$ and $M\&\neg T$ are in the same granule of the betting frame, and F has only two elements: $F = \{M,\ \neg M\}$.

The betting frame F is organized so that the granules of Ω are the elements of F. The problem is then to define bel^F on F given bel^{Ω}. This is achieved by applying a sequence of coarsenings and/or refinements on Ω. The only constraints that must hold between F and Ω is that the frames F and Ω are compatible, i.e., F and Ω have a common refinement (Shafer, 1976a page 114). The pignistic probability $BetP^F$ is then built from the belief function bel^F so derived on F from bel^{Ω}. Therefore we can write $BetP^F = \Gamma_F(bel^{\Omega})$ where it is understood that the Γ_F operator not only transforms a belief function into a probability function but it also transforms bel^{Ω} into bel^F (provided F and Ω are compatible, a constraint usually satisfied).

5.4.1 Betting under total ignorance.

To show the power of our approach, let us consider the next examples based on total ignorance and which solution in probability theory is often considered as disturbing.

Example 5.3. Betting and total ignorance. Consider a guard in a huge power plant. On the emergency panel, alarms A_1 and A_2 are both on. The guard never heard about these two alarms, they were hidden in a remote place. He takes the instruction book and discovers that alarm A_1 is on iff circuit C is in state C_1 or C_2 and that alarm A_2 is on iff circuit D is in state D_1, D_2

or D_3. He never heard about these C and D circuits. Therefore, his beliefs on the C circuit will be characterized by a 'vacuous' belief function on space $\Omega_C = \{C_1, C_2\}$, i.e., a belief function which bba satisfies $m^{\Omega_C}(\Omega_C) = 1$ (this particular belief function is the one that represents the state of total ignorance, as the only supported subset is the whole space Ω itself). By the application of (2) his pignistic probabilities will be given by

$$BetP^{\Omega_C}(C_1) = BetP^{\Omega_C}(C_2) = 1/2.$$

Similarly for the D circuit, the guard's belief on space $\Omega_D = \{D_1, D_2, D_3\}$ will be vacuous, i.e., $m^{\Omega_D}(\Omega_D) = 1$, and the pignistic probabilities are

$$BetP^{\Omega_D}(D_1) = BetP^{\Omega_D}(D_2) = BetP^{\Omega_D}(D_3) = 1/3.$$

Now, by reading the next page on the manual, the guard discovers that circuits C and D are so made that whenever circuit C is in state C_1, circuit D is in state D_1 and vice-versa. So he learns that C_1 and D_1 are equivalent (given what the guard knows) and that C_2 and (D_2 or D_3) are also equivalent as C is either C_1 or C_2 and D is either D_1 or D_2 or D_3. In the TBM, this information does not modify his belief about which circuit is broken.

If the guard had been a trained Bayesian, he would have assigned value for $P^{\Omega_C}(C_1)$ and $P^{\Omega_D}(D_1)$ (given the lack of any information, they would probably be 1/2 and 1/3, but any value could be used). Once he learns about the equivalence between $C_1$and D_1, he must adapt his probabilities as they must give the same probabilities to C_1 and D_1. Which set of probabilities is he going to update: P^{Ω_C} or P^{Ω_D}, and why?, especially since it must be remembered that he has no knowledge whatsoever about what the circuits are. In a probabilistic approach, the difficulty raised by this type of example results from the requirement that equivalent propositions should receive identical beliefs, and therefore identical probabilities.

Within the transferable belief model, the only requirement is that equivalent propositions should receive equal beliefs (it is satisfied as $bel^{\Omega_C}(C_1) = bel^{\Omega_D}(D_1) = 0$). Pignistic probabilities depend not only on these beliefs but also on the structure of the betting frame. The difference between $BetP^{\Omega_C}(C_1)$ and $BetP^{\Omega_D}(D_1)$ reflects the difference between the two betting frames. □

The fact the TBM can cope easily with such states of ignorance results from the partial dissociation between the credal and the pignistic levels. Bayesians do not consider such a distinction and therefore work in a more limited framework, hence the difficulty they encounter in the present example.

5.4.2 Undefined betting frame.

We consider now the problem where the betting frame is ill defined. Suppose bel^{Ω} is a belief function on a frame Ω and let F be a betting frame compatible with Ω. Let $BetP^F$ be the pignistic probability obtained by applying the pignistic transformation Γ_F to bel^Ω:

$$BetP^F = \Gamma_F(bel^\Omega).$$

Suppose another betting frame F' compatible with Ω. We build $BetP^{F'} = \Gamma_{F'}(bel^\Omega)$ in a way similar to the one used in the previous case. Consider now the family F_A made of all the betting frames F_1, $F_2 \ldots$ compatible with Ω and such that $A \subseteq F_i$ for all i. Compute $BetP^{F_i}(A)$ for all $F_i \in F_A$. Wilson (1993) shows that the minimum of $BetP^{F_i}(A)$ taken over the $F_i \in F_A$ is equal to $bel^\Omega(A)$:

$$\min\{BetP^{F_i}(A) : F_i \in F_A\} = bel^\Omega(A).$$

and that the set of pignistic probabilities $BetP^{F_i}$ that can be obtained from bel^Ω by varying the betting frame F_i is equal to the set $\Pi(bel^\Omega)$ of probability functions compatible with bel^Ω (see section 2.3).

So whatever the betting frame F compatible with Ω such that $A \subseteq F$,

$$BetP^F(A) \geq bel^\Omega(A), \ \forall A \subseteq \Omega.$$

Suppose You ignore what is the appropriate betting frame F. You nevertheless know that, for all $A \subseteq \Omega$, the lowest bound of $BetP^F(A)$ is $bel^\Omega(A)$. Therefore $bel^\Omega(A)$ can be understood as the lowest pignistic probability one could give to A when the betting frame is not fixed (Giles, 1982).

This set $\Pi(bel^\Omega)$ of probability functions compatible with a belief function bel^Ω gets a meaning within the TBM thanks to this result. It is the set of pignistic probability functions defined on betting frames F compatible with Ω that could be induced by bel^Ω when varying the betting frame. Its definition follows from bel^Ω, not the reverse as assumed by the authors who understand bel^Ω as the lower envelope of some class of probability functions. In the TBM, we derive $\Pi(bel^\Omega)$ from bel^Ω, not bel^Ω from $\Pi(bel^\Omega)$.

When betting must be done and the betting frame is totally unknown, all You know is that $BetP^?(A) \in [bel^\Omega(A), pl^\Omega(A)]$, where the ? superscript indicates that the betting frame is unknown. Such a case can be handled by using the procedure developed by Jaffray (1988) and Strat (1990b, 1990a), and detailed in section 6. In fact, if You only know that the betting frame belongs to a given subset F' of the set of all possible betting frames (and not necessarily the set of all possible betting frames), then You can compute the upper and lower bounds of $BetP^?(A)$ as

$$\begin{aligned} BetP_*(A) &= \min\{BetP^F(A) : F \in F'\} \\ BetP^*(A) &= \max\{BetP^F(A) : F \in F'\} \end{aligned}$$

Ordering these intervals is of course not obvious in general. Procedure based on weighted average of the limits of the intervals, like in the Jaffray - Strat solution, is a natural solution. Nevertheless we feel that the present problem is quite artificial (where F' comes from?), and we will not further consider it. Only the case where F' is the set of all possible betting frames is realistic, and it is discussed in section 6.

5.5 The impact of the two-level model

In order to show that the introduction of the two-level mental model is not just an intellectual game, we present an example where the results will be different if one takes the two-level approach as advocated in the transferable belief model or a one-level model like in probability theory.

5.5.1 The Peter, Paul and Marry Saga

Big Boss has decided that Mr. Jones must be murdered by one of the three people present in his waiting room and whose names are Peter, Paul and Marry. Big Boss has decided that the killer on duty will be selected by a throw of a dice: if it is an even number, the killer will be female, if it is an odd number, the killer will be male. You, the judge, know that Mr. Jones has been murdered and who was in the waiting room. You know about the dice throwing, but You do not know what the outcome was and who was actually selected. You are also ignorant as to how Big Boss would have decided between Peter and Paul in the case of an odd number being observed. Given the available information at time t_0, Your odds for betting on the sex of the killer would be 1 to 1 for male versus female.

At time $t_1 > t_0$, You learn that if Big Boss had not selected Peter, then Peter would necessarily have gone to the police station at the time of the killing in order to have a perfect alibi. Peter indeed went to the police station, so he is not the killer. The question is how You would bet now on male versus female: should Your odds be 1 to 1 (as in the transferable belief model) or 1 to 2 (as in the most natural Bayesian model).

Note that the alibi evidence makes 'Peter is not the killer' and 'Peter has a perfect alibi' equivalent. The more classical evidence 'Peter has a perfect alibi' would only imply P('Peter is not the killer' | 'Peter has a perfect alibi') = 1. But P('Peter has a perfect alibi' | 'Peter is not the killer') would be undefined and would then give rise to further discussion, which would be useless for our purpose. In this presentation, the latter probability is also 1.

5.5.2 The transferable belief model solution

Let k be the killer. The information about the waiting room and the dice throwing pattern induces the following basic belief assignment $m_{t_0}^{\Omega}$:

$$k \in \Omega = \{\text{Peter, Paul, Mary}\},$$

$$\begin{aligned} m_{t_0}^{\Omega}(\{\text{Mary}\}) &= .5 \\ m_{t_0}^{\Omega}(\{\text{Peter, Paul}\}) &= .5 \end{aligned}$$

The basic belief mass .5 given to {Peter, Paul} corresponds to that part of belief that supports 'Peter or Paul', could possibly support each of them, but given the lack of further information, cannot be divided more specifically between Peter and Paul.

Let $BetP_{t_0}^{\Omega}$ be the pignistic probability obtained by applying the pignistic transformation to $m_{t_0}^{\Omega}$ on the betting frame Ω. By relation (2), we get:

$$\begin{aligned} BetP_{t_0}^{\Omega}(\text{Peter}) &= .25 \\ BetP_{t_0}^{\Omega}(\text{Paul}) &= .25 \\ BetP_{t_0}^{\Omega}(\text{Mary}) &= .50 \end{aligned}$$

Given the information available at time t_0, the bet on the killer's sex (male versus female) is held at odds 1 to 1.

Peter's alibi induces a revision of $m_{t_0}^{\Omega}$ into $m_{t_1}^{\Omega}$ by Dempster's rule of conditioning:

$$\begin{aligned} m_{t_1}^{\Omega}(\text{Mary}) &= .50 \\ m_{t_1}^{\Omega}(\text{Paul}) &= .50 \end{aligned}$$

The basic belief mass that was given to 'Peter or Paul' is transferred to Paul.

Let $BetP_{t_1}^{\Omega}$ be the pignistic probability obtained by applying the pignistic transformation to $m_{t_1}^{\Omega}$ on the betting frame Ω^* whose elements are Paul and Marry.

$$\begin{aligned} BetP_{t_1}^{\Omega *}(Paul) &= .50 \\ BetP_{t_1}^{\Omega *}(Mary) &= .50 \end{aligned}$$

Your odds for betting on male versus female would still be 1 to 1.

5.5.3 The probabilistic solution

The probabilistic solution is not obvious as one data is missing: the value α of the probability that Big Boss selects Peter if he must select a male killer. Any value could be accepted for α, but given the total ignorance in which we are about this value, let us assume that $\alpha = .5$, the most natural solution (any value could be used without changing the problem we raise). Then the odds on male versus female before learning about Peter's alibi is 1 to 1, and after learning about Peter's alibi, it becomes 1 to 2. The probabilities are then:

$$\begin{aligned} P_{t_1}^{\Omega^*}(Paul) &= 0.33 \\ P_{t_1}^{\Omega^*}(Mary) &= 0.66. \end{aligned}$$

The 1 to 1 odds of the transferable belief model solution can only be obtained in a probabilistic approach if $\alpha = 0$. Some critics would claim that the transferable belief model solution is valid as it fits with $\alpha = 0$. The only trouble with this answer is that if the alibi story had applied to Paul, than we would still bet on the frame Ω^{**} ={Peter, Marry} at 1 to 1 odds within the TBM approach. Instead the probabilistic solution with $\alpha = 0$ would lead to a 0 to 1 bet, as the probabilities are:

$$\begin{aligned} P_{t_1}^{\Omega^{**}}(Peter) &= 0.00 \\ P_{t_1}^{\Omega^{**}}(Mary) &= 1.00 \end{aligned}$$

So the classical probabilistic analysis does not lead to the transferable belief model solution.

5.5.4 Which solution is 'good'?

We are facing two solutions for the bet on male versus female after learning about Peter's alibi: the 1 to 1 or the 1 to 2 odds? Which solution is 'good' is not decidable, as it requires the definition of 'good'.

Computer simulations have been suggested for solving the dilemma, but they are useless. In any finite sequence of simulations, the proportion of cases when Peter is selected when Big Boss must choose a male killer is well defined. If this proportion is close from the α used by the Bayesian, the Bayesian solution will be the best, otherwise the TBM can be the best. But this implies that we introduce a probability α equal to the probability that Peter is selected when the killer is a male. In that case the problem is no more the one we had consider in the initial story. If such an α were known, then it would have been included in the TBM analysis, and in that case the TBM and the Bayesian solutions become identical, as it should be.

So in order to compare the TBM and the Bayesian solution of the initial saga, we are only left over with a subjective comparison of the two solutions... or an in depth comparison of the theoretical foundations that led to these solutions.

Other examples illustrating the difference between the Bayesian approach and the TBM approach can be found in Smets (1994b) (see the breakable sensors example)

5.6 An operational definition of *bel*.

The pignistic transformation can be used in order to provide both an operational definition of the degrees of belief, and a method to assess them. The approach is essentially identical to the one encountered in subjective probability theory except we use the possibility to construct several betting frames (see section 3.1).

Operational definition of degrees of belief. Suppose a finite space Ω, a family of games $G = \{G_1, G_2 \ldots\}$ built on the betting frames $F_i, i = 1, 2 \ldots$, respectively, where each frame is compatible with Ω. Suppose a player and a banker. Consider one game $G_i \in G$ and its betting frame F_i. Suppose A is discerned by F_i. We have $'BetP^{F_i}_{You,t}(A) = x'$ iff You consider at time t that the player must pay \$$x$ to the banker to enter the game G_i where the player wins \$1 from the banker if the actual world belongs to A and \$0 otherwise, and You are ready to be any of the player or the banker. Consider then all possible games G_i on G. Then $bel^{\Omega}_{You,t}$ is the belief function on Ω such that:

1. $BetP^{F_i}_{You,t} = \Gamma_{F_i}(bel^{\Omega}_{You,t}), \ \forall i = 1, 2 \ldots.$
2. $bel^{\Omega}_{You,t}(A) = \min\{BetP^{F_i}_{You,t}(A) : i = 1, 2 \ldots\}.$

where the two cases are equivalent.

It is important to realize that the pignistic probability functions obtained with different frames are not necessarily related between them by the laws of probability. So you could bet on A versus B where $B = \overline{A}$ with pignistic probabilities of 1/2 and 1/2, and on A versus B_1 versus B_2 where $B_1 \cup B_2 = B$ with pignistic probabilities of 1/3, 1/3 and 1/3 (this is encountered in case of total ignorance on $\Omega = A \cup B$, (see (Smets & Kennes, 1994)).

5.7 The assessment of *bel*

In (Smets, 1998a), we explain in detail and illustrate how the bba's can be assessed. Here, we present only the general procedure.

The assessment of a belief function is essentially obtained through a schema based on preference between gambles (see section 3.2).

The method proposed in probability theory extends directly to belief functions. It is based on using several betting frames. Let a finite set Ω and a family of compatible betting frames F_1, F_2... For each F_i, we assess $BetP^{F_i}$ using the preference ordering between two bets as done in section 3.2. We then determine the set BF_i^Ω of belief function on Ω which pignistic transformation on F_i is $BetP^{F_i}$. We repeat the procedure with each F_i's. The bel^Ω belongs to the intersection of all the BF_i^Ω. If the intersection is empty, then it means the pignistic probability functions are inconsistent, what ideally should not occur, but it happens of course in practice, just as in probability theory where people assess probabilities that usually violate Kolmogorof axioms. It only translates the imprecision of the assessment tool. Thanks to the fact that a belief function is defined by a finite number of values and the possibility to build as many betting frames as one needs, the intersection can be such that it contains only one belief function.

The procedure is illustrated in the next example.

Example 5.4. Assessing *bel*. Suppose $\Omega = \{a, b\}$ where a denotes 'Circuit X is broken' and b denotes 'Circuit X is not broken'. Consider the betting frame F_1 with elements a and b. Suppose Your pignistic probabilities on that frame are:

$$\begin{aligned} BetP^{F_1}(a) &= 4/9 \\ BetP^{F_1}(b) &= 5/9. \end{aligned}$$

Suppose ψ and $\overline{\psi}$ are two complementary but otherwise unknown sets of worlds that denote that some circuit C whose properties are completely unknown to You is broken or not broken, respectively. The event $a \cap \psi$ will occur if circuits X and C are broken. The event $a \cap \overline{\psi}$ will occur if circuit X is broken and circuit C is not broken. Let us consider the betting frame F_2 with elements $\{a \cap \psi, a \cap \overline{\psi}, b\}$, and suppose Your pignistic probabilities on that new frame are:

$$BetP^{F_2}(a \cap \psi) = 7/27$$

$$\begin{aligned} BetP^{F_2}(a\cap\overline{\psi}) &= 7/27 \\ BetP^{F_2}(b) &= 13/27. \end{aligned}$$

Then it can be proven that the unique solution for m^Ω is:

$$\begin{aligned} m^\Omega(a) &= 2/9, \\ m^\Omega(b) &= 3/9 \\ m^\Omega(a,b) &= 4/9. \end{aligned}$$

To show it, let m' be the bba induces by m^Ω on F_2 by the uninformative refinement:

$$\begin{aligned} m'(a\cap\psi) &= 0 \\ m'(a\cap\overline{\psi}) &= 0, \\ m'(b) &= m^\Omega(b) \\ m'(a\cap\psi, a\cap\overline{\psi}) &= m^\Omega(a), \\ m'(a\cap\psi, b) &= 0 \\ m'(a\cap\overline{\psi}, b) &= 0 \\ m'(a\cap\psi, a\cap\overline{\psi}, b) &= m^\Omega(a,b). \end{aligned}$$

The solution for m^Ω must solve two linear equations derived from (2):

$$\begin{aligned} 4/9 &= m^\Omega(a) + \frac{m^\Omega(a,b)}{2} \\ 7/27 &= m'(a\cap\psi) + \frac{m'(a\cap\psi, a\cap\overline{\psi})}{2} + \frac{m'(a\cap\psi, b)}{2} + \frac{m'(a\cap\psi, a\cap\overline{\psi}, b)}{3} \\ &= \frac{m^\Omega(a)}{2} + \frac{m^\Omega(a,b)}{3}. \end{aligned}$$

The values of m^Ω are the only one that satisfy these two equations (given their sum is 1 as they are bbm). □

It might seem odd that b receives the pignistic probabilities $\frac{5}{9}$ or $\frac{13}{27}$ according to the betting context. It reflects the fact that a large amount ($\frac{4}{9}$) of Your initial belief was left unassigned, i.e., given to {a,b}. This example corresponds to a state in which You have very weak support for a and for b. You are not totally ignorant as in example 5.4.1, but still in a state of 'strong' ignorance. Part of $BetP^{F_1}(b) = \frac{5}{9}$ is due to justified beliefs ($\frac{3}{9}$) but the remainder results from a completely unassigned part of belief that You distribute equally by the pignistic transformation among the alternatives of Your betting frame.

5.8 Kinematic Dutch books

A classical criticism against any non probabilistic model for quantified beliefs is based on Dutch books arguments, i.e. on the possibility to build a set of forced bets such that the player will lose for sure. Dutch books are avoided only if beliefs, when used for decision making, are quantified by probability measures. The transferable belief model with its pignistic transformation resists to such a criticism. Static (also called synchronic) Dutch books are of course avoided inasmuch as bets are based on pignistic probabilities. The real delicate point is to resist diachronic Dutch books, i.e., those built when changes in beliefs are considered and bets can be reconsidered after new information has been collected by the participants in the betting game (Teller, 1973; Jeffrey, 1988).

In (Smets, 1993c), we show how the transferable belief model can resist diachronic Dutch books criticism, and how to build pignistic probabilities when the player knows that intermediate experiments will be run whose outcomes could affect the involved bets.

The overall principle is based on the decision tree. There are two types of nodes, the decision nodes and the uncertainty nodes, i.e., those usually called the 'chance' nodes, but we prefer to avoid the term 'chance' as it might create confusion. At each 'uncertainty' node, one conditions by Dempster's rule of conditioning the belief function that concerns the variable concerned by that node on all the pieces of evidence that will have been collected by the time You reach that node. You build the pignisitic probabilities on the betting frame encountered at that node. When the whole tree is built and all pignistic probabilities are established, the tree is folded back in order to select the best decision. We insist that the adequate choice of the betting frames is a delicate matter, and should be kept consistent for the whole tree.

The originality of the models we obtain in that way is that the player will use different probabilities depending on whether he knows about the experiments to be run or not. The transferable belief model analysis is rich enough to quantify the impact of the knowledge that some relevant intermediate experiments will be run, which is usually not the case within probability theory. Full details about the construction of the pignistic probabilities in a context of diachronic Dutch book are presented in (Smets, 1993c). Nevertheless the solution proposed to resist diachronic Dutch books still needs further developments. It will not be further discussed here as we focus only on static decision making.

5.9 Decision based on the maximum plausibility

Suppose a set H of n hypothesis $\{H_1, H_2, \ldots H_n\}$. In a context where You want to select the most 'probable/likely' hypothesis $H_i \in H$, authors like Appriou (1991) propose that one should select the most plausible hypothesis, a very natural proposal. Nevertheless we feel that this solution is poised by counterexamples like the next one.

Example 5.5. Decisions based on maximal plausibility. Suppose

$$\begin{aligned} m^H(H_1) &= .30, \\ m^H(H_2) &= .01, \\ m^H(H_2, H_3, \ldots, H_{70}) &= .69. \end{aligned}$$

Then

$$
\begin{aligned}
pl^H(H_1) &= .30, \\
pl^H(H_2) &= .70, \\
pl^H(H_3) = \ldots = pl^H(H_{70}) &= .69.
\end{aligned}
$$

So H_2 is the most plausible hypothesis, and according to that approach, the one to be selected.

With the pignistic transformation, we get:

$$
\begin{aligned}
BetP^H(H_1) &= .30, \\
BetP^H(H_2) &= .02, \\
BetP^H(H_3) = \ldots = BetP^H(H_{70}) &= .01.
\end{aligned}
$$

So now H_1 is the most 'probable' hypothesis. □

We feel the solution obtained with the pignistic transformation is better than the one based on the maximum plausibility. Of course, this is a matter of personal opinion, and we don't have a way to 'prove' which solution is definitively the best one.

5.10 An example: the Oil-Drilling Problem

In order to illustrate the use of the pignistic transformation, we present the classical Oil-Drilling example. It was analyzed in (Strat, 1994) within an upper and lower probability context. We present its analyze into the TBM context.

Example 5.6 The Oil-Drilling Problem. A wildcatter must decide whether or not to drill for oil. He is uncertain whether the hole will be dry, have a trickle of oil, or be a gusher. Drilling a hole costs \$70.000. The payoffs for hitting a gusher, a trickle, or a dry hole are \$270.000, \$120.000 and \$0, respectively. At a cost of \$10.000 the wildcatter could take seismic sounding that would help determine the underlying geological structure. The sounding will determine whether the terrain has no structure, open structure, or closed structure.

Let H be the set of hole state: $H = \{$Dry (Dr), Trickle (Tr), Gusher (Gu)$\}$. Let S be the set of terrain structures: $S = \{$No struct, Open, Closed$\}$.

The experts have provided their opinions about which state prevails given the result of the seismic soundings test (see table 1). These are represented by the bba $m^H[s]$ for $s \in S$. When $s =$ No Struct, a Dry hole is essentially expected (at level .45), but there is nevertheless some support (.40) that the the hole might also be Trickle, and there is some ignorance (.15). When $s =$ Open, there is also some support for Gusher, and when $s =$ Closed, Gusher gets some support.

Besides the experts have some a priori belief about what the outcome of the seismic soundings test might be. It is represented by the bba m^S with $m^S(\{$No struct}) = .5, m^S({No struct, Open}) = .3 and m^S({Open, Closed}) = .2. No struct (with Open) is supported, but there is also some support for Open or Closed. The way these bba can be assesses is discussed in section 5.7.

The bba $m^H[m^S]$ (presented in the 'Marginal' column of table 1) is computed by applying the disjunctive rule of combination (Smets, 1993a). One has:

$$b^H[m^S](h) = \sum_{X \subseteq S} m^S(X) b^H[X](h), \ \forall h \subseteq H,$$

with

$$b^H[X](h) = \prod_{s \in X} b^H[s](h),$$

where the b functions are the implicability functions with,

$$b(A) = bel(A) + m(\emptyset).$$

The first relation is just the explicit solution of the next relation:

$$m^H[m^S] = (m^{H \times S} \oplus m^{S \uparrow S \times H})^{\downarrow H},$$

where $m^{H \times S}$ is the bba on $H \times S$ that is built from the set of conditional bba $\{m^H[s], s \in S\}$ provided by the experts. The next one results from the disjunctive combination rule which is fully detailed in (Smets, 1993a). It corresponds in building $m[E_1$ or $E_2]$ from $m[E_1]$ and $m[E_2]$, just as the conjunctive combination rule consists in computing $m[E_1$ and $E_2]$ where E_1 and E_2 are two distinct pieces of evidence.

Figure 1 presents the decision tree for the present example. Decision nodes have their expected utilities in italics. Optimal decisions are indicated in capital letters. Suppose the test result is 'no structure' and drilling in done. The pignistic probabilities $BetP^H[No\ struct] = \Gamma_H(m^H[No\ struct])$ are indicated on the three possible branches. The expected utility is then $-\$36.500 = .05 \times 190.000 + .25 \times 40.000 + .70 \times (-80.000)$. The cost if one does not drill is -\$10.000 what is better, hence the optimal decision is not to drill. Identical computations are performed for the the other two results of the test. In these two cases, drilling is the optimal decision. The pignistic probabilities $BetP^S = \Gamma_S(m^S)$, presented at the bottom of table 1, are used to compute the expected utility when the test is performed. Its value is \$12.825.

We then proceed with the 'no test' option. One must first compute the bba $m^H[m^S]$ on H based on the conditional bba's $m^H[s], s \in S$, and the prior bba m^S on S. The column 'Marginal' in table 1 presents this bba. It is compute by the disjunctive combination rule detailed here above. Its pignistic transformation $BetP^H[m^S] = \Gamma_H(m^H[m^S])$ are given on the three related branches, and the expected utility is \$10.970. This result is not as good as the one obtained when performing the test, hence testing is the optimal decision.

In conclusions, the decision analysis shows that it is best to test, and that if the test result is open or closed structure, the optimal decision is to drill, whereas if the test result is no structure, the optimal decision is not to drill.

H State	No struct	Open	Closed	Marginal
Dry	.45	.10	0	.239
Trickle	0	0	0	0
Gusher	0	0	.25	0
Dr, Tr	.40	.30	0	.289
Dr, Gu	0	0	0	.005
Tr, Gu	0	.30	.30	.033
Dr, Tr, Gu	.15	.30	.45	.435
Dry	.70	.35	.15	.530
Trickle	.25	.40	.30	.306
Gusher	.05	.25	.55	.164
$BetP^S$	.65	.25	.10	

Table 1: The upper part presents the conditional bba $m^H[s]$ on the hole state H given the terrain structure $s \in S$. The 'Marginal' column presents the bba $m^H[m^S]$ on H given the prior belief m^S with $m^S(\{\text{No struct}\}) = .5$, $m^S(\{\text{No struct, Open}\}) = .3$ and $m^S(\{\text{Open, Closed}\}) = .2$. The middle part presents the pignistic probabilities $BetP^H[s]$ over H for each $s \in S$ and $BetP^H[m^S]$ for $m^H[m^S]$. The bottom part presents the pignistic probabilities $BetP^S$ over S computed from m^S.

This example is just given in order to illustrate the kind of computation to be performed.

Similar examples are studied by Xu (1992, 1993a), (Xu, Hsia, & Smets, 1993b). She explains the architecture of the software for decision making based on the valuation based system (Shenoy, 1991, 1992). In (Xu & Smets, 1996, 1995), the authors explain how to determine the sensitivity of the conclusions to variations in the bba.

6 Decision Making in the upper and lower probabilities case

6.1 Decisions based on upper and lower expectations

We consider the case where there is a probability function P^Ω that describes Your belief about which world in Ω is the actual world. The closed world assumption is accepted. It happens that You don't know what is exactly P^Ω, and all You know about P^Ω is that it belongs to a family of probability functions defined on Ω. Let Π denote this family. Furthermore assume the lower envelope of Π is a belief function, what is not a necessity, but there are cases where it happens.

To make optimal decision, one must compute the expected utility of each act (and chose the best accordingly). Normally this is achieved by computing for each act a in a set A of possible acts the expected utility $\overline{u}(a)$ of that act,

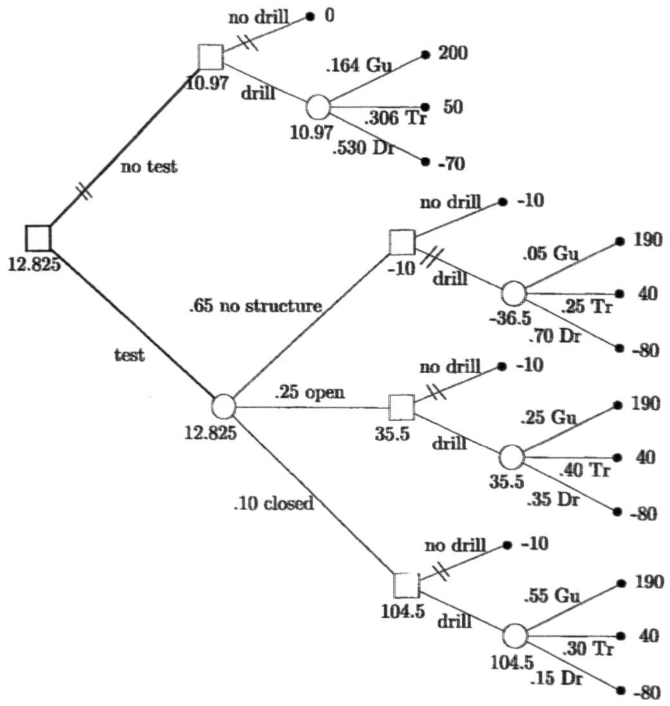

Figure 1: The decision tree for the Oil-Driling Problem, expectation in K$.

considering the utility $u(a, \omega)$ of each act $a \in A$ in each possible context $\omega \in \Omega$.

$$\overline{u}(a) = \sum_{\omega \in \Omega} u(a, \omega) P^{\Omega}(\omega) \ldots$$

Unfortunately $P^{\Omega}(\omega)$ is not available, as all we know is that $P^{\Omega} \in \Pi$. One approach consists in computing what would be $\overline{u}(a)$ if we consider all possible elements of Π. We can then compute the upper and the lower expectation of $\overline{u}(a)$, denoted $\overline{u}^*(a)$ and $\overline{u}_*(a)$, respectively. We have:

$$\begin{aligned}
\overline{u}^*(a) &= \max\{\sum_{\omega \in \Omega} u(a, \omega) P^{\Omega}(\omega) : P^{\Omega} \in \Pi\}, \\
\overline{u}_*(a) &= \min\{\sum_{\omega \in \Omega} u(a, \omega) P^{\Omega}(\omega) : P^{\Omega} \in \Pi\}.
\end{aligned}$$

So we know that $\overline{u}(a) \in [\overline{u}_*(a), \overline{u}^*(a)]$. Unfortunately, such an information does not lead to a total order, and ambiguities can appear when we have two acts a and b such that $\overline{u}_*(a) \leq \overline{u}^*(b)$ and $\overline{u}^*(a) \geq \overline{u}_*(b)$. In that case, Jaffray (1988, 1989a, 1989b, 1994) and Strat (Strat, 1990b, 1990a, 1994) have defended the suggestion to take a weighted average of the two expected utilities and select the best act using that value:

$$\overline{u}(a, \alpha) = \alpha \overline{u}_*(a) + (1 - \alpha)\overline{u}^*(a), \tag{3}$$

where α is an optimism/pessimism criteria. This solution is Hurwicz α-criteria (Luce & Raiffa, 1957).

Let m^Ω be the Möbius transform of P_*, the lower envelope of Π (just like the bba m^Ω is the Möbius transform of bel^Ω). It can be shown that:

$$\begin{aligned} \overline{u}^*(a) &= \sum_{X \subseteq \Omega} \max_{\omega \in X} u(a, \omega)\, m^\Omega(X) \\ \overline{u}_*(a) &= \sum_{X \subseteq \Omega} \min_{\omega \in X} u(a, \omega)\, m^\Omega(X) \end{aligned}$$

Using $\alpha = 1$ (0) means that You feel that the worst (best) possible outcome of X will occur when all You know is that $\omega \in X$. (Schubert, 1995) discusses about the choice of the value of α.(Nguyen & Walker, 1994) presents an overview of decision making with belief functions using Choquet integrals and random sets. Unfortunately, the nature of the uncertainty represented by the belief functions is not explained (see section 4).

Note: the expected utility one would obtain with the pignistic probabilities is:

$$\overline{u}(a) = \sum_{\omega \in \Omega} u(a, \omega) BetP^\Omega(\omega) = \sum_{X \subseteq \Omega} \sum_{\omega \in X} \frac{u(a, \omega)}{\mid X \mid} m^\Omega(X).$$

In that case, You consider that the utility when all You know is that $\omega \in X$ is the average of the utilities given to the elements of X.

Schmeidler (1989) had also proposed to chose the best act using the lower expectation (the case with $\alpha = 1$).

6.2 Justification of Jaffray-Strat's solution

Jaffray (1988, 1989a, 1989b), (Jaffray & Wakker, 1994) presents a justification for using the weighted average of the upper and lower expected utilities as given by relation (3) based on von Neumann-Morgenstern linear utility theory.

It is assumed that the decision maker bases his/her judgment on the sole comparison of the lower probabilities on the outcome set associated with each decision. Thus ordering can be defined directly on the set $\boldsymbol{F}$ of lower probabilities on Ω. Let f_1 and f_2 be the lower envelopes of the two convex sets Π_1 and Π_2 of probability functions defined on Ω, respectively. Let $\succeq$ denote the decision maker preference ordering., with $\succ$ denoting its asymmetric part). The axioms for $\succeq$ are (adapted from (Jaffray, 1994). They are the transposition to lower probability of the standard axioms for probability (Jensen, 1967). Note that their justification in (Jaffray, 1994) requires these lower probabilities to be at least 2-monotone.

Proposition 6.1 ***Transitivity and Completeness.*** $\succeq$ *is a transitive and complete relation on* $\boldsymbol{F}$.

Proposition 6.2 ***Independence.*** *For all* f_1 *and* f_2 *in* $\boldsymbol{F}$ *and* λ *in (0,1),*

$$f_1 \succ f_2 \Rightarrow \lambda f_1 + (1-\lambda)g \succ \lambda f_2 + (1-\lambda)g.$$

Proposition 6.3 ***Continuity.*** *For all f, g, k in* $\boldsymbol{F}$ *such that* $f \succ k \succ g$, *there exist* λ, μ *in (0,1] such that:*

$$\lambda f + (1-\lambda)g \succ k \succ \mu f + (1-\mu)g.$$

These three propositions are necessary and sufficient conditions for the existence of a linear utility V on $\boldsymbol{F}$ representing $\succeq$, i.e., for the existence of $V : \boldsymbol{F} \to \mathbf{R}$ (where $\mathbf{R}$ is the set of reals) satisfying;

$$V(f) \geq V(g) \Leftrightarrow f \succ g.$$

and

$$V(f) = \sum_{B \subseteq \Omega} V(1_B) m(B)$$

where m is the Möbius transform of f, and 1_B is the lower probability function that satisfies $1_B(A) = 1$ if $B \subseteq A$, $= 0$ otherwise. In fact 1_B is a belief function focused on B; it represents 'all You know is that the actual world belongs to B'. In the previous section, we had presented successively the following three solutions for V (where the act is not explicitated):

$$\begin{aligned} V^*(1_B) &= \max_{\omega \in B} u(\omega) \\ V_*(1_B) &= \min_{\omega \in B} u(\omega) \\ \overline{V}(1_B) &= \sum_{\omega \in B} u(\omega)/|B] \end{aligned}$$

If we add the next axiom, then V depends only on the upper and lower expected utilities.

Proposition 6.4 ***Dominance.*** *For all B', B" in* Ω,

$$V_*(1_{B'}) \geq V_*(1_{B''}) \text{ and } V^*(1_{B'}) \geq V^*(1_{B''}) \Rightarrow 1_{B'} \succeq 1_{B''}.$$

In (Cohen & Jaffray, 1985; Jaffray & Philippe, 1997), authors introduce some rationality axioms so that we get the solution based on Hurwicz α-criteria (see relation 3):

$$V(f) = \sum_{B \subseteq \Omega} (\alpha V_*(1_B) + (1-\alpha) V^*(1_B))\, m(B).$$

This derivation provides a justification for the Jaffray-Strat's solution. Note that the dominance axiom (6.4) is not satisfied in the TBM framework when using the pignistic transformation, but this should not be embarrassing as the TBM and the ULP model are not concerned with the same problem.

6.3 Ellsberg paradox revisited

It can been defended that Jaffray-Strat's solution has the advantage over the pignistic probability solution that the decision does not depend on any possible refinement of Ω. (This property is not shared by the solution based on the pignistic transformation). That this property is really worth defending might be challenged by the next example.

Let us suppose Ellsberg's urn made out of 90 balls colored red (R), black (B) and white (W). We only know that exactly 30 balls are R. We are offer four bets listed in the table 2.

bet	R	B	W	Value ULP	Value BetP
I	1	0	0	1/3	1/3
II	0	1	0	2(1-α)/3	1/3
III	1	0	1	1/3 + 2(1-α)/3	2/3
IV	0	1	1	2/3	2/3

Table 2: Set S_1 of four bets. Columns 2 to 4 present the gains according to the color of the randomly selected ball. The 'Value ULP' column gives the value of the game using the Jaffray-Strat's solution. The 'Value BetP' column gives the value of the game using the solution based on the pignistic probabilities.

It has been argued that people prefer bet I to bet II, and bet IV to bet III. There is no probability distribution on $\Omega = \{R, B, W\}$ that is compatible with these two preferences.

With Jaffray-Strat's solution, this ordering is satisfied when $\alpha > 1/2$ (so the decision maker is somehow pessimist). With the pignistic probabilities computed from the lower probabilities, this ordering is not found, and we face the same paradox as the classical Bayesians. This might be seen as a weakness of the pignistic transformation. Nevertheless, once we refine B or W, Jaffray-Strat's solution could be criticized.

bet	R	B_1	...	B_{1000}	W	Value ULP	Value BetP
I	1	0	...	0	0	1/3	1/3
II	0	1	...	1	0	2(1-α)/3	2/3 - ϵ
III	1	0	...	0	1	1/3 + 2(1-α)/3	1/3 + ϵ
IV	0	1	...	1	1	2/3	2/3

Table 3: Set of bets S_2. Gains according to the color of the randomly selected ball.ϵ denotes 1/1001.

Suppose the set of bets S_2 where B is refined into 1000 B_i's (see table 3). When facing the set of bets S_2, we personally feel people might prefer bet II to bet I, and bet IV to bet III.

bet	R	B	W_1	...	W_{1000}	Value ULP	Value BetP
I	1	0	0	...	0	1/3	1/3
II	0	1	0	...	0	2(1-α)/3	ϵ
III	1	0	1	...	1	1/3 + 2(1-α)/3	1 - ϵ
IV	0	1	1	...	1	2/3	2/3

Table 4: Set of bets S_3. Gains according to the color of the randomly selected ball.ϵ denotes 1/1001.

Suppose the set of bets S_3 where now W is refined into 1000 W_i's (see table 4). When facing the set of bets S_3, we personally feel people might prefer bet I to bet II, and bet III to bet IV.

It happens that in the three sets S_1, S_2 and S_3, the $\overline{u}(a)$ computed by Jaffray-Strat's formula give the same results, and therefore it does not produce the order that we have considered. Instead the pignistic probabilities are justifying the ordering for cases S_2 and S_3.

These examples only illustrate the difficulty to find 'rational' requirements that resist all criticisms. Cohen and Jaffray (1985) argue that it is 'rational' to require invariance to refinement, in which case their solution is appropriate. This sounds to be a good 'rational requirement', but its adequacy is nevertheless arguable as shown by our example.

Note: In the TBM, the Ellsberg's urn experiment is to be handled with care. In Ellsberg's problem, we are facing a problem of imprecise probabilities. Each ball has a fixed color. The selection procedure of the ball obeys to a probability law (that we know only partially) and this knowledge about the selection procedure has to be taken in consideration when building Your beliefs. The belief induced by the knowledge of the structure of Ellsberg's urn is not equal to the lower probability function. In (Smets, 1994a), we explain what is the belief induced on the $\{R, B, W\}$ space by the knowledge that the selection procedure is random and the probability law that governs that selection belongs to a subset of probability functions.

6.4 The pignistic transformation within the ULP context

Can we justify the applicability of the pignistic transformation within the ULP framework? This idea seems new. To check it, let us reconsider the example concerning the drink I have to buy for my friend (see section 5.1). Let $V = \{G, J\}$ and $D = \{c, w, b\}$ as before. Now we assume that there exists, for $v \in V$, probability functions $P^D[v]$, but their values are only known to belong to some given sets of probability functions, denoted $\Pi^D[v]$, respectively. Let us assume that these sets are uniquely characterized by their lower envelopes, denoted $P_*^D[v]$ for $v \in V$. We don't require that the lower envelopes $P_*^D[v]$ are belief functions as it is not important here.

The first approach consists in building, for each $v \in V$, the probability function $BetP^D[v]$ that will be used to make decisions. Let $BetP^D[v] = \Gamma_D(P_*^D[v])$, where Γ is still to be found. In fact all we need is to show that it satisfies the linearity constraint (see 5.2), the other assumptions being obviously satisfied.

By construction, the overall frame is $D \times V$, and $BetP^D[v]$ are the conditional probability functions over D given the visitor is v. Knowing the probability about who will be the visitor, then the probability function to be used to buy the drink is:

$$P^D = .5BetP^D[G] + .5BetP^D[J] = .5\Gamma_D(P_*^D[G]) + .5\Gamma_D(P_*^D[J]),$$

just as in the previous derivation.

Let us now consider the second approach. The probability distribution $P^{V \times D}$ on the product space $V \times D$ is known to belong to the set $\Pi^{V \times D}$ with:

$$\begin{aligned} \Pi^{V \times D} &= \{P^{V \times D} : P^{V \times D}(v, d) = .5P^D[v](d),\ \forall d \in D, \\ &\quad \text{where } P^D[v] \in \Pi^D[v],\ v \in V\}. \end{aligned}$$

In order to make a decision about which drink to buy, we need the probability function P^D obtained by marginalizing on D the probabilities defined on $V \times D$. The family of probability functions so derived from $\Pi^{V \times D}$ is:

$$\Pi^D = \{P^D : P^D = .5P^D[G] + .5P^D[J], \text{ where } P^D[v] \in \Pi^D[v], v \in V = \{G, J\}\}.$$

This family Π^D is convex and its lower envelope is given by:

$$P_*^D = .5P_*^D[G] + .5P_*^D[J].$$

The needed pignistic probability function is then $BetP^D = \Gamma_D(P_*^D)$. Therefore, the equality of the two approach implies that:

$$.5\Gamma_D(P_*^D[G]) + .5\Gamma_D(P_*^D[J]) = \Gamma_D(.5P_*^D[G] + .5P_*^D[J]).$$

Generalizing to any value for the probability that G comes tonight, we get the linearity constraint, and thus the pignistic transformation seems to be justified.

7 Conclusions

We have presented some of the procedures developed for the 'rational' decision making in the TBM context and in the ULP context. There are other proposals, but usually they are essentially *ad hoc* or proposed without justification.

We developed in full detail the pignistic transformation that provides, probably, the adequate way to build the probability function required for rational decisions. Its applicability seems not to be restricted to the TBM, and we feel it might also produce a useful tool in the upper and lower probabilities framework.

Using any other probability function would violate the requirement behind the justification of the pignistic transformation. We feel such a violation must be avoided, and therefore the pignistic transformation seems to be inevitable.

These non-probabilistic theories are young. So it should not be surprising that in some future some of the proposed solutions turned out to be inadequate. Only time will tell us how robust these solutions are. We feel nevertheless confident the justifications given to the various methods are strong enough to give us hope that the proposed procedures will resist to the test of time.

References

Appriou, A. (1991). Probabilités et incertitude en fusion de données multi-senseurs. *Revue Scientifique et Technique de la Défense, 11*, 27-40.

Ben Yaghlane, B., Smets, P., & Mellouli, K. (2000). Independence concepts for belief functions. In IPMU-2000 (Ed.), *Information processing and management of uncertainty* (Vol. 1, pp. 357–364).

Cohen, M., & Jaffray, J. Y. (1985). Decision making in a case of mixed uncertainty: a normative approach. *J. of Math. Psychology, 29*, 428–442.

De Finetti, B. (1974). *Theory of probability.* Wiley, London.

DeGroot, M. H. (1970). *Optimal statistical decisions.* McGraw-Hill, New York.

Dempster, A. P. (1967). Upper and lower probabilities induced by a multiple valued mapping. *Ann. Math. Statistics, 38*, 325–339.

Dempster, A. P. (1968). A generalization of Bayesian inference. *J. Roy. Statist. Soc. B., 30*, 205–247.

Dempster, A. P. (1972). A class of random convex polytopes. *Annals of Mathematical Statistics, 43*, 250–272.

Dubois, D., Prade, H., & Smets, P. (1996). Representing partial ignorance. *IEEE System Machine and Cybernetic, 26*, 361–377.

Dubois, D., & Pradre, H. (1982). On several representations of an uncertain body of evidence. In M. M. Gupta & E. Sanchez (Eds.), *Fuzzy information and decision processes* (pp. 167–181). North Holland, Amsterdam.

Dubois, D., Wellman, M. P., D'Ambrosio, B., & Smets, P. (Eds.). (1992). *Uncertainty in artificial intelligence 92.* Morgan Kaufman, San Mateo, Ca.

Fagin, R., & Halpern, J. (1991). A new approach to updating beliefs. In P. P. Bonissone, M. Henrion, L. N. Kanal, & J. F. Lemmer (Eds.), *Uncertainty in artificial intelligence 6* (pp. 347–374). North Holland, Amsteram.

Gardenfors, P., & Sahlin, N. E. (Eds.). (1988). *Decision, probability and utility.* Cambridge Univ. Press, Cambridge, G.B.

Gilboa, I., & Schmeidler, D. (1992). Updating ambiguous beliefs. In Y. Moses (Ed.), *Tark-92, theoretical aspects of reasoning about knowledge* (pp. 1xxx–Xxx). Morgan Kaufman, San Mateo, Ca.

Giles, R. (1982). Foundation for a possibility theory. In M. M. Gupta & E. Sanchez (Eds.), *Fuzzy information and decision processes* (pp. 83–195). North Holland, Amsterdam.

Gupta, M. M., & Sanchez, E. (Eds.). (1982). *Fuzzy information and decision processes.* North Holland, Amsterdam.

Hacking, I. (1988). Slightly mfore realistic personal probability. In P. Gardenfors & N. E. Sahlin (Eds.), *Decision, probability and utility* (pp. 118–135). Cambridge Univ. Press, Cambridge, G.B.

Harper, X., & Hooker, X. (Eds.). (1976). *Foundations of probability theory, statistical inference, and statistical theories of science.* Reidel, Doordrecht-Holland.

Heckerman, D., & Mamdani, A. (Eds.). (1993). *Uncertainty in artificial intelligence 93.* Morgan Kaufmann, San Mateo, Ca, USA.

Henrion, M., Shachter, R. D., Kanal, L. N., & Lemmer, J. F. (Eds.). (1990). *Uncertainty in artificial intelligence 5.* North Holland, Amsteram.

IJCAI-87 (Ed.). (1987). *Intern. joint conf. on artificial intelligence.* Morgan Kaufman, San Mateo, Ca.

Jaffray, J. Y. (1988). Application of linear utility theory for belief functions. In B. Bouchon, L. Saitta, & R. R. Yager (Eds.), *Uncertainty and intelligent systems* (pp. 1–8). Springer-Verlag, Berlin.

Jaffray, J. Y. (1989a). Coherent bets under partially resolving uncertainty and belief functions. *Theory and Decision, 26*, 99–105.

Jaffray, J. Y. (1989b). Linear utility theory for belief functions. *Op. Res. Letters, 8*, 107–112.

Jaffray, J. Y. (1992). Bayesian updating and belief functions. *IEEE Trans. SMC, 22*, 1144–1152.

Jaffray, J. Y. (1994). Dynamic decision making with belief functions. In R. R. Yager, J. Kacprzyk, & M. Fedrizzi (Eds.), *Advances in theDempster-Shafer theory of evidence* (pp. 331–352). Wiley, New York.

Jaffray, J. Y., & Philippe, F. (1997). On the existence of subjective upper and lower probabilities. *Mathematics of Operations Research, 22*, 165–185.

Jaffray, J. Y., & Wakker, P. (1994). Decision making with belief functions: compatibility and incompatibility with the sure-thing principle. *Journal of Risk and Uncertainty, 8*, 255–271.

Jeffrey, R. C. (1988). Conditioning, kinematics, and exchangeability. In B. Skyrms & W. L. Harper (Eds.), *Causation, chance, and credence* (pp. 21–255). Reidel, Dordrecht.

Jensen, N. E. (1967). An introduction to Bermoullian utility theory. I: Utility functions. *Swedish J. of Economics, 69*, 163–183.

Kohlas, J., & Monney, P. A. (1994). Theory of evidence: A survey of its mathematical foundations, applications and computations. *ZOR-Mathematical Methods of Operatioanl Research, 39*, 35–68.

Kohlas, J., & Monney, P. A. (1995). *A mathematical theory of hints: An approach to Dempster-Shafer theory of evidence.* Lecture Notes in Economics and Mathematical Systems No. 425. Springer-Verlag.

Kyburg, H. E., Jr. (1987a). Bayesian and non-Bayesian evidential updating. *Artificial Intelligence, 31*, 271–294.

Kyburg, H. E., Jr. (1987b). Objectives probabilities. In IJCAI-87 (Ed.), *Intern. joint conf. on artificial intelligence* (pp. 02–904). Morgan Kaufman, San Mateo, Ca.

Kyburg, H. E., Jr. (1988). Bets and beliefs. In P. Gardenfors & N. E. Sahlin (Eds.), *Decision, probability and utility* (pp. 101–117). Cambridge Univ. Press, Cambridge, G.B.

Levi, I. (1980). *The enterprise of knowledge.* MIT Press, Cambridge, Mass.

Luce, R. D., & Raiffa, H. (1957). *Games and decisions.* Wiley, New York.

Moral, S., & de Campos, L. M. (1990). Updating uncertain information. In B. Bouchon-Meunier, R. R. Yager, & L. A. Zadeh (Eds.), *Uncertainty in knowledge bases* (pp. 58–67). Springer Verlag, Berlin.

Nguyen, H. T., & Walker, E. A. (1994). On decision making using belief functions. In R. R. Yager, J. Kacprzyk, & M. Fedrizzi (Eds.), *Advances in theDempster-Shafer theory of evidence* (pp. 275–309). Wiley, New York.

Pearl, J. (1988). *Probabilistic reasoning in intelligent systems: Networks of plausible inference.* Morgan Kaufmann Pub. San Mateo, Ca, USA.

Ramsey, F. P. (1964). Truth and probability. In H. E. Kyburg, Jr. & H. E. Smokler (Eds.), *Studies in subjective probability* (pp. 61–92). Wiley, New York.

Rivett, B. H. P. (1975). Behavioural problems of utility theory. In D. J. White & K. C. Bowen (Eds.), *The role and effectiveness of theories of decision in practice* (pp. 21–27). Hodder and Stoughton, London.

Roth, A. E. (Ed.). (1988). *The Shapley value: Essays in honor of l.s. shapley.* Cambridge University Press, Cambridge, GB.

Ruspini, E. H. (1986). *The logical foundations of evidential reasoning* (Tech. Rep.). Technical note 408, SRI International, Menlo Park, Ca, US.

Ruspini, E. H. (1987). Epistemic logics, probability and the calculus of evidence. In IJCAI-87 (Ed.), *Intern. joint conf. on artificial intelligence* (pp. 924–931). Morgan Kaufman, San Mateo, Ca.

Savage, L. J. (1954). *Foundations of statistics.* Wiley, New York.

Schaller, J.-P. (1991). *Multiple criteria decision aid under incomplete information.* Unpublished doctoral dissertation, University of Fribourg, Switzerland.

Schmeidler, D. (1989). Subjective probability and expected utility without additivity. *Econometrica, 57*, 571–587.

Schubert, J. (1995). On rho in a decision-theoretic apparatus of Dempster-Shafer theory. *Int. J. Approx. Reas., 13*, 185–200.

Shafer, G. (1976a). *A mathematical theory of evidence.* Princeton Univ. Press. Princeton, NJ.

Shafer, G. (1976b). A theory of statistical evidence. In X. Harper & X. Hooker (Eds.), *Foundations of probability theory, statistical inference, and statistical theories of science* (pp. xx–xx). Reidel, Doordrecht-Holland.

Shapley, L. S. (1953). A value for n-person games. In H. Kuhn & A. W. Tucker (Eds.), *Contributions to the theory of games* (Vol. 2, pp. 307–317). Princeton University Press, NJ, US.

Shenoy, P. P. (1991). A fusion algorithm for solving bayesian decision problems. In B. D'ambrosio, P. Smets, & B. P. P. and (Eds.), *Uncertainty in artificial intelligence 91* (pp. 323–331). Morgan Kaufmann, San Mateo, Ca, USA.

Shenoy, P. P. (1992). Valuation-based systems for Bayesian decision analysis. *Operations Research, 40*, 463–484.

Smets, P. (1988). Belief functions. In P. Smets, E. H. Mamdani, D. Dubois, & H. Prade (Eds.), *Non standard logics for automated reasoning* (pp. 253–286). Academic Press, London.

Smets, P. (1990). Constructing the pignistic probability function in a context of uncertainty. In M. Henrion, R. D. Shachter, L. N. Kanal, & J. F. Lemmer (Eds.), *Uncertainty in artificial intelligence 5* (pp. 29–40). North Holland, Amsteram.

Smets, P. (1992a). The concept of distinct evidence. In IPMU-92 (Ed.), *Information processing and management of uncertainty* (pp. 89–94).

Smets, P. (1992b). The nature of the unnormalized beliefs encountered in the transferable belief model. In D. Dubois, M. P. Wellman, B. D'Ambrosio, & P. Smets (Eds.), *Uncertainty in artificial intelligence 92* (pp. 292–297). Morgan Kaufman, San Mateo, Ca.

Smets, P. (1993a). Belief functions: the disjunctive rule of combination and the generalized bayesian theorem. *International Journal of Approximate Reasoning, 9*, 1–35.

Smets, P. (1993b). Jeffreys rule of conditioning generalized to belief functions. In D. Heckerman & A. Mamdani (Eds.), *Uncertainty in artificial intelligence 93* (pp. 500–505). Morgan Kaufmann, San Mateo, Ca, USA.

Smets, P. (1993c). No Dutch book can be built against the TBM even though update is not obtained by bayes rule of conditioning. In R. Scozzafava (Ed.), *Workshop on probabilisitic expert systems* (pp. 181–204). Societa Italiana di Statistica , Roma.

Smets, P. (1993d). An axiomatic justifiaction for the use of belief function to quantify beliefs. In IJCAI-93 (Ed.), *Intern. joint conf. on artificial intelligence* (pp. 598–603). Morgan Kaufman, San Mateo, Ca.

Smets, P. (1994a). Belief induced by the knowledge of some probabilities. In D. Heckerman, D. Poole, & R. Lopez De Mantaras (Eds.), *Uncertainty in artificial intelligence 94* (pp. 523–530). Morgan Kaufmann, San Mateo, Ca.

Smets, P. (1994b). What is Dempster-Shafer's model? In R. R. Yager, J. Kacprzyk, & M. Fedrizzi (Eds.), *Advances in theDempster-Shafer theory of evidence* (pp. 5–34). Wiley, New York.

Smets, P. (1997). The normative representation of quantified beliefs by belief functions. *Artificial Intelligence, 92*, 229–242.

Smets, P. (1998a). The application of the transferable belief model to diagnostic problems. *Int. J. Intelligent Systems, 13*, 127–157.

Smets, P. (1998b). The transferable belief model for quantified belief representation. In D. M. Gabbay & P. Smets (Eds.), *Handbook of defeasible reasoning and uncertainty management systems* (Vol. 1, pp. 267–301). Kluwer, Doordrecht, The Netherlands.

Smets, P., & Kennes, R. (1994). The transferable belief model. *Artificial Intelligence, 66*, 191–234.

Smith, C. A. B. (1961). Consistency in statistical inference and decision. *J. Roy. Statist. Soc. B, 23*, 1–37.

Smith, P., & Jones, O. R. (1986). *The philosophy of mind, an introduction.* Cambridge University Press, Cambridge.

Strat, T. M. (1990a). Decision analysis using belief functions. *Int. J. Approx. Reasoning, 4*, 391–418.

Strat, T. M. (1990b). Making decisions with belief functions. In M. Henrion, R. D. Shachter, L. N. Kanal, & J. F. Lemmer (Eds.), *Uncertainty in artificial intelligence 5* (pp. 51–360). North Holland, Amsteram.

Strat, T. M. (1994). Decision analysis using belief functions. In R. R. Yager, J. Kacprzyk, & M. Fedrizzi (Eds.), *Advances in theDempster-Shafer theory of evidence* (pp. 275–309). Wiley, New York.

Suppes, P., & Zanotti, M. (1977). On using random relations to generate upper and lower probabilities. *Synthesis, 36*, 427–440.

Teller, P. (1973). Conditionalization and observation. *Synthesis, 26*, 218–258.

Teller, P. (1976). Conditionalization, observation and change of prefetrence. In X. Harper & X. Hooker (Eds.), *Foundations of probability theory, statistical inference, and statistical theories of science* (pp. 205–259). Reidel, Doordrecht-Holland.

Tsiporkova, E., Boeva, V., & De Baets, B. (1999). Dempster-Shafer's theory framed in modal logic. *Int. J. Approx. Reasoning, to appear.*

Tsiporkova, E., De Baets, B., & Boeva, V. (1999a). Dempster's rule of conditioning translated into modal logic. *Fyzzy Sets and Systems, 102*, 371–383.

Tsiporkova, E., De Baets, B., & Boeva, V. (1999b). Evidence theory in multivalued models of modal logic. *J. Appl. Non-Classical Logics, to appear.*

Voorbraak, F. (1993). *As far as i know: Epistemic logic and uncertainty.* Dissertation, Utrecht University.

Voorbracht, F. (1991). On the justification of Dempster's rule of combination. *Artificial Intelligence, 48*, 171–197.

Walley, P. (1987). Belief functions representations of statistical of evidence. *The Annals of Statistics, 15*, 1439–1465.

Walley, P. (1991). *Statistical reasoning with imprecise probabilities.* Chapman and Hall, London.

Williams, P. M. (1982). Discussion of Shafer's paper. *J. Roy. Statist. Soc.B, 44*, 322-352.

Wilson, N. (1993). Decision making with belief functions and pignistic probabilities. In *European conference on symbolic and quantitative approaches to reasoning and uncertainty* (pp. 364–371). Granada: Springer Verlag.

Xu, H. (1992). A decision calculus for belief functions in val
systems. In D. Dubois, M. P. Wellman, B. D'Ambrosio, & P. Smets (Eds.), *Uncertainty in artificial intelligence 92* (pp. 352–359). Morgan Kaufman, San Mateo, Ca.

Xu, H., Hsia, Y. T., & Smets, P. (1993a). A belief function based decision support system. In D. Heckerman & A. Mamdani (Eds.), *Uncertainty in artificial intelligence 93* (pp. 535–542). Morgan Kaufmann, San Mateo, Ca, USA.

Xu, H., Hsia, Y. T., & Smets, P. (1993b). A belief function based decision support system. In D. Heckerman & A. Mamdani (Eds.), *Uncertainty in artificial intelligence 93* (pp. 535–542). Morgan Kaufmann, San Mateo, Ca, USA.

Xu, H., & Smets, P. (1995). Generating explanations for evidential reasoning. In P. Besnard & S. Hanks (Eds.), *Uncertainty in artificial intelligence 95* (pp. 574–581). Morgan Kaufman, San Francisco, Ca.

Xu, H., & Smets, P. (1996). Some strategies for explanation in evidential reasoning. *IEEE Trans. SMC:*, *26*, 599–607.

Yager, R. R., Kacprzyk, J., & Fedrizzi, M. (Eds.). (1994). *Advances in the Dempster-Shafer theory of evidence*. Wiley, New York.

Empirical Models for the Dempster-Shafer-Theory

Mieczysław Alojzy Kłopotek[1,3] and Sławomir Tadeusz Wierzchoń[1,2]

[1] Institute of Computer Science, Polish Academy of Sciences, Warszawa, Poland
[2] Institute of Computer Science, Białystok University of Technology, Poland
[3] Institute of Computer Science, University of Podlasie, Poland

Abstract. In spite of many useful properties, the Dempster-Shafer Theory of evidence (DST) experienced sharp criticism from many sides. The basic line of criticism is connected with the relationship between the belief function (the basic concept of DST) and frequencies [65,18]. A number of attempts to interpret belief functions in terms of probabilities have failed so far to produce a fully compatible interpretation with DST - see e.g. [34,18,14] etc. As a way out of those difficulties, in the paper we will explain our three model proposals: (1) "the marginally correct approximation", (2) "the qualitative model", (3) "the quantitative model". All of them fit the framework of DST, especially the Dempster rule of combination of evidence that was the hardest point and the point of failure of previously known attempts.

1 Introduction

The Mathematical Theory of Evidence or MTE [50] known also as the Dempster-Shafer Theory, DST, has been deeply investigated with respect to formal properties. Hence its relation to Choquet capacities [67], the axiomatic systems for propagation of uncertainty by local computations [55] (in so-called Markov trees) and for graphoidal representation of belief functions [54] have been studied. Optimal query answering systems have been elaborated [68].

However, the relationship between experimental observations and the DST belief functions is still a hot topic of research. Establishing empirical models for belief functions may contribute strongly to future application of DST in many areas, including also economy [13,21,62].

By an appropriate empirical model for DST we understand the following (see fig.1 below):

We observe ("measure") a real world $state_1$, encode it as a belief function Bel_1, know that a real world process may be represented by a DST reasoning process Bel_p, run the reasoning while the real world process runs in the real world transforming it into the $state_2$. We observe (in exactly the same way as before) the real world and encode the $state_2$ as belief function Bel_2. Bel_2 shall coincide or at least be one of alternative predictions of the reasoning process.

In the past a number of different attempts has been made to identify a model like this. In the paper we will outline major attempts like lower

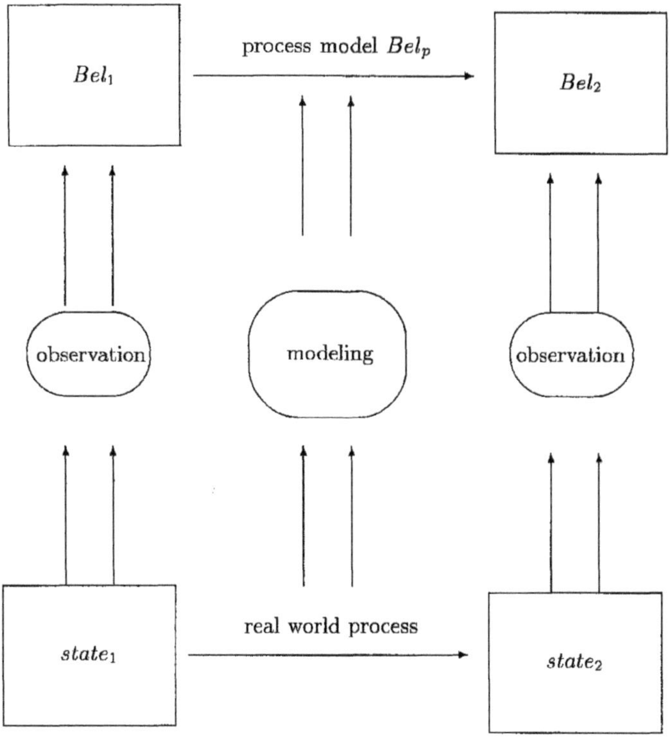

Fig. 1. Real World versus Dempster Shafer model

and upper probabilities, envelops of probability function families, probability structures approach, Shafer's Gamma mapping, rough set approaches etc. and point at their weaknesses and strengths. Though these approaches allow for derivation of a belief function describing the real world state properly, they fail in general to behave correctly under the reasoning (Bel_2 does not reflect a real world state even under "ideal" real world process).

It is still more dramatic if one attempts to identify graphoidal structures in the belief functions (needed in general to describe reasoning processes in a computationally efficient way). Conditional belief functions turn out to be negative-valued and hence cannot be interpreted by means of frequency-related concepts (like lower/upper conditional probabilities etc.). Still worse, combination of conditional belief functions in a graphoidal structure does not need to yield a proper joint belief function. Therefore the graphoidal structures of belief functions are poorly investigated and seldom used.

As a way out of those difficulties, in the chapter we will explain our three model proposals:

- "the marginally correct approximation".
- "the qualitative model"
- "the quantitative model"

The marginally correct approximation assumes that the belief function shall constitute lower bounds for frequencies, however only for the marginals, and not for the joint distribution. Then the reasoning process is expressed in terms of so-called Cano et al. conditionals - a special class of conditional belief functions that are positive. This approach implies modification of reasoning mechanism, because the correctness is maintained only by reasoning forward. Depending on the reasoning direction we need different "Markov trees" for the reasoning engine.

The qualitative approach is based on earlier rough set interpretations of DST, but makes a small and still significant distinction. All computations are carried out in strictly "relational" way that is indistinguishable objects in a database are merged (no object identities). The behavior under reasoning fits strictly to DST reasoning model. Factors of hypergraph representation can be expressed by relational tables. Conditional independence is well defined. However, there is no interpretation for conditional belief functions in this model.

The quantitative model assumes that during the reasoning process one attachs labels to objects hiding some of their properties. There is a full agreement with the reasoning mechanism of DST. Conditional independence and conditional belief functions are well defined. We have also elaborated processes that can give rise to well-controlled graphoidally structured belief functions. We elaborated also learning procedures for discovery of graphoidal structures from data.

The quantitative model seems to be the best fitting model for belief functions created so far.

1.1 Some Comments

The Dempster-Shafer Theory or the Mathematical Theory of Evidence (MTE) [50,9] is intended to be a generalization of bayesian theory of subjective probability [53]. This theory offers capability of representing ignorance in a simple and direct way, compatibility with the classical probability theory, compatibility with boolean logic and feasible computational complexity [45]. MTE may be applied for (1) representation of incomplete knowledge, (2) belief updating, (3) and for combination of evidence [43].MTE covers the statistics of random sets and may be applied for representation of incomplete statistical knowledge. Random set statistics is quite popular in analysis of opinion polls whenever partial indecisiveness of respondents is allowed

[11]. Practical applications of MTE include: integration of knowledge from heterogeneous sources for object identification [7], technical diagnosis under unreliable measuring devices [12], medical applications: [16,70], and for network reliability computation [42], reliability in real-time X-ray radioscopy and ultrasounds [10], multisensor image segmentation [2], safety control in large plants [20], map construction and maintenance [38], just to mention a few.

In spite of indicated merits, MTE experienced sharp criticism from many sides. The basic line of criticism is connected with the relationship between the belief function (the basic concept of MTE) and frequencies [65,18].

The problem of frequencies is not solely a scholar problem. It has significant knowledge engineering (expressive power, sources of knowledge, knowledge acquisition strategies, learning algorithms) and software engineering implications (internal representation, measure transformation procedures). First of all one should realize that a computer-based advisory system is rarely made for a single consultation. Hence we may (at least theoretically) obtain a statistics of cases for which the system has been applied. Life verifies also frequently enough the advices obtained from the advisory system. Hence after a long enough time one may pose at least partially the question whether or not the advices have been correct. A belief function (the basic concept of DST) without a modest frequency interpretation may be treated as a void answer in this context.

Therefore numerous probabilistic interpretations have been attempted since the early days of DST, see e.g. [9,51,34,19,40,42,35,58,14,18] and other.

But a number of attempts to interpret belief functions in terms of probabilities have failed so far to produce a fully compatible interpretation with DST - see e.g. [35,34,18,14] etc. As Smets [59] states "all these interpretations lead to different updating (conditioning) rules." [59, pp. 324-325]. Shafer [53] and Smets [59], in defense of MTE, dismissed every attempt to interpret MTE frequentistically. Shafer in [53] claims that probability theory developed over last years from the old-style frequencies towards modern subjective probability theory within the framework of bayesian theory. By analogy he claims that the very attempt to consider relation between DST and frequencies is old-fashioned and out of date. Wasserman opposes this view ([65], p.371) reminding "major success story in Bayesian theory", the exchangeability theory of de Finetti. It treats frequencies as special case of bayesian belief. "The Bayesian theory contains within it a definition of frequency probability and a description of the exact assumptions necessary to invoke that definition" [65]. Wasserman dismisses Shafer's suggestion that probability relies on analogy of frequency. .

1.2 Basics of the Dempster-Shafer Theory

Below we define the way we understand the basics of the Depster-Shafer theory (see [50]). On the one hand we include here the definitions of basic measures of uncertainty (belief, plausibility, mass function, commonality), operatorsd of marginalization and vacuous extension, the Dempster rule of evidence combination, rule of conditioning. Furthermore we consider as indispensible part of DST the Shafer's and Shenoy's representation of joint belief in terms of a decomposition and reasoning algorithms designed for that decomposition (see next subsection).

So let us start with basic notion.

Let Ξ be a finite set of elements called elementary events. Any subset of Ξ is a composite event, or hypothesis. Ξ be called also the frame of discernment.

Definition 1. [50] Let Ξ be a finite set of elements called elementary events. Any subset of Ξ be a composite event. Ξ be called also the frame of discernment.
A basic probability assignment (bpa) function (called also mass function) is any function m:$2^\Xi \rightarrow [0,1]$ such that

$$\sum_{A \in 2^\Xi} m(A) = 1 \qquad m(\emptyset) = 0, \qquad \forall_{A \in 2^\Xi} \quad 0 \leq \sum_{A \subseteq B} m(B)$$

We say that a bpa is vacuous iff $m(\Xi) = 1$ and $m(A) = 0$ for every $A \neq \Xi$.

Definition 2. [50] A belief function be defined as Bel:$2^\Xi \rightarrow [0,1]$ so that $Bel(A) = \sum_{B \subseteq A} m(B)$ A plausibility function be Pl:$2^\Xi \rightarrow [0,1]$ with $\forall_{A \in 2^\Xi}\ Pl(A) = 1 - Bel(\Xi - A)$ A commonality function be Q:$2^\Xi \rightarrow [0,1]$ with $\forall_{A \in 2^\Xi} \quad Q(A) = \sum_{A \subseteq B} m(B)$

Definition 3. [50] The Rule of Combination of two Independent Belief Functions Bel_{E_1}, Bel_{E_2} Over the Same Frame of Discernment (the so-called Dempster-Rule), denoted

$$Bel_{E_1,E_2} = Bel_{E_1} \oplus Bel_{E_2}$$

is defined as follows: :

$$m_{E_1,E_2}(A) = c \cdot \sum_{B,C;A=B \cap C} m_{E_1}(B) \cdot m_{E_2}(C)$$

(c - constant normalizing the sum of m to 1)

Furthermore, let the frame of discernment Ξ be structured in that it is identical to cross product of domains Ξ_1, Ξ_2, $\ldots \Xi_n$ of n discrete variables $X_1, X_2, \ldots X_n$, which span the space Ξ. Let $(x_1, x_2, \ldots x_n)$ be a vector in the space spanned by the variables $X_1,, X_2, \ldots X_n$. Its projection onto the subspace spanned by variables $X_{j_1}, X_{j_2}, \ldots X_{j_k}$ ($j_1, j_2, \ldots j_k$ distinct indices from the set 1,2,...,n) is then the vector $(x_{j_1}, x_{j_2}, \ldots x_{j_k})$. $(x_1, x_2, \ldots x_n)$ is also called an extension of $(x_{j_1}, x_{j_2}, \ldots x_{j_k})$. A projection of a set A of such vectors is the set $A^{\downarrow X_{j_1}, X_{j_2}, \ldots X_{j_k}}$ of projections of all individual vectors from

A onto $X_{j_1}, X_{j_2}, \dots X_{j_k}$. A is also called an extension of $A^{\downarrow X_{j_1}, X_{j_2}, \dots X_{j_k}}$. A is called the vacuous extension of $A^{\downarrow X_{j_1}, X_{j_2}, \dots X_{j_k}}$ iff A contains all possible extensions of each individual vector in $A^{\downarrow X_{j_1}, X_{j_2}, \dots X_{j_k}}$. The fact, that A is a vacuous extension of B onto space $X_1, X_2, \dots X_n$ is denoted by $A = B^{\uparrow X_1, X_2, \dots X_n}$

Definition 4. Let m be a basic probability assignment function on the space of discernment spanned by variables $X_1, X_2, \dots X_n$. $m^{\downarrow X_{j_1}, X_{j_2}, \dots X_{j_k}}$ is called the projection (or marginalization) of m onto subspace spanned by $X_{j_1}, X_{j_2}, \dots X_{j_k}$ iff

$$m^{\downarrow X_{j_1}, X_{j_2}, \dots X_{j_k}}(B) = \sum_{A; B = A^{\downarrow X_{j_1}, X_{j_2}, \dots X_{j_k}}} m(A)$$

Definition 5. Let m be a basic probability assignment function on the space of discernment spanned by variables $X_{j_1}, X_{j_2}, \dots X_{j_k}$. $m^{\uparrow X_1, X_2, \dots X_n}$ is called the vacuous extension of m onto superspace spanned by $X_1, X_2, \dots X_n$ iff

$$m^{\uparrow X_1, X_2, \dots X_n}(B^{\uparrow X_1, X_2, \dots X_n}) = m(B)$$

and $m^{\uparrow X_1, X_2, \dots X_n}(A) = 0$ for any other A.

Projections and vacuous extensions of Bel, Pl and Q functions are defined with respect to operations on m function. Notice that by convention if we want to combine by Dempster rule two belief functions not sharing the frame of discernment, we look for the closest common vacuous extension of their frames of discernment without explicitly notifying it.

Definition 6. (See [52]) Let B be a subset of Ξ, called evidence, m_B be a basic probability assignment such that $m_B(B) = 1$ and $m_B(A) = 0$ for any A different from B. Then the conditional belief function $Bel(.||B)$ representing the belief function Bel conditioned on evidence B is defined as: $Bel(.||B) = Bel \oplus Bel_B$.

1.3 Basics of Belief Function Decomposition and Reasoning

An integral part of DST is a particular type of inference engine - Shenoy-Shafer method of local computations (for presentation of this method the reader should consult the original paper of them [55]). The subsequent definitions of hypergraphs and operations on them are due to [55].

Hypergraphs: A nonempty set H of nonempty subsets of a finite set S be called a hypergraph on S. The elements of H be called hyperedges. Elements of S be called vertices. H and H' be both hypergraphs on S, then we call a hypergraph H' a *reduced hypergraph* of the hypergraph H, iff $H' \subseteq H$ holds, and for every $h \in H$ there exists such a $h' \in H'$ that $h \subseteq h'$.A hypergraph H *covers* a hypergraph H' iff for every $h' \in H'$ there exists such a $h \in H$ that $h' \subseteq h$.

Hypertrees: t and b be distinct hyperedges in a hypergraph H, $t \cap b \neq \emptyset$, and b contains every vertex of t that is contained in a hyperedge of H other than t; if $X \in t$ and $X \in h$, where $h \in H$ and $h \neq t$, then $X \in b$. Then we call t a twig of H, and we call b a branch for t. A twig may have more than one branch. We call a hypergraph a hypertree if there is an ordering of its hyperedges, say $h_1, h_2, ..., h_n$ such that h_k is a twig in the hypergraph $\{h_1, h_2, ..., h_k\}$ whenever $2 \leq k \leq n$. We call any such ordering of hyperedges a hypertree construction sequence for the hypertree. The first hyperedge in the hypertree construction sequence be called the root of the hypertree construction sequence.

Variables and valuations:Let $\mathbf{V}$ be a finite set. The elements of $\mathbf{V}$ are called variables. For each $h \subseteq \mathbf{V}$ there is a set VV_h. The elements of VV_h are called valuations. Let VV=$\bigcup\{VV_h | h \subseteq \mathbf{V}\}$ be called the set of all valuations.

In case of probabilities a valuation on h will be a non-negative, real-valued function on the set of all configurations of h(a configuration on h is a vector of possible values of variables in h). In the belief function case a valuation is a non-negative, real-valued function on the set of all subsets of configurations of h.

Proper valuation: for each $h \subseteq \mathbf{V}$ there is a subset P_h of VV_h elements of which are called proper valuations on h. Let P be the set of all proper valuations.

Combination: We assume that there is a mapping $\odot : VV \times VV \rightarrow VV$ called combination such that:
(i) if G and H are valuations on g and h respectively, then $G \odot H$ is a valuation on $g \cup h$
(ii) if either G or H is not a proper valuation then $G \odot H$ is not a proper valuation
(iii) if both G and H are proper valuations then $G \odot H$ may be or not be a proper valuation

Factorization: Suppose A is a valuation on a finite set of variables $\mathbf{V}$, and suppose HV is a hypergraph on $\mathbf{V}$. If A is equal to the combination of valuations of all hyperedges h of HV then we say that A factorizes on HV.

Let us remind also the following: (See [52]) Let B be a subset of Ξ, called evidence, m_B be a basic probability assignment such that $m_B(B) = 1$ and $m_B(A) = 0$ for any A different from B. Then the conditional belief function $Bel(.||B)$ representing the belief function Bel conditioned on evidence B is defined as: $Bel(.||B) = Bel \oplus Bel_B$.

The clue behind the uncertainty propagation method of Shenoy and Shafer is that if we make a factorization in terms along a hypertree structure (a Markov tree) then calculation of the joint belief distribution of variables belonging to a single hyperedge allows for a divide and conquer approach in that one considers this hyperedge as the root of a Markov tree the removal of which splits the Markov tree into as much disjoint Markov subtrees as there are twigs on the root etc. The calculation in the root requires only info from its twigs and the twigs calculate the info from their own Markov subtrees without any concern about other twigs of the root and their Markov subtrees. See [55] for detailed information.

2 Lower/Upper Bound Interpretation

Mathematical Theory of Evidence (MTE) is blamed to leave frequencies outside its framework. In this section we consider this problem from the point of view of conditioning in the MTE. We describe the class of belief functions for which marginal consistency with observed frequencies may be achieved and conditional belief functions are proper belief functions,and deal with implications for approximation of general belief functions by this class and for inference models in MTE.

belief

2.1 Case-based Understanding of Belief Functions

In an attempt to overcome the reason for those numerous failures to interpret consistently Dempster's rule of combination, a new frequency interpretation of MTE has been proposed in [29,30]. It has been demonstrated there that, in general, Dempster's rule has a destructive impact on the data so that whatever we expect calculation of conditional probabilities (given an event) differs from whatever we obtain under conditioning (given an event) in MTE (see the definition of aposteriorical conditioning of Shafer in [51].

Let us have a look at SQL [64] construct to calculate joint probability distribution from a database in two variables P(X,Y):

create view Total (Counted) as select count(*) from Cases;

create view Probability (X, Y,Prob) as select X, Y,count(*)/Counted from Cases, Total group by X, Y;

Let us look at calculation of conditional probability $P(X,Y|X \in A_X)$. We proceed as follows: we select first the proper subset of cases from the database and proceed to calculate the unconditional probability for the selected cases.

create view SelectedCases (X, Y) as select X, Y from Cases where X ∈ AX;

create view TotalCond (Counted) as select count(*) from SelectedCases;

create view CondProbability (X, Y, CondProb) as select Y,X,count(*)/Counted from SelectedCases, TotalCond where X ∈ AX group by X, Y;

If we calculate a conditional probability $P(X,Y|X \in A_X, X \in B_X)$ on a series of conditions $(X \in A_X, X \in B_X)$ we can proceed first by selecting cases for the first, then for the second condition etc., finding the intersection, and then calculating the probabilities (id - the identifier).

create view SelectedCasesA (id,X,Y) as select id,X,Y from Cases where $X \in AX$;

create view SelectedCasesB (id,X,Y) as select id,X,Y from Cases where $X \in BX$;

create view SelectedCases (id,X,Y) as select id,X,Y from SelectedCasesA intersection select id,X,Y from SelectedCasesB ;

create view TotalCond (Counted) as select count(*) from SelectedCases;

create view CondProbability (X,Y,CondProb) as select Y,X,count(*)/Counted from SelectedCases,TotalCond where $X \in AX$ *group by X, Y;*

Let us look at calculation of basic probability assignment (bpa) m(X,Y) from data :

create view Total (Counted) as select count(*) from Cases;

create view bpa (X,Y,m) as select X,Y,count(*)/TCounted from Cases,Total group by X,Y;

Let us look at calculation of aposterioric conditional bpa $m(X,Y||X \in A_X)$ We have to proceed as follows: we select first the proper subset of cases from the database and MODIFY the values for the variable X. Then we proceed to calculate the unconditional bpa for the selected and updated cases.

create view UpdatedCases (X,Y) as select $X \cap AX, Y$ *from Cases where* $X \cap AX \neq \emptyset$;

create view TotalCond (Counted) as select count(*) from UpdatedCases;

create view Cond_bpa (X,Y,Condbpa) as select X,Y,count(*)/Counted from UpdatedCases,TotalCond ;

If we calculate a conditional bpa $m(||X \in A_X, X \in B_X)$ on a series of conditions $(X \in A_X, X \in B_X)$ we CANNOT proceed by selecting cases for the first, then for the second condition etc., finding the intersection, and then calculating the bpa, because this would yield wrong results due to side effects stemming from case modifications.

This has a serious impact if we try to factorize a belief function into simpler components, e.g. for purposes of propagation of uncertainty (methods of propagation of uncertainty are presented e.g. in [4,55]. It turns out that:

- It is, in general, impossible to factoriz[illegible]t belief distribu[illegible]o components being conditional belief functions [1] (see eg. [4] for a discussion why two different notions of conditioning are needed for MTE: the posteriori-conditionals as conditionals in the sense of Shafer, and a priori-conditionals invented by Cano et al.,)
- A priori-conditional belief functions as proposed by Cano et al. in general do not exists (see a discussion on non-existence of a-priori conditionals in MTE presented by [54]) [2]
- What is more, it is often impossible to factorize a belief function Bel in variables p, q, r into two factors one Bel_1 in variables p, r and the second Bel_2 in variables q, r even if in conditional distribution given any value of the variable r, variables p, q are independent (see [63], that is when for every subset r_i of the domain of the variable r the following holds:

$$Bel(||r_i)^{\downarrow p,q} = Bel(||r_i)^{\downarrow p} \oplus Bel(||r_i)^{\downarrow q}$$

Therefore in papers [23,28,29] we have presented another approach to factorization of belief functions in terms of anticonditional belief functions. It turns out, however, that anticonditional belief functions are in general not belief functions but only pseudo-belief functions (that is ones with non-negative commonality functions). This means in practice, however, that anticonditional belief functions have no direct counterparts in the physical world, as the basic probability assignment may take negative values.

One can be tempted to suggest, that one shall then resign from modeling the joint belief distribution and instead try to find a marginally consistent decomposition of the joint belief distribution.

The natural question then arises:

- What is the class of Dempster-Shafer (DS) belief functions for which apriori-conditional belief functions exist ?
- How can general belief functions and uncertainty propagation for them be approximated by this class of belief functions and uncertainty propagation for them ?
- How can the belief functions and the reasoning with them be related to frequencies (cases)?

---

[1] Notice that in the domain of probability distributions, EVERY probability distribution may be represented by a composition of conditional probability distributions as so-called bayesian network

[2] In probability distributions, a-priori and a-posteriori conditionals from the point of view of frequencies coincide, and they always exist: Let us assume P(X,Y) is a frequency based (case-based) probability distribution of X,Y. A posteriori conditional distribution of variable X given variable Y=y is interpreted as uncertainty distribution of variable X $P'(X|Y=y)$ if we restrict ourselves only to cases for which Y=y. Apriori conditional distribution of X given Y is a function $P(X|Y)$ in X,Y defined as $P(X|Y) = P(X \cap Y)/P(Y)$ for all values of y for which $P(Y=y) > 0$. Obviously: $P'(X=x|Y=y) = P(X=x|Y=y)$ if $P(Y=y) > 0$.

2.2 Correct Approximation of Apriorical Conditional Belief Functions

Shafer [51] suggested that a belief function may emerge if we observe a variable X with domain of values Ξ_X indirectly (via a mapping f) by observing actually another variable Y with a domain Ξ_Y such that the mapping $f : \Xi_Y \to \Xi_X$ is not a function. Hence, in some cases, if we observe a single value ξ_Y of the variable Y, we can tell at most that the value of the variable X belongs to a non-empty set of elements $\{\xi_{X_1}, \xi_{X_2}, \ldots, \xi_{X_n}\}$. So a probability distribution P(Y) in Y translates into a basic belief assignment function, from which one calculates easily belief distribution Bel^X in X. In this way we could get a case-based distribution in variable X.

Variable Y	Corresponding set values of X (A)	frequency	$m^X(A)$	$Bel^X(A)$
y_1	$\{x_1\}$	10	.10	.10
y_2	$\{x_1, x_2\}$	20	.20	.30
y_3	$\{x_2, x_3\}$	30	.30	.70
y_4	$\{x_3\}$	40	.40	.40
-	$\{x_1, x_2, x_3\}$	-	.0	1.0

This could be extended simply to multivariate belief distributions. However, we encounter one interpretational problem:
Let us consider the following frequency table in variables X and Z:

X	Z	frequencies
$\{x_1, x_2\}$	$\{z_1, z_2\}$	20

What shall be the focal points of the multivariate belief function $Bel^{X,Z}$ in two variables X,Z ? Marginal consistency will be achieved either if we assume

$$m_1^{X,Z}(\{(x_1, z_1), (x_1, z_2), (x_2, z_1), (x_2, z_2)\}) = 1$$

and if we take

$$m_2^{X,Z}(\{(x_1, z_1), (x_2, z_2)\}) = 1$$

and if we suppose

$$m_3^{X,Z}(\{(x_1, z_2), (x_2, z_1)\}) = 1$$

and for many other belief functions. But which one is the best ? Let us try to calculate the conditional belief function $Bel_i(||X = x_1)^{\downarrow Z}$. (From Shafer's formula: $Bel_i(||X = x_1)^{\downarrow Z} = (Bel_i \oplus Bel_{X=x_i})^{\downarrow Z}$ with $Bel_{X=x_i}$ being a belief function with the only focal point $m_{X=x_i}(\{(x_1, z_1), (x_1, z_2)\}) = 1$). We get three totally different results - three belief functions with differing focal points: $m_1(||X = x_1)^{\downarrow Z}(\{z_1, z_2\}) = 1$, $m_2(||X = x_1)^{\downarrow Z}(\{z_1\}) = 1$, $m_3(||X = x_1)^{\downarrow Z}(\{z_2\}) = 1$.

You can easily see that it is next to impossible to decide which of these conditionals is the correct one from the point of view of the observed data. So which belief function shall be treated as the most representative for the data ? We suggest here the first one (Bel_1) for the following reasons:

1. if we observe X, Z separately, we have no reason to assume that x_1 must co-occur with z_1 but never with z_2 etc - we assume we have no more information than actually visible from the data,
2. the methods of uncertainty propagation suggested both by Cano et al. [4] and Shenoy & Shafer [55] implicitly assume that the joint belief in values of observed variables $X_1, X_2, ...X_n$ is the composition of the values of individual variables:

$$Bel_{observations} = Bel_{X_1=A_1} \oplus Bel_{X_2=A_2} \oplus \ldots \oplus Bel_{X_n=A_n}$$

with $A_i \subseteq \Xi_{X_i}$ being a subset of the domain of the ith variable. Violation of this assumption would invalidate the respective method of uncertainty propagation.

Let us consider now the following data in three (logical) variables X,Y,Z, giving the belief function Bel_{and}.

X=	Y=	Z=	fre-quen-cy	m_{and} $(A_X \times A_Y \times A_Z)$
$\{t_X\}$	$\{t_Y\}$	$\{t_Z\}$	10	.10
$\{t_X\}$	$\{f_Y\}$	$\{f_Z\}$	10	.10
$\{f_X\}$	$\{t_Y\}$	$\{f_Z\}$	10	.10
$\{f_X\}$	$\{f_Y\}$	$\{f_Z\}$	10	.10
$\{t_X\}$	$\{t_Y, f_Y\}$	$\{t_Z, f_Z\}$	10	.10
$\{f_X\}$	$\{t_Y, f_Y\}$	$\{f_Z\}$	10	.10
$\{t_X, f_X\}$	$\{t_Y\}$	$\{t_Z, f_Z\}$	10	.10
$\{t_X, f_X\}$	$\{f_Y\}$	$\{f_Z\}$	10	.10
$\{t_X, f_X\}$	$\{t_Y, f_Y\}$	$\{t_Z, f_Z\}$	20	.20

Let us consider calculation of an apriori conditional belief function in the sense of Cano et al. [4] such that it would imply the value of Z given X,Y. A look at the data would suggest that variables X,Y and Z are connected by the logical equation: $X \wedge Y = Z$ so that one might suggest a belief function with focal point

$$m_{\&}(\{(t_X, t_Y, t_Z), (t_X, f_Y, f_Z), (f_X, t_Y, f_Z), (f_X, f_Y, f_Z)\}) = 1$$

is the apriori conditional connecting X,Y and Z. But this is a wrong conclusion, because:

$$Bel_{and} \neq Bel_{and}^{\downarrow\{X,Y\}} \oplus Bel_{\&}$$

What is more, the Cano et al a priori conditional of Z given X,Y does not exist at all !!! Therefore, decomposition of a joint belief distribution into conditionals cannot in general be achieved. However, we must acknowledge that marginal consistency is actually achieved, that is :

$$(Bel_{and})^{\downarrow X} = (Bel_{and}^{\downarrow\{X,Y\}} \oplus Bel_{\&})^{\downarrow X}$$

$$(Bel_{and})^{\downarrow Y} = (Bel_{and}^{\downarrow\{X,Y\}} \oplus Bel_{\&})^{\downarrow Y}$$

$$(Bel_{and})^{\downarrow Z} = (Bel_{and}^{\downarrow\{X,Y\}} \oplus Bel_{\&})^{\downarrow Z}$$

Can we always construct a marginally consistent apriori-conditional ? We shall assume that we have found a marginally consistent apriori conditional $Bel^{|p}$ of Belief function Bel given set of variables p iff $Bel^{|p}$ is a belief function and for every variable X:

$$(Bel)^{\downarrow X} = (Bel^{|p} \oplus Bel^{\downarrow p})^{\downarrow X}$$

let us consider the following belief distribution in variables X,Z

X	Z	frequencies
$\{x_1\}$	$\{z_1\}$	40
$\{x_1, x_2\}$	$\{z_2\}$	60

It is easily to show that marginally consistent $Bel^{|X}$ does not exist.

What is then the class of belief functions possessing marginally consistent conditionals ? What is the class of marginally consistent conditional belief functions ?

It is easy to show that if there exists a marginally consistent conditional belief function $Bel^{|p}$ of the belief function Bel given set of variables p then there exists another marginally consistent conditional belief function $Bel^{|p}_{\Xi}$ of the belief function Bel given set of variables p such that $(Bel^{|p}_{\Xi})^{\downarrow p}$ has only one focal point $(m^{|p}_{\Xi})^{\downarrow p}(\Xi_p) = 1$ with Ξ_p being the joint domain of variables from set p. In other words, Cano et al. apriori-conditionals represent completely the class of marginally consistent conditional belief functions.

Hence it is nearly obvious that in general case-based (separately measured) belief functions do not possess marginally consistent conditional belief functions.

Therefore it is in general of primary interest to find an appropriate approximation of general belief functions by means of decompositions into Cano's et al apriori-conditionals. Let us say that an approximation Bel' of belief function Bel is correct iff for every set A $Bel'(A) <= Bel(A)$. An approximation Bel' of belief function Bel is marginally correct iff for every variable X and every set A $Bel'^{\downarrow X}(A)) <= Bel^{\downarrow X}(A)$.

Let us consider the following algorithm for calculation of a correct approximation of the function Bel in variables X,Y:

0. We initialize the basic probability assignment function m_{cond} defined over variables X,Y with 0 for every subset of $\Xi_X \times \Xi_Y$.
1. For each set $A_X \subseteq \Xi_X$ with $m^{\downarrow X}(A_X) > 0$ we calculate the quantity $g(A_X, A_Y) := m(A_X \times A_Y)/m^{\downarrow X}(A_X)$.
2. i:=1, q:=0
3. For each set $A_X \subseteq \Xi_X$ with $m^{\downarrow X}(A_X) > 0$ we select a set $r_i(A_X) \subseteq \Xi_Y$ with $g(A_X, r_i(A_X)) > 0$.
   $g_{i,r,min}$ be the minimum of $g(A_X, r_i(A_X))$ over all $A_X \subseteq \Xi_X$ with $m^{\downarrow X}(A_X) > 0$
4. For the relation r_i we select a function $a_i : \Xi_X \to 2^{\Xi_Y}$ such that for each set $A_X \subseteq \Xi_X$ with $m^{\downarrow X}(A_X) > 0$ we have $r_i(A_X) \subseteq \bigcup_{\xi_X \in A_X} a_i(\xi_X)$
5. We update the function m_{cond} as follows: We calculate the set $A = \bigcup_{\xi_X \in \Xi_X} \{\xi_X\} \times a_i(\xi_X)$. Then $m_{cond}(A) := m_{cond}(A) + g_{i,r,min}$.
6. We update the g function as follows: For each set $A_X \subseteq \Xi_X$ with $m^{\downarrow X}(A_X) > 0$ $g(A_X, r_i(A_X)) := g(A_X, r_i(A_X)) - g_{i,r,min}$
7. For each set $A_X \subseteq \Xi_X$ with $m^{\downarrow X}(A_X) > 0$

$$q := \frac{q + g_{i,r,min} * m^{\downarrow X}(A_X) * card(A_X)}{card(\bigcup_{\xi_X \in A_X} a_i(\xi_X))}$$

8. i:=i+1. If g is equal zero everywhere then terminate, otherwise continue with step 3.

The marginal quality of an approximation constructed by the above algorithm be the quantity q. The quality q can range from zero to one. If the quality is equal one then we have constructed a marginally consistent conditional of Bel given X. If Bel is a probabilistic belief function (with focal points being singleton sets), then a marginally consistent Cano's conditional of Bel given X always exists. If Bel is a general belief function possessing a marginally consistent Cano's conditional of Bel given X, then the construction by the above algorithm of the conditional is characterized by the fact that in step 4 we have $r_i(A_X) = \bigcup_{\xi_X \in A_X} a_i(\xi_X)$. However, the construction task as such is hard. In particular, we cannot assume that if there exists a Cano's conditional of Bel given X, and if and if for i=1,...,k we managed to obtain $r_i(A_X) = \bigcup_{\xi_X \in A_X} a_i(\xi_X)$, then we will get a $r_i(A_X) = \bigcup_{\xi_X \in A_X} a_i(\xi_X)$ for i=k+1. Consider the following (counter)example: Let *Bel* be a belief function separately measurable in X,Y, marginally consistent with $Bel_1 \oplus Bel_2$ where Bel_1 being a belief function in X, Bel_2 in X,Y with focal points:

A_X	$m_1(A_X)$
$\{x_1\}$	p_1
$\{x_2\}$	p_2
$\{x_3\}$	p_2
$\{x_1, x_2\}$	p_{12}
$\{x_1, x_3\}$	p_{13}
$\{x_2, x_3\}$	p_{23}

$A_{X,Y}$	$m_2(A_{X,Y})$
$\{(x_1, y_1), (x_2, y_1)(x_3, y_2)\}$	1/3
$\{(x_1, y_1), (x_2, y_2)(x_3, y_2)\}$	1/3
$\{(x_1, y_2), (x_2, y_1)(x_3, y_2)\}$	1/3

Obviously then Bel_2 is the marginally consistent Cano conditional of *Bel*. Let us select r_1 as follows:

A_X	$r_1(A_X)$
$\{x_1\}$	$\{y_1\}$
$\{x_2\}$	$\{y_1\}$
$\{x_3\}$	$\{y_1\}$
$\{x_1, x_2\}$	$\{y_1\}$
$\{x_1, x_3\}$	$\{y_1\}$
$\{x_2, x_3\}$	$\{y_1\}$

We can then easily construct function a_1 as $a_1(x_1) = y_1$, $a_1(x_2) = y_1$, $a_1(x_3) = y_1$ so that obviously $r_1(A_X) = \bigcup_{\xi_X \in A_X} a_1(\xi_X)$. However, if we increase in step 8 i to i=2 and reenter step 3, then it will not be possible any more to construct such an a_2 that $r_2(A_X) = \bigcup_{\xi_X \in A_X} a_2(\xi_X)$ because necessarily a fragment of r_2 will be:

A_X	$r_2(A_X)$
...	...
$\{x_1, x_2\}$	$\{y_1, y_2\}$
$\{x_1, x_3\}$	$\{y_1, y_2\}$
$\{x_2, x_3\}$	$\{y_1, y_2\}$

Hence in general finding a marginally consistent Cano's conditional, even if it exists, is hard and requires backtracking. So probably one will be satisfied already if one finds a high quality marginally correct approximate conditional belief distribution (Application of genetic algorithms is advised here.).

2.3 Impact on Reasoning

Let *Bel* be a belief function in X,Y and $Bel^{|X}$ its marginally correct approximate conditional belief distribution. Then $Bel^{\downarrow X} \oplus Bel^{|X}$ is a marginally correct approximation of *Bel*. Then Shafer's conditioning $Bel(||A_X \times \Xi_Y)$ with A_X being any non-empty subset of the domain Ξ_X of X is marginally correctly approximated by $(Bel^{\downarrow X} \oplus Bel^{|X})(||A_X \times \Xi_Y)$, that is given the "decomposition" of *Bel* into its marginal on X and the approximately correct conditional on X we can reason approximately correctly about the a posteriori distribution of Y given any event of observation of the intrinsic value of X. However, we cannot do it in the reverse direction: we cannot derive the aposterioric distribution of X by observation of Y because in general $Bel(||\Xi_X \times A_Y)$ with A_Y being any non-empty subset of the domain Ξ_Y of Y is NOT marginally correctly approximated by $(Bel^{\downarrow X} \oplus Bel^{|X})(||\Xi_X \times A_Y)$. What is worse, even if the conditionals are marginally consistent, we will not achieve marginal correctnesses, not to say marginal consistency.

This means that if we have a marginally consistent factorization (in terms of Cano's conditionals) of a belief function then we can in general use neither

Shafer & Shenoy nor Cano's at al. framework for propagation of uncertainty because the results will be inconsistent with the data. (If we are reasoning counter the stream of calculations of conditionals, we may fail to obtain correct result). A way out of this problem, for the framework of Cano, is to consider separate marginally correct approximations in each direction of reasoning. That is, given the polytree representing correctly dependencies among variables, we need to transform this polytree, for every variable the value of which we want to infer, into a such a (belief) network graph that every arrow points towards that variable. In case of plain directed trees the result of this transformation is a polytree (with undirected backbone identical with that of the original tree) such that edges connecting the target variable with its neighbous are reoriented to point at the target variable and every other variable is connected via a directed path with the target variable. In case of general polytree the result of the transformation is a network with more edges than the original polytree. Edges are added when an edge is reversed which originally pointed at a node with many ingoing edges. E.g. if we had the situation that $X- > Z < -Y$ and we want to invert the edge $Z < -Y$, then we need to add the edge $X- > Y$. In case of general polytree we obtain in this way networks with considerably different undirected backbones[3].

If we assume that we adopt a structure (factorization) of Cano type, that is in form of a generalized polytree (singly connected "bayesian" network), then products of above transformations are directly convertible into a Shenoy's and Shafer's Markov tree. Let us now shift to Shenoy's and Shafer's belief propagation in Markov tree: The general principle there is "message passing" - if a node of Markov-tree gets information from its all but one neighbors , then it sends, to the remaining node, a "message", that is $\oplus$ combination of those messages plus its own factor of the belief function factorization. In the original Shenoy/Shafer algorithm, this node's own factor of the belief function factorization is exactly the same independly to which neighbor the message is sent. We propose to have separate hypertrees for each target variable and to reason within each of them in one direction only (resp. modifications of propagation algorithm are known). Then it is guaranteed that the results of reasoning (a posteriori marginal distributions) will be marginally correct approximations with respect to the intrinsic distribution.

Let us now consider the meaning of Cano et al. conditionals. These are in fact sets of mappings between sets of variables selected with some probability. This gives a new meaning to the belief function. Instead of thinking in the way probability functions do that is that given some value of one variable, the conditional probability distribution assigns a value to another variable, we can think of objects that are assigned with some

[3] In case of a general belief network transformations aiming at creation of directed pathes from every node towards the target variable would result in still more complicated networks so that merits of reasoning in such networks would be questionable

probability a belief.

2.4 Summary of Lower/Upper Bound Approximation

1. The case-based derivation of aposteriori MTE belief function requires combination of operations of case selection with operation of case updating.
2. Therefore, marginally correct inference rules for MTE derived from data can be applied only unidirectionally - reversal of direction of reasoning leads to contradictions with the data. For this reason, original Cano et al. and Shenoy/Shafer uncertainty propagation methods are not suitable for case-based MTE belief functions.
3. Hence in case of direct dependence of a set of n variables, n inferences networks - one for each variable as dependent on the remaining ones - have to be established and used depending on target variable.

3 Qualitative Interpretation

Though a tendency to consider belief functions as subjective uncertainty measures is visible [53], the need for case-based interpretation as a pre-condition for practical applicability has been explicitly stressed [65]. Still this interpretation should be qualitative rather than quantitative in nature [59]. However, these requirements seem not to be met so far.

Apart from manageable interpretation, the MTE caused troubles of purely numerical nature. Unlike ordinary probabilities, which assign mass to each possible outcome, belief functions assign mass to each subset of the outcome space. As a consequence the amount of memory space required to store a belief function in a computer will grow exponentially with the size of the outcome space we consider. Searching for economical representation of a belief function, the researches made use of the already known concepts of sets factorisation analysed in the theory of relational databases. In our search for non-quantitative interpretation of MTE, our attention was attracted by the nature of the join operator of relational databases [3] or in general the multivalued dependency [8] the study of which led to invention of local computation method for uncertainty propagation of Shenoy and Shafer [54] for MTE. This in turn made the rough-set theoretic interpretation of MTE belief functions of Skowron and Busse [58] best choice for further investigation, as it was purely-case based and relational, though it is frequency based. The rough-set interpretation sheds some light onto what the concept of "evidence" may mean in experimental terms. The "evidence" there is the information part of a database record and it "supports" the decision part of a record. The complexity of combination of evidence according to the Dempster rule in [58] gave an impulse for search of a simpler way to accomplish it. It turns out that with frequency approach updating of decision parts of cases is needed (Dempster's combination is destructive). Out of this experience we decided to abandon the frequencies and concentrated on purely relational operations.

The section recalls traditional rough set theoretic frequency interpretation of DST from [58] and explains our insights of destructive nature of Dempster's combination with respect to frequencies. Then it presents our new qualitative interpretation. The section ends with some concluding remarks.

Throughout the section, as relational data tables are subject of rough set theory, SQL [64] query language is used to express semantics of DST measures and operators in terms of decision tables, both with respect to traditional and our rough sets based interpretation of DST, as SQL has the capability of expressing purely relational and frequentistic data processing.

3.1 Rough Set Theory. The Traditional Interpretation of Belief Functions

Skowron and Grzymala-Busse [58] and others studying rough sets developed more specifically the proposal of Shafer with respect to frequency interpretation of DST.

Let us introduce the following denotation concerning decision tables. Let a tuple μ mean a function $\mu : A \rightarrow DOM(A)$, with A being a set of attributes A_j, $DOM(A_j)$ being the domain of the attribute A_j, $DOM(A) = \bigcup_{A_j \in A} DOM(A_j)$. A be called the scheme of μ, $A = S(\mu)$. A relational table TAB be any set of tuples with identical scheme. This common scheme be denoted by $S(TAB)$. Let $\mu[R]$ with $R \subseteq S(\mu)$ denote the restriction of the tuple μ to the scheme R: $\mu[R] = \{(A_j, a_{jk}) | A_j \in R \wedge a_{jk} = \mu(A_j)\}$. The restriction of a relational table TAB to R, denoted $TAB[R]$, be defined $TAB[R] = \{\mu[R] | \mu \in TAB\}$. A relational join of two relational tables TAB_1, TAB_2 be defined as: $TAB_1 \otimes TAB_2 = \{\mu_1 \cup \mu_2 | \mu_1 \in TAB_1, \mu_2 \in TAB_2 \wedge \forall_{A_j \in S(\mu_1) \cap S(\mu_2)} \mu_1(A_j) = \mu_2(A_j)\}$.

A decision table is a relational table in which we split the scheme into two distinct parts: the information part **I** and the decision part **D**.

Let $card(SET)$ denote the cardinality of the set SET.

Let us assume that a decision table TAB of decisions D (atomic values) under conditions (information) **I** (atomic value vectors) is available. However, **I** may not contain the complete information to make decision D. This gives rise in a natural way to a mapping Γ assigning different values of D to the same value of **I**. Under these circumstances the belief in a set A (subset of the domain of D) $Bel(A)$ may be derived from a case database as follows: $Bel(A) = 1 - card(\{\mu | \mu \in TAB \wedge \mu(D) \notin A\}) / card(TAB)$, which may be implemented the SQL query language [64] as:

create view Total (Counted) as select count(*) from TAB;
*select count(*)/Counted from TAB, Total where not (***I** *in (select* **I** *from TAB where not (D in A)));*

Skowron and Grzymała-Busse[58] elaborated also a notion of conditioning under rough set interpretation [58, p.219 ff.] as respective measures for sub-tables (that is tables consisting of cases selected by a criterion). Let us condition on D belonging to the set B selecting tuples fitting the condition B $Subtable = \{\mu | \mu \in TAB \wedge \mu(D) \in B$ which may be implemented as

*create view SubtableTAB(D,***I** *) as select X,***I** *from TAB where not (***I** *in (select* **I** *from TAB where not (D in B)));*

The belief distribution for the subtable can be calculated from the view SubtableTAB in the same way as for the TAB database. However, it is a matter of a calculation exercise to show that their notion of conditionality does not agree with that of Shafer from Def.6.

Therefore, to achieve consistency with Shafer's conditioning from Def.6 we propose the following interpretation, derivable from our approach described in the paper [30]: Let $v \in B$. Then in SQL

update TAB set D=v where not (D in B) and **I** *in (select* **I** *from TAB where D in B);*
delete TAB where not (D in B);

Let c_1,c_2 be two cases from the database TAB such that $\mathbf{I}(c_1) = \mathbf{I}(c_2)$ but $D(c_1) \neq D(c_2)$ Let be $D(c_1) \in B$ and $D(c_2) \notin B$ Then after the above update and delete operations both cases c_1, c_2 are retained in the database TAB. c_1 has retained its value $D(c_1)$. But the case c_2 was subject to a metamorphose: its $D(c_2)$ has been changed (to v). This means that the Dempster rule of combination is "destructive". Preservation of frequency interpretation under conditioning enforces ignoring the intrinsic (observed) value of an attribute and replacement of it with some other value. It should be stressed at this point that the above SQL operation cannot be easily expressed in terms of sets and relations, because an update operation is engaged which may make distinct tuples identical.

A still more complex task is the interpretation of combination of two independent pieces of evidence. Skowron and Grzymała-Busse[58] elaborated a procedure consisting in transforming the combined decision tables into a kind of summary with multivalued decision columns (since non-relational) and then applying complex rational arithmetic to get finally a decision table (derived by so-called Ψ-independent combination) implementing Dempster combination of independent belief functions (consult [58] for details).

3.2 New Interpretation

Below we present a slight modification of the rough set interpretation of belief functions that surprisingly turns out to be both simple, elegant and straight forward and at the same time fulfils the requirement that was not matched by any known interpretations: it is qualitative and not quantitative in nature and still case-based. Furthermore we demonstrate that our new interpretation corresponds strictly to the notion of multivalued dependency, that is combination of belief functions parallels the relational join operator from database theory.

The results of any experiment with multiple outcomes can evaluated along two dimensions: the quantitative and the qualitative one. If we say e.g. that in a series of coin tossing experiments we got 57 heads and 43 tails, then this is a quantitative evaluation. But if we say that there were heads and tails (and not e.g. edges) then we say something about the qualitative aspects of the experiment. In the quantitative evaluation we say that 57 % of all the cases we got heads, in the qualitative evaluation we say that 50 % of all possibilities of diverse outcomes are heads. In most real life cases we are more interested in the quantitative aspects. Sometimes, however, the qualitative side may be of more interest. E.g. if 40 witnesses say that they saw the suspect had killed the victim, but their testimonies are suspiciously similar, and 20 say they saw the contrary, and their testimonies made impressions of individuality, then we would say that there are 1:20 chances of the guilt of the suspect rather than 40:20, because the qualitative aspects (diversity) are more important than quantitative ones (frequency).

Behaviour of frequencies under reasoning was historically the foundation of probability theory. As probabilistic (frequency based) models of MTE fail in general, we considered just the diversity as a possible alternative for a model of MTE. The diversity is well handled by relational model of databases. Though at a first glance the count of cases in a relational database may appear identical with counting frequencies of objects / events, the difference starts as soon as we make a projection on the subset of attributes. It turns out that projected frequencies differ significantly from the counts of cases in a projected relational database. Therefore we say that our approach is non-frequency, non-quantitative, that is qualitative one.

Let us define the plausibility $Pl_{TAB}(SET)$ derived from a decision table TAB with decision variable D and the set **I** of information variables as: $Pl_{TAB}(SET) = card(\{\mu[\mathbf{I}] | \mu \in TAB \wedge \mu(D) \in SET\})/card(TAB[\mathbf{I}])$, implemented as

create view tmpTAB(No) as select count(distinct **I***) from TAB;*
create view plTAB as select count(distinct **I***)/No from TAB,tmpTAB where TAB.D in SET;*

Example 1 explains the detailed numerical procedure for calculation of *Pl* from the above SQL expression.

Theorem 1. *The function $Pl_{TAB}(SET)$ derived from a decision table TAB with decision variable D and the set* **I** *of information variables is plausibility function $Pl(SET)$ in the sense of Dempster-Shafer theory.*

Proof. In DST, the plausibility of a set SET is just the sum of basic probability assignments $m(A)$ such that $SET \cap A \neq \emptyset$. Let r be a record, $I(r)$ its ation part and $D(r)$ its decision part. For the set SET, let us consider a subset R of all records from the decision table TAB such that: if $r \in R$ then $D(r) \in SET$ and for every $d \in SET$ there exists $r' \in R$ such that $D(r) = D(r')$ and there exists no record $r" \notin R$ such that $I(r") = I(r)$. Obviously, for two distinct sets SET' and $SET"$ their respective sets R' and $R"$ will share no records. Furthermore, $\bigcup_{SET \subseteq domain(D)} R(SET)$ will be the (relationally) identical with TAB. Hence we can consider the ratio number of records with distinct information part in $R(SET)$ divided by the number of records with distinct information parts in DT as the bpa function $m(SET)$ in the sense of DST. But the function $Pl_{TAB}(SET)$ counts (the relative share of) the records with distinct information part such that the decision part belongs to SET. Hence in practice it is just the sum of basic probability assignments $m(A)$ such that $SET \cap A \neq \emptyset$. Therefore it is a plausibility function.

Example 1. Let us first look at the relational table BUILD in tab. 1). The column D is the decision column, I is information part of the table. The domain of the decision variable D is {center, restaurant, school}.

Table 1. Example: Public offering: erection of buildings of a school, a restaurant and a shopping center. Decision table: BUILDing. "Information part" - the firm, "Decision part" - the object to be erected

	I	D
1.	ABD A.G.	center
2.	LQR Inc.	school
3.	PTS Ltd.	center
	PTS Ltd.	restaurant
4.	XYZ Inc.	center
5.	ZZZ Ltd.	restaurant
	ZZZ Ltd.	school

Let us calculate now the plausibility Pl({school, restaurant}) from this table. There are 7 cases (rows) in the dataset. But there are only 5 cases with distinct information part (firms) **I**. And there are only 3 cases with decision either ***school*** or ***restaurant*** with distinct information part **I** (LQR Inc., PTS Ltd., ZZZ Ltd).So the plausibility[4]is equal to Pl({school, restaurant})=3/5. One can check that Pl({school})=2/5 (LQR Inc., ZZZ Ltd) and Pl({restaurant})=2/5 (PTS Ltd., ZZZ Ltd).

Notice that from the calculational rules for Dempster-Shafer theory we can derive also relational views calculating other measures:

[4] Notice that under Skowron/Busse interpretation [58] we get $Pl = 4/7$ which is obviously a different value. The difference stems from the fundamental difference between frequency (Skowron/Busse) and relational(ours) view of the world.

Belief $Bel_{TAB}(SET) = 1 - card(\{\mu[\mathbf{I}] | \mu \in TAB \wedge \mu(D) \notin SET\})/card(TAB[\mathbf{I}])$, implemented as

create view belTAB as select 1-count(distinct **I***)/No from TAB,tmpTAB where not (TAB.D in SET);*

Commonality $Q_{TAB}(SET) = card(\{\mu[\mathbf{I}] | \forall_{d \in SET} \; \mu[\mathbf{I}] \cup \{(D,d)\} \in TAB\}) / card(TAB[\mathbf{I}])$, implemented as

create view tmp1TAB(CN) as select count(distinct D) from TAB where TAB.D in SET group by **I** *;*
create view qTAB as select count(*)/No from tmpTAB,tmp1TAB where CN=card(set); (card() is a function counting the elements of the set passed as its argument)

Basic belief assignment $m_{TAB}(SET) = card(\{\mu[\mathbf{I}] | \forall_{d \in SET} \; \mu[\mathbf{I}] \cup \{(D,d)\} \in TAB\} \wedge \forall_{d \notin SET} \; \mu[\mathbf{I}] \cup \{(D,d)\} \notin TAB\})/card(TAB[\mathbf{I}])$, implemented as

*create view tmp11TAB(***I***,D) as select TAB.***I***, TAB.D+XX.D from TAB, TAB XX where TAB.D in SET and XX.***I***=TAB.***I***;*
*create view tmp12TAB(***I***,CN) as select* **I***,count(distinct D) from tmp11TAB group by* **I***;*
*create view m as count(*)/No from tmpTAB, tmp12TAB where CN=card(SET)*card(SET);*

Theorem 2. *The functions $Bel_{TAB}(SET)$, $Q_{TAB}(SET)$, $m_{TAB}(SET)$ derived from a decision table TAB with decision variable D and the set* **I** *of information variables are belief, commonality, basic probability/belief assignment functions resp. $Bel(SET), Q(SET), m(SET)$ in the sense of Dempster-Shafer theory.*

Example 2. From table 1 we easily calculate that:
Commonality Q({school, restaurant}=1/5 (Number of firms ready to build either the school and the restaurant: ZZZ Ltd).
Belief Q({school, restaurant}=2/5 Number of firms ready to build nothing but the school or the restaurant (LQR Inc., ZZZ Ltd)
bpa - No of firms exactly offering erecting of: m({school, restaurant}=1/5 (ZZZ Ltd), m({restaurant}=0 (none), m({school}=1/5 (LQR Inc.)

Conditioning as Selection of a Subtable Let us define now the conditional belief function $Bel_{TAB}(.||B)$ representing the belief function Bel conditioned on evidence B as the belief function $Bel_{TAB\_B}(.)$ define over the view table

*create view TAB_B(***I***,D) as select* **I***,D from TAB where TAB.D in B;*

Table 2. Shafer's Conditioning. Relational Interpretation. Calculating $Bel(.||\{school, restaurant\})$ as a *Bel* from the table obtained by *select I,D from BUILD where D=school or D= restaurant*

	I	D
1.	LQR Inc.	school
2.	PTS Ltd.	restaurant
5.	ZZZ Ltd.	restaurant
	ZZZ Ltd.	school

Example 3. In our example, for the relational table BUILD from tab. 1, $Bel_{BUILD}(.||\{school, restaurant\})$ is just *Bel* calculated from the respective projection *select I,D from BUILD where D=school or D= restaurant* visible in tab. 2. It is easily seen that $Pl_{BUILD}(\{restaurant\}||\{school, restaurant\}) = 2/3$ (PTS Ltd.,ZZZ Ltd.) and $m_{BUILD}(\{restaurant\}||\{school, restaurant\}) = 1/3$ (PTS Ltd.).

Our conditional belief function matches perfectly the Shafer's definition of $Bel(.||B)$ cited above (Def.6).Notice that under Skowron/Busse interpretation (section 3), the matching of Shafer's conditionality definition had to be paid for with creating a physical copy of a relational table and updating it, whereas our notion works perfectly without any updates - only selection is used just as in probabilistic conditioning.

Table 3. Public offering: equipment for buildings of a school, a restaurant and a shopping center. Decision table: EQUIPment "Information part" - the firm, "Decision part" - the object to be equipped

	I2	D
1.	AAA GmbH	school
2.	BBB Ltd.	center
	BBB Ltd.	restaurant
3.	CCC Inc.	center
	CCC Inc.	restaurant

Combination as Relational Join Now let us discuss the most impressive property of the new interpretation: the Dempster's rule of combination interpreted as relational join.

Example 4. Let us consider the decision table EQUIP (tab. 3) and BUILD (tab. 1). We want to combine independent evidence from both tables to support a decision. Let us assume that independence of evidence means that no pair of firms (one from BUILD, one from EQUIP) refuse to cooperate on erecting and equipping an object. How many pairs of firms do we have to finish a set of objects mentioned in the offerings ? The answer lies in the relational table FINISH (tab. 4) obtained as a relational join of BUILD and EQUIP (over the common column D) so that the new decision table has as its decision column D and as its information part I,I2:

create table FINISH (I,I2,D);
insert into table FINISH from
select I,I2,D from BUILD, EQUIP where BUILD.D=EQUIP.D;

Notice that in BUILD, there were 5 cases with distinct information part, in EQUIP - 3, and in BUEQ there are only 10. We have here $Pl_{FINISH}(\{school, restaurant\}) = 8/10$ and $Bel_{FINISH}(\{school, restaurant\}) = 3/10$

You can easily check that $Bel_{FINISH} = Bel_{BUILD} \oplus Bel_{EQUIP}$.

Generally, we can formulate the theorem:

Theorem 3. *If the decision tables DT1(***I1***,D) and DT2(***I2***,D) with non-overlapping information parts* **I1**,**I2** *are combined by relational join operation* $DT1 \otimes DT2$*, implemented as*

select **I1**,**I2**,*DT1.D from DT1,DT2 where DT1.D=DT2.D;*

*yielding table DT12(***I***,D) with* **I**=**I1**∪**I2***, then* $Bel_{DT12} = Bel_{DT1} \oplus Bel_{DT2}$.

Proof. This can be demonstrated by considering the "fate" of records counted on calculation of m_i. If R_1 is the set of records counted when calculating $m_1(A)$ in DT1, and if R_2 is the set of records counted when calculating $m_2(B)$ in DT2, then upon join only records $\mu = (\mu_1[\mathbf{I1}], \mu_2[\mathbf{I2}], \mu_1[D])$ with $\mu_1 \in R_1$, $\mu_2 \in R_2$, $\mu_1[D] = \mu_2[D] \in A \cap B$ will be created, hence they will be counted in support of $m(A \cap B)$. Furthermore, their number will be exactly equal to the product of the number of distinct records in R_1 times the number of distinct records in R_2, so that the Dempster formula will be matched perfectly upon normalization.

Relational Marginalization and Decombination A further intriguing property, not present in any interpretation of MTE known so far, is the relationship between relational marginalization and MTE factorization ("decombination") of belief functions.

Example 5. Notice that BUILD and EQUIP in our example are both in first normal form and the domain of the attribute D is identical in both tables. Therefore we know from elementary properties of relational data tables that marginalization of FINISH over I,D

Table 4. Combination of Independent Evidence. Decision table FINISH obtained as *select I,I2,D from BUILD, EQUIP where BUILD.D=EQUIP.D*

	I	I2	D
1.	ABD A.G.	BBB Ltd.	center
2.	ABD A.G.	CCC Inc.	center
3.	LQR Inc.	AAA GmbH	school
4.	PTS Ltd.	BBB Ltd.	center
	PTS Ltd.	BBB Ltd.	restaurant
5.	PTS Ltd.	CCC Inc.	center
	PTS Ltd.	CCC Inc.	restaurant
6.	XYZ Inc.	BBB Ltd.	center
7.	XYZ Inc.	CCC Inc.	center
8.	ZZZ Ltd.	BBB Ltd.	restaurant
9.	ZZZ Ltd.	CCC Inc.	restaurant
10.	ZZZ Ltd.	AAA GmbH	school

select distinct I,D from FINISH;

is exactly identical with BUILD. and marginalization of FINISH over I2,D

select distinct I2,D from FINISH;

is exactly identical with EQUIP.

In general:

Theorem 4. *If the information part* **I** *of the decision table DT(***I***,D) can be split into two such parts* **I1**,**I2** *that* $\mathbf{I1} \cup \mathbf{I2} = \mathbf{I}$ *and* $\mathbf{I1} \cap \mathbf{I2} = \emptyset$ *and the relation DT is identical with DT1⊗DT2, implemented*

select **I1**,**I2**,*DT1.D from DT1,DT2 where DT1.D=DT2.D;*

*where DT1 and DT2 are DT1=DT[***I1***,D], DT2=DT[***I2***,D], implemented*

create view DT1 as select distinct **I1**,*D from DT;*
create view DT2 as select distinct **I2**,*D from DT;*

that is there is a multivariate dependency between **I1** *and* **I2** *given D, then* $Bel_{DT} = Bel_{DT^{\downarrow \mathbf{I1},D}} \oplus Bel_{DT^{\downarrow \mathbf{I2},D}}$.

Proof. Follows directly from theorem 3.

Let consider the unnormalized DST measures of decision tables m'_{TAB}, Bel'_{TAB}, Pl'_{TAB}, Q'_{TAB}, such that $f'_{TAB} = f_{TAB} \cdot card(TAB^{\downarrow I})$ (card - number of distinct rows, f - m or Bel or Pl or Q) and the unnormalized combination operator $\oplus'$ such that $Bel'_{E_1,E_2} = Bel'_{E_1} \oplus' Bel'_{E_2}$ is defined as follows: $m'_{E_1,E_2}(A) = \sum_{B,C;A=B\cap C} m'_{E_1}(B) \cdot m'_{E_2}(C)$.

What may be more surprising, a kind of a reverse theorem holds:

Theorem 5. *The information part I of the decision table DT(I,D) can be split into two such parts* **I1**,**I2** *that* **I1** $\cup$ **I2** $= I$ *and* **I1** $\cap$ **I2** $= \emptyset$ *and* $Bel'_{DT} = Bel'_{DT\downarrow I1,D} \oplus' Bel'_{DT\downarrow I2,D}$ *if and only if the relation DT is identical with DT1⊗DT2, implemented*

select **I1**,**I2**,*DT1.D from DT1,DT2 where DT1.D=DT2.D;*

*where DT1 and DT2 are DT1=DT[***I1***,D], DT2=DT[***I2***,D], implemented*

create view DT1 as select distinct **I1**,*D from DT;*
create view DT2 as select distinct **I2**,*D from DT;*

that is there is a multivariate dependency between **I1** *and* **I2** *given D,*

Proof. (An outline.) The if-part parallels exactly theorem 4. We need only pay attention to the fact that we never normalize.
The only-if-part follows from numerical calculations for Q-values of all the tables considered. If a record is counted in DT when calculating $Q'_{DT}(SET)$, then it is also counted when calculating both $Q'_{DT1}(SET)$ and $Q'_{DT2}(SET)$. If we form a join $DT1 \cdot DT2$ then $Q'_{DT1 \cdot DT2}(SET) = Q'_{DT1}(SET) \cdot Q'_{DT2}(SET)$. And this is the maximum value Q' can take in DT12. If there is ANY deviation from multivariate dependency concerning records with decision part in SET, then value of $Q'_{DT12}(SET)$ is smaller than $Q'_{DT1}(SET) \cdot Q'_{DT2}(SET)$. This proves our claim.

Remak: We can conclude that Dempster's rule of combination is equivalent with relational join and the Dempster-Shafer independence of evidence means multivalued dependence of evidence. We can also simulate other rules of combination of evidence. In the above, we assumed that given the decision, we cannot conclude from the information part **I1** the value of the information part **I2** in DT. This meant qualitative independence. Now let us assume the contrary in another decision table DT': given the decision d, we can totally predict **I2** from **I1** for all records r with D(r)=d in DT' or we can totally predict **I1** from **I2** for all records r with D(r)=d in DT'. It is immediately clear that in this case for any set of decisions the unnormalized plausibility is calculated as $Pl'_{DT'}(A) = max(Pl'_{DT'\downarrow I1,D}(A), Pl'_{DT'\downarrow I2,D}(A))$. We can conclude for normalized plausibility that we deal here with thc know rule of combination of dependent evidence: $Pl'_{DT'}(A) = max(\alpha \cdot Pl'_{DT'\downarrow I1,D}(A), (1-\alpha) \cdot Pl'_{DT'\downarrow I2,D}(A))$ where α ranges from 0 to 1 (depending on proportions between the numbers of distinct information parts **I1** and **I2**).

Multivariate Beliefs and Multidecision Tables We can extend our consideration to tables with multiple decision variables. In a straight forward way we can extend our definition of DST measures to such tables and consider multivariate belief distributions (in all the decision variables). It is trivial to see that dropping a decision variables does not diminish the diversity of

Table 5. Multivariate MTE. The table MADEOF and its projection *select distinct I,D from MADEOF*

Decision table MADEOF

	I	D	D2
1.	ABD A.G.	center	wooden
2.	LQR Inc.	school	stone
	LQR Inc.	school	wooden
3.	PTS Ltd.	center	stone
	PTS Ltd.	center	wooden
	PTS Ltd.	restaurant	stone
4.	XYZ Inc.	center	stone
5.	ZZZ Ltd.	restaurant	stone
	ZZZ Ltd.	restaurant	wooden
	ZZZ Ltd.	school	wooden

m({(center,wooden)})=1/5
m({(center,stone)})=1/5

Projected onto I,D:

	I	D
1.	ABD A.G.	center
2.	LQR Inc.	school
3.	PTS Ltd.	center
	PTS Ltd.	restaurant
4.	XYZ Inc.	center
5.	ZZZ Ltd.	restaurant
	ZZZ Ltd.	school

$m^{\downarrow D}$({(center)})=
m({(center,stone)})+
m({(center,wooden)})=2/ 5

Table 6. Variable Independence

D3 - heating

	I2	I3	D	D3
1.	AAA GmbH	EC	school	electric
2.	AAA GmbH	GC	school	gas
3.	BBB Ltd.	EC	center	electric
	BBB Ltd.	EC	restaurant	electric
4.	BBB Ltd.	GC	center	gas
	BBB Ltd.	GC	restaurant	gas
5.	CCC Inc.	EC	center	electric
	CCC Inc.	EC	restaurant	electric
6.	CCC Inc.	GC	center	gas
	CCC Inc.	GC	restaurant	gas

$$Bel = Bel^{\downarrow D} \oplus Bel^{\downarrow D2}$$

because the above table represents a cross product of the tables (without common columns)

	I2	D
1.	AAA GmbH	school
2.	BBB Ltd.	center
	BBB Ltd.	restaurant
3.	CCC Inc.	center
	CCC Inc.	restaurant

and

	I3	D3
1.	EC	electric
2.	GC	gas

Table 7. Conditional Variable Independence

I4 - painting company, D4 - color, D5 - finish,

	I2	I4	D	D5	D4
1.	AAA GmbH	Messer	school	wood	green
	AAA GmbH	Messer	school	wood	red
	AAA GmbH	Messer	school	plastic	green
	AAA GmbH	Messer	school	plastic	red
2.	BBB Ltd.	Messer	center	metallic	white
	BBB Ltd.	Messer	center	metallic	yellow
	BBB Ltd.	Messer	center	marble	white
	BBB Ltd.	Messer	center	marble	yellow
3.	BBB Ltd.	Gabel	restaurant	wood	red
4.	CCC Inc.	Messer	center	metallic	white
	CCC Inc.	Messer	center	metallic	yellow
	CCC Inc.	Messer	center	laminated	white
	CCC Inc.	Messer	center	laminated	yellow
5.	CCC Inc.	Gabel	restaurant	plastic	red

In Bel of the above table variables D4 and D5 are conditionally independent given D in the sense of Shenoy's valuation-based systems because the above table is a relational join of the tables below (with D as a common column)

	I2	D	D5
1.	AAA GmbH	school	wood
	AAA GmbH	school	plastic
2.	BBB Ltd.	center	metallic
	BBB Ltd.	center	marble
	BBB Ltd.	restaurant	wood
3.	CCC Inc.	center	metallic
	CCC Inc.	center	laminated
	CCC Inc.	restaurant	plastic

&

	I4	D	D4
1.	Gabel	restaurant	red
2.	Messer	school	green
	Messer	school	red
	Messer	center	white
	Messer	center	yellow

the information part. Hence dropping a decision variable Di from the set of decision variables **D** has the same effect as dropping a variable in the belief function. That is for any set B of decision vectors in variables **D**-{Di}: $m_{TAB\downarrow\mathbf{D}-\{Di\}}(B) = m_{TAB}^{\downarrow\mathbf{D}-\{Di\}}(B) = c \cdot \sum_{A;B=A^{\downarrow\mathbf{D}-\{Di\}}} m(A)_{TAB}$ (c - normalizing factor) See table 5 for an example.

The operator of projection $\downarrow$ should be understood as the DST projection operator applied to a belief function.

Let DTM be a decision table with decision variables D1 and D2. Let the information part consist of two disjoint parts I1 and I2. Let us consider the following views:

create view DTM1 (I1,D1) as select distinct I1,D1 from DTM;
create view DTM2 (I2,D2) as select distinct I2,D2 from DTM;
create view DTM12 as select distinct I1,I2,D1,D2 from DTM1,DTM2;

If now the table DTM12 is relationally identical with DTM, then we shall say that the decision variables D1 and D2 are independent in the decision table DTM. It is not surprising that: $Bel_{DTM} = Bel_{DTM}^{\downarrow D1} \oplus Bel_{DTM}^{\downarrow D2}$. This means that independence of decision variables in a decision table implies independence of variables in the corresponding belief function. See table 6 for an example.

Let DTX be a decision table with decision variables D1, D2 and D3. Let the information part consist of two disjoint parts I1 and I2. Let us consider the following views:

create view DTX1 (I1,D1,D3) as select distinct I1,D1,D3 from DTX;
create view DTX2 (I2,D2,D3) as select distinct I2,D2,D3 from DTX;
create view DTX12 as select distinct I1,I2,D1,D2,D3 from DTX1,DTX2 where DTX1.D3=DTX2.D3;

If now the table DTX12 is relationally identical with DTX, then we shall say that the decision variables D1 and D2 are independent given D3 in the decision table DTX. It is not surprising that: $Bel_{DTX} = Bel_{DTX}^{\downarrow D1,D3} \oplus Bel_{DTX}^{\downarrow D2,D3}$. But this means that the variables D1 and D2 are independent given D3 in the belief function Bel_{DTX} in the sense of Shenoy's VBS [54]. See table 7 for an example.

These results mean that analysis of independence and conditional independence of variables in a belief function corresponding to a decision table may serve as an indicator of presence or absence of independence or multivalued dependence in the decision table.

3.3 Summary of Qualitative Approach

A novel case-based interpretation of DST belief functions which is qualitative in nature and has the potential to represent a number of DST operations has been presented. The interpretation is based on rough sets (in connection with decision tables), but differs from previous interpretations of this type e.g. [58] in that it counts the diversity rather than frequencies in the decision table. The interpretation has the property that given a definition of the DST measure of objects in the interpretation domain (decision table) we can perform operations in the interpretation domain (e.g. combining decision tables) and the measure of the resulting object is derivable from measures of component objects via DST operator (e.g. combination). We demonstrated this property for Dempster rule of combination, marginalization, Shafer's conditioning, independent variables, Shenoy's notion of conditional independence of variables. Other known case-based (frequency or probabilistic) interpretations fall short of this property. E.g. in [58] complex rational number arithmetic, unnatural for decision tables, is needed to achieve compatibility of the final decision table with Dempster rule of combination. In [34] (probabilistic interpretation) only lower and upper bounds are found for Dempster rule. In [14] (probability structures interpretation) the belief function obtained from the Dempster rule is a potential, but not necessary result of the corresponding probabilistic structure combination operation. See also [59] for discussion of other interpretations.

As probabilistic (frequency based) models of MTE seem to fail in general, we looked for alternatives. The result of any experiment with multiple outcomes can evaluated along two dimensions: the quantitative and the qualitative one. In most real life cases we are more interested in the quantitative aspects. Sometimes, however, the qualitative side may be of more interest. E.g. legal applications we would treat suspiciously similar testimonies as a single argument in favour or against a hypothesis: we would rely on the count of diversity of arguments rather than on their actual counts. And MTE was claimed to be applicable just in legal reasoning [53]. Therefore we considered just the diversity as a possible alternative for a model of MTE and this idea turned out to very fruitful. The diversity is well handled by relational model of databases. Though at a first glance the count of cases in a relational database may appear identical with counting frequencies of objects / events, the difference starts as soon as we make a projection on the subset of attributes. It turns out that projected frequencies differ significantly from the counts of cases in a projected relational database. Therefore we say that our approach is non-frequency, non-quantitative, that is qualitative one.

The new interpretation may be directly applied in the domain of multiple decision decision tables: independence of decision variables or Shenoy's conditional independence in the sense of DST may serve as an indication of possibility of decomposition of the decision table into smaller but equivalent tables. Furthermore it may be applied in the area of Cooperative Query Answering [44]. The problem there is that a query posed to a local relational database system may contain an unknown attribute. But possibly other co-operating db systems know it and may explain it to the queried system in terms of known attributes, shared by the various systems. The uncertainties studied in the decision tables arise here in a natural way and our interpretation may be used to measure these uncertainties in terms of DST (as diversity of support). Furthermore, if several co-operating systems respond, then the queried system may calculate the overall uncertainty measure using DST combination of measures of individual responses.

Now we can ask how to understand then a DST belief function in the light of our experience. One possibility is to consider the belief function as a measure of diversity of support. This is an obvious departure from frequency interpretations proposed by Shafer and others. No mater how frequently the same piece of evidence is presented, it is counted once. This insight may encourage to revise other known interpretations of DST. In the "legal" interpretations e.g. [53], the witnesses in favor of a hypotheses should be counted separately, if their statements differ in unimportant details permitting to deduce that their statements are personal and not studied in. In the "probability of provability" approach [39] not a probability of correctness, but rather the number of distinct valid proofs of a statement should be counted. In the "possible world semantics" [46] the worlds should not be assigned a probability, but rather distinct possible worlds should be counted that differ in non-essential details. Then the operation of combination of independent evidence in the "legal" interpretation is just mixing compatible statements of two sets of witnesses (which saw the same event from different perspective) and counting different possible combinations. In the "probability of provability" approach the combination would mean putting together conclusion compatible proofs stemming from distinct domains (e.g. macro and microphysical observations) and counting legal combinations. In the possible worlds semantics we may combine worlds spanned over disjoined sets of dimensions.

Please notice also that the rough-set interpretation sheds some light onto what the concept of "evidence" may mean. The "evidence" are just different sets of information attributes and the "independence" means (deterministic) unpredictability of attribute values of the one set from the other set. This should not be confused with predictability of the decision variable. Nor with stochastic predictability which may be present. In the "legal" interpretation, independence would be measured with non-predictability of insignificant details. In the "provability" interpretation the independence may be measured by mutual non-derivability of the sets of underlying axioms. In the possible world semantics by possibility of putting together projections onto separated sets of dimension axes.

Further studies on interpreting other known DST operators in the spirit of qualitative interpretation presented in this section are needed and may reveal new potential applications of DST to real world problems.

4 Quantitative Interpretation

4.1 Introduction

The new interpretation of DST runs informally as follows: It is assumed that each object of a population is described by a set-valued attribute (with non-empty set as its value) and a set-valued label (having non-empty intersection with the attribute). Intuitively, the attribute represents objective observations, the label means the part of potential observations which one is ready to accept. Whenever belief (or mass or plausibility function) is calculated from data, it refers to the intersection of the label and the attribute value (and not to attribute value alone). Combination of evidence means a combined selection of a subpopulation and change (reduction) of the label of an object. Thus Dempster rule of combination is understood as data modification.

We introduce the "measurement function" M() (Def.7) which follows the idea of "lazy" observation of value of the object. It asks if any value from a set of values is the potential value of the object. It may be easier (cheaper) in practice to obtain an answer to the question about a set of values ("Are you busy ?") than to interrogate separately for each individual value ("Are you doing your lessons in mathematics?", "Are you washing your hands ?"

etc.) and the answer may be still sufficient for one's purposes (I want someone to go for a walk with me). The way from the M() function to Shafer's frequency interpretation [52] (Γ-function) is straight forward. But many authors [35,18] complained about Shafer's frequency interpretation due to its difficulties with Dempster's rule of combination. Therefore we introduce a generalization of Shafer's concept by adding the notion of "labeling" Def.8 and introduce the modified measurement function $M_l()$ Def.9. Using this notion we define frequency-based m, Bel and Pl functions in Def.10 Please notice that Def.10 relates belief and plausibility functions in a simple way to "lazy measurement". We show that the simple and general labeling processes (Def.11, Def.13) match the behaviour of the Dempster's rule of combination in terms of frequencies within the realm of frequency-based m, Bel and Pl functions under modified measurement of object values (see Theorem 8, Theorem 10).

Let us assume that we know that objects of a population can be described by an intrinsic attribute X taking exclusively one of the n discrete values from its domain $\Xi = \{v_1, v_2, ..., v_n\}$. Let us assume furthermore that to obtain knowledge of the actual value taken by an object we must apply a measurement method (a system of tests) M

Definition 7. X be a set-valued attribute taking as its values non-empty subsets of a finite domain Ξ. By a measurement method of value of the attribute X we understand a function:

$$M : \Omega \times 2^{\Xi} \rightarrow \{TRUE, FALSE\}$$

where Ω is the set of objects, (or population of objects) such that

- $\forall_{\omega;\omega \in \Omega} \quad M(\omega, \Xi) = TRUE$ (X takes at least one of values from Ξ)
- $\forall_{\omega;\omega \in \Omega} \quad M(\omega, \emptyset) = FALSE$
- whenever $M(\omega, A) = TRUE$ for $\omega \in \Omega$, $A \subseteq \Xi$ then for any B such that $A \subset B$ $M(\omega, B) = TRUE$ holds,
- whenever $M(\omega, A) = TRUE$ for $\omega \in \Omega$, $A \subseteq \Xi$ and if $card(A) > 1$ then there exists B, $B \subset A$ such that $M(\omega, B) = TRUE$ holds.
- for every ω and every A either $M(\omega, A) = TRUE$ or $M(\omega, A) = FALSE$ (but never both).

$M(\omega, A)$ tells us whether or not any of the elements of the set A belong to the actual value of the attribute X for the object ω.

The measuring function $M(\omega, A)$, if it takes the value TRUE, states for an object ω and a set A of values from the domain of X that the X takes for this object (at least) one of the values in A.

With each application of the measurement procedure some costs be connected, increasing roughly with the decreasing size of the tested set A so that we are ready to accept results of previous measurements in the form of pre-labeling of the population. So

Definition 8. A *label* L of an object $\omega \in \Omega$ is a subset of the domain Ξ of the attribute X.
A *labeling* under the measurement method M is a function $l : \Omega \rightarrow 2^{\Xi}$ such that for any object $\omega \in \Omega$ either $l(\omega) = \emptyset$ or $M(\omega, l(\omega)) = TRUE$.
Each *labelled object* (under the labeling l) consists of a pair (ω, L_ω), ω - the object, $L_\omega = l(\omega)$ - its label.
By a *population under the labeling* l we understand the predicate $P : \Omega \rightarrow \{TRUE, FALSE\}$ of the form $P(\omega) = TRUE\ iff\ l(\omega) \neq \emptyset$ (or alternatively, the set of objects for which this predicate is true)
If for every object of the population the label is equal to Ξ then we talk of an *unlabeled population* (under the labeling l), otherwise of a *pre-labelled* one.

Let us assume that in practice we apply a modified measurement method M_l being a function:

Definition 9. Let l be a labeling under the measurement method M. Let us consider the population under this labeling. The modified measurement method

$$M_l : \Omega \times 2^{\Xi} \rightarrow \{TRUE, FALSE\}$$

where Ω is the set of objects, is defined as

$$M_l(\omega, A) = M(\omega, A \cap l(\omega))$$

(Notice that $M_l(\omega, A) = FALSE$ whenever $A \cap l(\omega) = \emptyset$.)

For a labeled object (ω, L_ω) (ω - object, L_ω - its label) and a set A of values from the domain of X, the modified measurement method tells us that X takes one of the values in A if and only if it takes in fact a value from intersection of A and L_ω. Expressed differently, we discard a priori any value not in the label.

Please pay attention also to the fact, that given a population P for which the measurement method M is defined, the labeling l (according to its definition) selects a subset of this population, possibly a proper subset, namely the population P' under this labeling. $P'(\omega) = P(\omega) \wedge M(\omega, l(\omega))$. Hence also M_l is defined possibly for the "smaller" population P' than M is.

Let us define the following functions referred to as labelled Belief, labelled Plausibility and labelled Mass Functions respectively for the labeled population P: The predicate $\underset{\omega}{\mathfrak{Prob}}^{P(\omega)} \alpha(\omega)$ shall denote the probability of truth of expression $\alpha(\omega)$ over ω given population $P(\omega)$.

Definition 10. Let P be a population and l its labeling. Then

$$Bel_P^{M_l}(A) = \underset{\omega}{\mathfrak{Prob}}^{P(\omega)} \neg M_l(\omega, \Xi - A)$$

$$Pl_P^{M_l}(A) = \underset{\omega}{\mathfrak{Prob}}^{P(\omega)} M_l(\omega, A)$$

$$m_P^{M_l}(A) = \underset{\omega}{\mathfrak{Prob}}^{P(\omega)}\left(\bigwedge_{v;v\in A} M_l(\omega,\{v\}) \wedge \bigwedge_{v;v\in\Xi-A} \neg M_l(\omega,\{v\})\right)$$

$$Q_P^{M_l}(A) = \underset{\omega}{\mathfrak{Prob}}^{P(\omega)}\left(\bigwedge_{v;v\in A} M_l(\omega,\{v\})\right)$$

Theorem 6. *$m_P^{M_l}$, $Bel_P^{M_l}$, $Pl_P^{M_l}$ and $Q_P^{M_l}$ are the mass, belief, plausibility and commonality Functions in the sense of DST.*

Proofs of all the theorems are given in [32] Let us now assume we run a "(re-)labelling process" on the (pre-labelled or unlabeled) population P.

Definition 11. Let M be a measurement method, l be a labeling under this measurement method, and P be a population under this labeling. The *(simple) labelling process* on the population P is defined as a functional $LP : 2^{\Xi} \times \Lambda \to \Lambda$, where Λ is the set of all possible labelings under M, such that for the given labeling l and a given nonempty set of attribute values L ($L \subseteq \Xi$), it delivers a new labeling l' ($l' = LP(L,l)$) such that for every object $\omega \in \Omega$:

1. if $M_l(\omega, L) = FALSE$ then $l'(\omega) = \emptyset$
(that is l' discards a labeled object $(\omega, l(\omega))$ if $M_l(\omega, L) = FALSE$
2. otherwise $l'(\omega) = l(\omega) \cap L$ (that is l' labels the object with $l(\omega) \cap L$ otherwise.

Remark: It is immediately obvious, that the population obtained as the sample fulfills the requirements of the definition of a labeled population.

The labeling process clearly induces from P another population P' (a population under the labeling l') being a subset of P (hence perhaps "smaller" than P) labelled a bit differently. If we retain the primary measurement method M then a new modified measurement method $M_{l'}$ is induced by the new labeling.

Definition 12. "labelling process function" $m^{LP;L} : 2^{\Xi} \to [0,1]$: is defined as:

$$m^{LP;L}(L) = 1$$

$$\forall_{B;B\in 2^{\Xi},B\neq L}\, m^{LP;L}(B) = 0$$

It is immediately obvious that:

Theorem 7. *$m^{LP;L}$ is a Mass Function in sense of DST.*

Let $Bel^{LP,L}$ be the belief and $Pl^{LP,L}$ be the Plausibility corresponding to $m^{LP,L}$. Now let us pose the question: what is the relationship between $Bel_{P'}^{M_{l'}}$, $Bel_P^{M_l}$, and $Bel^{LP,L}$.

Theorem 8. *Let M be a measurement function, l a labeling, P a population under this labeling. Let L be a subset of Ξ. Let LP be a labeling process and let $l' = LP(L,l)$. Let P' be a population under the labeling l'. Then $Bel_{P'}^{M_{l'}}$ is a combination via Dempster's Combination rule of Bel^{M_l}, and $Bel^{LP;L}$., that is:*

$$Bel_{P'}^{M_{l'}} = Bel_{P}^{M_l} \oplus Bel^{LP;L}$$

Let us define a more general (re-)labeling process. Instead of a single set of attribute values let us take a set of sets of attribute values $L^1, L^2, ..., L^k$ (not necessarily disjoint) and assign to each one a probability $m^{LP,L^1,L^2,...,L^k}(A_i)$ of selection.

Definition 13. Let M be a measurement method, l be a labeling under this measurement method, and P be a population under this labeling (Note that the population may also be unlabeled). Let us take a set of (not necessarily disjoint) nonempty sets of attribute values $\{L^1, L^2, ..., L^k\}$ and let us define the probability of selection as a function $m^{LP,L^1,L^2,...,L^k} : 2^{\Xi} \to [0,1]$ such that

$$\sum_{A;A\subseteq\Xi} m^{LP,L^1,L^2,...,L^k}(A) = 1$$

$$\forall_{A;A\in\{L^1,L^2,...,L^k\}} m^{LP,L^1,L^2,...,L^k}(A) > 0$$

$$\forall_{A;A\notin\{L^1,L^2,...,L^k\}} m^{LP,L^1,L^2,...,L^k}(A) = 0$$

The *(general) labelling process* on the population P is defined as a (randomized) functional $LP : 2^{2^{\Xi}} \times \Phi \times \Lambda \to \Lambda$, where Λ is the set of all possible labelings under M, and Φ is a set of all possible probability of selection functions, such that for the given labeling l and a given set of (not necessarily disjoint) nonempty sets of attribute values $\{L^1, L^2, ..., L^k\}$ and a given probability of selection $m^{LP,L^1,L^2,...,L^k}$ it delivers a new labeling l" such that for every object $\omega \in \Omega$:

1. a label L, element of the set $\{L^1, L^2, ..., L^k\}$ is sampled randomly according to the probability distribution $m^{LP,L^1,L^2,...,L^k}$; This sampling is done independently for each individual object,

2. if $M_l(\omega, L) = FALSE$ then $l"(\omega) = \emptyset$
(that is l" discards an object $(\omega, l(\omega))$ if $M_l(\omega, L) = FALSE$

3. otherwise $l"(\omega) = l(\omega) \cap L$ (that is l" labels the object with $l(\omega) \cap L$ otherwise.)

Again we obtain another ("smaller") population P" under the labeling l" labelled differently. Also a new modified measurement method $M_{l"}$ is induced by the "re-labelled" population. Please notice, that l" is not derived deterministicly. Another run of the general (re-)labeling process LP may result in a different final labeling of the population and hence a different subpopulation under this new labeling.

Theorem 9. *$m^{LP,L^1,...,L^k}$ is a Mass Function in sense of DST.*

Let $Bel^{LP;L^1,...,L^k}$ be the belief and $Pl^{LP,L^1,...,L^k}$ be the Plausibility corresponding to $m^{LP,L^1,...,L^k}$. Now let us pose the question: what is the relationship between $Bel_{P''}^{M_{l''}}$, $Bel_P^{M_l}$, and $Bel^{LP,L^1,...,L^k}$.

Theorem 10. *Let M be a measurement function, l a labeling, P a population under this labeling. Let LP be a generalized labeling process and let l" be the result of application of the LP for the set of labels from the set $\{L^1, L^2, ..., L^k\}$ sampled randomly according to the probability distribution $m^{LP,L^1,L^2,...,L^k}$;. Let P" be a population under the labeling l". Then the expected value over the set of all possible resultant labelings l" (and hence populations P") (or, more precisely, value vector) of $Bel_{P''}^{M_{l''}}$ is a combination via Dempster's Combination rule of $Bel_P^{M_l}$, and $Bel^{LP,L^1,...,L^k}$., that is:*

$$E(Bel_{P''}^{M_l'}) = Bel_P^{M_l} \oplus Bel^{LP,L^1,...,L^k}$$

4.2 Independence and Shades of Conditionality

Let us turn now to multivariable setting of DST. As we defined combination rule of belief function in terms of frequencies, we may be tempted to define independence of belief functions (and conditional independence) following the remark of Shafer [51] that independence in DST shall be "understood traditionally". However, several peculiarities emerge. First, from probability theory, we associate independence of two variables X,Y both with unability to predict X,Y from one another and to represent joint distribution as a combination of marginal distributions. However, if, in DST, we parallel the first concept (mutual non-predictability) as in Def.14, we do not necessarily arrive at the second one (joint distribution from marginals) - see Theorem 11,Theorem 12. Hence, we need a stronger concept of independence, rooted in composite measurement of variables Def.15, which can lead then to decomposability of joint belief distribution see Theorem 13. A similar complexity emerges if we want to parallel the concept of a constant variable from probability. Given definition of independence of a distribution from a variable X from Def.16, we see from Theorem 15 and the subsequent ones that only the assumption of composite measurement of variables justifies dropping such a variable X from consideration.

If one turns to conditional independence, one has again to do with splitting of familiar probabilistic concepts: In probability, for the joint probability distribution $P(X, Y)$, distributions $f(X; Y)$ of X given a value of variable Y mean exactly the same as a function $g(X, Y)$ such that $P(X, Y) = g(X, Y) \cdot P(Y)$ that is $f(X, ; Y) = g(X, Y) = P(X|Y)$. But in DST, Shafer's conditional belief function $Bel(||Y) = Bel \oplus Bel_Y$ does not have the property that $Bel = Bel(||Y) \oplus Bel^{\downarrow X}$, so that two different concepts of conditionality emerge: the Shafer's conditional belief as defined in Def.6 and the anti-conditional belief function as defined in Def.18, introduced in this paper. If X,Y anre independent given Z then $P(X|Z,Y) = P(X|Z)$. This does hold for DST only existentially as described in Theorem 17 and Theorem 18. Shafer's conditional belief is the result of reasoning process - it appears "a posteriori"; whereas anticonditional belief function serves the purpose of decomposition (factorization) of a joint belief distribution - it is used "a priori".

Let us introduce the notion of quantitative independence for DS-Theory. We will fix the measurement method M we use and the population P we consider so that respective indices will be usually dropped.

Definition 14. Two disjoint sets of variables p, q are (mutually, marginally) independent when for objects of the population knowledge of the truth value of $M_l^{\downarrow p}(\omega, A^{\downarrow p})$ for all $A \subseteq \Xi_p \times \Xi_q$ does not change our prediction capability of the values of $M_l^{\downarrow q}(\omega, B^{\downarrow q})$ for any $B \subseteq \Xi_p \times \Xi_q$, that is

$$\underset{\omega}{\mathfrak{Prob}}^{P(\omega)}(M_l^{\downarrow q}(\omega, B^{\downarrow q}) = \underset{\omega}{\mathfrak{Prob}}^{P(\omega)}(M_l^{\downarrow q}(\omega, B^{\downarrow q})|M_l^{\downarrow p}(\omega, A^{\downarrow p}))$$

Theorem 11. *If sets of variables p, q are quantitatively independent, then for any $C \subseteq \Xi_q$, $A \subseteq \Xi_p$*

$$m^{\downarrow q}(C) \cdot m^{\downarrow p}(A) = \sum_{F;F^{\downarrow p}=A,F^{\downarrow q}=C} m(F)$$

Theorem 12. *If sets of variables p, q are quantitatively independent, then for any $C \subseteq \Xi_q$, $A \subseteq \Xi_p$*

$$Bel^{\downarrow q}(C) \cdot Bel^{\downarrow p}(A) = Bel(A \times C)$$

This actually expresses the relationship between marginals of two independent variables and their joint belief distribution. This relationship has one dismaying aspect: in general, we cannot calculate the joint distribution from independent marginals (contrary to our intuition connected with joint probability distribution).

In practical settings, however, we frequently have to do with some kind of composite measurement method, that is:

Definition 15. Two disjoint sets of variables p, q are measured compositely iff for $A \subseteq \Xi_p, C \subseteq \Xi_q$:

$$M(\omega, A \times C) = M(\omega, A \times \Xi_q) \wedge M(\omega, \Xi_p \times C)$$

and for $M(\omega, B)$, $B \subseteq \Xi_p \times \Xi_q$:

$$M(\omega, B) = \bigvee_{A,C;A\subseteq\Xi_p,C\subseteq\Xi_q,A\times C\subseteq B} M(\omega, A \times C)$$

Under these circumstances, it is easily shown that whenever $m(B) > 0$, then there exist A and C such that: $B = A \times C$.

So we obtain:

Theorem 13. *If sets of variables p, q are quantitatively independent and measured compositely, then*

$$m(A \times C) = m^{\downarrow p}(A) \cdot m^{\downarrow q}(C)$$

Hence the Belief function can be calculated from Belief functions of independent variables under composite measurement.:

Theorem 14. *If sets of variables p, q are quantitatively independent and measured compositely, then*

$$Bel = Bel^{\downarrow p} \oplus Bel^{\downarrow q}$$

Let us justify now the notion of empty extension:

Definition 16. The joint distribution over set of variables $X = p \cup q$ with sets p, q disjoint is independent of the variable set p when for objects of the population for every A,$A \subseteq \Xi_p \times \Xi_q$ knowledge of the truth value of $M_l^{\downarrow p}(\omega, A^{\downarrow p})$ does not change our prediction capability of the values of $M_l(\omega, A)$, that is

$$\underset{\omega}{\mathfrak{Prob}}^{P(\omega)}(M_l(\omega, A)) = \underset{\omega}{\mathfrak{Prob}}^{P(\omega)}(M_l(\omega, A)|M_l^{\downarrow p}(\omega, A^{\downarrow p}))$$

Theorem 15. *The joint distribution over $X = p \cup q$ with disjoint sets of variables p, q, measured compositely, is independent of the variable set p only if $m^{\downarrow q}(\Xi_q) = 1$ that is the whole mass of the distribution marginalized onto q is concentrated at the only focal point Ξ_q.*

Theorem 16. *If for $X = p \cup q$, p, q disjoint, $Bel = (Bel^{\downarrow p})^{\uparrow X}$ that is Bel is the vacuous extension of some Bel defined only over q, then the Bel is independent of the variable set q.*
If for a Bel over $X = p \cup q$ with disjoint sets p, q measured compositely Bel is independent of q, then $Bel = (Bel^{\downarrow p})^{\uparrow X}$.

Definition 17. Let Bel be defined over $X = p \cup q$, p, q disjoint. We shall speak that Bel is *compressibly independent* of q iff $Bel = (Bel^{\downarrow p})^{\uparrow X}$.

REMARK: $m^{\downarrow q}(\Xi_q) = 1$ does not imply empty extension as such, especially for non-singleton values of the variable p. As previously with marginal independence, it is the composite measurement that makes the empty extension a practical notion.

Let us introduce a concept of conditionality related to the above definition of independence. Traditionally, conditionality is introduced to obtain a kind of independence between variables de facto on one another. So let us define that:

Definition 18. For belief function *Bel* defined for discourse space over set of variables X let $s \subseteq X$. We define (anti-)conditional belief function $Bel^{|s}(A)$ as

$$Bel = Bel^{\downarrow s} \oplus Bel^{|s}$$

Let us notice at this point that the (anti-)conditional belief as defined above does not need to be unique, hence we have here a kind of pseudoinversion of the $\oplus$ operator. Furthermore, the conditional belief does not need to be a belief function at all, because some focal points m may be negative. But it is then the pseudo-belief function in the sense of the DS-theory, that is m,Bel,Pl take values from the interval [-1,1], and only the Q-measure remains non-negative. Please recall the fact that if $Bel_{12} = Bel_1 \oplus Bel_2$ then $Q_{12}(A) = c \cdot Q_1(A) \cdot Q_2(A)$, c being a proportionality factor (as all supersets of a set are contained in all intersections of its supersets and vice versa). Hence also for our conditional belief definition:

$$Q(A) = c \cdot (Q^{\downarrow s})^{\uparrow X}(A) \cdot Q^{X|s}(A)$$

We shall talk later of unnormalized conditional belief iff

$$Q_*^{|s}(A) = Q(A)/(Q^{\downarrow s})^{\uparrow X}(A)$$

Let us now reconsider the problem of independence, this time of a conditional distribution of $(p \cup q \cup r | p \cup r)$ from the third variable set r.

Theorem 17. *Let $X = p \cup q \cup r$, p, q, r pairwise disjoint, and let Bel be defined over X. Furthermore let $Bel^{|p\cup r}$ be a conditional Belief conditioned on variables p, r. Let this conditional distribution be compressibly independent of r. Let $Bel^{\downarrow p\cup q}$ be the projection of Bel onto the subspace spanned by p, q. Then there exists $Bel^{\downarrow p\cup q|p}$ being a conditional belief of that projected belief conditioned on the variable set p such that this $Bel^{|p\cup r}$ is the empty extension of $Bel^{\downarrow p\cup q|p}$*

$$Bel^{|p\cup r} = ((Bel^{\downarrow p\cup q})^{|p})^{\uparrow X}$$

Let us notice that under the conditions of the above theorem

$$Bel = Bel^{|p\cup r} \oplus Bel^{\downarrow p\cup r} = Bel^{\downarrow p\cup q|p} \oplus Bel^{\downarrow p\cup r}$$

and hence for any $Bel^{\downarrow p\cup r|p}$

$$Bel = Bel^{\downarrow p\cup q|p} \oplus Bel^{\downarrow p} \oplus Bel^{\downarrow p\cup r|p}$$

and therefore

$$Bel = Bel^{\downarrow p\cup q} \oplus Bel^{\downarrow p\cup r|p}$$

This means that whenever the conditional $Bel^{|p\cup r}$ is compressibly independent of r, then there exists a conditional $Bel^{|p\cup q}$ compressibly independent of q. But this fact combined with the previous theorem results in:

Theorem 18. *Let $X = p \cup q \cup r$, p, q, r pairwise disjoint, and let Bel be defined over X. Furthermore let $Bel^{|p \cup r}$ be a conditional Belief conditioned on variables p, r. Let this conditional distribution be compressibly independent of r. Then the empty extension onto X of any $Bel^{\downarrow p \cup q|p}$ being a conditional belief of projected belief conditioned on the variable p is a conditional belief function of X conditioned on variables p, r. Hence for every $A \subseteq \Xi$*

$$\frac{Q(A)}{Q^{\downarrow p \cup r}(A^{\downarrow p \cup r})} = \frac{Q^{\downarrow p \cup q}(A^{\downarrow p \cup q})}{Q^{\downarrow p}(A^{\downarrow p})}$$

In this way we obtained some sense of conditionality suitable for decomposition of a joint belief distribution.

4.3 Belief from Data

In this section we will show how the ideas of previous section will influence practical implementation of frequency-based belief functions in a relational database. We assume that attributes in the database may be set-valued and that set-theoretic operators are implemented for attributes (including ordering of sets).
First let us assume that we have a convenient situation that for each object $\omega \in \Omega$ and each value $\xi \in \Xi$ we have calculated $M(\omega, \xi)$ and, in the database Cases, the database attribute X stores for each object ω the set of those values ξ for which $M(\omega, \xi) = TRUE$ holds. Let us assume that we have also the database attribute *Lab* initially containing Ξ for each object.

Then let us construct a view bpa (in SQL[64]) reflecting the mass function for the population:

create view ModifiedCases (XMod) as select $X \cap Lab$ *from Cases where* $X \cap Lab \neq \emptyset$;
create view Total (Counted) as select count(*) from ModifiedCases;
create view bpa (X,m) as select XMod,count(*)/Counted from ModifiedCases, Total group by XMod;

(m in view bpa is our mass function assigned to the set X of the view bpa)
Now let us look what happens when we "condition" our databases Cases on the event that X stems from ACertainSet. We have to update our database Cases as follows:

update Cases set $Lab = Lab \cap ACertainSet$;

After this operation the view bpa defined above provides us with the resulting mass function $m' = m(||ACertainSet) = m \oplus m_{ACertainSet}$. Later on we may have a further "conditioning" of our databases Cases on the event that X stems from ACertainSet2. Then

update Cases set $Lab = Lab \cap ACertainSet2$;

After [illegible] ew bpa defined above provides us with the resulting mass function $m'' = m'(||ACertainSet2) = m(||ACertainSet, ACertainSet2) = m' \oplus m_{ACertainSet2}$. Calculations in case of general labeling process are more complicated and hard to express in interactive SQL (embedded SQL has to be used). We shall draw attention of the Reader to the fact that in cases of conditioning the group by phrase of an SQL query does not refer to the original value of X, but to its modification by the label Lab, which is updated.

Let us see how laziness of measurement method may be exploited for case-based calculation of belief function.
Let us assume that we have, in the database Cases, the database attribute id being object identity in the external world and a set-valued attribute *Lab* initially containing Ξ for each object and that we have a built-in function M such that for each object ω and each set $A \subseteq \Xi$ it provides us with the measurement value (by accessing e.g. the object by a robot handle) $M(\omega, A) =$ TRUE or FALSE. We have seen previously that the function Bel can be calculated by lazy measurement. For a concrete set A we can calculate Bel(A), after defining the view

create view Total (Counted) as select count(*) from Cases where $Lab \neq \emptyset$;

by issuing the query:

select count(*)/Counted from Cases,Total where (if $A \cap Lab \neq \emptyset$ *then* $\neg M(id, (\Xi - A) \cap Lab)$ *else false)* ;

If we want now to condition the Cases by the value set ACertainSet, then we have to update the label by

update Cases set Lab=if $M(id, Lab \cap ACertainSet)$ *then* $Lab \cap ACertainSet)$ *else* $\emptyset$;

Then the query above yields for a given set A $Bel'(A)$ with $Bel' = Bel(||ACertainSet)$.
Clearly, this "lazy" procedure with dynamic testing of M() is worth using only if there is really a dramatic difference in costs of applying M to sets of decreasing sizes.

4.4 Independence from Data

The preceding sections defined precisely what is meant by marginal independence of two variables in terms of the relationship between marginals and the joint distribution, as well as concerning the independence of a joint distribution from a single variable.

For the former case we can establish frequency tables with rows and columns corresponding to cardinalities of focal points of the first and the second marginal, and inner elements being cardinalities from the respective sum on DS-masses of the joint distribution. Clearly, cases falling into different inner categories of the table are different and hence χ^2 test is applicable. The match can be χ^2-tested. The following formula should be followed for calculation

$$\sum_{\substack{A;\\ A\subseteq \Xi_p,\\ m^{\downarrow p}(A)>0}} \sum_{\substack{B;\\ B\subseteq \Xi_q,\\ m^{\downarrow q}(B)>0}} \frac{\left(\left(\sum_{C;C\subseteq\Xi,A=C^{\downarrow p}B=C^{\downarrow q}} m(C)\right) - m^{\downarrow p}(A)\cdot m^{\downarrow q}(B)\right)^2}{m^{\downarrow p}(A)\cdot m^{\downarrow q}(B)}$$

The number of df is calculated as

$$(card(\{A; A\subseteq \Xi_p, m^{\downarrow p}(A)>0\})-1)\cdot(card(\{B; B\subseteq \Xi_q, m^{\downarrow q}(B)>0\})-1)$$

In case of independence of a distribution from one variable (set) one needs to calculate the marginal of the distribution of that variable (set), say s. Then the measure of discrepancy from the assumption of independence is given as:

$$1-m^{\downarrow s}(\Xi_s)$$

Statistically we can test, based on Bernoullie distribution, what is the lowest possible and the highest possible value of $1-m^{\downarrow s}(\Xi_s)$ for a given significance level of the true underlying distribution.

4.5 Conditional Independence from Data

In case of independence between the conditional distribution and one of conditioning variables, however, it is useless to calculate the pseudoinversion of $\oplus$, as we are working then with a population and a sample the size of which is not properly defined (by the "anti-labeling"). But we can build the contingency table of the unconditional joint distribution for the independent variable on the one hand and the remaining variables on the other hand, and compare the respective cells on how they match the distribution we would obtain assuming the independence. The number of degrees of freedom for the χ^2 test would then be the number of focal points of the joint distribution, minus the number of focal points within each of the multi-variable marginals plus one (for covering twice the total sum of 1 on all focal points).

If we test conditional independence of variables X and Y on the set of variables Z, then we have to compare empirical distribution $Bel^{\downarrow X,Y,Z}$ with $Bel^{\downarrow X,Z|Z} \oplus Bel^{\downarrow Y,Z|Z} \oplus Bel^{\downarrow Z}$. The traditional χ^2 statistics is computed (treating the latter distribution as expected one). If the hypothesis of equality is rejected on significance level $\alpha = 0.05$ then X and Y are considered dependent, otherwise independent.

4.6 Summary of Quantitative Approach

This section provides a frequency interpretation of MTE that covers simultaneously static and dynamic aspects of MTE. It is hoped that, though MTE may in fact be suitable for entirely different modes of uncertainty, the study of this interpretation will shed some light onto the nature of Dempster rule of combination of evidence.

The interpretation introduced here does not differ too much in defining the belief function in terms of frequency (or probability) from various other probabilistic approaches proposed in the past [51,58,18,14,34,35]. To pinpoint the essential new quality let us first remind the opinion expressed by Smets on probabilistic approaches proposed in the past. Smets states that "Far too often, authors concentrate on the static component (how beliefs are allocated?) and discover many relations between TBM (transferable belief model of Smets) and ULP (upper lower probability) models, inner and outer measures (Fagin and Halpern [14]), random sets (Nguyen [37]), probabilities of provability (Pearl [39]), probabilities of necessity (Ruspini [46]) etc. But these authors usually do not explain or justify the dynamic component (how are beliefs updated?), that is, how updating (conditioning) is to be handled (except in some cases by defining conditioning as a special case of combination). So I (that is Smets) feel that these partial comparisons are incomplete, especially as all these interpretations lead to different updating rules." [59][pp. 324-325]. We make here a break-through. The dynamic component of DST (Dempster rule) fits our frequency framework. And this is achieved by a simple trick: the label attached to the object. This label is modified by the re-labeling process, it prevents from reading the intrinsic value of the set-valued attribute when calculating the belief function. Thus it reveals two major aspects of DST which were apparently ignored in the past: (1) Dempster rule both selects and modifies objects of a population - differing just from proper probabilistic conditioning which only selects objects, (2) and belief function does not describe the reality as such (is not objective) but rather intermixes the description of real world with personal prejudices (vicious "labels" we attach to our surroundings) - just being a mixture of objective and subjective view of the world.

The new interpretation of DST has also consequences for multivariable considerations of DST. It has been demonstrated that there exists a much richer spectrum of shades of independence in DST than in probability calculus. Especially, non-predictability of one variable from marginal value of the other and vice versa does not imply that their joint distribution may be calculated from their marginals, unless they are compositely measured. This is due to the subtle structure of the space of discourse in DST. Furthermore, there is a split of concepts of conditionality, and hence complexities in conditional independence, compared to probability calculus, as Shafer's conditional belief function $Bel(||Y) = Bel \oplus Bel_Y$ does not have the property that $Bel = Bel(||Y) \oplus Bel^{\downarrow X}$. Hence two different concepts of conditionality emerge: the Shafer's conditional belief as defined in Def.6 and the anti-conditional belief function as defined in Def.18, introduced in this paper. Shafer's conditional belief is the result of reasoning process; whereas anticonditional belief function serves the purpose of decomposition (factorization) of a joint belief distribution. It turns out, however, that there exist a multitude of anticonditional belief functions for a given belief distribution, and even in cases, where variable X appears not to be influenced by a variable Y given a third variable Z, there may exist an anticonditional belief distribution of X given Y,Z such that X is influenced by Y. However important existential properties of anticonditional belief functions could be demonstrated in Theorem 17 and Theorem 18, relating anti-conditional belief distributions in all variables X,Y,Z and of a subset of variables X,Z after ignoring non-influential variable Y. These properties may serve as a foundation for decomposition of joint belief distribution into factors consisting of anti-conditional belief functions.These considerations extend radically the class of belief functions for which such decompositions can be considered, because previously Shenoy in [54] dealt only with so-called positive normal belief functions, which had unique anticonditional beliefs.

The existence of frequency interpretation and of statistical independence tests enables to acquire structural knowledge on Dempster-Shafer belief distribution from data. Several algorithms have been elaborated so far allowing to learn from data tree-structured, polytree-structured and network-structured decomposition of belief functions [?,24,25,28,29,31].

Also algorithms for the reverse process (sample generation from structured belief functions) have been elaborated for this quantitative model of belief functions [?,28,29,33]

5 Discussion and Concluding Remarks

The 32 years since the first publication of Dempster that initiated the Dempster-Shafer Theory of Evidence were scene of fierce discussion of the intrinsic meaning and significance of this new formalism of representation of uncertain knowledge. At least four distinct lines of development may be distinguished: (1) imprecise probabilities (with intuition saying that belief and plausibility were the lower and upper bound on some set of probabilities), (2) uncertainty about possible worlds (with intuition that basic probability assignment function assigning probabilities to completely deterministic possible states of the world) (3) uncertainty about propositional knowledge possessed by agents (beliefs being probabilities of provability), (4) uncertainty about proper decisions under incomplete knowledge of causal variables in decision tables (with plausibility being the relative count of cases supporting a set of decision).

All of these directions of development indicated some sets of expectations and intuitions about the applicability of the DST, but also were accompanied by fierce criticism, counter examples and misunderstandings. Some of them we have outlined in section 1.

But here we want to concentrate on the lesson we have learnt from this turbulent development. Nearly all of the approaches made the following crucial assumption: there is only one intrinsic state of the world, or one intrinsic probability distribution that one wants to approximate from incomplete and/or uncertain observations or enlightened insights. We think that this assumption may always lead to successful counter examples as can be seen from careful inspection of literature.

In order to be able to apply DST consistently, we insist that for the set A Bel(A) does not represent agent's belief that any element of A holds (without knowing which one), but rather that m(A) reflects the belief that exactly all elements of A hold or, alternatively, that one is unable to get the insight which of elements of A hold. What does it mean for a business in practical terms ? Let us assume we need to employ somebody with M.Sc. either in mathematics (e1), or computer science (e2), or physics (e3). "Normally", events cane1, e2 and e3 may be considered exclusive (so may be a basis for creation of a probability distribution to describe the possible stream of candidates).However, in some cases there are people having a degree e.g. both in mathematics and physics (hence we have to correct ourselves to generate a DST belief distribution over {e1,e2,e3} to describe the possible stream of candidates).

Furthermore this assumption is crucial in that it requires the revision of the intuition behind "belief revision" or the Dempster's conditioning rule. Usually the rhetorics of "independent" opinion (that the value domain is in fact restricted to some set) is used to justify the way of working of Dempster rule. This rhetorics may be justified if the "opinion" is logical in nature that is represented with a belief function with the whole mass concentrated on a single set. As soon as this is not the case, the counter examples can be transferred to nearly any interpretation of DST suggested so far, because any attempt of reasoning (belief revision) will materialize in assumption of underlying cases having values different for the intrinsic ones.

Our interpretations escape this pitfall. The application of the Dempster rule can be seen as follows: Assume two departments in our firm seek for new employees: one with M.Sc. in physics or computer science, the other in computer science or mathematics. The ingoing stream of candidates applying for a position in the firm is randomly served either by an officer of the one or the other department. In the distributed firmdatabase those that didn't fit the needs of the department of the actual serving officer are discarded, while those fitting are classified as having M.Sc. in physics, or computer science or both, in case of the first department, and in case of the second: as either having M.Sc. in computer science or mathematics or both. This database will of course reflect only the beliefs of the firm and not the real state of the world, because not only not all candidates having degrees both in mathematics and computer science will be registered as such (depending on the department, they will be register as either ones with M.Sc. in computer science or ones with M.Sc. both in mathematics and computer science), but also qualifications like M.Sc. both in mathematics and physics will be completely ignored, not to say about e.g. both M.Sc. in mathematics and history. But on the other hand notice that all candidates counted as support for m(comp.sci., mathem) will actually have both M.Sc. in mathematics and computer science.

Equipped with these basic assumptions we were capable to escape the most frequent point of attack on the Dempster-Shafer Theory of evidence - the claim of missing empirical interpretation.

In the chapter we have explained three different proposals of empirical models, meeting different expectations posed on DST:

- "the marginally correct approximation".
- "the qualitative model"
- "the quantitative model"

The marginally correct approximation assumes that the belief function shall constitute lower bounds for frequencies, however only for the marginals, and not for the joint distribution. Then the reasoning process is expressed in terms of so-called Cano et al. conditionals - a special class of conditional belief functions that are positive. This approach implies modification of reasoning mechanism, because the correctness is maintained only by reasoning forward. Depending on the reasoning direction we need different "Markov trees" for the reasoning engine.

Note that lower/upper bound interpretations have a long tradition for DST [9,34] and has been heavily criticezed [18]. The one that we presented here differs from the known ones significantly as we insist on different reasoning schemes (hypertrees) depending on which are our target variables values of which are to be inferred. This assures overcoming basic difficulties with lower/upper bound interpretations. In this way also we were able to outline an area where the intuition of lower/upper approximation is applicable.

The qualitative approach is based on earlier rough set interpretations of DST, but makes a small and still significant distinction. All computations are carried out in strictly "relational" way that is indistinguishable objects in a database are merged (no object identities). The behavior under reasoning fits strictly to DST reasoning model. Factors of hypergraph representation can be expressed by relational tables. Conditional independence is well defined. However, there is no interpretation for conditional belief functions in this model.

Rough set interpretations [58] were primarily interested in interpreting the belief function in terms of decision tables. However, the Dempster-rule of evidence combination was valid there only for "extended decision tables", not easily derived from original ones. In our interpretation, both the original tables and the resultant tables dealt with when simulating Dempster-rule are conventional decision tables and the process of decision table merging in a natural one (relational join operator).

With our interpretation we show what kind of "possible worlds semantics" may be used consistently with DST: the basic hint when measuring uncertainty is to think in terms of "diversity" (number of different worlds) and not in terms of "frequency" (number of worlds).

The quantitative model assumes that during the reasoning process one attachs labels to objects hiding some of their properties. There is a full agreement with the reasoning mechanism of DST. Conditional independence and conditional belief functions are well defined. We have also elaborated processes that can give rise to well-controlled graphoidally structured belief functions. We elaborated also learning procedures for discovery of graphoidal structures from data.

The quantitative model seems to be the best fitting model for belief functions created so far.

This frequency model differs from what was previously considered [59–61] in that it assumes that reasoning in DST is connected with updating of variables for individual cases. This is different from e.g. reasoning in probability where reasoning means only selection of cases. And just in this way failures of previous approaches could be overcome. A new flavor of the word "belief" comes with this interpretation: we maintain in our section of database only data that we believe are important for a particular local application (like in the above case of two departments looking for job candidates) without bothering of sufficiency of the data for the whole database.

Many authors [53,59] question the need for an empirical model for DST and point rather to theoretical properties of DST considered within an axiomatic framework seeking parallels with the probability theory. Though it is true that the probability theory may be reasoned with within the framework of Kolmogorov axioms and quite useful results derived in this way, one shall still point out that the applicability of probability theory is significanlty connected with frequencies. Both frequencies considered as "naive probabilities", ore ones being probabilities "in the limit". Statistics is clearly an important part of the probabilistic world.

We suspect that a similar relation exists between the axiomatic framework of DST and empirical models for DST. We have just shown that at least three empirical types models with properties postulated in section 1 exist. They may constitute some hints for future search for more application areas of DST. And, as the general human experience demonstrates, practical applications would inevitably lead to further theoretical progress.

References

1. A. Acid , L.M. deCampos, A. Gonzales, R. Molina, N. Perez de la Blanca: Learning with CASTLE. In:Kruse R., Siegel P., eds, *Symbolic and Quantitative*

Approaches to Uncertainty. Lecture Notes In Computer Science 548, Springer-Verlag (1991), 99-106
2. A. Bendjebbour, W. Pieczynski: *Traitement du Signal*, Vol. 14, No.5, 1997, pp. 453-464.
3. C. Beeri, R. Fagin, D. Maier, Y. Yannakakis: On the desirability of acyclic database schemes, *J. Assoc. Comput. Mach.*, vol. 30, no 3, 1983, 479-513.
4. Cano J., Delgado M., Moral S.: An axiomatic framework for propagating uncertainty in directed acyclic networks, *Int. J. of Approximate Reasoning.* 1993:8, 253-280.
5. C.K. Chow, C.N. Liu: Approximating discrete probability distributions with dependence trees. *IEEE Transactions on Information Theory* **IT-14**(1968), 462-467
6. G.F. Cooper, E. Herskovits: A Bayesian method for the induction of probabilistic networks from data, *Machine Learning* **9** (1992), 309-347.
7. deKorvin A., Kleyle R., Lea R.: The object recognition problem when features fail to be homogeneous, *IJAR* 1993:8, 141-162.
8. C. Delobel: Normalization and hierarchical dependencies in the relational data model, *ACM Transactions on Database Systems*, vol. 3, no 3, 1978, 201-222.
9. A.P. Dempster: Upper and lower probabilities induced by a multi-valued mapping. *Ann. Math. Stat.*. **38**(1967), 325-339.
10. A DromignyBadin,S Rossato,Y.M. Zhu: Radioscopic and ultrasonic data fusion via the evidence theory, *Traitement du Signal*, Vol. 14, No.5, 1997, pp.499-510.
11. Dubois D., Prade H.: Evidence, knowledge and belief functions, *International Journal of Approximate Reasoning*, 1992:6, 295-319.
12. Durham S.D., Smolka J.S., Valtorta M.: Statistical consistency with Dempster's rule on diagnostic trees having uncertain performance parameters, *International Journal of Approximate Reasoning* 1992:6, 67-81.
13. Dutta, S. K., K. Harrison, and R. P. Srivastava, "The Audit Risk Model Under the Risk of Fraud," in Applications of Fuzzy Sets & The Theory of Evidence to Accounting II, Vol. 7, edited by P. Siegel, K. Omer, A. Korvin, and A. Zebda, published by Jai Press Inc., 1998, pp. 221-244.
14. R. Fagin, J.Y. Halpern: Uncertainty, belief, and probability. *Comput. Intell.* **7**(1991), 160-173.
15. Geiger D., Verma T., Pearl J.: d-Separation: From theorems to algorithms. In:Henrion M., Shachter R.D., Kamal L.N. and Lemmer J.F., eds, *Uncertainty in Artificial Intelligence 5.* Elsevier Science Publishers B.V. (North-Holland), 1990, 139-148.
16. Gordon J., Shortliffe E.H.: The Dempster-Shafer theory of evidence, in: Shafer G., Pearl J.,eds, *Readings in Uncertain Reasoning.* Morgan Kaufmann Pub.Inc., San Mateo CA, (1990), 529-539.
17. J.W. Grzymala-Busse: *Managing Uncertainty in Expert Systems*, Kluwer, 1991.
18. J.Y. Halpern, R. Fagin: Two views of belief: belief as generalized probability and belief as evidence.*Artificial Intelligence* **54**(1992), 275-317
19. R. Hummel, M. Landy: A statistical viewpoint on the theory of evidence. *IEEE Trans.PAMI* (1988), 235-247.
20. M. Itoh, T. Inagaki: Evidential theoretic revision of beliefs under a mixed strategy for safety-control of a large-complex plant. *Transactions of the Society of Instrumental and Control Engineering*, Vol. 34, no.5, 1998, pp. 415-421
21. Jafray, J.Y. (1989) Coherent bets under partially resolving uncertainty and belief functions. Theory and Decisions, 26,99-105

22. M.A. Kłopotek: Partial dependency separation - a new concept for expressing dependence/independence relations in causal networks. *Demonstratio Mathematica.* Vol XXXII No 1,1999, pp. 207-226.
23. M.A. Kłopotek: Beliefs in Markov trees - From local computations to local valuation. In:Trappl R., ed., *Cybernetics and Systems Research.* Vol.1., World Scientific Publishers (1994), pp. 351-358
24. M.A. Kłopotek: Learning belief network structure from data under causal insufficiency. In:Bergadano F., DeRaed L., eds, *Machine Learning ECML-94.* Lecture Notes in Artificial Intelligence 784, Springer-Verlag (1994), 379-382.
25. M.A. Kłopotek: Handling Causal Insufficiency in Dempster-Shafer Belief Networks. *Posters of Information Processing and Management of Uncertainty, Paris, 4-8 July 1994.* 41-42.
26. M.A. Kłopotek: Restricted Causal Inference Algorithm, In:Pehrson B., Simon I., eds, *Proc. World Computer Congress of IFIP, Hamburg 28 August - 2 September 1994, Vol.1* . Elsevier Scientific Publishers (North-Holland), Amsterdam (1994), 342-347
27. M.A. Kłopotek: On a Deficiency of the FCI Algorithm Learning Bayesian Networks from Data. to appear in *Demonstratio Mathematica.* Vol. XXXIII, 2000.
28. M.A. Kłopotek: Reasoning from Data in the Mathematical Theory of Evidence, In:*Proc. Eighth International Symposium On Methodologies For Intelligent Systems (ISMIS'94), Charlotte, North Carolina, USA, October 16-19, 1994.* Oak National Laboratory Publishers (1994), 71-84.
29. M.A. Kłopotek: Testumgebung für Entwicklung eines Beratungssystems auf der Basis der Mathematischen Theorie der Evidenz, *Öster. Zeitschrift für Statistik und Informatik, 1994*
30. M.A. Kłopotek: Interpretation of belief function in Dempster-Shafer Theory. *Foundations of Computing & Decision Sciences* **20**(1995)4, pp. 287-306.
31. M.A. Kłopotek: Identification of belief structure in Dempster-Shafer Theory. *Foundations of Computing & Decision Sciences* **21**(1996)1, pp. 35-54.
32. M.A. Kłopotek: *Methods of Identification and Interpretations of Belief Distributions in the Dempster-Shafer Theory* (in Polish). Publisher: Institute of Computer Science, Polish Academy of Sciences, Warsaw, Poland, 1998, ISBN 83-900820-8-x.
33. M.A. Kłopotek, S.T. Wierzchoń: An Interpretation for the Conditional Belief Function in The Theory of Evidence. In:: Z.Ras, A. Skowron eds: *Foundations of Intelligent Systems.* Lecture Notes in Artificial Intelligence 1609, Springer-Verlag, Berlin, 1999, 494-502.
34. H.E. Kyburg Jr: Bayesian and non-Bayesian evidential updating. *Artificial Intelligence* **31**(1987), 271-293.
35. Y. Ma, D.C. Wilkins: Induction of uncertain rules and the sociopathicity property in DST . In:Kruse R., Siegel P.,eds, *Symbolic and Quantitative Approaches to Uncertainty.* Lecture Notes In Computer Science 548, Springer-Verlag (1991), 238-245.
36. Michalewicz M., Wierzchoń S.T., Kłopotek M.A.: Knowledge Acquisition, Representation & Manipulation in Decision Support Systems. In:, M. Dąbrowski Michalewicz M., Raś Z., eds, *Intelligent Information Systems.* Proceedings of a Workshop held in Augustów, Poland, 7-11 June, ICS PAS (1993), 210- 238, .
37. Nguyen H.T.: On random sets and belief functions, *J. Math. Anal. Appl.* **65**(1978), 539-542.

38. , D Pagac,E.M. Nebot,H Durrant-Whyte: An evidential approach to map-building for autonomous vehicles. IEEE Transactions on Robotics & Automation, vol.14, no. 4, 1998, pp.623-629.
39. J. Pearl: *Probabilistic Reasoning in Intelligent Systems: Networks of Plausible Influence.* Morgan and Kaufmann, 1988
40. J. Pearl: Bayesian and Belief-Function formalisms for evidential reasoning:A conceptual analysis. In: Shafer G., Pearl J.,eds, *Readings in Uncertain Reasoning.* Morgan Kaufmann Pub.Inc., San Mateo CA, (1990), 540-569.
41. J. Pearl, T. Verma: A theory of inferred causation. In:Allen J., Fikes R., Sandewell E., eds, *Principles of Knowledge Representation and Reasoning.* Proc. of the Second IOnternational Conference, Cambridge, Massachusetts, April 22-25, 1991, San Mateo CA:Morgen Kaufmann (1991), 441-452.
42. G.M. Provan: A logic-based analysis of Dempster-Shafer Theory, *International Journal of Approximate Reasoning* **4**(1990), 451-495.
43. Provan G.M.: The validity of Dempster-Shafer belief functions, *International Journal of Approximate Reasoning,* 1992:6, 389-399.
44. Z.W. Ras: Query processing in distributed information systems, *Fundamenta Informaticae Journal,* Special Issue on Logics for Artificial Intelligence, IOS Press, Vol. XV, No. 3/4, 1991, 381-397
45. Ruspini E.H., Lowrance D.J., Strat T.M.: Understanding evidential reasoning, *International Journal of Approximate Reasoning,* 1992:6, 401-424.
46. E.H. Ruspini: The logical foundation of evidential reasoning, Tech. Note 408, SRI International, Menlo Park, Calif. USA, 1986.
47. G. Rebane, J. Pearl: The recovery of causal poly-trees from statistical data. In:Kanal L.N., Levit T.S., Lemmer J.F., eds, *Uncertainty in Artificial Intelligence 3.* Elsevier Science Publishers B.V., (North Holland) (1989), 175-182
48. M. Singh, M. Valtorta: Construction of bayesian network structures from data: A brief survey and an efficient algorithm. *International Journal of Approximate Reasoning* , **12**(1995), 111-131
49. Spirtes P., Glymour C., Scheines R.: *Causation, Prediction and Search.* Lecture Notes in Statistics 81, Springer-Verlag, 1993.
50. G. Shafer: *A Mathematical Theory of Evidence.* Princeton University Press, Princeton, 1976.
51. G. Shafer: Belief functions: An introduction. In: Shafer G., Pearl J.,eds, *Readings in Uncertain Reasoning.* Morgan Kaufmann Pub.Inc., San Mateo CA, (1990), 473-482.
52. G. Shafer, R. Srivastava: The Bayesian and Belief-Function Formalisms. A General Prospective for Auditing. In: Shafer G., Pearl J.,eds, *Readings in Uncertain Reasoning.* Morgan Kaufmann Pub.Inc., San Mateo CA, (1990), 482-521.
53. G. Shafer: Perspectives on the theory and practice of belief functions. *International Journal of Approximate Reasoning* **4**(1990), 323-362.
54. P.P. Shenoy: Conditional independence in valuation based systems. *International Journal of Approximate Reasoning* **109**(1994),
55. Shenoy P., Shafer G.: Axioms for probability and belief-function propagation, in: Shachter R.D., Levitt T.S., Kanal L.N., Lemmer J.F. (eds): *Uncertainty in Artificial Intelligence 4,* Elsevier Science Publishers B.V. (North Holland), 1990,
56. A. Skowron: Boolean reasoning for decision rules generation, J. Komorowski, Z.W.Raś (Eds): *Methodologies for Intelligent Systems,*

7th International Symposium, ISMIS'93, Torndheim, Norway, June 1993, Proccedings, Lecture Notes in Artif.Intel.689, Springer-Verlag, 1993, 295-305

57. A. Skowron: A synthesis of decision rules: applications of discernibility matrix properties, In:M. Dąbrowski, M. Michalewicz, Z. Raś eds: ***Intelligent Information Systems***, Proceedings of a Workshop held in Augustów, Poland, 7-11 June, 1993, ISBN 83-900820-2-0, 30-46
58. A. Skowron, J.W. Grzymała-Busse: From rough set theory to evidence theory. In:Yager R.R., Kasprzyk J. and Fedrizzi M., eds, *Advances in the Dempster-Shafer Theory of Evidence.* J. Wiley, New York (1994), 193-236.
59. Ph. Smets: Resolving misunderstandings about belief functions. *International Journal of Approximate Reasoning* **6**(1992), 321-344.
60. Ph. Smets, R. Kennes: The tranferable belief model. *Artif.Intel.* **66**(1994), 191-234.
61. Smets Ph.: Numerical represenation of uncertainty. In: Gabbay DF.M., Smets Ph. Eds.: Handbook of defeasible reasoning and uncertainty management systems. Vol. 3. Kluwer, Doordrecht, 1998, 265-309.
62. Srivastava, R. P., "Decision Making Under Ambiguity: A Belief-Function Perspective," Archives of Control Sciences, Vol. 6 (XLII), 1997, No. 1-2, pp. 5-27.
63. M. Studeny: Formal properties of conditional independence in different calculi of AI, Sonderforschungsbericht 343, Diskrete Strukturen in der Mathematik, Universität Bielefeld
64. A. Vang: *SQL and Relational Databases.* Microtrend Books, Slawson Communications Inc., 1991
65. L. Wasserman: Comments on Shafer's "Perspectives on the theory and practice of belief functions", *International Journal of Approximate Reasoning* 1992:6:367-375.
66. S.T. Wierzchoń: On plausible reasoning, in: M.M.Gupta, T.Yamakawa eds.: *Fuzzy Logic in Knowledge Based Systems, Decision and Control* , North-Holland Amsterdam, 1988, 133-152.
67. K. Weichselberger, S. Poehlmann, *A Methodology for Uncertainty in Knowledge-Based Systems.* . Lecture Notes in AI 419, Springer Verlag, 1990.
68. S.T. Wierzchoń, M.A. Kłopotek, Modified Component Valuations in Valuation Based Systems As A Way to Optimize Query Processing *Journal of Intelligent Information Systems* 9, 157-180 (1997).
69. S.T. Wierzchoń: *Metody repreyentacji i pryetwaryania informacji niepewnej w ramach teorii Dempstera-Shafera*, monography, Instytut Podstaw Informatyki PAN, 1996.
70. Zarley D.K., Hsia Y, Shafer G.: Evidential reasoning using DELIEF. In:*Proc. of the Seventh National conference on Artificial Intelligence (AAAI-88), 1.* Minneapolis MN (1988), 205-209.
71. Q. Zhu, E.S. Lee: Dempster-Shafer Approach in Propositional Logic. *International Journal of Intelligent Systems* **8**(1993), 341-349.

The Descriptive Ability of Models of Audit Risk

Gary Monroe[1] and Juliana Ng[2]

[1] School of Accounting, Edith Cowan University, Churchlands, 6018 Western Australia.
[2] Department of Accounting and Finance, The University of Western Australia, Nedlands, 6907 Western Australia.

Abstract. Auditors are required to perform assessments of risk during the planning stages of an audit. Consequently, the efficiency and effectiveness of audits should be affected by risk assessments. Various models that could assist auditors in the risk assessment task have been discussed in the auditing literature.

This study investigated the degree of consistency between auditors' intuitive assessments of audit risk and the audit risk values generated by various models. In addition to the traditional audit risk model, this study was interested in the performance of models that allowed for belief revision.

Sixty-nine auditors in Western Australia participated in this study. The auditors were required to complete two experimental booklets. The first booklet was designed to elicit the auditors' intuitive judgments concerning audit risk. The second booklet was used to extract estimates of the components required to generate model values. The auditors' judgments were then compared to the model-generated responses.

The results of this study indicated inconsistencies between auditors' intuitive assessments and the traditional audit risk model. Tests based on absolute mean differences indicated inconsistencies also existed between auditors' intuitive assessments and the belief revision models. Paired t-tests confirmed these inconsistencies, with the exception of the Belief Function model. The paired t-test showed no significant difference between auditors' intuitive assessments and the values generated by the Belief Function model.

1 Introduction

Australian Auditing Standards AUS 302, *Planning*, and AUS 402, *Risk Assessments and Internal Controls*, prescribe risk assessment as part of the audit planning routine. The adoption of this risk analysis approach to auditing means that auditors' assessments of risk will impact on the efficient and effective conduct of an audit and, consequently, influence the allocation of scarce audit resources.

The auditing literature indicates efforts to develop models that can be used for risk assessment. Although the assessment of audit risk is an intuitive task based on professional judgment, models that can assist auditors with the risk assessment task would serve to provide a general risk level which the auditor can then review and adjust accordingly to reflect his/her own professional judgment.

Much of the literature has focused on the theoretical aspects of these models, and a few have examined these models empirically. For example, earlier empirical studies that compared auditors' intuitive assessments with estimates generated by the traditional audit risk model revealed that there were significant differences (e.g., Jiambalvo and Waller, 1984; Daniel, 1988). More recently, Dusenbury, Reimers and Wheeler (1996) compared the risk assessments generated using the traditional audit risk model with a firm-specific model and a belief-based model. They reported that the belief-based model provided the most conservative assessments of the three models tested. In a more comprehensive study, Krishnamoorthy, Mock and Washington (1999) examined the descriptive ability of various belief revision models to reflect auditors' judgments pertaining to risk assessment using an inventory valuation task. The models examined were: a Bayesian model based on Cascaded Inference Theory; a Belief Function model; and two versions of the Belief-Adjustment model. One version of the Belief-Adjustment model examined consistently positive evidence, while the other version incorporated negative and positive evidence.[1] Krishnamoorthy et al. reported that these models reflected the direction of the auditors' judgments. However, the only model that reflected both the magnitude and direction of auditors' judgments was the Belief-Adjustment model incorporating both negative and positive evidence. The predictions of the remaining models were higher than the judgments of the auditors.

The present study examines the overall audit risk judgment and contributes to the literature in several ways. Firstly, it extends the literature by examining the descriptive ability of a number of models applicable to this task. Specifically, this study focuses on six models described in the literature as being adaptable for audit risk assessment. The models examined are: (1) the traditional audit risk model; (2) The Canadian Institute of Chartered Accountants (CICA) model; (3) the extended CICA model (Skerratt and Woodhead, 1992); (4) Skerratt and Woodhead's (1992) combined model of posterior risk; (5) the Belief-Adjustment model (Hogarth and Einhorn, 1992); and (6) the Belief Function model (Srivastava and Shafer, 1992). These models differ in terms of the way in which information is perceived to be integrated. Since the assessment of risk must ultimately be dependent on professional judgment, a comparison of the models' performances with the auditors' professional assessments is essential. Therefore, this study investigates the degree of consistency between auditors' intuitive assessments of audit risk and the audit risk values generated by the models. It should be noted, however, that although this study compares auditors' intuitive assessments to the model-generated estimates, the study makes no comment on which is the correct or appropriate assessment. This research is solely concerned in determining if

[1] In the context of the Belief-Adjustment model, the term "positive evidence" is used to describe evidence that supports the hypothesis under consideration, while negative evidence refers to evidence that disconfirms or refutes the hypothesis.

any particular model reflects more accurately auditors' audit risk judgments. As with many aspects of auditing, there is usually no immediate feedback to determine if auditors' assessments of audit risk are appropriate. The auditor has to rely on his professional judgment, and whether this assessment is "right" or "wrong" may only be judged in the long run if the client suffers financial problems and legal action is brought against the auditor.

Secondly, a review of the published literature reveals that some of the models in this study have either not been empirically tested or have had limited testing. For example, the applicability of the combined model of posterior risk (Skerratt and Woodhead, 1992) has been illustrated using only hypothetical values and not demonstrated using empirical data. This study contributes to the literature by providing further empirical evidence of the suitability of the six models chosen.

Thirdly, since this study compares auditors' intuitive assessments with assessments generated by the selected models, an understanding of the judgment process may be obtained. A model that can descriptively represent auditors' subjective audit risk judgments could provide insights into their judgment processes. Specifically, since the models differ in their assumptions regarding the integration of information, this study may provide some information regarding the manner in which auditors integrate the various risk components.

This paper is sequenced as follows. The audit risk model is briefly discussed first as it is the traditional approach to risk assessment. The literature has recognised that there are certain deficiencies in this model and these deficiencies provide the incentive to examine other models. The models selected for examination in this paper are also briefly reviewed. Following this, the research method used to investigate the consistency between auditors' intuitive assessments of audit risk and the audit risk estimates generated using the selected models is described. The analysis and results are then discussed, followed by the conclusions and limitations of this paper.

2 Models

2.1 Audit Risk Model

The authoritative literature defines audit risk as "the risk that auditors may express inappropriate opinions on financial information that is materially misstated. Audit risk has three components: inherent risk, control risk, and detection risk" (AUS 402, 1995). The Standard defines these components as follows:

- inherent risk (IR) is defined as the "susceptibility of an account balance or class of transactions to misstatement that could be material ... assuming that there are no related internal controls",

- control risk (CR) is "the risk that misstatements that could occur in an account balance or class of transactions and that could be material ... will not be prevented or detected on a timely basis by the system of internal control", and
- detection risk (DR) is defined as "the risk that auditors' substantive procedures will not detect a misstatement that exists in an account balance or class of transactions that could be material..."

The literature presents the audit risk model as:

$$AuditRisk = IR \times CR \times DR \tag{1}$$

The auditor is interested in detection risk as this aids in ascertaining the nature, timing and extent of substantive procedures required for that particular engagement (Libby, Artman and Willingham, 1985). Thus, the audit risk model can be used to determine the required level of detection risk. However, the audit risk model can also be used to determine the reasonableness of a proposed audit plan (Arens, Loebbecke, Best and Shailer, 1990). In this context, an auditor would first determine the inherent risk, control risk and detection risk for a proposed audit plan. Based on these assessments, the achieved audit risk value can then be calculated. This value would then be compared to the desired audit risk for the client to determine if the preliminary audit plan was appropriate.

In addition to the authoritative literature and articles that have provided general descriptions of audit risk and the audit risk model (e.g., Adams, 1989; Grobstein and Craig, 1984), some researchers have critically evaluated its suitability as a model for risk assessment and empirically investigated its performance against auditors' judgments. Empirical studies that compared auditors' risk assessments with risk estimates calculated using the audit risk model (e.g., Jiambalvo and Waller, 1984; Daniel, 1988; Strawser, 1990; Strawser, 1991) have shown that the multiplicative form of the audit risk model is inconsistent with auditors' judgments.

Other researchers have commented on the deficiencies of the audit risk model. For example, Cushing and Loebbecke (1983) identified several conceptual problems associated with the audit risk model. Primarily, they argued that the risk analysis model provided an oversimplification of the task.[2] Researchers have also argued that the audit risk model is incomplete as it fails to consider all possible audit outcomes. For instance, Kinney (1989) commented that this resulted in the understatement of achieved audit risk. Specifically, Kinney argued that the audit risk formula did not provide for "conditioned audit strategies" (i.e., alternative routes to reaching an opinion), nor did it

[2] Several issues were discussed including: the problem of aggregating risk assessments; the independence of risk components; and differences between real and assessed risks.

provide for the risk of incorrect rejection.[3] Kinney's stance was that it was the omission to incorporate audit outcomes pertaining to incorrect rejection that led to the understatement of achieved audit risk.

2.2 Alternative Models

The preceding discussion highlighted researchers' concerns on the suitability of the traditional audit risk model as a tool for risk assessment and on its ability to reflect auditors' risk assessments. In the present study, several alternative models that can be applied to the audit risk assessment were examined to determine their descriptive validity: the Canadian Institute of Chartered Accountants (CICA) model; the extended CICA model; Skerratt and Woodhead's (1992) combined model of posterior risk; the Belief-Function model; and the Belief-Adjustment model. These alternative models were chosen as they allow for the revision of beliefs, which the traditional audit model does not.

In this section, a brief overview of the models is provided, and concludes with a comparison of the models discussed. The application of these models to the experimental task are discussed in a later section.

CICA Risk Model

The Canadian Institute of Chartered Accountants (CICA) risk model (1980) identifies the same risk components as the audit risk model, but adopts Bayesian principles to calculate the posterior probability of material misstatement. Under this model, the audit risk assessment task is viewed as a sequential procedure, starting with the assessment of inherent risk. This is followed, in order, by: (1) internal control evaluation; (2) analytical review procedures; and (3) substantive tests of details (Leslie, Anderson and Teitlebaum, 1979).

The model presented in CICA (1980) is an adoption of Leslie et al.'s (1979) posterior risk model. The model is presented as:[4]

$$OverallRisk = \frac{JointRisk}{JointRisk + InherentConfidence} \tag{2}$$

or, written alternatively,

$$OverallRisk = \frac{IR \times CR \times AR \times TD}{IR \times CR \times AR \times TD + (1 - IR)} \tag{3}$$

[3] The audit risk model focuses on the likelihood that audit tests will fail to detect material error when it is present (i.e., audit tests will incorrectly accept an assertion), but does not consider the risk of incorrect rejection.

[4] The CICA model, in essence, represents a two-state Bayesian model (Smieliauskas, 1989). The two states are the "exactly material errors" state and the "zero-errors" state. The audit risk model considers only the former state.

where:

OR = overall risk (or posterior risk), and represents "the auditor's assessment of the risk that the audited financial statements contain material error after all the audit work is completed, given that no material errors were detected during the audit" (Smieliauskas, 1989, p. 720);

IR = prior probability of irregularities initially occurring in the financial data (CICA, 1980);

CR = the risk that material irregularities will not be detected by the system of internal controls;

AR = analytical review risk; and

TD = substantive testing of details risk.

Extended CICA Model and Combined Model of Posterior Risk (Skerratt and Woodhead, 1992)

Skerratt and Woodhead suggested that the CICA model was incomplete as it failed to incorporate the possibility of a situation where a misstatement has occurred but has been detected and corrected by the system of internal controls.[5] Extending the CICA model to incorporate the possibility results in the following equation (Skerratt and Woodhead, 1992):

$$OverallRisk = \frac{IR \times CR \times AR \times TD}{IR \times CR \times AR \times TD + 1 - (IR \times CR)} \quad (4)$$

Using the above equation as a framework, Skerratt and Woodhead then incorporated Kinney's suggestion pertaining to the risk of incorrect rejection.

Skerratt and Woodhead used a tree-diagram to illustrate their combined model of posterior audit risk, which indicated the audit outcome space for three possible events: (1) material misstatements exist and are not corrected by the system of internal controls; (2) material misstatements exist but have been detected and corrected by the system of internal controls; and (3) material misstatements do not exist. Extracting the relevant paths of the tree-diagram that are consistent with the definition of audit risk, the following formula is obtained (Skerratt and Woodhead, 1992):

$$PosteriorRisk = \frac{IR \times CR \times AR \times TD}{IR \times CR \times AR \times TD + (1 - IR \times CR) \times AR^{*} \times TD^{*}} \quad (5)$$

[5] In the CICA model, this possibility is excluded because it is assumed that the auditor would conduct an investigation to determine if the internal controls detected a material misstatement (Leslie, 1984). The auditor would, therefore, be in a position to know whether the event had occurred. Skerratt and Woodhead argued that, from a practical perspective, it was unlikely that the auditor would investigate all errors detected by the internal controls during the year. They suggested that the auditor would prefer to determine, ex ante, the likelihood that the internal controls would detect material misstatements.

where:

AR* = the probability that analytical procedures would not signal material error when it had not occurred.

TD* = the probability that substantive tests of details would not signal a material error when it had not occurred.

The Belief-Adjustment Model

The Belief-Adjustment model, developed by Hogarth and Einhorn (1992), attempts to provide a general framework that could be used for belief revision. Underlying the Belief-Adjustment model is the notion that individuals have limited information-processing capabilities and exhibit adaptive behavior to ease cognitive strain. The Belief-Adjustment model assumes that beliefs change via a sequential anchoring-and-adjustment process. That is, an individual's current belief provides an anchor, and this anchor is adjusted by succeeding pieces of evidence or information.

The model is presented in Hogarth and Einhorn's (1992) paper as:

$$S_k = S_{k-1} + w_k(S(X_k) - R) \tag{6}$$

where:

S_k = the degree of belief in some hypothesis after evaluating k pieces of information or evidence ($0 \leq S_k \leq 1$);

S_{k-1} = the anchor or prior opinion. (The initial strength of belief is represented by S_0);

w_k = the adjustment weight for the kth piece of information or evidence;

$S(X_k)$ = the subjective evaluation (persuasiveness) of the kth piece of information or evidence. Boundaries on the value of $S(X_k)$ are described later; and

R = the reference point or background against which the impact of the kth piece of information or evidence is evaluated.

Three sub-processes are incorporated in this model: (1) the encoding process; (2) the adjustment process; and (3) how the information is processed (Hogarth and Einhorn, 1992). The encoding process focuses on how new information is encoded before it is integrated with the prior opinion, and is denoted as $(S(X_k) - R)$ in the model. The difference between the subjective evaluation of the kth piece of evidence (i.e., $S(X_k)$) and some reference point or background (i.e., R) is described as "the impact of the new evidence."

In the adjustment process, individuals adjust their opinions to adapt to new information. However, Hogarth and Einhorn argued that this adaptation was sensitive to the sign of the adjustment and that the adaptation rate changes over time (Asare and Messier, 1991). Adaptive behavior was introduced into the Belief-Adjustment model by assuming a "contrast" effect. The model hypothesised that the adjustment weight (w_k) is a function of both the sign of the impact of the evidence $((S(X_k) - R))$ and the level of the current opinion (S_{k-1}). The contrast assumption provides certain expectations about the relationship between the extent of the belief revision and the preceding anchor. Specifically, the contrast assumption states that "negative evidence induces greater belief change the larger the preceding anchor; for positive evidence it is the reverse" (Hogarth and Einhorn, 1992). In essence, Hogarth and Einhorn assumed that, given the same negative information, "large anchors are 'hurt' (i.e., revised downwards) more than smaller ones" (p. 14). By analogy, for positive evidence, small anchors are 'helped' (i.e., revised upwards) more than larger ones.

Relating this back to the adjustment weight (w_k), Hogarth and Einhorn argued that for situations where $S(X_k) \leq R$, w_k should be proportional to S_{k-1}. Where $S(X_k) > R$, w_k should be inversely proportional to S_{k-1}. Mathematically, Hogarth and Einhorn represented this assumption as:

$$w_k = \alpha S_{k-1} \quad for S(X_k) \leq R \tag{7}$$

$$w_k = \beta(1 - S_{k-1}) \quad for S(X_k) > R \tag{8}$$

where α and β are constants ($0 \leq \alpha, \beta \leq 1$).

In the above equations, α and β represent an individual's receptiveness to negative and positive evidence, respectively, such that high (low) values of α and β suggest high (low) sensitivity to new information. Hogarth and Einhorn acknowledged that individuals differ in their receptiveness to positive and negative new information and assumed that α and β are dependent on both individual and situational variables.

In describing the manner in which new evidence is processed, the Belief-Adjustment model allows for two processing methods: Step-by-Step (SbS) processing and End-of-Sequence (EoS) processing. The SbS processing mode assumes that individuals use an anchoring-and-adjustment process, and adjust their anchor after each piece of new information is received. The EoS processing method assumes that individuals make only one adjustment to their initial anchor.

The Belief Function Model

Srivastava and Shafer (1992) focused on belief-function theory in developing a descriptive model of belief revision. They argued that the use of probability theory may not be an appropriate representation of the auditor's notion of audit risk[6], and advanced the use of "belief-function plausibility." Under the

[6] In an earlier paper, Shafer and Srivastava (1990) criticised the additivity rule in probability theory. Shafer and Srivastava Shafer (1990) and Shafer (1976) claimed that the Bayesian formulation required the allocation of the total probability among the elements of the hypothesis set. This was required even though there may be a lack of evidence or knowledge about one of the elements. In such a

belief-function approach, the plausibility of a statement refers to the "extent that we lack evidence against the statement. (Hence) high plausibility of error indicates only a lack of assurance, not positive evidence that there is an error" (Srivastava and Shafer, 1992).

In essence, the belief-function framework differs from the Bayesian framework in that it allows a term for ignorance or a lack of knowledge to be incorporated. The difference in the two frameworks can be illustrated as follows. Under Bayesian principles, the sum of the probability of a particular state, (s), and its complement, ($\bar{s}$), must equal 1. The belief-function framework, however, recognises that there is a third element; the element that reflects the individual's uncertainty about the "true" state as a result of a lack of knowledge or evidence. This element is denoted (s,$\bar{s}$) and represents an uncommitted belief. Thus, the belief-function framework differs from the Bayesian framework in that the sum of: (i) the probability of state (s); (ii) the probability of its complement ($\bar{s}$); and (iii) the ignorance term (s,$\bar{s}$), must equal 1 (Srivastava, 1993).

Srivastava and Shafer argued that the use of plausibility functions represents conceptually the auditor's cognitive process when assessing audit risk.[7] Srivastava (1993) documented a simple approach for combining evidence in the audit risk assessment[8] and illustrated the applicability of the Belief Function model for audit risk assessment through the use of numerical examples based on fictitious values.

Comparisons Between the Models

To conclude this section, a summary of the main differences between the various models is provided. The CICA model is based on Bayesian principles as is the combined model of posterior risk. However, the latter model extends the CICA framework by addressing the issues raised by Kinney (1989) concerning audit outcome space. The Belief Function model also focuses on probability theory. However, the model recognises that individuals may lack knowledge or evidence concerning an event and, unlike the Bayesian framework, allows

situation, it was common to evenly distribute the probability among the elements. However, Srivastava and Shafer argued that "...doing so seems to be a positive expression of belief, not an expression of ignorance" (p. 131).

[7] The application of plausibility functions to the assessment of audit risk was provided in two examples from Srivastava and Shafer (1992).

[8] Srivastava and Shafer (1992) described an overall model of audit risk by incorporating the impact of evidence at three levels (the financial statement level, the account balance level and the audit objectives level), and provided belief function formulae on the basis of the resulting complex structure. Srivastava (1993) illustrated a less complex approach by focusing on only one level. In the present study, subjects were asked to direct their attention to the accounts receivable account, and to assess audit risk for the account. Consequently, Srivastava's approach was appropriate for the study.

individuals to provide an expression of ignorance or uncommitted belief. The Belief-Adjustment model differs from the Bayesian-based models in that it permits individuals to evaluate evidence with regard to a single hypothesis (Asare and Messier, 1991).

Unlike the traditional audit risk model, these models are all models of belief revision. This may be viewed as an improvement on the audit risk model, which is multiplicative in nature. The belief revision models may more appropriately reflect the procedural stages of the audit risk assessment task. Specifically, the risk assessment task is a sequential process, and the belief revision models enable the auditor to aggregate evidence obtained via a sequential process with earlier evidence, thus allowing the auditor to revise his beliefs.

3 Research Method

This study was predominantly exploratory in nature, and was aimed at comparing auditors' intuitive assessments of audit risk to the audit risk estimates generated by the models described above models.

To generate the values, subjects were required to provide estimates of the various components of the models. Consequently, two case booklets were used for this experiment. In the first booklet, a holistic approach was adopted. Subjects were provided with information pertaining to a hypothetical client, and were asked to reach a conclusion regarding audit risk. This represented their intuitive judgments. Subjects' responses to the second booklet provided the necessary estimates from which the model-generated values of audit risk could be calculated. The second booklet contained the same information as the first booklet. However, the information was separated into different sections, and the subjects were required to provide estimates based on each separate section. Thus, each subject's intuitive assessment could then be compared with the values generated by the various models using the individual subject's component estimates.

A description of the tasks and procedures used in this study is provided below. Details pertaining to the first booklet are presented first. Booklet 2 is then described.

3.1 Booklet 1

In Booklet 1, subjects were told that they were to provide an assessment of the level of audit risk for the accounts receivable section. Subjects were provided with information pertaining to: inherent risk, the internal control environment, the results of the analytical review of account balances, and a review of proposed substantive tests of details.[9] The inherent risk information

[9] The work of Chang and Monroe (1991) and Monroe and Therry (1993) were used in developing these scenarios.

and the internal control information were manipulated at two levels: relatively high and low (for inherent risk), and relatively low and high (for control risk).[10]

At the beginning of this task, subjects were told that their firm had been retained as the continuing auditors for a hypothetical client. The auditor who had conducted the preceding year's audit had since left the firm. However, prior to his departure, he had completed an initial audit plan for the current year's audit. Subjects were told that they had been assigned to the audit of the client, and the audit partner's instructions were for them to evaluate the proposed audit plan. Specifically, they were asked to direct their attention to the accounts receivable account and determine the likelihood (risk) that the account balance contained material errors or was materially misstated after the audit has been completed and an unqualified opinion has been reached.[11] Subjects were also told to assume that the information contained in the case had been gathered by the subject using the same procedures and with the same thoroughness as they normally would in practice.

Subjects were initially provided with information pertaining to inherent risk through the background information for the hypothetical client. Subjects were provided with a general description of the client, and information pertaining to market share, financial position, management, the accounts receivable department, prior years' audit opinions, and any changes in these areas since the last audit.[12]

---

[10] Subjects were randomly assigned to the manipulated levels. In designing the experiment, extreme manipulations were avoided as these would overshadow any compensatory factors.

[11] In applying the concept of audit risk to planning judgments, detection risk is usually the variable of interest. However, it is possible for the audit risk model to be used to determine the audit risk value. Arens et al. (1990) commented that the audit risk model can be used to evaluate the reasonableness of an audit plan. To do this, an auditor would determine the inherent risk, control risk and detection risk for a proposed audit plan and obtain an audit risk value. This value would then be compared to the desired audit risk for the client to determine if the preliminary audit plan was appropriate. To encourage subjects to use the concept of audit risk in this manner for the experiment, subjects were informed that they were required to evaluate the reasonableness of a proposed audit plan.

[12] Subjects in the low inherent risk scenario were told that no changes had occurred since the last audit that would have some bearing on the company's operations, financial position, market share, management and/or accounts receivable department. Subjects in the high inherent risk scenario were informed that several changes had occurred in these areas since the last audit. For the high risk scenario, subjects were informed that sales had fallen in the previous financial year; the previous year's provision for doubtful debts was inadequate; both the credit manager and the controller had retired during the current financial year; and that errors discovered in accounts receivable in the previous year pertaining to arithmetic errors and amounts wrongly allocated to customer accounts recurred in a sample of accounts receivable taken from the current financial year.

After reviewing this information, subjects were asked to assess the "likelihood (risk) that the accounts receivable account may contain material errors or be materially misstated after the audit has been completed and an unqualified opinion has been reached." Responses were recorded on the same scale as that used for the inherent risk task. This response represented subjects' initial responses.

Subjects were then reminded that they would be presented with three sets of additional information pertaining to the internal control environment, analytical review procedures for account balances and a review of proposed substantive tests of details. They were told that, after reviewing all the information, they would be required to update their initial response. They were also reminded not to make changes to their initial response.

On the next page, subjects were presented with information pertaining to the control environment. A description of the environment in prior years was provided along with any changes that had occurred since the last audit.[13] Next, subjects were provided with information pertaining to analytical procedures. This consisted of unaudited financial statements for the current financial year, audited financial statements for the previous two years, and financial ratios based on this information. Subjects were also provided with industry ratios for comparative purposes.[14]

Subjects were then given information pertaining to the proposed substantive tests. Specifically, the subjects were provided with a list of planned substantive procedures to test six financial statement assertions: measurement; existence; occurrence; completeness; valuation; and presentation and disclosure. Moreover, subjects were informed that while time constraints had prevented them from conducting the more time-consuming procedures, they had completed some tests to check for the mathematical accuracy, ownership

[13] In the low control risk scenario, subjects were informed that no changes to the control environment had occurred. Subjects were also provided with a partial internal control checklist relevant to the internal controls for credit sales. Subjects were informed that the checklist had been completed after compliance testing and that the results from compliance testing had revealed that prescribed controls were in place. Subjects were told that, while some errors were discovered, these were significantly less than the maximum tolerable deviation rate. In the high control risk scenario, subjects were reminded that the controller and credit manager had retired. The internal control checklist revealed a lack of controls over credit approval and no follow-up procedures for customer enquiries and disputed amounts. Subjects were informed that compliance testing had revealed that some prescribed internal controls were not functioning properly and that some procedural deviations were found to be higher than the tolerable rate.

[14] In order to manipulate inherent risk at high and low levels, information pertaining to the level of sales and the provision for doubtful debts was used as differentiating factors. Consequently, two versions of the financial statements were designed; one that matched with the information provided for the low inherent risk scenario, and the other for the high inherent risk scenario.

and classification of a sample of accounts receivables. A few minor errors were revealed from conducting those tests.

Having reviewed all the information pertaining to control risk, analytical procedures and proposed tests of details, subjects were asked to update their original response concerning the "likelihood (risk) that the accounts receivable account may contain material errors or may be materially misstated after the audit has been completed and an unqualified opinion has been reached." The same response scale was used, and the responses represented the final judgment.

It was necessary to elicit one more response from the subjects in order to test Skerratt and Woodhead's (1992) combined model of posterior risk. The combination model incorporated the risk of incorrect rejection as discussed by Kinney (1989). To examine this issue, subjects were asked to assume that they had reported back to the audit partner with their final judgment only to be told that, based on previous experience with the client, the partner believed that there was a 20% chance that analytical procedures would indicate material errors when none existed, and a 5% chance that substantive tests of details would indicate material errors when none existed. Subjects were then asked if this information would cause them to revise their final judgment. If they responded in the affirmative, they were asked to provide the revised likelihood assessment. After completing Booklet 1, the subjects were asked to proceed to Booklet 2.

3.2 Booklet 2

Booklet 2 was designed to elicit information from subjects so that model-generated audit risk values could be calculated. The subjects were provided with the same information as in Booklet 1. However, this information was separated into passages, and responses were elicited after each passage in order to obtain the estimates of the components required for the various models.

In the instructions to Booklet 2, subjects were informed that they would receive the same information as in Booklet 1. However, they were told that there was no need to refer back to Booklet 1 nor change their responses in that booklet. Furthermore, subjects were informed that, in Booklet 2, they would receive several passages of information. While Booklet 1 required subjects to update their beliefs in light of new information, subjects were told that Booklet 2 did not require them to revise their responses. Rather, each passage was to be evaluated on its own merits, independently of other passages.[15] Finally, subjects were again reminded that they were to assume

[15] Since the assessment of audit risk followed a sequential pattern starting with the inherent risk assessment, the passages were presented in a different order than that presented in Booklet 1 to reduce the possibility that subjects may try to update their beliefs after each passage.

that the information contained in the case had been gathered by the subject using the same procedures and degree of thoroughness as they normally would in practice.

In total, subjects were provided with five randomly-ordered passages pertaining to inherent risk (background information), the internal control environment, analytical procedures, inherent risk and internal control environment combined, and substantive tests of details. After each passage, subjects were required to answer two questions. The subjects were asked to indicate either:

- the likelihood that material errors or misstatements would occur in the accounts receivable account, assuming that there were no related internal controls;
- the likelihood that material errors or misstatements that could occur in the accounts receivable account would be prevented or detected by the system of internal controls;
- the likelihood that analytical review procedures would detect any material errors or misstatements in the accounts receivable account;
- the likelihood that the accounts receivable account contained material errors or was materially misstated given both inherent risk and internal control information; or
- the level of risk that the subject was willing to accept that the substantive tests of details would detect material errors or misstatements in the accounts receivable account.

In each passage, subjects were asked to record their responses on a number line ranging from '0' to '100'.

The second question in each passage asked subjects to indicate how confident they were of the estimate they had provided in the first question. Again, a number line ranging from '0' to '100' was used. This confidence measure was used to estimate the "ignorance" (or uncommitted belief) variable in the Belief Function model.

3.3 Transformation of Risk Components

To apply the models, it was necessary to restate the subjects' responses so that they were consistent with the definitions of the risk components used in the various models. The questions in Booklet 2 pertaining to internal controls, analytical procedures and substantive tests of details were expressed in terms opposite to that required in the definitions stated in the models. For example, control risk was defined above as the risk that misstatements that could occur will not be prevented or detected. Subjects, however, were required to provide a response pertaining to the likelihood that misstatements that could occur will be prevented or detected.[16] Consequently, subjects' responses

[16] This was done to maintain uniformity in the phrasing of the questions since earlier questions used affirmative expressions.

to the questions pertaining to the internal control environment, analytical procedures and substantive tests of details were transformed to conform with the definitional requirements.

4 Analysis and Results

In this section, the results of statistical tests used in this study are presented. This section is organised as follows. In the first part, demographic details of the participants in this experiment are provided. The second part discusses the procedures used to calculate audit risk values for each of the models. In the third part, the results of comparisons between the model-generated audit risk values and the auditors' intuitive assessments are reported.

4.1 Subjects

Sixty-nine auditors from accounting firms in Western Australia participated in this experiment.[17] The average number of years of audit experience was approximately six and a half years, and ranged from two and a half years to 33 years. Fifty-four percent of the auditors were from Big 6 firms, and the average audit experience of this group of auditors was approximately five and a half years. For non-Big 6 firms, the average number of years of audit experience was approximately eight years. In the total sample, 46.4% of the auditors held the position of manager or partner, 11.6% held the position of supervisor, and 40.6% were seniors. One subject was classified as an assistant with 2.5 years of experience.

The subjects were required to complete the case materials under supervised conditions, and were compensated for their time.

4.2 Calculation of Audit Risk

To determine the audit risk values under each of the six models, it was first necessary to ascertain estimates of the components of each model. The models predominantly required the same inputs (i.e., the components of inherent risk, control risk, the risk associated with analytical procedures and the risk pertaining to substantive tests of details), but differed in the manner in which the components were combined. The specific requirements for each model are described below.

Audit Risk Model, CICA Model and Extended CICA Model

The audit risk model, the CICA model, and its extended version are relatively straightforward in their application. To apply these models, subjects'

[17] The original sample consisted of 70 subjects. However, one subject received non-matching booklets for this study and was excluded.

estimates of the following risk components were required: inherent risk (IR); control risk (CR); substantive tests of details risk (TD); and analytical procedures risk (AR), and were combined in accordance with the formulae requirements of the three models.

Skerratt and Woodhead's (1992) Combined Model of Posterior Risk

Skerratt and Woodhead's combined model of posterior risk integrated a measure for the risk of incorrect rejection within the CICA framework. In addition to the common components of IR, CR, AR and TD, the combined model required two additional elements: the probability that analytical procedures would not signal material error when it had not occurred (denoted AR* in the model); and the probability that substantive tests of details would not signal a material error when it had not occurred (denoted TD*).

These two estimates were provided to the subjects as part of the information associated with the task. To avoid any potential misinterpretation or confusion due to the subjects' unfamiliarity with these definitions of AR* and TD*, the information pertaining to these two elements that was provided to the subjects was expressed differently. The subjects were informed that there was a 20% chance that the analytical procedures would indicate material errors when none had occurred, and a 5% chance that substantive tests of details would indicate a material error when none had occurred. Estimates of AR* and TD* as required by the model were obtained by transforming the given probabilities. Specifically, the estimate of AR* was set at 80% and TD* was set at 95%. The values of these estimates were constant for all subjects.

The Belief-Adjustment Model

To account for the different impact of positive and negative evidence using the SbS processing model, the Belief-Adjustment model can be re-written as (Hogarth and Einhorn, 1992):

$$S_k = S_{k-1} + \alpha S_{k-1}(S(X_k) - R) \quad for\ negative\ evidence \tag{9}$$

$$S_k = S_{k-1} + \beta(1 - S_{k-1})(S(X_k) - R) \quad for\ positive\ evidence \tag{10}$$

In adopting the model for the audit risk judgment, there were three items of evidence that needed to be integrated with the auditor's initial opinion. The audit risk assessment was viewed as a sequential process whereby the auditor initially determined the level of inherent risk. This assessment was then updated in light of information pertaining to control risk, analytical review procedures and substantive tests of details. Hence, the subjects' responses to the inherent risk component represented their initial belief in the hypothesis that the account contains material errors or material misstatements after the audit was completed and an unqualified opinion was reached. The remaining three components were viewed as representing the first, second, and third items, respectively. The final assessment after incorporating all the pieces of evidence represented audit risk.

Positive and negative evidence for the Belief-Adjustment model To apply the Belief-Adjustment model, it was necessary to differentiate between positive (supporting the hypothesis or assertion) and negative (refuting the hypothesis or assertion) evidence.

Thus, in addition to eliciting a response for the risk components from subjects, it was also necessary to determine if subjects viewed the components as representing negative or positive evidence. To categorise the three components as either positive or negative, the following procedure was implemented. Subjects were required to record their responses to questions concerning these components on a number line that ranged from 0 (extremely unlikely) - 100 (extremely likely). The mid-point (50) was arbitrarily chosen as the benchmark. Consequently, after transforming each subject's responses to bring them in line with the definitions of control risk, analytical review procedures risk and substantive tests of details risk, if a subject's responses for any of the three components was 50 or greater, that component was coded as positive evidence (i.e., evidence that confirmed the assertion). Conversely, responses less than 50 were treated as negative evidence (i.e., refuting the assertion). So, for example, if a subject's responses (after transformation) were 70%, 40%, and 60% for control risk, analytical review procedures risk, and substantive tests of details risk, respectively, these items were classified as positive, negative, and positive.

Sensitivity to positive and negative evidence Using the Belief Adjustment model as a judgment model required an estimation of each individual's sensitivity to negative (α) and positive (β) evidence. Low sensitivity to positive (negative) information was implied by smaller values of $\beta(\alpha)$. In their framework, Hogarth and Einhorn (1992) identified five main attitudes: (i) advocate ($\alpha = 0$, $\beta = 1$); (ii) sceptic ($\alpha = 1$, $\beta = 0$); (iii) insensitive ($\alpha = 0$, $\beta = 0$); (iv) highly sensitive ($\alpha = 1$, $\beta = 1$); and (v) semi-sensitive ($\alpha = 0.5$, $\beta = 0.5$).

Earlier studies testing the order effect predictions of the Belief-Adjustment model attempted to infer values for auditors' sensitivity to evidence. Johnson (1989) ruled out the use of direct measures of individuals' sensitivity on the basis that such a measure was subject to several biases, which, if attempts were made to control for, would result in little useful data, and he suggested that previous studies had not considered individuals' sensitivities because of the measurement difficulties.

Similarly, in this study, auditors' sensitivity to evidence were not elicited directly from subjects in this experiment. Values for sensitivity were estimated by manipulating information sensitivity at various values such that $0 \leq \alpha, \beta \leq 1$.

To determine if the subjects were more sensitive to positive or negative evidence, a debriefing questionnaire was used to ask subjects to rank 10 items in order of the importance that they attached to those items in their evaluation of risk. These 10 items consisted of five variables that included inherent risk factors, control risk factors and analytical procedures, and which were each manipulated to indicate a high and low level of risk (see Table 1).

There were two approaches that subjects may have adopted to complete this task. One strategy would have been to treat the 10 items individually. Using this approach, it was expected that individuals who exhibited a tendency to be more attentive to items that indicated potential problems would list more high risk items as the five more important variables, and more low risk items as the five less important variables.[18] An alternative strategy that could have been adopted by the subjects would have been to first identify the underlying five factors and then rank each item in the pair according to the perceived importance. Five subjects adopted this strategy. Under the alternative approach, if subjects had a tendency to be more attentive towards items that suggested potential problems, it was expected that the high risk item in each pair would be ranked higher. Four of the five subjects exhibited this behavior.

The list of items is provided in Table 1. The items are presented in order of their perceived importance in risk evaluation, from the most important item to the least important item. The mean rank for each item is also reported. From the Table, it can be seen that the five most important (influential) items were all high risk items.[19] This finding suggests a conservatism bias, and is consistent with prior research (e.g., Kida, 1984; Ashton and Ashton, 1990) that indicated that auditors were more attentive to evidence that suggested potential problems. Restating this in terms of the Belief-Adjustment model and this study, subjects appeared to be more attentive to evidence that supported the hypothesis that the account may contain material misstatements after the audit is completed and an unqualified opinion is reached (i.e., $\beta > \alpha$).

Based on the findings, various combinations of α and β were examined to determine if any particular combination generated audit risk values that corresponded closer to the intuitive judgments. Theoretically, α and β can extend over a range of values from $0 \leq \alpha, \beta \leq 1$. Given this range of values, numer-

[18] The mid-point ranking of 5 was arbitrarily chosen as the cut-off.

[19] A statistical test was also performed to determine if there were similarities in the order in which the subjects ranked the 10 items. A Kendall coefficient of concordance, W, revealed that there was a high degree of agreement among the subjects in their rankings of the 10 items ($W = .490$; $p \leq .001$).

Table 1. Mean Ranks for High/Low Risk Items

Rank	Description of Item	High/Low Risk	Mean Rank [a]
1.	The client's cash flows are not adequate to cover current expenditures and debt commitments.	high	2.39
2.	The client's personnel are not experienced and lack competence.	high	2.71
3.	There has been a high turnover of key personnel.	high	4.11
4.	The client does not maintain adequate separation of duties.	high	4.23
5.	Ratio analysis of profitability and liquidity reveals that the client is performing worse than the industry.	high	4.77
6.	The client's personnel are experienced and competent.	low	6.45
7.	The client maintains adequate separation of duties.	low	7.20
8.	The client's cash flows are adequate to cover current expenditures and debt commitments.	low	7.26
9.	Ratio analysis of profitability and liquidity reveals that the client is performing better than the industry.	low	7.73
10.	There has been a low turnover of key personnel.	low	8.15

[a]The subjects were asked to rank the items from 1 (most influential) to 10 (least influential).

ous possible combinations exist. Hogarth and Einhorn (1992) described an individual who was semi-sensitive towards evidence as having α and β values of 0.5. Based on the preceding discussion pertaining to auditors' sensitivity to evidence and, in particular, the results of prior research and the responses of the auditors in Table 1, the semi-sensitivity α and β combination was used as the starting point. Four combinations trialed were selected to reflect an increasing sensitivity towards positive evidence but a decreasing sensitivity towards negative evidence.[20] The five different combinations of α and β levels

[20] It is acknowledged, however, that it was possible for individuals to exhibit signs of increased sensitivity towards positive evidence yet maintain constant levels of sensitivity towards negative evidence. Consequently, the combinations selected

were used in this experiment. The selected combinations were: (1) $\alpha = 0.5$; $\beta = 0.5$; (2) $\alpha = 0.4$; $\beta = 0.6$; (3) $\alpha = 0.3$; $\beta = 0.7$; (4) $\alpha = 0.2$; $\beta = 0.8$; and (5) $\alpha = 0.1$; $\beta = 0.9$.

Belief Function Model

Srivastava (1993) described the applicability of the Belief Function model to the audit risk judgment using hypothetical estimates. To apply the Belief Function model, four items of evidence had to be integrated. These four items pertained to information concerning the internal control environment, analytical procedures, substantive tests of details, and background information regarding the client. For each item, estimates for three variables had to be established. Specifically, it was necessary to obtain an estimate that: (1) the accounts receivable account was not materially misstated after evaluating information pertaining to that item (denoted as m(ar)); (2) the accounts receivable account was materially misstated after evaluating information pertaining to that item (denoted as $m(\overline{ar})$); and (3) a measure of the extent to which the subject was uncommitted to his or her belief (denoted as $m(ar,\overline{ar})$).

To obtain these estimates based on the subjects' responses in the case study, it was necessary to use a two-step procedure that involved using the principles of probability theory in the first stage, and then converting the outcomes into the Belief Function framework in the second step. In the first stage, probability theory was used to determine (ar) and its complement $(\overline{ar})$ for each item of evidence such that $P(ar) + P(\overline{ar}) = 1$.

Unlike probability theory, which allows for the occurrence of only two possible states (i.e., material misstatements or no material misstatements), the Belief Function framework allows for the expression of some level of uncommitted belief. Consequently, it was necessary to obtain a measure of uncommitted belief or "ignorance" for each item of evidence. A surrogate for the "ignorance" variable was obtained by asking subjects to provide expressions of their confidence in their estimates of inherent risk, control risk, analytical review procedures risk and substantive tests of details risk. This confidence estimate was used to provide a measure of the uncommitted belief or "ignorance" such that (1 - confidence estimate $= m_i(ar,\overline{ar})$). The term $m_i(ar)$ was calculated using $(1 - m_i(\overline{ar}))$. The three terms for each item of evidence were then proportionally adjusted to give the sum of 1.

Using the notation described earlier, the Belief Function model specifies that $m(ar) + m(\overline{ar}) + m(ar,\overline{ar}) = 1$. Thus, to apply the Belief Function model, it was necessary to modify the probability estimates to comply with the specifications of the model. This was accomplished by proportionally adjusting the estimates as illustrated in the following example. Using the internal control item for illustrative purposes, assume a subject had provided a

may reflect a bias in that an increase (or decrease) in one variable was balanced with a decrease (or increase) in the corresponding variable.

response of 40% after evaluating the pertinent information. Given the wording of question used to elicit the response, this was the subject's estimate that the accounts receivable account was not materially misstated after evaluating information pertaining to the internal control environment. Thus, this response was used to establish the subject's estimate of m(ar). If the subject believed that there was a 40% chance that the account was not materially misstated, this would imply a 60% chance that the account was materially misstated using the principles of probability theory. Assume further that the subject placed an 80% confidence estimate on their response. The subject's responses had to be adjusted to reflect their confidence level and to conform with the specifications of the model. This was achieved by multiplying the unadjusted responses by the confidence estimate. Thus, in this example, the estimates of m(ar) and m($\overline{ar}$) as defined by the Belief Function model were 0.32 and 0.48, respectively. The estimate of m(ar,$\overline{ar}$) was computed as 0.2 (i.e., m(ar,$\overline{ar}$) = 1 - confidence level). Note that, after the adjustment, m(ar) + m($\overline{ar}$) + m(ar,$\overline{ar}$) = 1.

Having identified m($\overline{ar}$), m(ar) and m(ar,$\overline{ar}$) for each item of evidence, it was necessary to combine the items of evidence. This was accomplished using Dempster's rule of combination. Dempster's rule is expressed as follows:[21]

$$m(A) = K^{-1}\sum\{m_1(B_1)m_2(B_2)|B_1 \cap B_2 = A, A \neq \phi\} \tag{11}$$

where $K = 1 - \sum\{m_1(B_1)m_2(B_2)|B_1 \cap B_2 = \phi\}$

4.3 Results

The results of comparisons between the subjects' intuitive assessment and the values generated by the various models are summarised in Table 2. It can be seen that the values generated by the various models were in the same direction as the intuitive assessments. However, there were differences in the magnitude. On average, the Belief-Adjustment model combinations provided the highest audit risk values while the audit risk model, the CICA model and its variations provided the lowest audit risk values. The values generated by the audit risk model, CICA model, extended CICA model and combined model were the most divergent from the subjects' intuitive assessments. Paired *t*-tests revealed significant differences between the intuitive assessments and the values generated by the audit risk model, the CICA model and its variations, and the Belief-Adjustment model ($p < .001$). The paired *t*-test indicated that there was no significant difference between the intuitive assessments and the values generated by the Belief Function model.

[21] While this formula applies to circumstances involving a two items of evidence, the same formula can be used to combine more than two items of evidence. This is achieved by combining the first two items to obtain an intermediate m-value which is then combined with the third item of evidence, and so on (Srivastava, 1993).

Table 2. Comparisons of Models with Intuitive Assessments

	Mean	Mean Difference[c]	Paired t-value	p	Absolute Mean Difference[b]
Intuitive Assessment	0.40				
Audit Risk Model	0.04	0.36	12.35	$< .001$	0.86
CICA Model	0.11	0.29	9.19	$< .001$	0.78
Extended CICA	0.05	0.35	11.60	$< .001$	0.84
Combined Model of Posterior Risk	0.07	0.33[a]	10.83	$< .001$	0.80
B-A Model (α=0.5, β=0.5)	0.58	-0.18	-5.03	$< .001$	1.73
B-A Model (α=0.4, β=0.6)	0.62	-0.22	-6.37	$< .001$	1.90
B-A Model (α=0.3, β=0.7)	0.67	-0.27	-7.69	$< .001$	2.07
B-A Model (α=0.2, β=0.8)	0.71	-0.31	-9.01	$< .001$	2.26
B-A Model (α=0.1, β=0.9)	0.76	-0.36	-10.31	$< .001$	2.45
BF Model	0.41	-0.003	-0.01	.947	1.08

[a] compared to intuitive assessments after adjusting for AR^* and TD^*. Interestingly, only 10 subjects opted to revise their assessments. This could reflect two possible causes. First, the information relating to AR^* and TD^* are not considered in the conventional models, and the subjects may have been uncertain of the implications associated with the information provided. Consequently, they may have chosen to ignore the information. Alternatively, the subjects may have perceived that the risk values indicated in the information provided to them was not sufficiently high enough to warrant any revision of their assessment. Specifically, the information that was provided indicated that there was a 20% and 5% chance that the analytical procedures and substantive tests of details, respectively, would indicate material errors when none existed. Thus, it was possible that the subjects may have perceived that the risk of incorrect rejection was not sufficiently high.

[b] absolute mean error difference calculated as the absolute model generated value minus intuitive assessment divided by the intuitive assessment.

[c] mean difference is calculated as the difference between intuitive assessments and model values.

Absolute mean differences were calculated, and these revealed that none of the models were consistent with the subjects' intuitive assessments. Interestingly, the greatest variation occurred when the Belief Adjustment model and the Belief Function model were used. The CICA model had the lowest error. Further analysis using demographic factors was performed. Specifically, comparisons on the basis of firm (Big 6 or non-Big 6) and experience[22] were performed. The results were consistent with those reported in Table 2.

The results of this study can be compared with the results reported by Krishnamoorthy et al. (1999). Krishnamoorthy et al. used a risk-related task to examine the descriptive ability of a Bayesian model based on Cascaded Inference Theory, the Belief-Adjustment model, and the Belief Function model, and it is interesting to compare the two studies to see whether the models can be applied across a range of tasks. In both studies, the models generated predictions that were in the same direction as the subjects' intuitive assessments. However, the magnitude of differences varied in the two studies. Krishnamoorthy et al. reported no significant differences, using paired t-tests, between the subjects' intuitive assessments and the version of the Belief-Adjustment model incorporating both positive and negative evidence. Krishnamoorthy et al also found that the Bayesian model, the version of the Belief-Adjustment model incorporating positive evidence, and the Belief Function model predicted higher values than the intuitive assessments. These results differ from those presented in this study. Paired t-tests indicated that there were no significant differences between the subjects' intuitive assessments and the Belief Function model. However, significant differences were found for the other models examined. The CICA model and its variations predicted lower values than the intuitive assessments, while the Belief-Adjustment model predicted higher values than the intuitive assessments.

5 Conclusions and Limitations

This study investigated the degree of consistency between auditors' intuitive assessment of audit risk and the audit risk values generated by various models. In addition to the traditional audit risk model, this study was interested in the performance of models that allowed for belief revision (i.e., the CICA model and its variations, the Belief-Adjustment model and the Belief Function model).

The results of this study were consistent with earlier research (e.g., Daniel, 1988) that noted that there were inconsistencies between auditors' intuitive

[22] Experience was measured using auditors' position. Two separate analyses were performed. In the first analysis, the responses of partners and managers were compared against the responses of supervisors and below. In the second analysis, partners, managers and supervisors were treated as one group and compared against the seniors and the assistant.

assessments and the traditional audit risk model. Tests of absolute mean differences also indicated inconsistencies between auditors' intuitive assessments and the values generated by the belief revision models examined. Paired t-tests, however, showed no significant differences between auditors' intuitive assessments of audit risk and the Belief Function. This result differs from Krishnamoorthy et al.'s (1999) finding that the Belief-Adjustment model incorporating positive and negative evidence reflected the direction and magnitude of auditors' intuitive assessments. A possible explanation for the different results could be related to differences in the nature of the tasks.

There are also several limitations that could have affected the results of this study. Firstly, some mention must be made about the generalisability of the results. Given that the selection of auditors was limited to one geographical area, caution should be exercised in generalising the results of this study.

Secondly, in the case materials, auditors were required to provide quantitative assessments of risk. However, researchers have noted that individuals may have difficulty in quantifying subjective probabilities (e.g., Chesley, 1975; Hogarth, 1975; Daniel, 1988). Reimers et al. (1993) reported differences in the control risk assessments of subjects who provided linguistic assessments (high, low or moderate risk) and those who provided numerical probabilities. Future studies could examine whether the use of linguistic assessments provide different results to those reported in this study.

Ashton and Ashton (1988) recognised that subjects may be hesitant to use the extreme points of response scales. This could be another possible explanation for the difference between the intuitive assessments and the model-generated values. The auditors were required to provide an intuitive assessment as well as assessments for individual risk components. In essence, if the auditors had avoided using extreme values on the response scale for these assessments, the multiplicative nature of the audit risk model and the Bayesian approach adopted by the CICA model and its variant models would have diluted the effect of the individual components. However, the intuitive assessment would have remained unchanged.

Again, on measurement, another limitation that warrants stating pertains to the arbitrary methods used to obtain the required inputs for the various models examined. Specifically, for the Belief-Adjustment model, an arbitrary midpoint of 50 was used to label evidence items as either positive or negative. In addition, values for the sensitivity to evidence were inferred rather than directly elicited from the subjects. As such, these estimates may not appropriately reflect the subjects' views. A measurement issue also arises in the estimation of the m-values for the Belief Function model. In this paper, the required m-values were not directly elicited from the subjects. Rather, a probability framework was used to infer the m-values. The application of these arbitrary methods to obtain the necessary measurements for the models must be viewed as a limitation to the results of this paper, and future studies could explore more direct methods of eliciting the required inputs.

A further limitation was that this study adopted a simplified view of the audit risk assessment task. The experiment required auditors to focus on assessing audit risk only at the account balance level. As such, the task adopted a simplified approach to audit risk evaluation as it failed to extend the analysis to the financial statement level and the assertion level.

Finally, a potential weakness with experimental case studies is that only a limited amount of information can be incorporated. It is possible that the risk assessment task is dependent on a variety of factors that cannot be integrated in the format of an experimental case. For example, a few of the auditors who participated in the experiment commented that they would have liked to have some additional information or to explain their responses. Consequently, the auditors' responses to the experiments could reflect potential ambiguities arising from insufficient information. Future studies could look at ways of implementing more realistic audit scenarios.

References

1. Arens, A., Loebbecke, J., Best P., and Shailer, G. (1990):Auditing in Australia: An integrated approach , 2nd edition, (Prentice Hall: Australia)
2. Asare, S.K. and Messier, W. (1991): A review of audit research using the Belief-Adjustment model in: L. Ponemon and D.R. Gerhart, eds., Auditing: Advances in behavioral research (Springer-Verlag:New York)
3. Ashton, A., and Ashton, R. (1988): Sequential belief revision in auditing, The Accounting Review, October, 623-41
4. Canadian Institute of Chartered Accountants. (1980): Extent of audit testing, The Canadian Institute of Chartered Accountants
5. Chang, M., and Monroe, G. (1991): An experimental study on the impact of inherent risk, control risk analytical review procedures, and experience on the auditors' planning process, Honours thesis (The University of Western Australia)
6. Chesley, G. (1975): Elicitation of subjective probabilities: A review, The Accounting Review, April, 325-37
7. Cushing, B., and Loebbecke, J. (1983): Analytical approaches to audit risk: A survey and analysis, Auditing: A Journal of Practice and Theory, Vol. 3, No. 1, 23-41
8. Daniel, S. (1988): Some empirical evidence about the assessment of audit risk in practice, Auditing: A Journal of Practice and Theory, Vol. 7, No. 2, 174-81
9. Dusenbury, R., Reimers, J., and Wheeler, S. (1996): An empirical study of belief-based revision and probability-based specifications of audit risk, Auditing: A Journal of Practice and Theory, Vol. 15, No. 2, 12-28
10. Grobstein, M., and Craig, P. (1984): A risk analysis approach to auditing, Auditing: A Journal of Practice and Theory, Vol. 3, No. 2, 1-16
11. Hogarth, R. (1975,): Cognitive processes and the assessment of subjective probability distributions, Journal of the American Statistical Association, Vol. 70, No. 350, 271-89

12. Hogarth, R., and Einhorn, H. (1992): Order effects in belief updating: The Belief-Adjustment model, Cognitive Psychology, 24, 1-55
13. Jiambalvo, J., Waller, W. (1984): Decomposition and assessments of audit risk, Auditing: A Journal of Practice and Theory, Vol. 3, No. 2, 80-88
14. Johnson, E. (1989): Effects of experience, task variables, and prior beliefs on auditors' Sequential Judgments, Working paper (UMI: Ann Arbor)
15. Kida, T. (1984): The impact of hypothesis-testing strategies on auditor use of judgement data, Journal of Accounting Research, Vol. 22, 96-108
16. Kinney, W. (1989): Achieved audit risk and the audit outcome space, Auditing: A Journal of Practice and Theory, Vol. 8 Supplement, 67-84
17. Krishnamoorthy, G., Mock, T., and Washington, M. (1999): A comparative evaluation of belief revision models in auditing, Auditing: A Journal of Practice and Theory, Vol. 18, No. 2, 105-27
18. Leslie, D. (1984): An analysis of the audit framework focusing on inherent risk and the role of statistical sampling in compliance testing, Touche Ross University of Kansas Symposium on Auditing Problems, 89-125
19. Leslie, D., Teitlebaum, A., and Anderson, R. (1979): Dollar unit sampling (Copp Clark Pittman: Toronto)
20. Libby, R., Artman, J., and Willingham, J. (1985): Process susceptibility, control risk, and audit planning, The Accounting Review, April, 212-30
21. Monroe, G., and Therry, L. (1993): The impact of inherent risk, control risk and analytical review results on auditors' planning decisions for the revenue cycle, Working paper (The University of Western Australia)
22. Reimers, J., Wheeler, J., and Dusenbury, R. (1993): The effect of response mode on auditors' control risk assessments, Auditing: A Journal of Practice and Theory, Vol. 12, No. 2, 62-78
23. Shafer, G. (1976): A mathematical theory of evidence (Princeton University Press)
24. Shafer, G. (1982): Belief functions and parametric models, Journal of the Royal Statistical Society, Series B, Vol. 44, No. 3, 322-52
25. Shafer, G., and Srivastava, R. (1990): The Bayesian and Belief-Function formalisms: A general perspective for auditing, Auditing: A Journal of Practice and Theory, Vol. 9 Supplement, 110-48
26. Skerratt, L C., and Woodhead, A. (1992): Modelling Audit Risk, The British Accounting Review, Vol. 24, No. 2, pp. 119-37
27. Smielauskas, W. (1989): A note on bayesian revision models of audit risk practice, Contemporary Acounting Research, Vol. 5, No. 2, 720-32
28. Srivastava, R. (1993): Belief functions and audit decisions, The Auditor's Report, Vol. 17, No. 1, American Accounting Association: Auditing Section
29. Srivastava, R., and Shafer, G. (1992): Belief-function formulas for audit risk, The Accounting Review, April, 249-83
30. Strawser, J. R. (1990): Human information processing and the consistency of audit risk judgments, Accounting and Business Research, Vol. 21, No. 18, 67-75
31. Strawser, J. R. (1991): Examination of the effect of risk model components on perceived audit risk, Auditing: A Journal of Practice and Theory, Vol. 10, No. 1, 126-35
32. Waller, W. S. (1993): Auditors' assessments of inherent and control risk in field settings, The Accounting Review, October, 783-803

The Effectiveness and Efficiency of Belief Based Audit Procedures

Maximilian K. P. Jung and Herwig E. Fink

Department of Accounting and Auditing, University of Graz, Universitaetsstrasse 15/F1, A-8010 Graz, Austria

Abstract. A series of simulation experiments has been carried out in order to compare the effectiveness and efficiency of three different approaches for determining audit risk in complex audit situations. The first approach uses probability theory and the audit risk model to combine two different items of audit evidence from analytical procedures and tests of details. The second approach is based on the belief function framework and uses the Dempster-Shafer rule for combining the two items of evidence. In the third approach, information from analytical procedures is neglected and audit risk is simply determined by tests of details. The results indicate that the belief based audit is always more efficient than a simple one and can be less efficient than the traditional approach. With respect to audit effectiveness, the belief based approach turns out to be best. Furthermore, the results show that the belief based audit is more robust when there are small failures in interpreting information provided by analytical procedures.

1 Introduction

The goal of a financial audit is to express a competent opinion about the fairness of the financial statements. For this purpose, the auditor has to perform effective and efficient audit procedures. Effectiveness in this context means that the auditor will issue an unqualified audit opinion if the financial position is indeed fairly stated. If financial statements are materially misstated, the auditor should either issue a qualified or an adverse opinion. The efficiency of audit procedures is defined as the auditor's ability to express a correct audit opinion about the financial statements at minimum costs. In order to plan an appropriate audit program, the auditor has to know in advance the individual and collective effectiveness and efficiency of the intended audit procedures.

The purpose of this study is to compare the effectiveness and efficiency of three different approaches to handling complex audit situations. In complex audit situations, various items of evidence have to be considered at different levels in order to express an overall opinion about the financial statements. The first (traditional) approach uses the framework of probability theory to plan the nature, timing and extent of several audit procedures and to evaluate the results of the audit. The second (belief based) approach employs the mathematical theory of evidence developed by Shafer [16] and applied to auditing by Srivastava [18] to determine the overall audit risk. In the third (simple) approach, the auditor is restricted to using only one single audit procedure. In the traditional as well as in the belief based audit, the auditor performs a statistical analytical review and a sample-based test of details. In the simple audit, the auditor just uses audit sampling.

The traditional audit approach and especially the audit risk model has long been criticized in literature. Its main drawbacks are usually summarized by the assertion that it is very difficult to interpret the uncertainties included in audit evidence as probabilities. To avoid this weakness the belief based audit approach has been suggested (e.g. [18]).

This study compares the three audit approaches in a series of computer simulations in order to answer the following three research questions:

1. Is the belief based audit approach more effective than the traditional or the simple one?

2. Is the belief based audit more efficient than the other two approaches?

3. Is the belief based audit less sensitive to small errors in interpreting the information provided by analytical procedures?

If it is indeed true that the notion of beliefs provides the better framework for the formalization of audit evidence, then the belief based audit should reveal itself to be more effective than the other two approaches. When compared with the simple or traditional approach, the belief function formalism should cause the actual frequencies of issuing wrong audit opinions approach the values planned by the auditor. Observe that a seemingly high degree of efficiency need not be an argument in favour of a certain audit approach under all circumstances since gains in efficiency can also lead to losses in effectiveness. A good audit approach is characterized by its ability to realize situations in which an increase of efficiency will not harm effectiveness.

Section 2 of this paper gives an overview of the related literature. Section 3 outlines the structure of the simulation experiments. The main results are discussed in section 4. Section 5 provides a summary of our experimental case and a discussion of the appropriateness of belief functions in audit situations.

2 Related Literature

Simulation experiments have a long tradition in audit research. Most of these studies are characterized by the assumption of simple audit structures. This means that it is usually supposed that the auditor employs only one single audit procedure. Grimlund and Felix [9], Mandl and Jung [13], Neter and Loebbecke [14] and Reneau [15], for example, evaluate the performance of statistical sampling techniques, such as mean per unit or dollar unit sampling, in typical audit environments. Chen and Leitch [5] and Knechel [11] are prominent examples for investigations dealing with the effectiveness of statistical procedures for analytical review. The audit situation supposed in this study is more complex. The auditor first carries out an analytical review, the results of which are then used to determine the necessary extent of statistical sampling techniques performed at stage two. The results of both audit procedures are combined to formulate the auditor's final opinion.

Audit risk models are presented by the AICPA in [1], [2] and [3] as well as by the CICA in [6]. They suggest that the extent of statistical tests of details may depend on the information provided by preceeding audit procedures and can be derived on the grounds of traditional probability theory. Elliott and Rogers [8] suggest a heuristic to derive the allowed risk for tests of details. In this study we use the framework of the audit risk model in the context of the traditional approach for combining the two items of evidence. Two ways of combining these items are considered: In the no cutoff case, the probabilities of material overstatements as provided by the analytical review are always used to compute the sample size of the subsequent test of details regardless of their amounts. In the cutoff case, the sample size of the test of details are not reduced if the analytical review indicates a high probability of material overstatements.

The formal aspects of belief functions are developed by Shafer [16]. They have been applied to auditing by Srivastava [18], [19], [20], Srivastava and Shafer [22], [23] and Dutta [7]. Shafer and Srivastava [17] argue that the application of probability theory can mislead the auditor to regard problems as problems of statistical evidence in a too restrictive way, so that nonstatistical evidence, which is especially frequent in auditing, could be taken into the traditional framework in an incorrect way. Another shortcoming of the traditional probability based framework is the difficulty it has in handling ignorance or lack of evidence. Srivastava and Shafer [22] discuss how using belief functions to represent uncertainties in the audit evidence can help to overcome those limitations. Additionally, they assert that taking into consideration all the evidence gathered by the auditor and thinking of it as a network of variables may lead to more efficiency and effectiveness in the planning and evaluation of an audit. Srivastava [19] also claims that the uncertainties included in audit evidence can be better described in terms of belief functions. This study employs the belief function formalism in the context of the belief based audit approach for combining the two items of evidence. In contrast to some studies in the related literature, the evidential network used is fairly simple as it consists of only two items of evidence.

3 Research Methodology

In order to compare the effectiveness, efficiency and robustness of the belief based and the traditional audit approach, a series of computer simulations is carried out. From an overall perspective, each individual simulation consists of two different phases: In phase 1, financial information as presented by the auditee's management is generated. In phase 2, the audit is conducted and an opinion about the fairness of the financial information is expressed.

3.1 Generation of Financial Information (Phase 1)

It is assumed that the auditee has to provide one single piece of financial information for the public (e.g. sales or revenues). The amount of sales or revenues as asserted by the auditee depends on several factors: Firstly, the amount of sales is systematically influenced by the level of economic activity. Secondly, sales or revenues depend on further exogeneous forces which are assumed to be random. Thirdly, irregularities in the auditee's accounting system may cause misstatements of the asserted sales. Phase 1 includes three steps: In step 1, correct monthly sales are computed. In step 2, correct sales are allocated to individual transactions. In step 3, random errors that cause misstatements in some of the transaction are generated.

Step 1: Generation of Correct Monthly Sales or Revenues
Random sequences consisting of 48 correct amounts of monthly sales, y_t with $t = 1, .., 48$, are generated using the following linear relation (see [11], p. 80):

$$y_t = a + bz_t + \epsilon \tag{1}$$

where

$$\begin{aligned} \epsilon &\sim N(0, \sigma_\epsilon^2), \\ z_t &\sim N(u_t, \sigma^2), \\ u_t &\doteq u_0 + \sum_{i=0}^{t-1} gu_i \end{aligned}$$

Here, a and b denote parameters specifying the assumed linear dependency of sales on actual economic activity, z_t. g measures the growth of average economic activity, u_t, which has an initial value of u_0. All other exogeneous forces randomly affecting monthly sales are summarized and designated by the parameter ϵ. The riskiness of the economic environment is expressed by the variances σ_ϵ^2 and σ^2. The audit period lasts from $t = 37, .., 48$. Thus, the correct total revenues of the audit period are $Y = \sum_{t=37}^{48} y_t$.

Step 2: Generation of Correct Sales per Transaction
It is supposed that N individual sales transactions take place in the audit period. In order to derive correct sales per transaction, y_i, with $i = 1, .., N$, the correct total revenues of the audit period, Y, have to be allocated appropriately. It is assumed that the derived sales per transaction are exponentially distributed with mean $\bar{y} = Y/N$ and variance $\sigma_y^2 = (\lambda_y \bar{y})^2$, wherein λ_y denotes some scaling factor. Empirical studies (e.g. [14]) indicate that distributions of real world transactions are frequently positively skewed. Therefore, the exponential distribution seems to be a more realistic model than any symmetrical distribution.

Step 3: Generation of Asserted Sales or Revenues
Asserted sales may differ from the correct amounts due to random errors occurring in the auditee's accounting system. To generate the auditee's assertions, a set of transactions $\mathbf{M}$ is chosen from the population of N. For each selected transaction an amount of error, v_i, is determined, i.e. $v_i \neq 0 \ \ \forall y_i \in \mathbf{M}$. It is supposed that errors are exponentially distributed with mean $\bar{v} = V/M$ and variance $\sigma_v^2 = (\lambda_v \bar{v})^2$ where V denotes the total amount of error, M is the number of incorrect transactions and λ_v is some scaling factor. Empirical studies (e.g. [10]) demonstrate that the exponential distribution is realistic. Transactions not selected do not contain any error, i.e. $v_i = 0 \ \ \forall y_i \notin \mathbf{M}$. Asserted sales per transaction, x_i, and asserted total revenues, X, are calculated by $x_i = y_i + v_i$ for $i = 1, .., N$ and $X = \sum_{i=1}^{N} x_i$, respectively. Furthermore, the parameter m is used to denote the percentage of incorrect transactions in the population, i.e. $m = M/N$, whereas ρ labels the relative amount by which the sales of the audit period are misstated, i.e. $\rho = V/Y$.

3.2 Audit (Phase 2)

It is the auditor's task to express an opinion about the correctness of the asserted sales. In particular, the auditor has to decide whether the hypothesis H_0^A : *Revenues are not misstated* $(X = Y)$ or its alternative H_A^A : *Revenues are materially misstated* $(X \geq Y + V_m)$ is supported by audit evidence. In order to accumulate the necessary information, the auditor carries out two different audit procedures under the traditional as well as the belief based audit approach: A statistical analytical review and a sample-based test of details. If the auditor uses the third (simple) audit approach, he performs the sample based test of details alone. This third approach is analysed for reasons of comparison, only. Its sample sizes will be larger than those of the other two approaches as it uses less information. However, by considering the simple approach the benefits of employing analytical reviews can be demonstrated.

Analytical Review:
The purpose of analytical procedures is to assess the plausibility of asserted

revenues. The auditor first uses the observations of $t = 1, .., 36$ of each sales sequence to compute the coefficients of a linear regression equation:

$$\hat{y}_t = \hat{a} + \hat{b}z_t + \hat{\epsilon} \tag{2}$$

Then, he uses in the monthly economic activities of the audit period to derive predictions for the monthly sales, $\hat{y}_t$ in the periods $t = 37, .., 48$. Estimated total revenues of the audit period, $\hat{Y} = \sum_{t=37}^{48} \hat{y}_t$, are normally distributed according to:

$$\hat{Y} \sim N(\mu_{\hat{Y}}, \sigma^2_{\hat{Y}}) \tag{3}$$

where

$$\mu_{\hat{Y}} = 12(\hat{a} + \hat{b}\bar{z}),$$
$$\sigma^2_{\hat{Y}} = 144(\sigma^2_{\hat{a}} + \bar{z}^2\sigma^2_{\hat{b}} + 2\bar{z}\sigma_{\hat{a}\hat{b}} + \sigma^2_{\hat{\epsilon}})$$

The difference between X and $\hat{Y}$ measures the plausibility of X. In the traditional framework, the degree of plausibility is interpreted as the probability of a material misstatement:

$$\mathbf{P}(incorrect) = \mathbf{P}(\mid \hat{Y} - X \mid \geq V_m) \tag{4}$$

Whereby, V_m denotes the material amount of misstatement. Within the framework of belief functions the degree of plausibility is expressed by beliefs:

$$\mathbf{Bel}(correct),\ \mathbf{Bel}(incorrect) \tag{5}$$

The computation of those beliefs is shown in the Appendix.

Test of Details:
Tests of details are performed to evaluate the amount of the misstatement of the asserted revenues. In order to be confident with either his hypothesis H_0 or alternative H_1, the auditor randomly selects a sample of n transactions from the population of N and expresses an overall opinion based on the realization of the appropriate mean per unit test statistic. The calculation of sample sizes as well as the decision rules employed are outlined in the Appendix.

3.3 Parameter Values

It is assumed throughout the simulations that the auditor's objective is to accept asserted revenues, which are not misstated, with probability $1-\alpha = 0.95$. If sales are materially misstated the auditor wants to reject them with probability $1 - \beta = 0.95$. α (β) designates the risk of incorrect rejection (acceptance). The materiality threshold is fixed at $\rho_m = 0.1$ of asserted sales and

$V_m = \rho_m$ X. The values for α, β and ρ_m are arbitrary. It is assumed that the results will not change their characteristics if those amounts are altered.
Actual misstatements are taken from the set $\rho \in \{0, 0.\dot{1}\}$ of correct sales. If $\rho = 0$, then sales are correctly stated. If $\rho = 0.\dot{1}$, they are materially overstated, since $0.\dot{1}Y = 0.1X$. Houghton and Fogarty [10] report that overstatements of net income account for approximately two-thirds of the weighted errors detected in real audit situations. Overstatements were both more frequent and larger than errors of understatement.
In generating monthly sales sequences, eight different cases, as summarized in Table 1, are considered. Here, cases I - IV are high growth settings, whereas

Table 1. Parameter Values for Monthly Sales Sequences

No.	u_0	g	σ_u^2	a	b	σ_ϵ^2
I	100	0.005	100	500	5	10000
II	100	0.005	100	500	2.5	10000
III	100	0.005	25	500	5	2500
IV	100	0.005	25	500	2.5	2500
V	100	0.0025	100	500	5	10000
VI	100	0.0025	100	500	2.5	10000
VII	100	0.0025	25	500	5	2500
VIII	100	0.0025	25	500	2.5	2500

V - VIII are characterized by low average economic growth. Settings I and II (V and VI) are considerably riskier than II and III (VII and VIII). In I and III (V and VII), the amount of variance which is unexplained by a linear regression equation is substantially lower than in the corresponding settings II and IV (VI and VIII). Linear regression should work best in III (VII) and worst in II (VI).
It is supposed that the scaling factors used for the allocation of periodical sales on populations of individual transactions and for the step of error generation are $\lambda_y \in \{0.25, 0.5\}$ and $\lambda_v \in \{0.25, 0.5\}$, respectively.
The number of transactions is set to $N = 1000$. The fraction of incorrect transactions is taken from $m \in \{0.4, 0.8\}$.
If $\lambda_y = 0.5$ or $\lambda_v = 0.5$, the distributions of sales per transaction and errors are strongly (positively) skewed. If $m = 0.8$, errors are distributed over a large number of transctions. The individual amount of error is small. If $m = 0.4$, errors are more concentrated. The total number of simulated parameter combinations is 128 ($= 2 \times 8 \times 2 \times 2 \times 2$). For each parameter combination, 10000 audit situations are simulated and evaluated. The software is programmed using Visual Basic 5.0 and runs under Windows NT.

Since the focus of this study is on the combination of audit evidence from different sources and not on the quality of evidence provided by one single audit procedure, the sampling technique as well as the method used for analytical review is held constant. It is assumed that in reality the characteristics of the results also hold if other, more sophisticated audit techniques are employed.

4 Results

Efficiency is measured by comparing sample sizes. An audit approach is more efficient if a smaller sample is needed to formulate a correct audit judgement. The effectiveness of an audit approach is measured by comparing the actual probabilities of acceptance with the objectives stated by the auditor. The abiltity of an audit approach to remain efficient and effective if the auditor makes small errors in interpreting the information provided by analytical procedures, is called robustness. The two types of the traditional audit approach considered, i.e. the cutoff and the no cutoff case, are described in the Appendix.

4.1 Efficiency

To provide a first illustrative insight, Tables 2 - 4 compare the average sample sizes necessary for the three audit approaches under consideration. In the tables, the term "cutoff" is used to indicate that under the traditional approach with cutoff (TRA2) the results of the analytical review are used to reduce subsequent sample sizes if they do not indicate a high risk of material overstatements. Formally, under (TRA2) the results of the analytical review will not be used if estimated revenues exceed the book value plus the materiality threshold. For details refer to the appendix.
The results indicate that average sample sizes strongly depend on the three parameters λ_y, λ_v and m. The intuition is straightforward: As λ_y, λ_v and m influence the variance of the distribution of asserted revenues per transaction, and as this variance plays a key role in computing the sample size, the average sample size must increase if λ_y, λ_v and m do.
If sales are not misstated, Table 2 shows that the traditional audit without cutoff (TRA1) leads to smaller sample sizes than the belief based audit (BEL). Due to the fact that this approach does not use the results of the analytical review, the highest sample sizes are needed under the simple approach (NAP). The sample sizes of the traditional audit with cutoff (TRA2) are only slightly smaller than those of the (NAP). This implies that the analytical review frequently indicates the existence of material overstatements and that, therefore, the auditor is not willing to reduce the sample sizes of the subsequent tests of details. Sample sizes of (TRA2) are also higher than those of (TRA1) and (BEL).
Further insights can be gained by observing that sample sizes for both the

Table 2. Average Sample Sizes for Correctly Stated Sales

	I	II	III	IV	V	VI	VII	VIII
No Misstatements ($\rho = 0$)								
$\lambda_y = 0.25$								
NAP	81.03	81.05	81.08	81.08	81.08	81.05	81.06	81.07
TRA1	53.72	63.37	24.77	36.44	54.29	64.09	24.69	35.56
TRA2	80.92	81.01	80.88	80.86	81.25	81.00	80.76	80.91
BEL	71.41	76.92	31.60	56.39	71.33	77.27	31.27	55.25
$\lambda_y = 0.5$								
NAP	324.15	324.05	324.16	324.19	324.15	324.20	324.20	324.09
TRA1	214.74	253.48	98.99	145.76	217.05	256.22	98.72	142.17
TRA2	323.70	324.02	323.21	323.44	323.84	324.16	323.15	323.87
BEL	285.48	307.56	126.42	225.45	285.04	308.99	125.06	220.95

NAP ... No Analytical Procedures, TRA1 ... Traditional Approach without Cutoff
TRA2 ... Traditional Approach with Cutoff, BEL ... Belief Functions Approach

belief based and the traditional audit approach without cutoff are substantially smaller in cases III and VII than in all other cases considered whereas under the simple as well as the traditional approach with cutoff, sample sizes in cases III and VII seem to be equal to the others. The first part of this observation is due to the fact that cases III and VII are those which are most favourable to the application of linear regression techniques. Analytical procedures will correctly indicate low probabilities (or beliefs) of material misstatements of revenues and sample sizes can be reduced accordingly. If those low probabilities are still higher than the threshold used in the traditional approach with cutoff or if they are not used at all, sample sizes will not be adapted. This explains the second part of the observation.

If revenues are materially overstated, Tables 3 and 4 show that the traditional approach without cutoff leads to the smallest sample sizes followed by the belief based audit, the traditional approach with cutoff and the simple audit. To sum up, we conclude that, corresponding to intuition, audit efficiency can be increased substantially by using analytical procedures. In addition, the following two central statements seem to be supported:

1. Average sample sizes are smaller under both the belief based and the traditional approach without cutoff than under a simple audit.
2. Average sample sizes are smaller under the traditional approach without cutoff than under the belief based approach.

Table 3. Average Sample Sizes for Overstated Sales

	I	II	III	IV	V	VI	VII	VIII
Material Overstatements ($\rho = 0.1$)								
$(m, \lambda_y, \lambda_v) = (0.8, 0.25, 0.25)$								
NAP	70.49	70.49	70.49	70.50	70.48	70.50	70.46	70.50
TRA1	54.39	56.87	52.93	52.42	55.43	57.42	53.45	53.38
TRA2	70.46	70.41	70.46	70.50	70.46	70.47	70.39	70.45
BEL	68.75	68.94	68.47	68.28	69.22	69.12	68.93	68.75
$(m, \lambda_y, \lambda_v) = (0.8, 0.25, 0.5)$								
NAP	73.49	73.48	73.51	73.50	73.49	73.49	73.49	73.47
TRA1	56.83	59.36	55.23	54.72	57.86	59.93	55.78	55.75
TRA2	73.49	73.37	73.49	73.49	73.47	73.45	73.49	73.44
BEL	71.68	71.98	71.32	71.14	72.14	72.06	71.84	71.69
$(m, \lambda_y, \lambda_v) = (0.8, 0.5, 0.25)$								
NAP	267.68	267.71	267.71	267.74	267.77	267.75	267.71	267.71
TRA1	207.20	216.38	201.54	199.48	210.80	218.60	203.33	203.17
TRA2	267.65	267.70	267.61	267.65	267.64	267.67	267.60	267.71
BEL	261.75	261.78	260.56	259.30	263.17	262.72	262.13	261.73
$(m, \lambda_y, \lambda_v) = (0.8, 0.5, 0.5)$								
NAP	270.85	270.87	270.92	270.85	270.76	270.88	270.74	270.72
TRA1	209.65	218.64	203.66	201.82	213.05	221.07	205.65	205.73
TRA2	270.80	270.89	270.86	270.88	270.90	270.57	270.80	270.83
BEL	264.53	265.10	263.39	262.34	266.55	265.65	262.13	264.55

NAP ... No Analytical Procedures, TRA1 ... Traditional Approach without Cutoff
TRA2 ... Traditional Approach with Cutoff, BEL ... Belief Functions Approach

Table 4. Average Sample Sizes for Overstated Sales

	I	II	III	IV	V	VI	VII	VIII
Material Overstatements ($\rho = 0.1$)								
$(m, \lambda_y, \lambda_v) = (0.4, 0.25, 0.25)$								
NAP	87.76	87.69	87.72	87.71	87.70	87.72	87.72	87.67
TRA1	67.83	70.79	65.90	65.33	69.00	71.51	66.58	66.53
TRA2	87.70	87.63	87.70	87.71	87.70	87.67	87.76	87.67
BEL	85.60	85.80	85.21	84.91	86.11	85.94	85.70	85.72
$(m, \lambda_y, \lambda_v) = (0.4, 0.25, 0.5)$								
NAP	93.67	93.61	93.65	93.66	93.61	93.65	93.65	93.62
TRA1	72.44	75.69	70.53	69.85	73.77	76.48	71.17	71.08
TRA2	93.66	93.65	93.69	93.74	93.66	93.64	93.62	93.67
BEL	91.48	91.74	91.06	90.86	92.12	91.89	91.74	91.56
$(m, \lambda_y, \lambda_v) = (0.4, 0.5, 0.25)$								
NAP	285.22	285.22	285.22	285.22	285.22	285.22	285.22	285.22
TRA1	220.62	230.35	214.40	212.59	224.32	232.50	216.64	216.37
TRA2	285.39	285.12	285.20	285.32	285.21	285.75	285.13	285.05
BEL	278.07	278.89	277.29	276.09	280.02	279.53	278.78	278.64
$(m, \lambda_y, \lambda_v) = (0.4, 0.5, 0.5)$								
NAP	291.22	291.16	291.12	291.22	291.18	291.12	291.12	291.16
TRA1	225.08	235.15	218.87	216.90	229.08	237.55	221.24	221.13
TRA2	291.00	291.42	291.37	291.09	291.19	290.98	291.10	290.95
BEL	284.47	284.89	283.09	281.77	285.86	285.28	284.79	284.27

NAP ... No Analytical Procedures, TRA1 ... Traditional Approach without Cutoff
TRA2 ... Traditional Approach with Cutoff, BEL ... Belief Functions Approach

To be more exact, these findings are tested by means of t-Tests. The corresponding hypotheses are:

H_0^1: *Average sample size is not larger under the belief-based approach than under the traditional approach without cutoff*
H_0^2: *Average sample size is not lager under the simple audit than under the belief-based approach*
H_0^3: *Average sample size under the traditional audit approach equals that of the simple audit*

For the first two hypotheses the test statistics range form 4.4 to 126.4 under all circumstances considered. Therefore, both hypotheses are rejected at high levels of significance. For the third hypothesis, test statistics range from -0.93 to 1.35 implying that this hypothesis cannot always be rejected with high significance.
This strongly confirms the assumption that the efficiency of the belief based audit lies somewhere between the efficiency of an audit not employing analytical procedures and the efficiency of the traditional audit approach without cutoff. Furthermore, the gain in efficiency from the employment of the traditional approach with cutoff appears to be rather small.

4.2 Effectiveness

The effectiveness of an audit approach is expressed by the degree with which it is able to meet the auditor's objectives. Under the parameter values set for these simulations, a certain approach is qualified as effective if it leads the auditor to accept correctly stated (materially misstated) revenues with a probability of at least 0.95 (at most 0.05).
Table 5 shows the frequencies of acceptance for the three audit approaches if sales are not misstated. Frequencies of acceptance higher than 0.95 are labeled with ** in order to indicate full compliance with the auditor's objectives. Frequencies within a region of tolerance of 0.01, i.e. frequencies higher than 0.94 and not higher than 0.95, are labeled with *. It can be seen from Table 5 that the auditor completely omitting analytical procedures (NAP) will not be able to meet his objectives if revenues are correctly stated and $\lambda_y = 0.25$. If $\lambda_y = 0.5$, then the results all lie within the region of tolerance. The performance of the traditional approach without cutoff (TRA1) is poor. It is never able to completely satisfy the auditor and, if $\lambda_y = 0.25$, it does not even 'touch' the region of tolerance. Furthermore, the traditional approach without cutoff performs worst in cases III and VII. The last finding strongly indicates that incorrect information processing is taking place under this audit approach.
The results improve, if the auditor employs the traditional approach with cutoff (TRA2). This means that the auditor will not use the results of the

Table 5. Frequency of Acceptance of Correctly Stated Sales Depending on the Audit Approach Employed

	I	II	III	IV	V	VI	VII	VIII
No Misstatements ($\rho = 0$)								
$\lambda_y = 0.25$								
NAP	0.9366	0.9370	0.9371	0.9379	0.9379	0.9377	0.9374	0.9359
TRA1	0.9335	0.9335	0.9127	0.9220	0.9328	0.9327	0.9121	0.9202
TRA2	0.9373	0.9388	0.9355	0.9381	0.9398	0.9366	0.9358	0.9352
BEL	0.9425*	0.9398	0.9511**	0.9445*	0.9411*	0.9421*	0.9521**	0.9451*
$\lambda_y = 0.5$								
NAP	0.9449*	0.9436*	0.9436*	0.9447*	0.9438*	0.9439*	0.9444*	0.9441*
TRA1	0.9428*	0.9476*	0.9387	0.9404*	0.9452*	0.9465*	0.9376	0.9436*
TRA2	0.9464*	0.9454*	0.9460*	0.9433*	0.9478*	0.9443*	0.9438*	0.9433*
BEL	0.9481*	0.9484*	0.9486*	0.9491*	0.9467*	0.9494*	0.9507**	0.9479*

NAP ... No Analytical Procedures, TRA1 ... Traditional Approach without Cutoff
TRA2 ... Traditional Approach with Cutoff, BEL ... Belief Functions Approach
* ... within one percent of auditor's objectives
** ... meeting auditor's objectives

analytical review to justify a reduction of subsequent sample sizes if they indicate a high probability of material overstatements. He is then able to come close to the simple audit, which means that the results are inside the region of tolerance at least for $\lambda_y = 0.5$. Table 2 shows the losses in efficiency associated with the use of the simple audit and the traditional approach with cutoff.

In contrast, the belief based audit (BEL) comes close to compliance with the auditor's objectives under almost all circumstances considered. In cases III and VII, the auditor's objectives are completely met, if $\lambda_y = 0.25$. In case II, the frequency of acceptance only just misses the specified region of tolerance for $\lambda_y = 0.25$.

Tables 6 and 7 show the frequencies of incorrect acceptances if sales are materially overstated. If $m = 0.8$, the simple audit (NAP) never comes close to meeting the auditor's objectives. HOwever, if $m = 0.4$, it either fully satisfies the auditor or is in the region of tolerance.

The same can be said of the the traditional audit approach with cutoff (TRA1): If $m = 0.8$, the auditor's objectives are missed. If $m = 0.4$ they are more or less met.

Table 6. Frequency of Acceptance of Misstated Sales Depending on the Audit Approach Employed

	I	II	III	IV	V	VI	VII	VIII
Material Overstatements ($\rho = 0.1$)								
$(m, \lambda_y, \lambda_v) = (0.8, 0.25, 0.25)$								
NAP	0.0793	0.0786	0.0789	0.0804	0.0783	0.0798	0.0796	0.0799
TRA1	0.1489	0.1329	0.1632	0.1656	0.1433	0.1331	0.1587	0.1575
TRA2	0.0780	0.0794	0.0764	0.0744	0.0796	0.0792	0.0792	0.0806
BEL	0.0348**	0.0367**	0.0378**	0.0359**	0.0362**	0.0341**	0.0321**	0.0351**
$(m, \lambda_y, \lambda_v) = (0.8, 0.25, 0.5)$								
NAP	0.0668	0.0657	0.0660	0.0660	0.0654	0.0654	0.0654	0.0669
TRA1	0.1373	0.1202	0.1416	0.1566	0.1233	0.1211	0.1431	0.1427
TRA2	0.0698	0.0646	0.0666	0.0656	0.0686	0.0670	0.0664	0.0684
BEL	0.0354**	0.0348**	0.0413**	0.0393**	0.0326**	0.0353**	0.0376**	0.0362**
$(m, \lambda_y, \lambda_v) = (0.8, 0.5, 0.25)$								
NAP	0.0718	0.0731	0.0728	0.0723	0.0723	0.0720	0.0719	0.0713
TRA1	0.1386	0.1213	0.1437	0.1571	0.1347	0.1164	0.1411	0.1497
TRA2	0.0726	0.0716	0.0724	0.0704	0.0708	0.0658	0.0714	0.0720
BEL	0.0472**	0.0402**	0.0444**	0.0443**	0.0405**	0.0423**	0.0424**	0.0443**
$(m, \lambda_y, \lambda_v) = (0.8, 0.5, 0.5)$								
NAP	0.0627	0.0627	0.0631	0.0627	0.0633	0.0630	0.0632	0.0633
TRA1	0.1304	0.1228	0.1573	0.1552	0.1287	0.1174	0.1484	0.1440
TRA2	0.0634	0.0628	0.0642	0.0626	0.0622	0.0632	0.0634	0.0626
BEL	0.0418**	0.0401**	0.0411**	0.0448**	0.0422**	0.0414**	0.0424**	0.0387**

NAP ... No Analytical Procedures, TRA1 ... Traditional Approach without Cutoff
TRA2 ... Traditional Approach with Cutoff, BEL ... Belief Functions Approach
* ... within one percent of auditor's objectives
** ... meeting auditor's objectives

Table 7. Frequency of Acceptance of Misstated Sales Depending on the Audit Approach Employed

	I	II	III	IV	V	VI	VII	VIII
Material Overstatements ($\rho = 0.1$)								
$(m, \lambda_y, \lambda_v) = (0.4, 0.25, 0.25)$								
NAP	0.0459**	0.0446**	0.0450**	0.0436**	0.0444**	0.0436**	0.0439**	0.0435**
TRA1	0.0910	0.0838	0.1055	0.1026	0.0868	0.0792	0.0976	0.0982
TRA2	0.0420**	0.0422**	0.0436**	0.0436**	0.0432**	0.0426**	0.0444**	0.0440**
BEL	0.0363**	0.0386**	0.0405**	0.0404**	0.0342**	0.0354**	0.0396**	0.0407**
$(m, \lambda_y, \lambda_v) = (0.4, 0.25, 0.5)$								
NAP	0.0313**	0.0314**	0.0292**	0.0309**	0.0308**	0.0322**	0.0298**	0.0307**
TRA1	0.0787	0.0686	0.0856	0.0902	0.0721	0.0613	0.0842	0.0837
TRA2	0.0324**	0.0294**	0.0324**	0.0268**	0.0276**	0.0316**	0.0280**	0.0322**
BEL	0.0399**	0.0400**	0.0360**	0.0371**	0.0332**	0.0368**	0.0352**	0.0385**
$(m, \lambda_y, \lambda_v) = (0.4, 0.5, 0.25)$								
NAP	0.0566*	0.0583*	0.0576*	0.0566*	0.0583*	0.0576*	0.0566*	0.0583*
TRA1	0.1194	0.1095	0.1397	0.1328	0.1167	0.1079	0.1276	0.1327
TRA2	0.0600	0.0550*	0.0560*	0.0562*	0.0586*	0.0570*	0.0594*	0.0564*
BEL	0.0450**	0.0393**	0.0440**	0.0487**	0.0398**	0.0431**	0.0450**	0.0454**
$(m, \lambda_y, \lambda_v) = (0.4, 0.5, 0.5)$								
NAP	0.0553*	0.0532*	0.0540*	0.0565*	0.0538*	0.0562*	0.0549*	0.0530*
TRA1	0.1136	0.1022	0.1276	0.1315	0.1079	0.1059	0.1252	0.1245
TRA2	0.0578*	0.0552*	0.0582*	0.0574*	0.0570*	0.0578*	0.0564*	0.0560*
BEL	0.0415**	0.0421**	0.0453**	0.0446**	0.0400**	0.0410**	0.0443**	0.0463**

NAP ... No Analytical Procedures, TRA1 ... Traditional Approach without Cutoff
TRA2 ... Traditional Approach with Cutoff, BEL ... Belief Functions Approach
* ... within one percent of auditor's objectives
** ... meeting auditor's objectives

The traditional audit without cutoff (TRA2) is revealed to be worst under all circumstances as it is never able to come near the region of tolerance. Again, the belief based approach (BEL) is the only one that is able to meet the auditor's objectives under all circumstances considered.

4.3 Robustness

In order to analyse the robustness of the three audit approaches considered, the simulations are repeated under the assumption that revenues of the audit period do not follow the same trend as sales of prior periods. It is supposed that the parameters a, b and σ_ϵ^2 of (1) have different values in months $t = 37, ..., 48$ than in $t = 1, ..., 36$. Using the regression procedure described above will lead the auditor to derive poor predictions of the revenues in the audit period. Table 8 shows the parameter values actually assumed. All cases are

Table 8. Parameter Values for Monthly Sales Sequences

No.	u_0	g	σ_u^2	a	b	σ_ϵ^2
Periods t = 1, ..., 36						
III	100	0.005	25	500	5	2500
Periods t = 37, ..., 48						
IIIa	100	0.005	25	525	5	2500
IIIb	100	0.005	25	475	5	2500
IIIc	100	0.005	25	500	5.25	2500
IIId	100	0.005	25	500	4.75	2500
IIIe	100	0.005	25	500	5	2756
IIIf	100	0.005	25	500	5	2256

derived from case III of Table 1, by changing only one of the parameters. In IIIa, IIIc and IIId the values are increased by a small percentage of 5Table 9 demonstrates the effects on sample sizes. If no misstatements are present, an increase of a, b and σ_ϵ^2 has the consequence that sales of the audit period tend to move away from the mean estimated by regression analysis. Thus, the auditor observing these results provided by analytical procedures is induced to think that the risk of a material misstatement is higher. The auditor will increase sample sizes on average.

If misstatements exist, the revenues of the audit period also move away from the prediction as derived from linear regression. If this move is positive as in case IIIa and IIIc, and if the material overstatement is added, the analytical procedures lead the auditor to assume a very high risk. Average sample size

Table 9. Average Sample Sizes

	III	IIIa	IIIb	IIIc	IIId	IIIe	IIIf
No Misstatements ($\rho = 0$)							
$\lambda_y = 0.5$							
NAP	324.16	324.06	324.28	324.21	324.31	324.19	324.12
TRA1	98.99	100.20	118.33	101.99	123.47	100.22	99.34
TRA2	323.21	323.16	324.23	323.61	323.77	322.94	323.91
BEL	126.42	132.09	185.51	140.63	199.19	130.19	127.03
Material Overstatements ($\rho = 0.1$)							
$(m, \lambda_y, \lambda_v) = (0.4, 0.5, 0.5)$							
NAP	291.12	291.10	291.12	291.03	291.15	291.19	291.12
TRA1	218.87	248.53	172.60	255.40	160.51	216.15	217.40
TRA2	291.37	291.21	291.21	291.14	291.17	291.23	291.11
BEL	283.09	289.97	257.51	290.42	248.07	281.75	282.67

NAP ... No Analytical Procedures, TRA1 ... Traditional Approach without Cutoff
TRA2 ... Traditional Approach with Cutoff, BEL ... Belief Functions Approach

is increased. If this move is negative, as it is in case IIIb and IIId, the effect is compensated by the existing material overstatements. Then, the analytical review induces the auditor to think that the risk of a misstatement is low. He will reduce the sample size. In cases IIIe and IIIf, sales of the audit period are not shifted in any systematic manner and the effect on average sample size is comparatively small.

Table 10 demonstrates the effect on effectiveness. The belief based audit (BEL) reacts to small errors in interpreting the information provided by analytical procedures in the least sensitive way. In almost all cases it comes close to meeting the auditor's objctives. However, in the two situations, in which the revenues are shifted away from the mean prediction in a negative direction and this effect is compensated by the material error, even the belief based approach fails compliance. Under these circumstances the performance of the traditional approach without cutoff (TRA1) is inferior. As can be seen from Table 10, the auditor employing the traditional approach without cutoff would run an actual risk of committing an error of incorrect rejection of 0.2133 in case IIIb or 0.2397 in case IIId. The auditor carrying out a belief based audit is confronted with an actual risk of 0.0716 or 0.0857. The planned risk is 0.05. If the auditor uses the simple approach (NAP) or the traditional

Table 10. Frequency of Acceptance

	III	IIIa	IIIb	IIIc	IIId	IIIe	IIIf
No Misstatements ($\rho = 0$)							
$\lambda_y = 0.5$							
NAP	0.9436*	0.9445*	0.9441*	0.9431*	0.9413*	0.9434*	0.9470*
TRA1	0.9387	0.9381	0.9389	0.9371	0.9415*	0.9417*	0.9358
TRA2	0.9460*	0.9464*	0.9438*	0.9470*	0.9440*	0.9442*	0.9432*
BEL	0.9486*	0.9491*	0.9510**	0.9512**	0.9520**	0.9487*	0.9471*
Material Overstatements ($\rho = 0.1$)							
$(m, \lambda_y, \lambda_v) = (0.4, 0.5, 0.5)$							
NAP	0.0540*	0.0547*	0.0549*	0.0541*	0.0533*	0.0522*	0.0552*
TRA1	0.1276	0.0944	0.2133	0.0814	0.2397	0.1338	0.1331
TRA2	0.0582*	0.0518*	0.0530*	0.0514*	0.0506*	0.0516*	0.0530*
BEL	0.0453**	0.0401**	0.0716	0.0392**	0.0857	0.0450**	0.0440**

NAP ... No Analytical Procedures, TRA1 ... Traditional Approach without Cutoff
TRA2 ... Traditional Approach with Cutoff, BEL ... Belief Functions Approach
* ... within one percent of auditor's objectives
** ... meeting auditor's objectives

approach with cutoff (TRA2) he is able to achieve results lying in the region of tolerance but not fully meeting his objectives.

5 Summary

Following the results presented above, the belief based audit approach has to be judged to be the most appropriate tool for the purpose of conducting financial audits. It is not the the most efficient approach, but it clearly outperforms the traditional approach in terms of effectiveness. In situations in which financial statements are materially misstated, the auditor using the traditional approach without cutoff is confronted with unintentionally large risks of committing errors of incorrect rejection. These errors could eventually lead to losses due to costly court cases or due to damage to the auditor's reputation. The auditor can avoid these risks by employing the traditional audit approach with cutoff or the belief based audit approach. Of these two approaches the belief based audit appears to be the more efficient one. Further advantages of the belief based audit are: The smaller risk of errors of incorrect acceptance and the robustness with respect to errors in interpreting the information provided by analytical procedures. The assertion that beliefs better represent the uncertainties included in audit evidence is confirmed.

The simulations carried out are simplified in various ways in order to handle the computational complexities. Nevertheless, the audit situations generated remain realistic with respect to the key assumptions regarding the distributions of transactions and errors. The simulations of more complex and therefore even more realistic circumstances is open to further research.

6 Appendix

This appendix outlines the formalisms underlying the traditional and the belief based audit approaches as applied in the simulations described above.

6.1 Traditional Approach

If revenues predicted by means of regression analysis, $\hat{Y}$, are distributed according to (3) and if X is the asserted amount of sales, the probability of a misstatement that is larger than the materiality threshold is computed by:

$$\mathbf{P}(incorrect) = \mathbf{P}(\mid \hat{Y} - X \mid \geq V_m) \tag{6}$$

In terms of the audit risk model, this probability is equivalent to the risk that a material error occurred and was not detected by the auditee's internal controls, or

$$\mathbf{IR} \times \mathbf{CR} \doteq \mathbf{P}(incorrect) \tag{7}$$

If the auditor is willing to accept a total audit risk of **AR** or β, the neccessary detection risk of the subsequent tests of details, **DR** or $\hat{\beta}$ is calculated by:

$$\hat{\beta} \doteq \mathbf{DR} = \frac{\mathbf{AR}}{\mathbf{IR} \times \mathbf{CR}} \tag{8}$$

In the simulations, $\hat{\beta}$ was not allowed to decrease below a level of 0.5. In the traditional approach without cutoff (TRA1 in the text) formula (8) is applied regardless of the results achieved by analytical procedures. If a cutoff level is added to the traditional approach (TRA2 in the text), detection risk is calculated according to (8) only if $\mid X - \hat{Y} \mid \leq V_m$. If this difference is larger, the detection risk is set equal to the overall audit risk ($\hat{\beta} = \beta$). This means that the results of the analytical review are only used if the do not indicate a high probability of material overstatements. The traditional sample size necessary to achieve the desired audit risk is calculated by:

$$n_{tr} = \frac{\sigma_x^2 \times (u_{1-\alpha/2} + u_{\hat{\beta}})^2}{V_m^2} \tag{9}$$

Here, σ_x^2 is the variance of the distribution of asserted sales. $u_{1-\alpha/2}$ and $u_{\hat{\beta}}$ denote quantiles of the standard normal distribution. The evaluation of the sample results is standard. If the test statistic lies inside (outside) the acceptance region a positive (adverse) opinion is expressed. The test statistic for mean per unit sampling is approximately normally distributed and given by:

$$T = \frac{\bar{X} - \mu}{\sigma^2} \times \sqrt{n} \tag{10}$$

Here, μ and σ designate the sample mean and variance.

6.2 Belief Functions

The basic notions necessary in the belief function framework, such as **m**-values, belief and plausibility are outlined elsewhere (eg. [16], [18], [23]). If the auditor's desired level of audit risk is **AR** or β, his desired overall level of belief, **Bel**(*overall*), is

$$\mathbf{Bel}(overall) = 1 - e^{-\frac{u_\beta^2}{2}} \tag{11}$$

Furthermore, if revenues predicted by means of regression analysis, $\hat{Y}$, are distributed according to (3) and if X is the asserted amount of sales, the belief for correctly stated revenues depending on the results of the analytical procedures is given by:

$$\mathbf{Bel}(correct) = \begin{cases} 1 - e^{\frac{(V_m - |X-\hat{Y}|)^2}{2\sigma_{\hat{Y}}^2}} & \text{if } | X - \hat{Y} | \leq V_m \\ 0 & \text{otherwise} \end{cases} \tag{12}$$

The belief for incorrect sales derived by analytical review is:

$$\mathbf{Bel}(incorrect) = \begin{cases} 1 - e^{\frac{(V_m - (X-\hat{Y}))^2}{2\sigma_{\hat{Y}}^2}} & \text{if } X - \hat{Y} < -V_m \\ 1 - e^{\frac{(-V_m + (X-\hat{Y}))^2}{2\sigma_{\hat{Y}}^2}} & \text{if } X - \hat{Y} > V_m \\ 0 & \text{otherwise} \end{cases} \tag{13}$$

The necessary amount of belief, which has to be contributed by tests of details in order to be able to reach the overall desired belief is calculated using Dempster's rule:

$$\mathbf{Bel}(necessary) = \begin{cases} \frac{\mathbf{Bel}(overall) - \mathbf{Bel}(correct)}{1 - \mathbf{Bel}(correct)} & \text{if } | X - \hat{Y} | < V_m \\ \frac{\mathbf{Bel}(overall)}{1 - \mathbf{Bel}(incorrect) \times [1 - \mathbf{Bel}(overall)]} & \text{otherwise} \end{cases} \tag{14}$$

Bel(*necessary*) was not allowed to exceed **Bel**(*overall*). Sample size is calculated according to

$$n_{bel} = \frac{\sigma_x^2 \times [u_{1-\alpha/2} + \sqrt{-2 \times ln(1 - \mathbf{Bel}(necessary)}]^2}{V_m^2} \tag{15}$$

The evaluation of the sample results uses the same test statistic (10) as the traditional audit approach. The rejection region starts at

$$\frac{V_m \times \sqrt{n}}{\sigma} - \sqrt{-2 \times ln[1 - \mathbf{Bel}(overall)]} \quad (16)$$

which approximates the β quantil of the standard normal distribution.

References

1. AICPA (1973) Statement on Auditing Procedures No. 54: The Auditor's Study and Evaluation of Internal Control. Journal of Accountancy. **135**, March, 56–71
2. AICPA (1981) Statement on Auditing Standards No. 39: Audit Sampling. Journal of Accountancy. **152**, August, 106–110
3. AICPA (1984) Statement on Auditing Standards No. 47: Audit Risk and Materiality in Conducting an Audit. Journal of Accountancy. **157**, February, 143–146
4. Arens A. A., Loebbecke J. K. (1996) Auditing an Integrated Approach. 7th edition. Englewood Cliffs
5. Chen, Y., Leitch R. A. (1998) The Error Detection of Structural Analytical Procedures: A Simulation Study. Auditing: A Journal of Practice and Theory. **17**, 36–70
6. CICA (1980) The Extent of Audit Testing. A Research Study, Toronto
7. Dutta S.K. (1991) Evidence Aggregation for Planning and Evaluation of Audit: A Theoretical Study. University of Kansas
8. Elliott R. K., Rogers J. R. (1972) Relating Statistical Sampling to Audit Objectives. Journal of Accountancy. **134**, July, 46–55
9. Grimlund R. A., Felix W. L. (1987) Simulation Evidence and Analysis of Alternative Methods of Evaluation Dollar-Unit Samples. Accounting Review. **62**, 455–479
10. Houghton C. W., Fogarty J. A. (1991) Inherent Risk. Auditing: A Journal of Practice and Theory. **10**, 1–21
11. Knechel R. W. (1988) The Effectiveness of Statistical Analytical Review as a Substantive Audit procedure: A Simulation Analysis. Accounting Review. **63**, 74–95
12. Lapin L. L. (1987) Statistics for Modern Business Decisions. 4th edition. San Diego
13. Mandl G., Jung M. (1997) Effizienz und Effektivität statistischer Stichprobenverfahren. Betriebswirtschaftliche Forschung und Praxis. 229–243
14. Neter J., Loebbecke J. K. (1975) Behavior of Major Statistical Estimators in Sampling Accounting Populations. New York
15. Reneau J. H. (1978) CAV Bounds in Dollar-Unit Sampling: Some Simulation Results. Accounting Review. **53**, 669–680
16. Shafer G. (1976) A Mathematical Theory of Evidence. Princeton
17. Shafer G., Srivatava R. (1990) The Bayesian and Belief-Function Formalisms: A General Perspective for Auditing. Auditing: A Journal of Practice and Theory. **9**, Supplement, 110–137
18. Srivastava R. P. (1993) Belief Functions and Audit Decisions. The Auditors Report. **17**, 8–12

19. Srivastava R. P. (1995) The Belief Functions Approach to Aggregating Audit Evidence. International Jounal of Intelligent Systems. **10**, 329–356
20. Srivastava R. P. (1997) Audit Decisions Using Belief Functions: A Review. Control and Cybernetics. **26**, 135–160
21. Srivastava R. P., Dutta S. K., Johns R. W. (1996) An Expert System Approach to Audit Planning and Evaluation in the Belief-Function Framework. Intelligent Systems in Accounting, Finance and Management. **5**, 165–185
22. Srivastava R. P., Shafer G. R. (1992) Belief-Function Formulas for Audit Risk. Accounting Review. **67**, 249–283
23. Srivastava R. P., Shafer G. R. (1994) Integrating Statistical and Nonstatistical Audit Evidence Using Belief Functions: A Case of Variable Sampling. International Jounal of Intelligent Systems. **9**, 519–539
24. Stringer K. W., Stewart T. R. (1996) Statistical Techniques for Analytical Review in Auditing. 2nd edition. New York

Auditors' Evaluations of Uncertain Audit Evidence: Belief Functions versus Probabilities

Keith E. Harrison, Rajendra P. Srivastava, R. David Plumlee

Truman State University, University of Kansas, University of Utah[1]

Abstract

Recently, Shafer and Srivastava [1], Srivastava and Shafer [2], Srivastava [3]-[4], and Van den Acker [5] have identified appealing features of belief function evidential networks. These networks can express the support that audit evidence provides for assertions, accounts and financial statements. These networks can also aggregate many pieces of evidence into an overall level of support for a particular assertion, account or an entire set of financial statements.

There is little empirical evidence about the ability of practicing auditors to express their evaluations of the strength of audit evidence in terms of belief functions. Many traditional models assume the use of probabilities. These might be called the traditional type of subjective probabilities. They are additive by definition, i.e. $\mathbf{P}(a) + \mathbf{P}(\sim a) = 1$. Throughout the remainder of this paper they will simply be referred to as probabilities. This study examines the question of expressing the support provided by audit evidence empirically. Auditors are asked to express the level of support that evidence provides for or against an assertion or account and the ignorance that remains about the assertion or account after considering the evidence.

Many auditors who use probabilities to measure risk express ignorance by giving equal weight to support for and support against the objective. Belief functions express ignorance by allocating mass to all elements of the frame (all possible outcomes), an alternative that is distinct from assigning equal mass to each element of the frame. Thus, belief functions show ignorance as an amount separate from the amounts of support for and against the objective.

---

1 The authors would like to acknowledge the generous support of the Deloitte & Touche Foundation through their Doctoral Fellowship program that supported the research in this project.

Forty-nine experienced auditors were asked to estimate the strength of the evidence provided in twenty-eight different audit situations. These auditors were given the opportunity to model their estimates of support and ignorance in ways that were consistent either with belief functions or with Probabilities. In this study, a statistically significant percentage of the auditors represented their estimates in ways that were consistent with belief functions and were inconsistent with probabilities. This suggests that future practitioner decision aids may include belief functions as a way of naturally expressing the ignorance and risk that persist in many audit engagements.

1. Introduction

Evidence is a key component of any audit process. Professional standards require that audit conclusions be supported by enough persuasive evidence to survive a challenge from skeptical critics. It seems natural to consider Dempster-Shafer belief functions as a way to describe the support provided by evidence as well as the ignorance that one feels even after gathering that evidence. Beginning with Shafer and Srivastava [1] and Srivastava and Shafer [2], Srivastava and his colleagues have explored the theoretical possibilities of designing belief function models for expressing audit evidence. Some of these papers include Srivastava [3-4], Van den Acker [5], Srivastava and Lu [6], Dutta, Harrison and Srivastava [7], Gillett [8] and Srivastava, Dutta and Johns [9]. This paper will begin to examine the empirical issues of whether auditors express their evaluations about the strength of evidence and the existence of ignorance in ways that are similar to belief functions.

First, the paper provides some background information on financial statement audits. Next, there is a section discussing the semantics of belief functions, The following section reviews the literature about empirical investigations of the use of belief functions including the application of belief functions to auditing situations. Then there is a section that develops the hypothesis of this paper, a section that describes the methods used in the experiment, a section that presents results and briefly discusses them and the paper ends with a brief conclusion.

2. Financial Statement Audits

Financial statement audits are a key component of the American and world economies. Arens and Loebbecke [10] provide a useful definition of a financial statement audit in a leading auditing textbook:

> Auditing is the accumulation and evaluation of evidence about information to determine and report on the degree of correspondence between the information and established criteria. Auditing should be done by a competent independent person.

Auditors examine financial statements and issue an auditor's report on them. To issue such a report, the auditors must be reasonably sure that the financial statements are correct. To do this, they must gather, evaluate and aggregate evidence about the financial aspects of the company. Gathering evidence about the financial statements as a whole is important and necessary, but more specific information about the company's financial aspects requires examination of individual accounts and various dimensions of those accounts.

An account is a record of the business transactions that affect one specific asset, liability, equity, revenue or expense. The cash account is an account that records the affects of all of the business transactions that involve a company's cash. Most companies report sales and this appears as a revenue account. Effective evidence gathering procedures require that auditors subdivide accounts. Each account has various dimensions, each of which must be tested by the auditors. These dimensions are called management assertions because management asserts that all dimensions of the account are correct when they give the financial statements to the auditors to be audited.

Auditors create a set of objectives to test each of these management assertions called audit objectives. There may be one or more than one audit objective for each management assertion.

The audit process consists of gathering enough evidence to support each one of these audit objectives for each account in the financial statements. Different types of evidence provide different levels of support for audit objectives.

The support that audit evidence provides is almost never certain. Some doubt remains about all evidence because people make mistakes or intentionally mislead others for their own advantage. The process of combining pieces of evidence also contributes to uncertainty because there are not uniform procedures for combining different items of evidence that relate to a single audit objective or a single account.

Auditors are to consider audit risk in every audit. Professional auditing standards [11, paragraph .02] define audit risk as "the risk that the auditor may unknowingly fail to appropriately modify his opinion on financial statements that are materially misstated." One aspect of audit risk is <u>inherent risk</u>. Professional auditing standards [11, paragraph .20] also define this risk, "inherent risk is the susceptibility of an assertion to a material misstatement, assuming that there are no related internal control structure policies or procedures." Assessing inherent risk for a particular assertion may involve many factors about the company, its operating environment and the overall economy. Making this assessment for every assertion in the financial statements may be very costly and time consuming. In such cases, the professional standards suggest [11, paragraph .22]:

> If an auditor concludes that the effort required to assess inherent risk for an assertion would exceed the potential reduction in the extent of his auditing procedures derived from such an assessment, he should assess inherent risk as being at the maximum when designing auditing procedures.

If one is using probabilities to represent audit risks, this leads to the inherent risk component of audit risk being set at 1.0 or 100%. Srivastava and Shafer [2, p. 252] use this situation to point out one of the difficulties in using probabilities to express audit risk:

> We advance belief functions ... because we believe that the usefulness of the Bayesian approach is limited by divergences between the intuitive and Bayesian interpretations of audit risk. For example, according to SAS No. 47, if an auditor decides not to consider inherent factors, then the inherent risk is set equal to 1. Since a probability measure of 1 means certainty, this seems to be saying that it is certain that the account is materially in error. But this is not what the auditor has in mind when deciding not to depend on inherent factors. The auditor's intention is represented better by a belief-function plausibility of 1 for material error, which says only that the auditor lacks evidence based on inherent factors.

Professional standards ask auditors to proceed with an open mind. They should neither assume that an amount is correct nor assume that an amount is incorrect before gathering evidence. The auditor simply has a high level of ignorance about all types of risk, including inherent risk, at the beginning of the audit. If this problem is viewed from a belief function perspective, Inherent Risk is the plausibility of material misstatement due to inherent factors. Under this consideration, IR = 1 implies that the plausibility of material missttatement due to inherent factors is 1, i.e. $\mathbf{PL}_{IF}$(Material mistatement) = 1, where IF stands for inherent factors.

With the probability framework, most decision-makers will use the convention of assigning equal probability to each alternative to express ignorance. For example, if there are only two alternatives, 50% is assigned to each alternative. However, several interpretations of this information are possible. It is not possible to distinguish between 50% support for each alternative, complete ignorance, or some situation in-between. These different interpretations lead auditors to different conclusions. Clarity about which of them exists improves an auditor's understanding of audit risk. Belief functions can provide this clarity because belief functions express ignorance separately from the support for any of the alternatives in a situation. With belief functions, the inherent risk example can be modeled by setting ignorance of inherent risk at 100% and then seeking evidence to provide support for lowering audit risk in other areas such as internal controls.

Auditors also face difficult issues in knowing how to model the relationship between evidence and the audit objective or account that it supports. For example, analytical procedures are audit tests that examine the relationships between various pieces of financial (and non-financial) information about a company. Some relationships can be predicted because of industry trends and other internal and external factors. Analytical procedure tests provide evidence not only about audit objectives but also about accounts and financial statements as a whole. This means that an auditor must be able to consider evidence that supports different types of variables (financial statements, accounts and audit objectives) simultaneously. Again Srivastava and Shafer [2] demonstrate that a belief function model arranged in tree-type structures can handle evidence that supports multiple levels of financial variables.

Another issue that auditors frequently face is the problem of one piece of evidence that supports more than one audit objective simultaneously, often with differing levels of support for each. One type of evidence about accounts receivable, a confirmation letter, is usually thought to provide evidence for both the existence audit objective and the valuation audit objective. Many auditors think that it provides a higher level of support for existence than for valuation. In such a case, the tree-type structures developed in Srivastava and Shafer [2] are not theoretically applicable because this one piece of evidence would need to be treated as though it were two independent pieces of evidence. In practice, the independence assumption cannot always be made. In this case, an evidential network can be used. Such a network allows an item of evidence to support multiple audit objectives with a different level of support for each. Srivastava [3] develops such an evidential network for the belief function framework.

Almost all of the work in belief function evidential networks (for example, Srivastava and Shafer [2], Srivastava [3], [4] and Mock, Wright and Srivastava [12]) has been theoretical and not empirical. The theoretical arguments for using belief function evidential networks have been strong and intuitively appealing, but no empirical testing of the use of belief functions in an audit setting has been performed. This paper addresses that need for empirical testing.

3. The Semantics of Belief Functions

Background on the basic elements of belief functions can be found in the introductory chapters of this volume. In this section, one perspective for interpreting and understanding belief functions from a semantic perspective will be presented. The experiment described in this paper is related to this understanding and interpretation of belief functions.

Shafer and Tversky [13] and Shafer [14] clearly describe belief functions as an alternate language of probability, not as something distinct from probability. Each language permits the user to construct different types of analogies between evidence and mental models that the user may be familiar with from past experience.

Shafer and Tversky [13] also redirect the traditional argument between the subjective and objective understandings of probability into a middle-ground interpretation of probability where the meaning of the probability data is constructed each time the decision-maker encounters a situation requiring reasoning with uncertain information. The meaning is constructed from canonical examples that the decision-maker has learned from his or her experience or has been taught in the past. These examples can be frequency events for physical objects such as tosses of fair coins. They can also be subjective judgments about mental experiments such as the relationship between management displaying certain attitudes and the increased risk of fraud. Shafer and Tversky [11, p. 336] describe probability judgment in this way:

> Probability judgment is a process of construction rather than elicitation. People may begin a task of probability judgment with some beliefs already formulated. But the process of judgment, when successful, gives greater content and structure to these beliefs and tends to render initial beliefs obsolete. It is useful, in this respect, to draw an analogy between probability and affective notions such as love and loyalty. A declaration of love is not simply a report on a person's emotions. It is also a part of a process whereby an intellectual and emotional commitment is created; so too with probability.

Shafer and Srivastava [1, p. 119] state this point somewhat more directly:

> Numerical probabilities usually do not have objective reality independent of human judgment. Nor do they exist in people's minds prior to deliberation. But people can construct numerical probabilities on the basis of objective evidence.

The constructive interpretation gains depth from the idea that probability judgment involves matching practical problems to abstract canonical examples. Shafer and Tversky describe canonical examples in the following way [11, 310-311]:

> We also need canonical examples for each degree of probability on this scale–examples where it is agreed what degree of probability is appropriate.

They continue [11, p. 311]:

> Using a theory of subjective probability means comparing the evidence in a problem with the theory's scale of canonical examples and picking out the canonical example that matches it best.

Belief functions differ from probabilities in the type of canonical examples they use, but not in the process of constructing analogies. Belief functions use indirect canonical examples because they establish a relationship between a situation with known probabilities and a situation with unknown probabilities. The situation with the unknown probabilities is the situation of interest. Belief functions become useful when the decision-maker cannot estimate the probabilities to the question of interest, but can estimate probabilities for some related question. The example below illustrates this point.

Company X has a control procedure where a computer program verifies the general ledger account coding for transactions prepared in the field by sales representatives. Different types of sales receive different types of commissions. Auditor testing shows that on days with a lot of sales activity across the country, the director of computing can disable the general ledger coding control procedure in order to get customer orders processed and shipped in a timely fashion. This means that the general ledger code supplied by the sales person will automatically be used without being checked by the computer. The auditor estimates that the control operates for 85% of all sales transactions. The auditor is not primarily interested in the control procedure itself. The auditor wishes to give an opinion on the financial statements and whether or not the amount of commission expense is correctly stated. The auditor believes that if the control is operating, the amount of commission is calculated correctly. However, it may also be calculated correctly if the control is not functioning. No individual sales representative will know when the system has been turned off since the transactions are coded during the day on a laptop computer and transmitted to headquarters in the evening. The sales representative codes the transaction assuming that the control will be in effect. If the control is in effect, attempts to create overstated commissions will be detected and stopped.

Belief functions are useful in this example because the auditor is unable to gather direct evidence about the fact that really concerns the auditor, the existence of errors in the sales commission amount shown in the financial statements. Evidence can be gathered on the related question of whether the control was operating at the time of the event. The auditor has developed the relationship that if the control was turned on, the amount in the financial statement is correct. If the control was not turned on, the data may either be correct or incorrect. Suppose that the auditor estimates that the control is in operation 85% of the time. Combining the facts and the relationship between sets of facts gives the auditor a belief that at least 85% of the commissions are processed correctly and no belief that the commissions are processed incorrectly. Up to 15% of the transactions may be processed either correctly or incorrectly when the controls are not in operation. This judgment can be expressed in terms of ***m***-values as $\boldsymbol{m}(a) = 0.85$, $\boldsymbol{m}(\sim a) = 0$, and $\boldsymbol{m}(\{a,\sim a\}) = 0.15$, or in terms of beliefs as $\boldsymbol{Bel}(a) = 0.85$ and $\boldsymbol{Bel}(\sim a) = 0$, where "$a$" represents the situation that sales commissions are fairly stated and "$\sim a$" represents the situation that sales commissions are not fairly stated.

This example can be described using a belief function canonical example because belief functions do not require additivity. In other words, Bel [A] + Bel [~A] $\leq$ 1. This is one of the properties that makes belief functions particularly useful in audit settings. Many of the situations that auditors encounter can best be modeled by this sort of canonical example. A belief function canonical example is designed to take evidence that is known to the decision-maker but is only indirectly relevant and relate it to the question of interest for which the decision-maker has less ability to gather information. Shafer describes one type of canonical example that can be used for belief functions [12, 338]:

> In my mind, the simplest and most effective metaphor for belief functions is the metaphor of the witness who may or may not be reliable. In many cases, the example of such a witness can serve as a standard of comparison for the strength of evidence. We can assess given evidence by saying that it is comparable in strength to the evidence of a witness who has a certain chance of being reliable.
>
> A witness testifying to a specific proposition leads to a relatively simple belief function—one that gives a specified degree of belief to that proposition and its consequences and zero degree of belief to all other propositions.

Shafer and Tversky [13] suggest that probability is a useful canonical example for expressing frequencies. To illustrate this, a decision-maker might say that the probability of finishing the current project in less than one week is 25% and the probability of finishing in one week or more is 75%. She bases this evaluation on similar projects with similar amounts of work to complete that she has led. She is using past frequencies to model this uncertainty and expressing this as a probability.

As Shafer and Srivastava [1] note, some situations that decision-makers face can best be handled by probabilities. If this is the case, they should be used. Probabilities and belief functions can be used together in the same model of evidence because probabilities are a subset of belief functions. Probabilities are belief functions that follow the rule of additivity (they can be called Bayesian belief functions). Shafer and Srivastava [1, p. 130] provide some additional insight about how probabilities are related to belief functions. For example, they state "The Bayesian formalism has two elements—the idea of a probability measure and the rule of conditioning. Both of these elements have their place in the belief-function formalism." They also discuss additivity, "The general point is that both (Bayesian) additivity and (non-Bayesian) nonadditivity are permitted in the belief function formalism. A belief function does not have to be a probability measure, but it can be one."

4. Empirical Investigations into the Use of Belief Functions

Experiments that explore the empirical use of belief functions are very limited at this time. Several bear mentioning, Curley and Golden [15], Krishnamoorthy, Mock and Washington [16] Dusenbury, Reimers and Wheeler [17] and Monroe and Ng [18].

Curley and Golden [15] explored the use of belief functions within a simulated legal context. Business students acted as jurors hearing a case with four possible suspects and up to four pieces of evidence that supported one or more of these suspects. With four suspects, "a", "b", "c" and "d", many different subsets of guilty suspects could be created. For example, evidence item one might implicate subjects "a" and "d" but not the other suspects. While many subsets of subjects potentially could be assigned mass, under belief function theory only {a}, {d}, {a,d} and {a,b,c,d} should be assigned mass. Curley and Golden measured which frames were assigned mass by the participants. The researchers grouped responses into categories. For example, all responses that assigned mass only to {a,d} were included in one category. Other responses that chose only {a} and {d} were included in another category.

The researchers were able to identify patterns in the ways that participants assigned mass. With this level of complexity, the researchers wished merely to understand whether participants assigned mass in a manner consistent with Dempster-Shafer belief-function theory.

Their results show that the participants did assign mass to subsets that were logically consistent with Dempster-Shafer belief functions. This is important because it provides a basis for the current study. It is consistent with what the auditors were expected to do. However, participants in the Curley and Golden study did not combine evidence in ways that also were consistent with Dempster's Rule for the combination of belief functions. Since Dempster's Rule of combination is one of the mathematical requirements of belief functions, this difference between theory and observed behavior should be explored in future research.

Krishnamoorthy, Mock and Washington [16] compared four theoretical models for revising belief with the results produced by auditors combining pieces of evidence in an experimental setting. The four methods included Cascaded Inference Theory (Bayesian inference), Dempster-Shafer belief functions and two versions of Einhorn and Hogarth's Belief Adjustment Model. Although both belief functions and cascaded inference correctly predicted the direction of the auditor assessments, they produced results that were overly conservative when compared to the participants' responses and to the results from the Belief Adjustment Models. However, information about the values of some inputs to the models was not elicited from the participants and was assumed or interpolated. While this may be reasonable in a situation where several competing models are being tested, it appears that further work could help to determine the usefulness of belief functions for auditors. The current study addresses this issue.

Dusenbury, Reimers and Wheeler [17] asked experienced auditors from a major auditing firm to assess inherent risk, control risk and analytical procedures risk for two accounting cycles. The allowed test of details risk (TDR) was derived from these assessments. The allowed TDR was derived using three separate audit risk models. The models were (1) the model described in Statements on Auditing Standards, (2) a model developed by the auditing firm and (3) a belief-based specification of the audit risk model.

This study also asked auditors to assess two other constructs. Participants rated the sufficiency of the evidence and their own confidence ratings of their assessments of risk. The authors used these constructs to construct a belief ratio that reflected an estimate of the ignorance that auditors felt about the evidence and their evaluation of the evidence. This study differs from the current work in this key dimension. The researchers created the belief-based measures based on inputs rather than asking the participants to estimate support and ignorance directly.

The results of this study show some of the potential benefits of a belief-based model [15, p. 12]. It demonstrated that "a belief-based model can incorporate qualities of evidence into risk assessments and that belief-based assessments can be combined to derive and allowed test of details risk." Neither of the other models captured the uncertainty that the auditors felt about the evidence that they had gathered. Similar to [16], the belief-based model in [17] produced results that were more conservative than the other models examined.

Monroe and Ng [18] compared the intuitive assessments of audit risk made by 69 practicing Australian auditors to the assessments provided by various audit risk models, including a belief function audit risk model. The estimates for the component inputs to these models were elicited from the same auditors. The results reported indicate that all of the models produced a risk assessment that was inconsistent with the risk assessment produced intuitively by the auditors. Fairly large errors were reported for the Belief-Adjustment and Belief function models. The authors identify several possible reasons for the limitations of all of the models, including the use of the assessment of risk only at the account-balance level. This study raises the possibility that many levels of risk and many characteristics of an engagement may need to be evaluated simultaneously in order to achieve an acceptable risk assessment from any audit risk model.

This paper expands the work of these studies by giving auditors the opportunity to directly assess the ignorance that remains in their minds after evaluating evidence.

5. Hypotheses

Shafer and Tversky recognize that no one model of uncertainty will fit all problems. They state [11, p.311]:

> Proponents of different theories of subjective probability have often debated which theory best describes human inductive competence. We believe that none of these theories provide an adequate account of people's intuitive judgments of probability. On the other hand, most of these theories can be learned and used effectively. Consequently, we regard these theories as formal languages for expressing probability judgments rather than as psychological models, however idealized.
>
> The usefulness of these formal languages for a specific problem may depend both on the problem and on the skill of the user. There may not be a single probability language that is normative for all people and all problems. A person may find one language better for one problem and another language better for another. Furthermore, individual probability judgments made in one language may not be directly translatable into another.

This leads to a testable hypothesis for this study. If one formulates uncertain situations that the theory suggests should be expressed more effectively in one probability language as opposed to another, subjects presented with that situation should choose to model the problem using the preferred probability language. If the theory is not supported, subjects may randomly choose a particular probability language for expressing uncertainty or may consistently choose a probability representation because of its greater familiarity.

In the specific case of audit evidence, many procedures provide one-sided evidence. Often, evidence supports the audit objective being tested and provides no support for contradicting the audit objective being tested. This was true in the internal control example given earlier. This sort of one-sided support is described in the belief function framework as a simple support function. Theoretically, it would seem that participants should have a clear preference for using belief functions in auditing because simple support functions describe many auditing situations. Therefore, it becomes important to determine if the theory is consistent with practice.

This presents the basic research question of this experiment. When faced with evidence that provides support for an audit objective or account and no support against this objective or account, do auditors model the support provided by evidence through the use of belief functions? Said another way, will the auditors choose to represent ignorance as a separate, specific part of their evaluation of the audit evidence?

In the experiment, auditors were asked to determine whether a piece of evidence supported or did not support a particular audit objective (or account in the case of a combined evaluation of several pieces of evidence). They also were asked if a separate amount of ignorance remained about the audit objective or account. Auditors that chose to represent a separate amount of ignorance showed a preference for a belief function representation because it is easier to represent ignorance in belief functions than in probabilities.

Auditors that chose to identify no separate ignorance category may have been showing a preference for a probability representation. Probability is discussed in college statistics classes and included in guidance in the professional literature. Note however, that the representations that exclude a separate ignorance category can easily be modeled using belief functions and are completely consistent with a belief function approach.

If auditors were indifferent between a belief function approach and a probability approach for modeling the strength of evidence, one would expect to find that auditors choose to use them about equally. One might even expect that the probability approach might show up more frequently, since some professionals are familiar with this approach from training. However, if separate identification of ignorance occurs, this provides evidence that auditors are choosing a belief function representation over a probability representation.

Let p_{bf} represent the proportion of the auditors' evaluations that are consistent with a belief functions representation and inconsistent with a Bayesian representation. Let p_p represent the proportion of the auditors' evaluations that are consistent with a probability representation[2]. If there were a preference for a probability representation, or indifference between the two representations, one would expect that the proportion of evaluations that are consistent with a belief function representation, p_{bf}, would be less than or equal to ½. This is equivalent to $p_{bf} \leq p_p$. However, if auditors use a representation consistent with belief functions, we would expect that p_{bf} would be greater than ½ and $p_{bf} > p_p$. The hypothesis can be stated as follows:

$$H_0: p_{bf} \leq 0.5 .$$

$$H_A: p_{bf} > 0.5 .$$

The next sections of this paper will describe how the experiment was conducted.

6. Methods Used in this Experiment

6.1. Participants

In this section, the participants in the experiment are identified and the accounting firms that they represent are described. Accounting firms in Missouri and Iowa were contacted. One office from six different firms agreed to participate in the research. Of these, two firms only participated during the design phase and are not included in the table. The type of firm and the number of participants that participated in the experiment are listed in Table 1.

A reasonable level of experience in evaluating and combining audit evidence is necessary in order for an individual to complete the experiment successfully. Partners and managers from several firms and the experimenters agreed that a

[2] Representations where the auditor feels that the evidence completely supports (or completely refutes) the audit objective or account can be represented equally well under belief functions or subjective probabilities. In this paper they have been arbitrarily assigned to the subjective Bayesian probability case because this will make it harder to reject the null hypothesis and provides a stronger test of the hypothesis.

minimum of one year of audit experience would be needed to carry out these tasks. All 49 met that requirement.

Table 1: Summary by Firm of the Participants in the Study

Firms participating in the experiment	Number of Participants
"Big Five" firms	26
Large regional firm	15
Large local firm	8
Total number of participants in the experiment	49

Auditors assisting during the design phase evaluated whether the descriptions of the pieces of evidence made sense and asked the participants to identify the audit objective or objectives that they believed each piece of evidence supported. Most of these auditors were seniors or managers with three to six years' experience.

The pilot-testing phase used auditors from a large national accounting firm to test the accuracy and quality of the experimental materials. These auditors ranged in experience from one to five years.

Participants in the experiment came from four CPA firms located in Missouri. Two of these firms are "Big Five" accounting firms. One of the "Big Five" firms employed sixteen of the participants and the second "Big Five" firm employed ten of the participants. These participants had between one and four years of auditing experience.

Fifteen auditors from a large national firm (i.e. a firm located throughout the United States but not a "Big Five") also participated in this study. These auditors ranged in experience from three to twenty years' experience.

Finally, eight auditors from a very large one-office firm completed the experiment. These auditors ranged in experience from one to four years.

Auditors from one of the "Big Five" firms and from the National firm completed the experiment as part of a training meeting. Auditors from the other firms completed the experiment individually. They returned the experiment to a local manager or partner who returned the completed experiments to the researchers.

6.2. Materials Used in the Experiment

The purpose of the experiment is to determine whether auditors express their evaluations of the strength of audit evidence in terms that are more consistent with belief functions or probabilities. This requires the use of items of audit evidence. To save time, auditors were given brief descriptions of typical items of audit evidence rather than the actual audit evidence. Five descriptions of audit evidence were provided in four different audit areas. Figure 1 shows one of these descriptions.

In designing the descriptions of the evidence for the experiment, certain simplifying features were implemented. First, all of the areas of evidence pertain to one company, Midwest Industries. This company was designed to be familiar to a wide range of auditors. It is involved in a traditional, profitable industry that does not involve high-risk business or accounting activities. It was designed to have strong management and strong internal control.

This type of company provides a relatively familiar environment for the participants to work with. It allows them to focus on the particular pieces of evidence that are presented in each evidence set without having a large number of other variables influencing their decision in ways that could be hard to predict or control. Such variables could include a high risk of fraud or increased risks of litigation. This positive set of conditions would exist on some but certainly not all of an auditor's clients. At the same time, they are not unrealistic.

Four different audit areas were used in this experiment. They include accounts receivable, accounts payable, plant, property and equipment and inventory quantities. These areas were chosen for several reasons. These areas generally are familiar to most auditors. Accounts receivable is the audit area where the amount owed to a company is tested. Accounts payable is the audit area where the amount owed by a company is tested. Plant, property and equipment is the audit area where tangible assets with long lives such as machinery and buildings are tested. All three of these areas would be involved in almost every audit, regardless of the industry or type of business.

Inventory is the audit area where the assets that are available for sale to customers are tested. Inventory can be either purchased or manufactured. Inventory will not be involved in every audit because some companies provide services instead of goods. The inventory evidence set was limited to "quantity" issues and did not discuss the cost or value of the inventory. Eliminating the cost and value issues makes it possible for more auditors to understand the evidence because most auditors will have observed a physical inventory count.

Within each of the audit areas, the participants saw five individual pieces of evidence. They were asked to evaluate the strength of each of these pieces of evidence individually. They also were asked to evaluate the combined strength of the first four pieces of evidence before they saw the fifth piece of evidence. After evaluating the fifth piece of evidence, they evaluated the combined strength of all five pieces of evidence.

For two of the four areas, the last piece of evidence provided support for two different audit objectives within the area. This difference is not significant to the results of this experiment.

Each auditor that participated in the study received a folder of materials. These materials included:

1. Two copies of an informed consent.[3]

2. An introduction to the research project explaining what the research was being conducted to study.

3. A practice set of materials for notes payable, an area that is not included in the experiment.

4. Experimental materials for four audit areas. These materials included:

   a) Background information for the hypothetical company, Midwest Industries.

   b) Four sets of audit evidence. Each set includes:

      i) Four pieces of evidence, each on a separate page.

      ii) A page for providing an evaluation of the combined strength of the first four pieces of evidence.

      iii) A fifth page of evidence.

      iv) A page for providing an evaluation of the combined strength of all five pieces of evidence.

5. A demographic information page that collected data related to professional characteristics of the individual involved.

---

[3] The experimental materials and consent forms were approved through the institutional review process for human experimentation at a major midwestern university.

A sample page for recording the level of support provided by the first piece of evidence for the inventory audit area is shown in Figure 1.

Figure 1: A Sample Page for Collecting Information about the Support that Evidence Provides

Midwest Industries Audit December 31, 1998 Working Paper I-1 Audit Objective: Existence

The audit team members observing the inventory count selected a sample of tags listed on the used tag summary sheet and found that a copy of all of these tags were attached to actual inventory. Tags not attached to inventory were all designated as unused. The staff noted that all inventory movement was halted during the count to minimize the risk of double counting inventory. Later, once the inventory had been summarized, a staff auditor reviewed the inventory summary listed by tag number and found that none of the unused tags were included. The staff auditor also verified that used tags appeared only once on the inventory summary listing.

0 | 1 | 2 | 3 | 4 | 5 | 6 | 7 | 8 | 9 | 10

6.3. Experimental Procedures

Each auditor was asked to complete the twenty-eight individual and combined evidence evaluation tasks that were described in the previous section. Auditors at two of the firms completed the exercise during a firm training sessions and auditors at the other two firms completed the exercise individually and returned the materials to a firm coordinator. The coordinators returned the materials to the researchers. Oral instructions were provided during the firm training sessions and written instructions were provided for auditors completing the evaluations independently. The same set of instructions was provided in both cases. There was no significant statistical difference between the evaluations of auditors performing the task in training sessions and the evaluations of auditors performing the task individually.

Each of the auditors completed an informed consent form, provided some demographic data, reviewed some instructions and completed a practice exercise before beginning the experimental evidence evaluation task. No significant questions were raised during the practice exercise and none of the auditors appeared to have difficulty with the task. It appears that the materials were clear and easy for the auditors to understand.

Auditors were asked to document their evidence evaluations by dividing the judgement box at the bottom of each page. Figure 2 shows a sample judgment box. Each piece of evidence was identified with one or two audit objectives that related to the evidence. Groups of four or five pieces of evidence were associated with an account that related to all of the evidence for that area.

Figure 2: Judgment Box

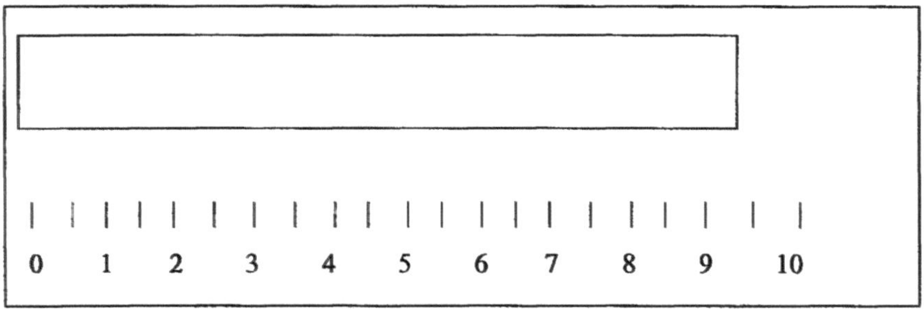

Participants were asked to completely fill the large box at the bottom of each page by dividing the box into one, two or three sections and then labeling each box with a letter related to the way they thought the uncertainty in each situation would be resolved. Participants were asked to fill in the judgment box with one, two or all three of the following choices. Choice "A" represented the amount of support that the evidence set provided for the audit objective identified in the scenario. Choice "B" represented the amount of support that the evidence provided against the audit objective. Choice "C" represented the amount of ignorance that the auditor continued to have about the audit objective after seeing the piece of evidence.

The auditors divided the judgement box to show the amount they wished to assign to each of the choices. For example, the auditor drew a line at "6" if she or he wished to allocate 60% of the box to "A" and 40% of the box to "C". The auditor labeled the larger section of the box with an "A" and the smaller section of the box with a "C". The judgment box remained undivided if the auditor wished to allocate the entire box to just one of the three choices. Table 2 summarizes the choices of "A", "B", and "C" made by the auditors.

Table 2: Summary of Auditors Assignment of Support for Individual Evidence and Combinations of Evidence

	Choices that auditors made to record their support for the evidence in the various scenarios*						
Column Number	I	II	III	IV	V	VI	VII
Choice from Instructions	A	B	C	AB	BC	AC	ABC
Probability Representation	P(a)	P($\sim a$)		P(a), P($\sim a$)			
Belief function Representation (non-zero m-values)	$m(a)$	$m(\sim a)$	$m(\{a, \sim a\})$	$m(a)$ and $m(\sim a)$	$m(\sim a)$ and $m(\{a,\sim a\})$	$m(a)$ and $m(\{a,\sim a\})$	$m(a)$, $m(\sim a)$ and $m(\{a,\sim a\})$
Firm 1, $N = 450$	50	1	0	4	3	356	36
Percentage	11.1%	0.2%	0.0%	0.9%	0.7%	79.1%	8.0%
Firm 2, $N = 480$	49	1	1	24[a]	1	300	104
Percentage	10.2%	0.2%	0.2%	5.0%	0.2%	62.5%	21.7%
Firm 3, $N = 239$	51	0	1	20[b]	0	134	33
Percentage	21.3%	0.0%	0.4%	8.4%	0.0%	56.1%	13.8%
Firm 4, $N = 300$	71	0	4	10	1	136	78
Percentage	23.7%	0.0%	1.3%	3.3%	0.3%	45.3%	26.0%
Total, $N = 1,469$	221	2	6	58	5	926	251
Percentage	15.0%	0.1%	0.4%	3.9%	0.3%	63.0%	17.1%

*The letters in these columns correspond to the types of support. Choice A shows support for the audit objective being true, choice B shows support for the audit objective not being true and choice C shows the amount of ignorance the auditor feels about the situation. Columns that have multiple letters indicate that the auditor used all of the letters shown. Each evaluation appears in only one column. For example, no evaluations included in the column labeled "A" are included in the column labeled "AC". An auditor that used "AC" thought that the evidence provided some support for the audit objective or account but also left some ignorance about the audit objective or account.

[a] One individual recorded ten items in this category.

[b] One individual recorded ten items in this category and another individual recorded seven items in this category.

7. Results and Discussion

The evaluations of the evidence are presented in Table 2. Each auditor assigned one, two or all three of the letters (A,B,C) described above to each evidence evaluation. Any evaluation that involves letter C represents an evaluation that is consistent with a belief function representation of the evidence and inconsistent with a Bayesian representation of the evidence. Each evaluation is included in only one column. For example, if an auditor thought that evidence provided some positive support for the auditor objective but felt that some ignorance remained, that individual would choose to use both A and C and their choice would be included in column VI in the table. That evaluation would not be included in columns I or III.

In total, 1,469 evaluations were made. Each of the 49 auditors evaluated 26 items where the evidence supported one assertion or account and two items where the evidence supported two different assertions and a separate evaluation was made for each. This means that each auditor made 30 evaluations. This gives a theoretical total of 1,470 evaluations (49 x 30 = 1,470). One auditor omitted one evaluation and the total of 1,469 in Table 2 reflects this omission.

Evaluations that appear in columns I, II and IV are consistent with a probability representation. Items in columns III, V, VI, and VII are only consistent with a belief function representation of uncertainty. Table 3 summarizes the choices that are consistent with belief functions and probabilities.

Table 3: Summary of Results by Representation

	Belief Function Columns III, V, VI, VII	Probability Columns I, II, IV	Total
Number of items	1,188	281	1,469
Proportion	0.81	0.19	1.00
Probability that (p_{bf} 0.50) = .0000			

The results from Table 3 provide strong evidence that the null hypothesis that the proportion of evaluations using a belief function representation will be less than or equal to ½ (i.e. p_{bf} 0.50) is rejected. This probability is nearlyzero and is zero to four decimal places. Over 4/5 of the evaluations use a belief function representation to express the auditor's evaluation of the evidence. This indicates that these auditors think about the evidence problem in terms of support and ignorance rather than in terms of support for and support against the audit objective being true.

Perhaps this is most clearly demonstrated in the data that suggests that just a few auditors do use a probability representation for the evidence. Three auditors accounted for 27 of the 58 uses of the "AB" category. This category shows that the evidence provides some support for and some support against but leaves no ignorance about the evidence. It appears that these three auditors were most comfortable using a probability approach to modeling evidence. Since three auditors provide almost half of the responses in the "AB" category, other auditors use it very infrequently. Most auditors used a belief function representation. For those auditors that use a Bayesian representation, a belief function representation approach can be used since all Bayesian representations can also be represented in belief functions as described earlier. Gillett [8] also found similar results with a very small sample of auditors that he contacted during his research.

This research does not address the issue of whether auditors combine evidence in a manner consistent with the axioms of belief functions. Results from Curley and Golden [15], and Krishnamoorthy, Mock and Washington [16] suggest that more work may need to be performed to understand how auditors do combine pieces of evidence. It also suggests that training of auditors might be needed if an auditing firm wished to utilize a belief function model to combine evidence and arrive at an overall evaluation for an audit area or the financial statements as a whole. This is not unusual. Most decision aids require some training before they can be properly utilized by decision-makers. Srivastava, Dutta and Johns [9] demonstrate that a realistic audit process for one portion of an audit can be constructed using a belief function based expert system. This current research suggests that auditors will be comfortable in providing inputs to such a system in a belief function format. Further work remains to develop a full-scale belief function expert system capable of modeling an entire audit.

8. Conclusion

This paper has shown that a clear majority of the auditors in this study chose to represent the uncertainty inherent in audit evidence through belief functions rather than through probabilities, when both choices were available to them. Two reasons appear to explain this preference. First, belief functions represent ignorance as a separate explicit component of the evaluation, rather than describing it indirectly by assigning some ignorance to each of the possible outcomes. Second, belief functions can represent support for an audit objective or account without showing any support against the audit objective or account. This is not surprising since Shafer [19] designed belief functions as a mathematical theory of evidence.

This result will advance the research into developing a belief function expert system for audit decisions. It now appears that auditors can provide evaluations of evidence in ways that are consistent with belief functions and it also appears that these evaluations will be useful for these auditors. Further research is needed to determine the type of training that would be needed to improve the use of belief functions by auditors. Auditors are willing to express support for audit objectives in a belief function framework because ignorance is specifically quantified.

References

[1] G. Shafer and R. P. Srivastava, (1990) The Bayesian and belief-function formalisms: A general perspective for auditing. *Auditing: A Journal of Theory and Practice*, vol. 9 (Supplement), pp. 110-148.

[2] R. P. Srivastava and G. R. Shafer, (1992) Belief-function formulas for audit risk. *The Accounting Review*, vol. 67 (April), pp. 249-283.

[3] R. P. Srivastava, (1995a) A general scheme for aggregating evidence in auditing: Propagation of beliefs in networks. In *Artificial Intelligence in Accounting and Auditing*, vol. 3. Miklos A. Vasarhelyi, Ed. Princeton, NJ: Markus Wiener Publishers

[4] R. P. Srivastava, (1995b) The belief-function approach to aggregating audit evidence. *International Journal of Intelligent Systems*, vol. 10 (March) pp. 329-356.

[5] C. Van den Acker, (1999) A Belief-Function Model for the Representation and the Combination of Uncertain Audit Evidence. *Intelligent Systems in Accounting, Finance and Management*, vol. 8 (3), pp. 215-224.

[6] R. P. Srivastava and H. Lu, (2000) Evidential Reasoning Under Uncertainty Using Belief Functions: A Structural Analysis of Audit Evidence. *Fuzzy Sets and Systems*, Forthcoming.

[7] S. K. Dutta, K. E. Harrison and R. P. Srivastava, (1998) The audit risk model under the risk of fraud. *Applications of Fuzzy Sets and the Theory of Evidence to Accounting, II* (vol. 7 in the *Studies in Managerial and Financial Accounting* series). Philip H. Siegel, Khursheed Omer, Andre de Korvin and Awni Zebda, Eds. Stamford Connecticut: JAI Press Inc.

[8] P. R. Gillett, (1996) *A Comparative Study of Audit Evidence and Audit Planning Models Using Uncertain Reasoning.* Doctoral dissertation. University of Kansas, Lawrence, KS.

[9] R. P. Srivastava, S. K. Dutta and R. W. Johns, (1996) An Expert System Approach to Audit Planning and Evaluation in the Belief-Function

Framework. *Intelligent Systems in Accounting, Finance and Management*, vol. 5, pp. 165-183.

[10] A. A. Arens and J. K. Loebbecke, (1997) *Auditing: An integrated approach*. 7th ed. Englewood Cliffs, NJ: Prentice Hall.

[11] American Institute of Certified Public Accountants, (1983) *Statement on Auditing Standards No. 47: Audit Risk and Materiality in Conducting an Audit*. New York: AICPA.

[12] T. Mock, A. Wright and R. Srivastava, (1998) Audit Program Planning Using a Belief Function Framework. *AUDITING SYMPOSIUM XIV; Proceedings of the 1998 Deloitte & Touche/University of Kansas Symposium on Auditing Problems. pp. 115-142.*

[13] G. Shafer, and A. Tversky, (1985) Languages and designs for probability judgment. *Cognitive Science*, vol. 9, pp. 309-339.

[14] G. Shafer, (1990) Perspectives on the theory and practice of belief functions. *International Journal of Approximate Reasoning*, vol. 4 pp. 323-362.

[15] S. P. Curley and J. I. Golden, (1994) Using belief functions to represent degrees of belief. *Organizational Behavior and Human Decision Processes*, vol. 58, pp. 271-303.

[16] G. Krishnamoorthy, T. J. Mock, and M. T. Washington, (1999) A Comparative Evaluation of Belief Revision Models in Auditing. *Auditing: A Journal of Theory and Practice*, vol. 18 (Fall), pp. 104-127.

[17] R. Dusenbury, J. L. Reimers, and S. Wheeler, (1996) An Empirical Study of Belief-Based and Probability-Based Specifications of Audit Risk. *Auditing: A Journal of Theory and Practice*, vol. 15 (Fall), pp. 12-28.

[18] G. Monroe and J. Ng, (2000) The Efficacy of Models of Audit Risk. *Belief-Functions in Business Decisions,* edited by R. Srivastava and T. Mock.

[19] G. Shafer, (1976) *A Mathematical Theory of Evidence*. Princeton, NJ: Princeton University Press.

Conflict, Consistency and Consonance in Belief Functions: Coherence and Integrity of Belief Systems

Peter R. Gillett

Associate Professor, Rutgers: The State University of New Jersey[1]

Abstract

This paper discusses how the belief function formalism gives rise to new concepts of conflict and nonspecificity that are more important than conflict in the case of probability theory; assessing this conflict can be important for the strategic choices of whether to seek additional evidence or to discount or retract existing evidence, and which beliefs to retract; it is important to consider not just the external conflict between beliefs, but the internal conflict within belief functions arising from masses assigned to non-intersecting focal elements. The paper considers six measures of conflict: two that apply only to separable belief functions, and that require the canonical decomposition to be found (based on Shafer's work), and four based on extension of the entropy concept (by Yager, Höhle, Ramer, Klir and others). Detailed computations of the various measures are exhibited for two illustrative examples. Axioms for conflict in the context of its intended use are given, and it is argued that dissonance may be the conflict measure that fits them most closely. Finally, a method is given for using conflict to decide which of a set of beliefs to retract (or discount).

1. Introduction

In recent years there has been increased interest in the use of belief functions to represent the assurance provided by various items of audit evidence, and to generate a combined level of assurance. Akresh, Loebbecke and Scott [1] have commented on the flexibility and adaptability of the belief function representation. Shafer and Srivastava [2], Srivastava and Shafer [3] and Srivastava [4-6], have described ways in which, in general, belief functions may be used to model

---

[1] Comments provided by Prakash Shenoy and Keith Harrison are gratefully acknowledged. Support for this research was provided by Hughes Research Laboratories under grant No. GP3044.94-075.

networks of audit evidence, and to propagate the resulting assurance derived from performing various audit procedures. Part of the appeal of belief functions in this context is that they are able to represent ignorance in a way that appears intuitively more appealing to some commentators than a probability-based representation (e.g., Gillett [7]).

1.1. The Representation of Ignorance

The auditor, for example, who performs a limited audit procedure that is deemed to provide a level of assurance assessed as 0.6 will generally not have achieved sufficient assurance to satisfy the relevant audit objective. Nevertheless, the shortcoming may arise from an insufficiency of evidence in support of the assertion being audited – not an accumulation of evidence against the assertion. If a standard probability-based model is used, it may be appropriate to claim that, based on the evidence, the probability of the assertion being true is 0.6. The auditor will be less sanguine, however, about a concomitant claim that there is a probability of 0.4 that the assertion is false. Of course, there may be situations where this would be an appropriate representation: for example, where many respondents to a confirmation of accounts receivable confirm the recorded balance, while a number of others claim that there is a material error. When the limited assurance in support of the correctness of the balance is based on the fact that only some, but not all, of the customers responded to the confirmation, the auditor may be more comfortable with a knowledge representation that in some way attributes belief of 0.6 to the truth of the assertion, and represents the remaining 0.4 as simply a level of ignorance that remains to be resolved by additional audit work or follow-up procedures, and that may in the end be allocated either in support of the assertion or as evidence against it.

The desirability of such an approach becomes more apparent when the evidence in favor of the assertion is based on such a small number of responses that the auditor attributes belief of only 0.4 to the truth of the assertion. Given that all the available evidence, limited though it is, supports the veracity of the assertion subject to audit, a probability-based model that ascribes a probability of 0.6 to the falsity of the assertion would not seem to correspond naturally to the auditor's intuition. There is, after all, no audit evidence against the assertion – merely insufficient evidence in support of it.

The belief function approach described by Shafer & Srivastava [2] has, therefore, as one of its claimed advantages, a more natural representation of ignorance, allied with an ability to differentiate in a useful way between disconfirming evidence and the insufficiency (at some juncture) of supporting evidence.

Shafer and Srivastava claim that by representing a network of audit evidence using belief functions, they derive formulae for the aggregation of audit evidence that differ significantly from the Audit Risk Model that is most often used in practice (AICPA [8-9]). Contrary to this, Efrim Boritz has suggested[2], based on conversations with Anderson, that belief functions do not, and will not, generate results that differ substantively from probability-based approaches. It may be useful to discuss briefly how this diversity of viewpoints has arisen. It is evident from their paper that Shafer and Srivastava do in fact derive formulae that differ analytically from the Audit Risk Model. However, it is fair to say that the differences are entirely attributable (discounting notational variation) to their decision to consider evidence arising at multiple levels within their model. There is no formal reason why the AICPA's Audit Risk Model could not be further developed to consider this possibility.

On the other hand, Boritz's argument is that the Shafer and Srivastava model associates an Audit Risk of 0.05 with the plausibility of error being 0.05 or less. Consequently, the required Belief in the assertion subject to audit is 0.95 – and if this is achieved, it is of no consequence whether the remaining 0.05 or less is allocated to the falsity of the assertion, is allocated to ignorance, or is divided between these alternatives. In any event, sufficient assurance in support of the assertion has been achieved. This, too, seems on its face reasonable.

One of the dilemmas faced in developing and exposing a belief function model of the audit evidence aggregation process has arisen as a result of the need to begin with simple models as a consequence of the relative unfamiliarity of the formalism. Unfortunately, the simple models have not been best designed to take advantage of the expressive power of belief functions. Only when models are considered that combine evidence in support of assertions with evidence against them can the consequences of the different formalisms for the achievement of a specified level of belief (such as 0.95) be appreciated.

In showing how belief functions might be used to represent the aggregation of audit evidence there are many issues to be addressed besides the construction of an appropriate network. Some audit evidence of a judgmental nature may best be described in belief functions terms directly by the auditor. For quantitative audit evidence, Srivastava and Shafer [10] have shown how evidence based on Variables Sampling may be converted to belief in a financial interval. Gillett [11] examines similar issues for Monetary Unit Sampling, and Gillett and Srivastava [12] discuss how evidence based on attribute sampling (for example, of internal controls) may be incorporated via belief functions.

Models of audit assurance that incorporate both positive and negative evidence, whether at the planning stage or as evaluation tools, will naturally produce results

---

[2] Personal communication

that differ from probability-based models, even when evidence at only a single level is considered.

1.2. The Notion of Conflict in Evidence

The representation of audit assurance in probability models is done in such a way that each piece of audit evidence has components of both confirmation and disconfirmation; in other words, we assign to each piece of evidence some probability p that the appropriate assertion is true, together with a concomitant probability (whether or not explicitly stated) of $q = 1 - p$ that the assertion is false. Of course, we may classify the evidence as "confirming" or "disconfirming" based on the relative sizes of p and q but, in any event, in giving a value for either p or q for any particular item of audit evidence, we implicitly or explicitly ascribe a value to the other.

The situation for the belief function representation, on the other hand, is somewhat different. For an assertion with a frame of discernment providing for just truth or falsity, we need to give a mass p in support of truth, and a mass q in support of falsity; the measure of ignorance is then $1 - p - q$, the mass attributed to the frame. However, in this case neither p nor q may in general be derived from the other. This gives rise to a richer representation of the evidence, and to a number of interesting questions. Except in trivial cases (where $p = 0$ or 1), every item of evidence in probability models may be said to contain both positive and negative evidence – although how we classify the item may depend on the relative sizes of p and q. In the belief function framework, however there are new possibilities. An item of evidence may be entirely positive (if $p > 0$ and $q = 0$), entirely negative (if $p = 0$ and $q > 0$), or a mixture (if $p > 0$ and $q > 0$). Suppose we have two separate items of audit evidence. In the case of probability models, we usually consider conflicting evidence only in terms of the relative sizes of p and q for each item; for example, if $p_1 > 0.5$ and $p_2 < 0.5$ we may say the audit evidence provides conflicting results. But this is, in a sense, only a matter of degree – since each item of evidence in this framework has both positive and negative components (apart from trivial cases).

In the case of the belief function framework, however, we may consider two items of evidence with $p_1 > 0.5$ and $p_2 < 0.5$ – and yet there may be no conflict between them: they may simply be stronger and weaker items of supporting evidence Whether or not the evidence is conflicting depends on whether one item provides support for the truth of the assertion while the other provides support for its falsity; i.e., either $p_1 > 0$ and $q_2 > 0$, or $p_2 > 0$ and $q_1 > 0$. In the case of belief functions, evidence may be entirely positive, entirely negative, or a mixture of both – in which case it becomes relevant to consider the internal conflict within an individual item of evidence. For example, when $p_1 > 0$ and $p_2 > q_2 > 0$, the negative evidence in the second belief conflicts not only with the positive evidence in the first belief, but also with the positive evidence in its own belief. The present paper considers how, within the belief function framework, conflict within items of audit evidence should be evaluated and interpreted.

In the context of probability-based models of audit assurance, it is natural to consider evidence as positive or negative in terms of the "balance" between p and q (i. e., whether $p > q$ or $p < q$). Balanced evidence might be said to occur when $p = q$; however, given that $p + q = 1$, this can only occur when $p = q = 0.5$. On the other hand, within the belief function framework there are many possible ways in which the evidence may be evenly balanced between support for the truth and support for the falsity of a proposition or audit assertion; specifically, any basic probability assignments with $p = q$ and $p, q \leq 0.5$ will be evenly balanced. Questions may therefore be posed in this context that do not arise in the probability models. What is the practical significance of the difference between audit evidence modeled by a belief function where $p = q = 0.02$, and another where $p = q = 0.48$? It seems reasonable to suppose that the answer is in some way related to the strength of audit evidence.

The first of these two cases suggests that there is currently inadequate audit evidence, a situation that might be considered resolved if the mass of 0.96 currently assigned to the whole frame were subsequently re-allocated (on the arrival of further evidence) either to p or to q. In fact, this cases arises from combining two belief functions providing belief of 0.0204 respectively for truth and falsity. The second case, however, is potentially more problematic for the auditor. It represents a situation where little ignorance remains ($1 - p - q = 0.04$) but the evidence that has been obtained displays considerable internal conflict. In fact, this case arises from combining two belief functions providing belief of 0.9231 respectively for truth and falsity, suggesting considerable evidence in support of each position. If further evidence were gathered and continued to provide support for both truth and falsity of the assertion, the level of assurance that is normally required to warrant acceptance of the assertion subject to audit would not be obtained. On the other hand, further evidence might eventually resolve the conflict definitively. An alternative response, however, might be to wonder whether the selected audit procedures were failing, for some reason, to provide reliable cues as to the truth or falsity of the assertion. Analytical procedures that are normally reliable, for example, might fail to provide reliable cues if significant unknown events have not been taken into account in developing expectations. The practical problem for the auditor, to which we return later, is whether to seek to overwhelm the problems of the existing evidence by gathering further evidence, or to seek to identify and remove the sources of conflict in the existing evidence.

In the audit environment, therefore, conflict within the belief functions representing the audit evidence may be interpreted either as an accurate representation of an unclear situation, or as a consequence of the failure of the selected audit procedures to provide reliable evidence. The difference between these two interpretations is clearly significant, and has serious consequences for the appropriate audit response. The auditor needs to be able to identify, interpret and respond to conflict within the audit evidence obtained. In probability-based models, $p = q = 0.5$ may represent ignorance or conflict; in belief function representations, however, $p = q = 0$ represents complete ignorance, and $p = q = 0.5$ represents not ignorance but conflict. At intermediate levels, $p = q =$ (say) 0.25 represents a mixture of conflict and ignorance requiring careful interpretation.

1.3 Using Measures of Conflict

The auditor encountering conflict thus faces a strategic choice. At low levels of conflict it may be most appropriate to extend the gathering of audit evidence until the target level of assurance is achieved. At high levels of conflict, it may be more appropriate to seek to identify and remove the sources of conflict. If it is concluded that some of the evidence is providing inaccurate signals as to the target assertion, it may be appropriate either to discount the belief it supports, or to retract the evidence. A suitable measure of conflict, therefore, may be potentially useful in making this strategic choice. If discounting or retraction is chosen, the auditor needs to identify which of a set of conflicting belief functions should be discounted or retracted. Measures of conflict, therefore, have a role to play in identifying belief functions responsible for conflict. Discounting and retraction (invoking defeasible reasoning) are more subtle strategies than seeking to overwhelm conflict by means of additional evidence, and are the subject of ongoing research. The focus of the present paper is the consideration of appropriate measures of conflict, and procedures for using them to assign responsibility for conflict to specific belief functions. As the paper illustrates, these issues are not peculiar to auditing, and arise in other contexts where belief functions are used to model the aggregation of evidence.

1.4 Belief Functions

Before considering examples in which conflict arises, and different ways to measure such conflict, it may be useful to review certain terminology relating to different types of belief functions. Full details may be found in Shafer [13] or Yager [14]. Alternative presentations of belief functions may be found in Kohlas and Monney [15] and Smets and Kennes [16].

A belief function on a frame Θ is a function $\boldsymbol{Bel}: 2^{\Theta} \rightarrow [0, 1]$ satisfying the conditions:

(1) $\boldsymbol{Bel}(\varnothing) = 0$ (1)

(2) $\boldsymbol{Bel}(\Theta)=1$ (2)

(3) for every positive integer n and every collection $A_1,\ldots,A_n$ of subsets of Θ,

$$\boldsymbol{Bel}(A_1 \cup \ldots \cup A_n) \geq \sum_i \boldsymbol{Bel}(A_i) - \sum_{i<j} \boldsymbol{Bel}(A_i \cap A_j) + \ldots + (-1)^{n+1} \boldsymbol{Bel}(A_1 \cap \ldots \cap A_n). \tag{3}$$

We may then define the plausibility function as a function $\boldsymbol{Pl}: 2^\Theta \rightarrow [0, 1]$ given by:

$$\boldsymbol{Pl}(A)=1-\boldsymbol{Bel}(A) \text{ for } A \subseteq \Theta. \tag{4}$$

An alternative formulation of belief functions begins with a *basic probability assignment*, which is a function $\boldsymbol{m}: 2^\Theta \rightarrow [0, 1]$ such that:

(1) $\boldsymbol{m}(\varnothing)=0$ and (5)

(2) $\sum_{A\subseteq\Theta} \boldsymbol{m}(A)=1.$ (6)

Then we may define a belief function by:

$$\boldsymbol{Bel}(A)=\sum_{B\subseteq A} \boldsymbol{m}(B). \tag{7}$$

Furthermore, the basic probability assignment is unique, and can be recovered from:

$$\boldsymbol{m}(A)=\sum_{B\subseteq A} (-1)^{|A-B|} \boldsymbol{Bel}(B) \text{ for all } A \subseteq \Theta. \tag{8}$$

Given a belief function ***Bel*** on the frame Θ represented by a basic probability assignment (bpa) ***m***, we define a *focal element* as:

any subset $X \subseteq \Theta$ such that $\boldsymbol{m}(X) > 0$. (9)

The core $\mathcal{C}$ of ***Bel*** is defined as the union of all the focal elements; i.e.:

$$\mathcal{C}=\{X \subseteq \Theta : \boldsymbol{m}(X) > 0\}. \qquad (10)$$

Belief functions may be combined using Dempster's Rule (see Shafer [13]), as follows. Suppose that $\boldsymbol{m}_1$ and $\boldsymbol{m}_2$ are basic probability assignments with focal elements $A_1,\ldots,A_k$ and $B_1,\ldots,B_l$ respectively, and that they do not flatly contradict each other; i.e., $\kappa = \sum_{\substack{i,j \\ A_i \cap B_j = \varnothing}} \boldsymbol{m}_1(A_i)\cdot \boldsymbol{m}_2(B_j) < 1$. Then the function $\boldsymbol{m} : 2^{\Theta} \rightarrow [0, 1]$ defined by:

$$(1) \quad \boldsymbol{m}(\varnothing) = 0 \text{ and} \qquad (11)$$

$$(2) \quad \boldsymbol{m}(A) = \frac{1}{1-\kappa} \sum_{\substack{i,j \\ A_i \cap B_j = A}} \boldsymbol{m}_1(A_i)\cdot \boldsymbol{m}_2(B_j) \qquad (12)$$

is a basic probability assignment. We call this the orthogonal sum of $\boldsymbol{m}_1$ and $\boldsymbol{m}_2$ and write $\boldsymbol{m} = \boldsymbol{m}_1 \oplus \boldsymbol{m}_2$. Clearly, this orthogonal sum is associative and commutative, so that it does not matter in what order items of evidence are presented and combined.

Where one belief $\boldsymbol{Bel} : 2^{\Theta} \rightarrow [0, 1]$ in a set of beliefs conflicts strongly with the others, we may elect to *discount* it by a factor $a \in [0, 1]$ (cf. Shafer [13]) to produce a new belief function $\boldsymbol{Bel}^a : 2^{\Theta} \rightarrow [0, 1]$, before combining it with the others, as follows:

$$(1) \quad \boldsymbol{Bel}^a(\Theta) = 1 \qquad (13)$$

$$(2) \quad \boldsymbol{Bel}^a(A) = (1-a)\cdot \boldsymbol{Bel}(A) \text{ for all proper } A \subset \Theta. \qquad (14)$$

A belief function $\boldsymbol{Bel}$ is a *vacuous support function* if

$$\boldsymbol{m}(\Theta) = 1 \qquad (15)$$

(which implies that for all other $X \subseteq \Theta$, $\boldsymbol{m}(X) = 0$).

A belief function ***Bel*** is a *simple support function* if for some $A \subseteq \Theta$, and for some s,

$$\boldsymbol{Bel}(X) = \begin{cases} 0 \text{ if } A \not\subset X \\ 1 \text{ if } X = \Theta \\ s \text{ if } A \subseteq X \neq \Theta \end{cases} \tag{16}$$

or alternatively,

$$\begin{aligned} &\boldsymbol{m}(A) = \boldsymbol{Bel}(A) = s \\ &\boldsymbol{m}(\Theta) = 1 - s \\ &\boldsymbol{m}(X) = 0 \text{ if } X \neq A,\ \Theta. \end{aligned} \tag{17}$$

If s = 1, we describe ***Bel*** as a *certain support function*.

A belief function ***Bel*** is a *separable support function* if

$$\boldsymbol{Bel} = S_1 \oplus \ldots \oplus S_n \tag{18}$$

where each S_i is a simple support function. In general, this decomposition is not unique. However, if ***Bel*** is non-vacuous with core $\mathcal{C}$ there is a unique canonical decomposition where the focus of each S_i is contained in $\mathcal{C}$ and distinct elements have distinct foci; i.e., $i \neq j \Rightarrow$ focus of $S_i \neq$ focus of S_j.

A belief function ***Bel*** is a *support function* if there is some refinement Ω of the frame Θ (i.e., with some of the elements of Θ subdivided), and a separable support function S on Ω such that ***Bel*** is equal to the restriction of S to Θ (i.e., $\boldsymbol{Bel} = S^{\downarrow\Theta}$). See Shafer [13] for an example of a support function that is not separable.

A belief function ***Bel*** is a *quasi-support function* if it is not a support function. Quasi-support functions may be represented as the limits of sequences of support functions.

A belief function ***Bel*** is a *Bayesian support function* if :

$$
\begin{aligned}
&\boldsymbol{Bel}(\varnothing)=0\\
&\boldsymbol{Bel}(\Theta)=1\\
&\boldsymbol{Bel}(\mathrm{X}\cup\mathrm{Y})=\boldsymbol{Bel}(\mathrm{X})+\boldsymbol{Bel}(\mathrm{Y})\ \text{if X, Y}\subseteq\Theta\ \&\ \mathrm{X}\cap\mathrm{Y}\neq\varnothing\ \text{or, equivalently:}\\
&\boldsymbol{Bel}(\mathrm{X})+\boldsymbol{Bel}(\sim\mathrm{X})=1\ \text{if X}\subseteq\Theta.
\end{aligned}
\tag{19}
$$

The focal elements of a Bayesian support function are singletons. Bayesian support functions are quasi-support functions. Shafer views these as in a sense idealized belief functions defined as limiting results that cannot arise in practice as a result of finitary evidence-gathering processes.

Finally, a belief function ***Bel*** is a ***consonant belief function*** if its focal elements are nested. Equivalently,

$$
\boldsymbol{Bel}(\mathrm{X}\cap\mathrm{Y})=\boldsymbol{min}(\boldsymbol{Bel}(\mathrm{X}),\ \boldsymbol{Bel}(\mathrm{Y}))\ \text{or}\ \boldsymbol{Bel}(\mathrm{X}\cup\mathrm{Y})=\boldsymbol{max}(\boldsymbol{Pl}(\mathrm{X}),\ \boldsymbol{Pl}(\mathrm{Y})).
\tag{20}
$$

Every simple support function is consonant. The only belief functions that are both consonant and Bayesian are the certain support functions. If ***Bel*** is a consonant support function then for any $\mathrm{X}\subseteq\Theta$ either ***Bel***(X) = 0 or ***Bel***(~X) = 0. Shafer regards consonant belief functions as: "true support functions; in fact, they are separable support functions. And they are distinguished by their failure to betray even a hint of conflict in the evidence. The evidence underlying a consonant support function is not necessarily homogeneous. But it can be described as 'pointing in a single direction'; it is heterogeneous only in that it varies in the precision of its focus. (Shafer 1976)"

1.5 Missile Defense Applications

The aggregation of audit evidence, the resolution of conflicts in that evidence, and the consequential audit decisions, are real and practical problems of considerable importance and significant financial implications. Models of these processes to date, however, whether based on belief functions or probabilities, have been based on considering the presence or absence of material misstatements, and for these purposes binary frames of discernment suffice. Other applications of belief functions require larger frames, and the resulting conflicts among the items of evidence are richer and more complex. One such application is the development of missile defense systems. The real-world application in which the issues addressed in this paper first arose are the subject of non-disclosure agreements that prevent their description, and the discussion in the paper is therefore based on a stylized example of the recognition of a potential missile. Nevertheless, the simplified nature of the fictional example is not intended to suggest that the application issues are anything but real: clearly, the financial burdens of developing such systems are huge, and the potential implications of poor performance potentially tragic. Approiu [17] describes an unrelated application of belief functions to multisensor data fusion.

The next section of this paper examines the idea of conflict in belief functions in more detail, discusses internal and external conflict, provides several alternative definitions of conflict, and sets out two examples of sets of conflicting beliefs that are used to illustrate the various alternative measures. The third section discusses desirable properties for definitions of conflict, evaluates the various proposed measures of conflict in relation to these properties, and examines how measures of conflict might be used to identify "outliers" in a set of beliefs so that they may be discounted or retracted. Finally, the last section summarizes the main arguments and results of the paper, and considers potential future research issues.

2. Conflict and Consonance

2.1. Conflicting Beliefs on Binary Frames

As Gillett [7] has observed, the auditor does not usually plan to obtain conflicting evidence. Nevertheless, conflict may arise when planned audit procedures are performed. Consider, for example, a case where an auditor seeks to confirm the management assertion that Accounts Receivable exist. Let us refer to this assertion in abbreviated form as ARE, and assign to it a frame of discernment $\Theta_{ARE} = \{e, \sim e\}$ representing the possibilities that Accounts Receivable, as stated in the Financial Statements, do or do not exist, respectively. Suppose also that the application of analytical procedures based on ratio analysis provides assurance assessed as 0.60 that Accounts Receivable as stated do indeed exist. The evidence provided by analytical procedures can be represented by a belief function μ_1 described by giving its basic probability assignment:

$$\boldsymbol{m}_1(\{e\}) = 0.60, \boldsymbol{m}_1(\{\sim e\}) = 0.00, \boldsymbol{m}_1(\{e, \sim e\}) = 0.40. \tag{21}$$

Now suppose, additionally, that the auditor performs the usual confirmation procedures in order to obtain additional assurance in support of ARE, but that, contrary to expectations, customers dispute the amounts in question, so that the auditor has evidence supporting ~e, represented as a belief function μ_2 by the bpa:

$$\boldsymbol{m}_2(\{e\}) = 0.00, \boldsymbol{m}_2(\{\sim e\}) = 0.80, \boldsymbol{m}_2(\{e, \sim e\}) = 0.20. \tag{22}$$

Thus μ_1 and μ_2 are both simple support functions. The standard application of Dempster's Rule gives the combined bpa (or orthogonal sum):

$$m_1 \oplus m_2(\{e\}) = (0.60*0.20)/(1-0.60*0.80),$$
$$m_1 \oplus m_2(\{\sim e\}) = (0.40*0.80)/(1-0.60*0.80),$$
$$m_1 \oplus m_2(\{e, \sim e\}) = (0.40*0.20)/(1-0.60*0.80) \quad (23)$$

i.e., $m_1 \oplus m_2(\{e\}) = 0.23$, $m_1 \oplus m_2(\{\sim e\}) = 0.62$, $m_1 \oplus m_2(\{e, \sim e\}) = 0.15$,

leading to beliefs

$$Bel(\{e\}) = 0.23, Bel(\{\sim e\}) = 0.62, Bel(\{e, \sim e\}) = 1.00. \quad (24)$$

In arriving at the combined bpa, a considerable amount of evidence is "discarded" as a result of the conflict created by the impossibility of e and ~e both being true (0.60*0.80). In addition, the resulting bpa now demonstrates internal conflict, being evidence supporting both e and ~e. One question to be considered in this paper is how to measure the external and internal conflict arising in this example. Note also that the combined belief function is (by definition) a separable support function, although it is not simple. However, since $\{e\} \not\subset \{\sim e\}$ and $\{\sim e\} \not\subset \{e\}$ it is not a consonant support function.

In calculating the combined bpa $m_1 \oplus m_2$ the values were normalized by dividing through by (1 - 0.60*0.80), where $\kappa = 0.60*0.80$ represents the mass that would otherwise have been assigned to impossible conditions identified by empty intersections such as $\{e\}\cap\{\sim e\}$. The sum of such masses (i.e., κ = 1 - the normalizing constant used in Dempster's Rule) represents a natural initial measure of the conflict between m_1 and m_2, in this case equal to 0.48[3]. Clearly, the measure κ has a range of values from 0 to 1. Effectively, the sum of the masses that would otherwise be assigned to empty intersections is proportionally allocated to the focal elements of the combined belief. As a result, this mass no longer appears explicitly as conflict in the combined belief. However, since the remaining bpas are increased by this normalization process, the effect is to increase the conflict between the combined belief and any subsequent belief functions. (It may be seen from the discussion below that measures of internal conflict within the combined belief are also increased by the conflict dissipation inherent in Dempster's Rule.)

2.2. Conflicting Beliefs on General Frames

A more complex situation arises where the frame of discernment is larger than a binary set. Consider, for example, a system designed to detect and analyze airborne threats, where the frame of discernment $\Theta = \{f, e, c, n\}$. The intended interpretation is:

---

[3] In some alternative versions of belief functions, such as the transferable belief model described by Smets and Kennes [16], there is no normalization, and the corresponding degree of conflict is represented by the bpa assigned to the empty set.

f friendly aircraft

e enemy aircraft

c enemy missile – conventional warhead

n enemy missile – nuclear warhead.

Suppose that belief functions are generated from a number of different sources:

μ_1 from an advanced radar system

μ_2 from a spy satellite system

μ_3 from a computer-based intelligence system

μ_4 from reports by the pilots of military aircraft.

Suppose also that at some point in time an incoming object is detected by advanced radar, traveling at high speed on a path potentially directed towards the White House. Interpretation of the radar signals might suggest a low belief that the object is an aircraft (friendly or enemy), a higher belief that the object is a missile (conventional or nuclear) together with some residual uncertainty (ignorance). Signals from an overhead spy satellite might suggest, based on trajectory and velocity, that the object is definitely a missile, with a low belief that it is conventional, a higher belief that it is nuclear, and some belief distributed between the two options (with some residual ignorance based on potential unreliability of the equipment). Military intelligence, however, might suggest that the apparent country of origin is without nuclear capability; in conjunction with a certain modest recognition of past failings, this might be represented by a small belief that the object is, in fact, a friendly aircraft, a larger belief that it is an unfriendly projectile (whether aircraft or missile), and some belief that it must at least be one or other of these as it cannot possibly be nuclear (along with residual uncertainty naturally accruing to military intelligence processes!). Finally, however, suppose the pilot of a high speed interceptor plane reports that the object looks like a friendly aircraft (but might not be, as it is a bright sunny day and difficult to see the projectile clearly).

A set of belief functions corresponding to this scenario might be given by the following basic probability assignments:

$$\mu_1 \quad \boldsymbol{m}_1(\{f, e\}) = 0.2. \ \boldsymbol{m}_1(\{c, n\}) = 0.75, \boldsymbol{m}_1(\{f, e, c, n\}) = 0.05 \qquad (25)$$

μ_2 $\boldsymbol{m}_2(\{c\}) = 0.3, \boldsymbol{m}_2(\{n\}) = 0.6, \boldsymbol{m}_2(\{c, n\}) = 0.05, \boldsymbol{m}_2(\{f, e, c, n\}) = 0.05$ (26)

μ_3 $\boldsymbol{m}_3(\{f\}) = 0.1, \boldsymbol{m}_3(\{e, c\}) = 0.6, \boldsymbol{m}_3(\{f, e, c\}) = 0.25, \boldsymbol{m}_3(\{f, e, c, n\}) = 0.05$ (27)

μ_4 $\boldsymbol{m}_4(\{f\}) = 0.6, \boldsymbol{m}_4(\{f, e, c, n\}) = 0.4.$ (28)

This evidence is less than ideal. Quite apart from the fact that the different sources of evidence do not appear to be sending consistent signals, none of the individual belief functions except the last is consonant. μ_1, μ_2 and μ_3 are separable support functions, and μ_4 is simple.

The combined belief from advanced radar and spy satellite evidence (μ_1 and μ_2) is given by the bpa:

$$\boldsymbol{m}_1 \oplus \boldsymbol{m}_2(\{c\}) = 0.2963, \boldsymbol{m}_1 \oplus \boldsymbol{m}_2(\{n\}) = 0.5926, \boldsymbol{m}_1 \oplus \boldsymbol{m}_2(\{f, e\}) = 0.0123,$$
$$\boldsymbol{m}_1 \oplus \boldsymbol{m}_2(\{c, n\}) = 0.0957, \boldsymbol{m}_1 \oplus \boldsymbol{m}_2(\{f, e, c, n\}) = 0.0031. \quad (29)$$

Following incorporation of the evidence μ_3 from military intelligence, we obtain:

$$\boldsymbol{m}_1 \oplus \boldsymbol{m}_2 \oplus \boldsymbol{m}_3(\{f\}) = 0.0039, \boldsymbol{m}_1 \oplus \boldsymbol{m}_2 \oplus \boldsymbol{m}_3(\{e\}) = 0.0186,$$
$$\boldsymbol{m}_1 \oplus \boldsymbol{m}_2 \oplus \boldsymbol{m}_3(\{c\}) = 0.8747, \boldsymbol{m}_1 \oplus \boldsymbol{m}_2 \oplus \boldsymbol{m}_3(\{n\}) = 0.0745,$$
$$\boldsymbol{m}_1 \oplus \boldsymbol{m}_2 \oplus \boldsymbol{m}_3(\{f, e\}) = 0.0093, \boldsymbol{m}_1 \oplus \boldsymbol{m}_2 \oplus \boldsymbol{m}_3(\{e, c\}) = 0.0047,$$
$$\boldsymbol{m}_1 \oplus \boldsymbol{m}_2 \oplus \boldsymbol{m}_3(\{c, n\}) = 0.0120, \boldsymbol{m}_1 \oplus \boldsymbol{m}_2 \oplus \boldsymbol{m}_3(\{f, e, c\}) = 0.0019,$$
$$\boldsymbol{m}_1 \oplus \boldsymbol{m}_2 \oplus \boldsymbol{m}_3(\{f, e, c, n\}) = 0.0004. \quad (30)$$

Finally, after inclusion of the belief μ_4 generated by the report from the pilot of the interceptor plane we obtain the combined bpa:

$$\boldsymbol{m}_1 \oplus \boldsymbol{m}_2 \oplus \boldsymbol{m}_3 \oplus \boldsymbol{m}_4(\{f\}) = 0.0265, \boldsymbol{m}_1 \oplus \boldsymbol{m}_2 \oplus \boldsymbol{m}_3 \oplus \boldsymbol{m}_4(\{e\}) = 0.0182,$$
$$\boldsymbol{m}_1 \oplus \boldsymbol{m}_2 \oplus \boldsymbol{m}_3 \oplus \boldsymbol{m}_4(\{c\}) = 0.8548, \boldsymbol{m}_1 \oplus \boldsymbol{m}_2 \oplus \boldsymbol{m}_3 \oplus \boldsymbol{m}_4(\{n\}) = 0.0728,$$
$$\boldsymbol{m}_1 \oplus \boldsymbol{m}_2 \oplus \boldsymbol{m}_3 \oplus \boldsymbol{m}_4(\{f, e\}) = 0.0091, \boldsymbol{m}_1 \oplus \boldsymbol{m}_2 \oplus \boldsymbol{m}_3 \oplus \boldsymbol{m}_4(\{e, c\}) = 0.0045,$$
$$\boldsymbol{m}_1 \oplus \boldsymbol{m}_2 \oplus \boldsymbol{m}_3 \oplus \boldsymbol{m}_4(\{c, n\}) = 0.0118, \boldsymbol{m}_1 \oplus \boldsymbol{m}_2 \oplus \boldsymbol{m}_3 \oplus \boldsymbol{m}_4(\{f, e, c\}) = 0.0019,$$
$$\boldsymbol{m}_1 \oplus \boldsymbol{m}_2 \oplus \boldsymbol{m}_3 \oplus \boldsymbol{m}_4(\{f, e, c, n\}) = 0.0004. \quad (31)$$

Full details of the bpas, beliefs and plausibilities for the combined belief functions in this example are given in Table 1. Panel A shows μ_1 in ***m***, ***Bel*** and ***Pl*** forms, followed by four associated measures of conflict and nonspecificity (discussed in section 2.5 below). The same information is then provided for μ_2 and for their combination $\mu' = \mu_1 \oplus \mu_2$. Panel B shows this information for μ', μ_3, and their combination $\mu'' = \mu_1 \oplus \mu_2 \oplus \mu_3$. Finally, Panel C shows this information for μ'', μ_4 and their combination $\mu = \mu_1 \oplus \mu_2 \oplus \mu_3 \oplus \mu_4$.

It may be seen, for example, that:

$$\boldsymbol{Bel}(\{c, n\}) = \boldsymbol{Bel}_1 \oplus \boldsymbol{Bel}_2 \oplus \boldsymbol{Bel}_3 \oplus \boldsymbol{Bel}_4(\{c, n\}) = 0.9393, \boldsymbol{Pl}(\{c, n\}) = 0.9462 \tag{32}$$

$$\boldsymbol{Bel}(\{n\}) = \boldsymbol{Bel}_1 \oplus \boldsymbol{Bel}_2 \oplus \boldsymbol{Bel}_3 \oplus \boldsymbol{Bel}_4\ (\{n\}) = 0.0728, \boldsymbol{Pl}(\{n\}) = 0.0849, \tag{33}$$

$$\boldsymbol{Bel}(\{e\}) = \boldsymbol{Bel}_1 \oplus \boldsymbol{Bel}_2 \oplus \boldsymbol{Bel}_3 \oplus \boldsymbol{Bel}_4\ (\{e\}) = 0.0182, \boldsymbol{Pl}(\{e\}) = 0.0341. \tag{34}$$

Although there is no intention in this study to suggest that this is in any way a realistic example, it appears that the possibility of a missile attack (either conventional or nuclear) is strongly suggested by the evidence. Interception and/or evacuation of the President and his staff might be appropriate. However, a nuclear attack is only weakly indicated, and evacuation of Washington DC does not seem necessary. Of course, the landing of an enemy plane on the White House lawn seems most unlikely. Issues of realism notwithstanding, our confidence in the outcome of this analysis may be somewhat mitigated by the apparent confusion in the evidence, which we discuss below.

In the earlier auditing example, each of the two possible outcomes opposed the other, and conflict was obvious. In the present case, there are four mutually exclusive possible outcomes, and evidence for any one of them presumably conflicts with evidence for any of the others. This alone, however, is not sufficient for an understanding of either the vagueness or the conflict in the example. The mass attributed by μ_1 to the pair of outcomes {f, e} also apparently conflicts with the mass attributed by μ_2 to the pair {c, n} – the incoming object may be an aircraft, or a missile, but cannot be both. We might conclude that there is conflict between any two non-identical focal elements; in the case of, say, {n} and {f, e, c} this seems reasonable, but more generally the position is less clear. For example, how should we categorize the interaction between {f} and {f, e}. One of the distinguishing features of belief functions, as opposed to probability theory, is the possibility of committing mass to subsets of the frame other than singletons. Mass attributed to {f, e} is committed to either f or e, although we cannot yet say which. This nonspecificity does not necessarily constitute conflict in an intuitive sense, and the focal elements {f} and {f, e} are not inconsistent; their combined mass would be ascribed to the element {f}. In the spirit of the definition of consonant belief functions given earlier, we see that since $\{f\} \subseteq \{f, e\}$ it may be appropriate to describe these two elements as *consonant*. What are we to say, then, regarding elements such as {f, e, c} and {c, n}? Certainly there is nonspecificity here, although the elements are not consonant; their combined belief would be ascribed to a third element, {c}. On the other hand, this narrowing down of choices as a result of additional evidence seems entirely natural, and not necessarily a situation of conflict. Our intuitions regarding when we might or might not want to declare conflict between two elements may be intimately tied up with the purpose for which conflict is to be assessed.

2.3. Internal Conflict

Consider again the example of two conflicting beliefs for Accounts Receivable described above. In arriving at the combined belief a bpa mass of $\kappa = 0.48$ was redistributed across the focal elements of the combined belief. Nevertheless, the orthogonal sum $m_1 \oplus m_2$ still represents the conflict in the original items of evidence. Recall that the combined bpa was:

$$\boldsymbol{m}_1 \oplus \boldsymbol{m}_2(\mathrm{e}) = 0.23,\ \boldsymbol{m}_1 \oplus \boldsymbol{m}_2(\sim\mathrm{e}) = 0.62,\ \boldsymbol{m}_1 \oplus \boldsymbol{m}_2(\mathrm{e}, \sim\mathrm{e}) = 0.15. \tag{35}$$

There is less ignorance represented here than in either of the original beliefs, as a consequence of the obtaining of additional evidence. However, the additional evidence has largely refuted the original evidence, and as a result the combined bpa itself contains conflict because it assigns masses to focal elements that cannot be true simultaneously. We refer to this as "internal conflict". In the simple case where two conflicting belief functions are combined, the internal conflict in the resulting combined bpa is evident: {e} and {~e} are in a natural sense opposites (each element is the negation of the other). As we have seen, a little more care is needed in considering the case of combined beliefs on larger than binary frames of discernment.

2.4. External Conflict and Shafer's Weight of Conflict

For the auditing example above, we defined an intuitive measure of conflict between two belief functions as the sum of the masses assigned to empty intersections (e.g., $\{e\} \cap \{\sim e\}$):

$$\kappa = \sum_{\substack{i,j \\ A_i \cap B_j = \varnothing}} \boldsymbol{m}_1(\mathrm{X}_i) \cdot \boldsymbol{m}_2(\mathrm{Y}_j). \tag{36}$$

The calculated value was $\kappa = 0.48$. For the airborne threats example, the values of κ calculated at each stage of the combination process are shown in Table 1. For example, when μ_1 and μ_2 are combined (see Panel A), $\kappa = 0.19$. In the final step, when $(\mu_1 \oplus \mu_2 \oplus \mu_3)$ and μ_4 are combined (Panel C), $\kappa = 0.5907$. At each stage in the application of Dempster's Rule, however, the conflict mass in the current combination measured by κ is re-distributed among the focal elements of the combined belief function, so that the masses on focal elements are inflated accordingly, leading to correspondingly higher values for κ at subsequent stages of combination.

A cumulative measure discussed by Shafer [13] is based on the total sum of the masses that would be allocated to cells corresponding to empty intersections in the hyper-cube created if all the orthogonal sums were carried out simultaneously (as opposed to sequentially). This cumulative κ may be calculated from the sequential values as follows:

if $\kappa_1, \ldots, \kappa_{n-1}$ are the values derived from the (n-1) steps in forming the orthogonal sum (in any order) of belief functions $\mu_1, \ldots, \mu_n$, then the combined

$$\kappa = 1 - \prod_{1}^{n-1} (1-\kappa_i). \tag{37}$$

This cumulative measure is also shown in Table 1. Thus, for the airborne threats example, the combined value of $\kappa = 0.8681$. However, this intuitive measure is not itself a completely satisfactory measure of conflict. It is a measure only of "external conflict"; i.e., it measures the conflict between $\mu_1, \ldots, \mu_n$, but does not capture the internal conflict between the masses assigned to different focal elements within each belief function.

Our first measure of (external) conflict, κ, has values in the range [0, 1]. Shafer prefers to treat his measure of conflict as a weight, and uses instead of κ the log of the normalizing constant

$$\boldsymbol{Con}(\mu_1, \ldots, \mu_n) = \boldsymbol{log}\left(\frac{1}{1-\kappa}\right) = -\boldsymbol{log}(1-\kappa). \tag{38}$$

This has values in the range $[0, \infty]$. Shafer also shows that the cumulative conflict may be calculated by summing the values of this function: i.e.:

$$\boldsymbol{Con}(\mu_1, \ldots, \mu_{n+1}) = \boldsymbol{Con}(\mu_1, \ldots, \mu_n) + \boldsymbol{Con}(\mu_1 \oplus \ldots \oplus \mu_n, \mu_{n+1}). \tag{39}$$

Using this result, cumulative values can be calculated without the product formula given earlier. Like κ, however, $\mathrm{Con}(\mu_1, \ldots, \mu_n)$ measures only the *external* conflict between $\mu_1, \ldots, \mu_n$, and does not measure the complete conflict in the combined belief function because it fails to include the *internal* conflict within the original belief functions.

For a separable belief function μ, Shafer defines a measure W_μ of *internal* conflict as follows:

$$W_\mu = \begin{cases} 0 \text{ if } \mu \text{ is a simple support function} \\ \text{the infimum of the quantities } \boldsymbol{Con}(\mu_1,\ldots,\mu_n) \text{ for the various possible} \\ \text{decompositions } \mu = \mu_1 \oplus \ldots \oplus \mu_n \text{ into simple support functions} \\ \text{if } \mu \text{ is not simple.} \end{cases} \tag{40}$$

This is equivalent to $W_\mu = \boldsymbol{Con}(\mu_1, \ldots, \mu_n)$ for the canonical decomposition of μ.

The belief functions in the auditing example considered earlier were both simple support functions, with *internal* conflict $W_\mu = 0$. For the airborne threats example, the measures of *internal* conflict (not shown in Table 1) may be computed from the canonical decompositions as follows:

μ_1 has the canonical decomposition

$$\begin{aligned} &\boldsymbol{m}_1(\{f, e\}) = 4/5,\ \boldsymbol{m}_1(\{f, e, c, n\}) = 1/5 \\ &\boldsymbol{m}_2(\{c, n\}) = 15/16,\ \boldsymbol{m}_2(\{f, e, c, n\}) = 1/16 \end{aligned} \tag{41}$$

giving $\kappa = 0.75$ and $W_\mu = 1.3863$.

μ_2 has the canonical decomposition

$$\begin{aligned} &\boldsymbol{m}_1(\{c\}) = 3/4,\ \boldsymbol{m}_1(\{f, e, c, n\}) = 1/4 \\ &\boldsymbol{m}_2(\{n\}) = 6/7,\ \boldsymbol{m}_2(\{f, e, c, n\}) = 1/7 \\ &\boldsymbol{m}_3(\{c, n\}) = 1/2,\ \boldsymbol{m}_3(\{f, e, c, n\}) = 1/2 \end{aligned} \tag{42}$$

giving $\kappa = 0.6429$ and $W_\mu = 1.0296$.

μ_3 has the canonical decomposition

$$\begin{aligned} &\boldsymbol{m}_1(\{f\}) = 1/4,\ \boldsymbol{m}_1(\{f, e, c, n\}) = 3/4 \\ &\boldsymbol{m}_2(\{e, c\}) = 2/3,\ \boldsymbol{m}_2(\{f, e, c, n\}) = 1/3 \\ &\boldsymbol{m}_3(\{f, e, c\}) = 5/6,\ \boldsymbol{m}_3(\{f, e, c, n\}) = 1/6 \end{aligned} \tag{43}$$

giving $\kappa = 0.1667$ and $W_\mu = 0.1823$.

μ_4 is a simple support function so that

$$W_\mu = 0. \tag{44}$$

As shown in Table 1 – Panel C, the *external* conflict ***Con***$(\mu_1, \ldots, \mu_4) = 2.0257$ for the combination of $\mu_1, \ldots, \mu_4$; in order to obtain a measure of the *total* conflict in the combined $\mu = \mu_1 \oplus \ldots \oplus \mu_4$ we must add to this the *internal* conflicts, giving:

$$W_\mu = 2.0257 + 1.3863 + 1.0296 + 0.1823 + 0 = 4.6239; \tag{45}$$

this corresponds to a combined *total* conflict, from equation (38), $\kappa = 0.9902$.

This result confirms our earlier feeling of unease: 99.02% of the combined mass of the belief functions in the example is assigned to empty intersections, and is proportionally re-allocated to the masses constituting the remaining 0.98%. Effectively, 99.02% of the original mass is treated as noise.

Note that Shafer's measure of internal conflict is defined only for separable support functions, and not for non-separable support functions or quasi-support functions. It is natural to wonder under what conditions the definition of W_μ might be extended; however, for the present we pursue an alternative course. Even for separable support functions, it is necessary to obtain the canonical decomposition of the combined (or the original) belief functions before this measure can be used. Smets [18] has developed an extended method for defining a canonical decomposition of belief functions, and recommends using this to determine a measure of conflict [19]. This decomposition requires the use of "inverse support functions" which are not belief functions as defined in this paper; consequently, this line of inquiry is not pursued here.

Since Shannon's entropy has had such a significant impact on probability and information theory, we now examine attempts to generalize entropy to belief functions so as to give measures of conflict that are defined for general belief functions. Note, however, that the measures we have been considering define conflict relative to a particular rule for the combination of belief functions – Dempster's Rule. Zadeh [20] and others have questioned whether Dempster's Rule is appropriate in circumstances where it has been found to give counter-intuitive results. Alternative proposals, based on amended treatments of the closed-world assumption used by Shafer, and the way in which conflict is handled, have been proposed by a number of writers (Zadeh [21], Yager [22], Smets [23]), and may be presumed to have significant implications for definitions of conflict. These issues have not yet been fully explored in the literature.

2.5. Entropy-Like Measures of Conflict

Shannon's measure of entropy for a probability distribution (Shannon [24]) is given by the formula

$$H=\sum_{i} -p(x_i)\cdot \boldsymbol{log}_2\, p(x_i) \tag{46}$$

and has been extensively used in information theory. Several writers have proposed generalizations to belief functions. For example, Yager [14] proposes

$$\text{Em}=\sum_{A\subseteq\Theta} \boldsymbol{m}(A)\cdot \boldsymbol{Con}(\boldsymbol{Bel},\ \boldsymbol{Bel}_A) \tag{47}$$

where $\boldsymbol{Bel}_A$ is the certain support function focused at A. Equivalently:

$$\text{Em}=-\sum_{A\subseteq\Theta} \boldsymbol{m}(A)\cdot \boldsymbol{log}(\boldsymbol{Pl}(A)). \tag{48}$$

For Bayesian belief functions, this definition reduces to the Shannon entropy. Em = 0 for simple support functions, for consonant belief functions and, indeed, for any belief structure where no two focal elements are disjoint. Bayesian belief functions are thus prototypical examples of disjoint belief structures with non-zero entropy. Em is maximal if all the focal elements are disjoint.

In the remainder of this paper we use a slightly modified version of this measure discussed by Klir [25] in which, as for Shannon's H, the base of logarithms is 2:

$$E(\boldsymbol{m})=-\sum_{A\subseteq\Theta} \boldsymbol{m}(A)\cdot \boldsymbol{log}_2(\boldsymbol{Pl}(A)). \tag{49}$$

This measure is a natural extension of Shafer's measure of internal conflict insofar as it defines as conflicting only those elements that are disjoint. $E(\boldsymbol{m})$ has values in the range $[0, \boldsymbol{log}_2 |\Theta|]$, and is sometimes called a measure of *dissonance*.

We saw earlier that for consonant elements such as $\{f\} \subseteq \{f, e\}$ it seems appropriate not to define conflict; however, some authors have suggested that our intuition suggests that conflict nevertheless exists where, for example, $\{f, e\} \not\subset \{f\}$ even though these subsets are not disjoint. A broader entropy-like measure of conflict defining conflict for any two elements X, Y where $X \not\subset Y$ was given by Höhle [26] (often called a measure of *confusion*):

$$C(\boldsymbol{m})=-\sum_{A\subseteq\Theta} \boldsymbol{m}(A)\cdot \boldsymbol{log}_2(\boldsymbol{Bel}(A)). \tag{50}$$

Unfortunately, the values of C(m) are not confined to the range [0, log_2 |Θ|], and C(m) takes no account of the *degree* of non-inclusion of conflicting subsets. A modification to deal with this was proposed by Klir and Ramer [27]:

$$D(m) = -\sum_{A \in F} m(A) \cdot log_2 \left[1 - \sum_{A \in F} m(B) \cdot \frac{|B - A|}{|B|} \right] \tag{51}$$

where F is the set of focal elements of m. Equivalently:

$$D(m) = -\sum_{A \in F} m(A) \cdot log_2 \left[\sum_{A \in F} m(B) \cdot \frac{|A \cap B|}{|B|} \right]. \tag{52}$$

D(m) has values in the range [0, log_2 |Θ|], and is called a measure of *discord*. Further details are given in Ramer and Klir [28].

Although D(m) incorporates a measure of non-inclusion and has the desirable property $E(m) \leq D(m) \leq S(m)$, it does not scale correctly in the case of nested elements (i.e., where one is a subset of the other. More recently, Klir and Parviz [29] and Vejnarova and Klir [30] have proposed an alternative which is scaled differently to correct this shortcoming :

$$S(m) = -\sum_{A \in F} m(A) \cdot log_2 \left[1 - \sum_{A \in F} m(B) \cdot \frac{|A - B|}{|A|} \right] \tag{53}$$

where F is the set of focal elements of m. Equivalently:

$$S(m) = -\sum_{A \in F} m(A) \cdot log_2 \left[\sum_{A \in F} m(B) \cdot \frac{|A \cap B|}{|A|} \right]. \tag{54}$$

S(m) has values in the range [0, log_2 |Θ|], and is called a measure of *strife*.

Reference was made earlier (see section 2.2) to nonspecificity in belief functions; entropy-like measures have been used successfully to assess nonspecificity. For example, the function proposed by Dubois and Prade [31], and now widely accepted, is:

$$N(m) = \sum_{A \subseteq \Theta} m(A) \cdot log_2 (|A|). \tag{55}$$

For probability functions, this measure has value 0. Since belief functions may exhibit both conflict and nonspecificity, it is reasonable to consider measures of

Aggregate Uncertainty based on E($\boldsymbol{m}$) + N($\boldsymbol{m}$), D($\boldsymbol{m}$) + N($\boldsymbol{m}$) or S($\boldsymbol{m}$) + N($\boldsymbol{m}$). As discussed below, however, these functions lack the property of subadditivity, and research has focused on studying alternative approaches to total uncertainty. Harmanec and Klir [32] (in conjunction with a number of other authors) propose as a measure of Aggregate Uncertainty:

$$\mathrm{Au}(\boldsymbol{Bel}) = \underset{P_{\mathrm{Bel}}}{\boldsymbol{max}} \left[-\sum_{\theta \in \Theta} p_\theta \cdot \boldsymbol{log}_2 p_\theta \right] \tag{56}$$

where the maximum is taken over all the probability distributions $\langle p_\theta | \theta \in \Theta \rangle$ that are consistent with the given belief measure; i.e., that satisfy the constraints:

$$\text{(1)} \quad p_\theta \in [0, 1] \text{ for all } \theta \in \Theta \text{ and } \sum_{\theta \in \Theta} p_\theta = 1 \tag{57}$$

$$\text{(2)} \quad \boldsymbol{Bel}(\mathrm{A}) \leq \sum_{\theta \in \mathrm{A}} p_\theta \leq 1 - \boldsymbol{Bel}(\overline{\mathrm{A}}) \text{ for all } \mathrm{A} \subseteq \Theta . \tag{58}$$

AU($\boldsymbol{Bel}$) is defined in terms of the solution to a nonlinear optimization problem; fortunately, relatively simple algorithms are available for computing the measure (see Harmonec et al. [33]). Current research interest focuses on AU($\boldsymbol{Bel}$) as a measure of total aggregate uncertainty; it seems natural, therefore, to consider AU($\boldsymbol{Bel}$) - N($\boldsymbol{m}$) as a another candidate for a measure of conflict. However, the properties of such a measure have not yet been fully explored, and we will not consider it further in this paper. Klir and Wierman [34] summarizes most of the research to date on these topics.

Table 1 shows details of the computation of the four (entropy-like) measures of conflict for the airborne threats example discussed earlier, together with the measure of nonspecificity; the amount that each element contributes to the total measure is shown to facilitate an intuitive understanding of the differences in how these measures are defined. Note, for example, that the strife S($\boldsymbol{m}$) for the final combined belief function is 0.7050 (Panel C). This is less than after only the first two functions have been combined (0.8768). The table also shows the measures re-scaled to take values in the range [0, 1] by normalizing by the maximum value, in order to facilitate comparison with belief functions on other frames of different cardinalities (in this example, of course, this is not strictly necessary, since all belief functions discussed are on the same frame). Note that the final results are naturally independent of the order in which the beliefs are combined.

Table 1 is presented in a format that explicitly shows the contribution of each focal element to the various measures of conflict. For example, the element {n} contributes 0.2590 to the total strife S($\boldsymbol{m}$) = 0.7050 for the final combined belief function (Panel C). Thus differences and similarities between the four entropy-like measures, based on differences in what is considered conflict, as described above, are clearly visible. Section 3 below further discusses the choice from among these four possible measures.

We have already seen that this example incorporates significant degrees of conflict, however measured. Nevertheless, it is a carefully constructed example that avoids some of the more serious effects of conflict. For example, although μ_3 purported to be based on intelligence that the country of origin did not have nuclear capability, there was still some mass attributed to the potential fallibility of intelligence. Suppose that μ_3 were modified to:

$$\boldsymbol{m}_3(\{f\}) = 0.1,\ \boldsymbol{m}_3(\{e, c\}) = 0.6,\ \boldsymbol{m}_3(\{f, e, c\}) = 0.30. \tag{59}$$

Then external conflict increases to give $\kappa = 0.8777$; internal conflict (as measured e.g. by strife) in the final combined belief, however, is reduced to 0.3610, and there is now no belief at all in the possibility that the incoming object is a nuclear missile.

Suppose further that μ_2 were also modified to

$$\boldsymbol{m}_2(\{c)) = 0.3,\ \boldsymbol{m}_2(\{n\}) = 0.6,\ \boldsymbol{m}_2\ (\{c, n\}) = 0.10. \tag{60}$$

This somewhat more devastating change is shown in Table 2. Note that two of the input beliefs (μ_1 and μ_4) no longer impact the final combined result at all, that the result is a certain belief function focused on {c}, that external conflict may be assessed by $\kappa = 0.8848$, but that there is no internal conflict in the final result.

3. Measures of Conflict and Coherence of Beliefs

We now have six competing measures of conflict to consider: κ and W_μ, based on Dempster's Rule, and entropy-like measures: dissonance – E($\boldsymbol{m}$), confusion – C($\boldsymbol{m}$), discord – D($\boldsymbol{m}$) and strife – S($\boldsymbol{m}$). We may reasonably pose a number of questions regarding their competing merits. Are any or all of them useful in distinguishing low and high levels of conflict to aid strategic choices in evidence gathering such as whether to extend the process or to discount or retract evidence? Are any or all of them useful in identifying which belief functions to discount or to retract? Which measures perform best? Future empirical studies will be needed to assess usefulness and performance, but theoretical considerations may also play a part in suggesting answers and directing research studies. We state below a number of desirable properties for a measure of conflict ***Conflict***($\mu_1, \ldots, \mu_n$) between belief functions. Of course, these properties are not theoretically derived, but are based on intuition and consideration of the intended use of the measure. These properties may be considered as axioms for a theory of conflict in the intended domain. Theory can tell us whether or not any of the measures discussed obey these axioms. Empirical studies will tell us whether or not this is a successful theory of conflict.

3.1. Properties of Conflict

A1 ***Conflict***($\mu_1, \ldots, \mu_n$) should be defined for all finite sets of belief functions.

A2 ***Conflict***($\mu_1, \ldots, \mu_n$) should be symmetric; i.e., ***Conflict***($\mu_1, \ldots, \mu_n$) should have the same value for all permutations of $\mu_1, \ldots, \mu_n$.

A3 ***Conflict***(μ) = 0 whenever μ is a simple support function.

A4 ***Conflict***(μ) has maximum value when μ is a uniform Bayesian support function.

Axiom A1 merely provides that our measure of conflict will be available whenever we need it; axiom A2 is a plausible enough requirement, given that Dempster's Rule is itself symmetric.

Axiom A3, however, is rather more demanding, and incorporates part of our intuition as to what is, and what is not, conflict. In general, a simple support function will have two focal elements, one of which is the frame itself; i.e., part, but not all, of the belief is assigned to some element, and the remainder is assigned to the frame. This clearly generates nonspecificity. The issue is whether or not we want to declare that the mass assigned to the frame conflicts with the mass assigned to the other focal element. Many authors (e.g., Klir and Wierman [[34]) do in fact treat this as conflict, and require instead of Axiom A3 only the weaker condition:

A3° ***Conflict***(μ) = 0 whenever μ is a certain support function.

In the case of the auditing example, however, which is typically modeled using a binary frame, we would have no interest in retracting or discounting an item of evidence merely because it failed to be adequately specific (although it might have been more cost-effective to have avoided collecting it in the first instance). For more general frames, such as in the airborne threats example, our intuitions may vary. Many of the measures of conflict discussed earlier define conflict for any two elements X, Y where $X \not\subset Y$. One area which does not yet seem to have been researched is the possibility of defining conflict only for two elements neither of which is a subset of the other; i.e., when $X \not\subset Y$ and $Y \not\subset X$.

Axiom A4 reflects the intuition that the "worst case" of conflict occurs when every member of the frame is individually supported, to the same degree, with no nonspecificity at all.

As we have already seen, κ and W_μ are not defined for quasi-support functions such as Bayesian support functions (but see the extensions by Smets referenced earlier), whereas dissonance, confusion, discord and strife each satisfy axioms A1-A2. However, confusion fails to satisfy A4, and only dissonance satisfies A3; this is because each of the other entropy-like measures treats the mass assigned to the frame as conflicting, to a greater or lesser extent, with the mass assigned to the other focal element. Note also that in fact dissonance satisfies the stronger condition:

A3* **_Conflict_**(μ) = 0 whenever μ is a consonant belief function

but that it is not necessary to invoke this stronger condition in order to distinguish dissonance from the other measures.

Harmanec and Klir [33] document a number of additional, more technical properties which are desirable in measures of uncertainty (including conflict and nonspecificity), which are listed below:

A5 For *Bayesian support functions*, **_Conflict_**(μ) should collapse to the Shannon entropy

$$H=\sum_i -p(x_i)\cdot \boldsymbol{log}_2\, p(x_i),.$$

A6 For *certain support functions*, **_Conflict_**(μ) should collapse to the Hartley measure of set-theoretic certainty $H=\boldsymbol{log}_2|A|$.

A7 When uncertainty is given in bits, the range should be given by $0 \leq$ **_Conflict_**(μ) $\leq \boldsymbol{log}_2 |\Theta|$.

A8 For non-interacting bodies of evidence, **_Conflict_**(μ) should exhibit additivity;
i.e., if ***Bel*** is a joint belief function on the frame $X \times Y$, and $\boldsymbol{Bel}_X$ and $\boldsymbol{Bel}_Y$ are the associated marginal belief functions on X and Y, respectively, then **_Conflict(Bel)_** = **_Conflict_**($\boldsymbol{Bel}_X$) + **_Conflict_**($\boldsymbol{Bel}_Y$).

A9 More generally, **_Conflict_**(μ) should exhibit subadditivity;
i.e., **_Conflict(Bel)_** $\leq$ **_Conflict_**($\boldsymbol{Bel}_X$) + **_Conflict_**($\boldsymbol{Bel}_Y$).

These axioms are not discussed in detail in the present paper. All four entropy-like measures obey axioms A5, A6 and A8, and all but confusion obey axiom A7 (see Klir and Folger [35], p. 176 for details of the maximum value for confusion). None of them, however, obeys axiom A9. Of the measures discussed in this paper, only AU(***Bel***) obeys axiom A9. It is not known whether this measure is uniquely defined by these axioms (without A3).

In the auditing context, the dissonance measure E(***m***) emerges from this discussion as the preferred candidate for a measure of conflict, although perhaps not fully justified; it obeys Axioms A1–A5, A7 and A8 (axioms A3 and A6 should be seen as alternatives: A3 is stated for measures of conflict alone, and A6 for measures of Aggregate Uncertainty). The difference between this measure and the others considered here is in the definition of conflict itself. E(***m***) essentially measures conflict only between disjoint focal elements, whereas to a greater or lesser extent the others include intersecting focal elements in the definition of conflict. Klir [25] writes:

"... we feel intuitively that ***m***(B) conflicts with ***m***(A) whenever $B \not\subset A$, not only when $B \cap A = \emptyset$." The present author does not share Klir's intuition, and takes a view more consistent with Shafer's position that consonant belief functions exhibit no conflict. Our preferred measure of conflict between a set of belief functions is therefore the measure of dissonance in the combined belief function following the application of Dempster's Rule. In more general contexts, however, strife (S(***m***)) is the measure of conflict favored by most authors. Current research is focused on AU(***Bel***) as a measure of Aggregate Uncertainty because it is the only measure so far found to obey Axiom A9.

3.2 Assigning Responsibility for Conflict

In the Introduction to this paper, we wondered what could be said about the difference between two balanced belief functions on a binary frame: one with $p = q = 0.02$, and another with $p = q = 0.48$. We can now see that the former has E(***m***) = 0.0012 and N(***m***) = 1.9200 (low internal conflict and high nonspecificity), whereas the latter has E(***m***) = 0.9057 and N(***m***) = 0.0800 (high internal conflict and low nonspecificity). In this way, dissonance may be used to identify situations of (relatively) high conflict. In comparing belief functions with different frames of discernment, it may be more convenient to normalize the dissonance by dividing by the maximum possible values. It remains an open question how different levels of dissonance might impact the strategic decision as to whether to seek further evidence, or to retract existing evidence. Nevertheless, the auditor frequently has at least the option of seeking to diffuse conflict by gathering additional evidence.

In other contexts, however, a decision may have to be made, perhaps in near real time, based on a fixed set of available evidence; i.e., while we may elect to discard evidence, we do not have the option of seeking additional evidence. Suppose, for example, that we conclude that one of the signals regarding the airborne threats must be misleading – perhaps due to badly calibrated instruments – and that we decide to retract the belief function in question. How can we use measures of conflict to identify the "problem" Belief?

The solution is to determine which of the four Beliefs, when removed, would show the greatest reduction in our chosen measure of conflict. This is an application of an arbitration principle known as the *principle of minimum uncertainty* (see, for example, Klir and Wierman [[34]). Naturally, some information is lost when the belief function representing an item of evidence is retracted (or discounted). The principle of minimum uncertainty seeks to ensure that as little as possible is discarded. The nature of the information retained is, of course, related to the type of uncertainty that is minimized. Naturally, the principle may be applied to any of the measures of conflict considered in this paper, such as dissonance or strife (or even measures not discussed here, such as AU(***Bel***) - N(***m***)).

For instance, the final level of dissonance in our airborne threats example is 0.6785 regardless of the sequence of the Beliefs (in accordance with axiom A2). The greatest reduction, then, corresponds to the sequence with the smallest dissonance immediately prior to the final combination of Beliefs. From Table 1, when μ_4 is combined last, the dissonance of $\mu_1 \oplus \mu_2 \oplus \mu_3$ prior to its inclusion is 0.5627; repeating these computations in different sequences shows that the dissonance of $\mu_1 \oplus \mu_2 \oplus \mu_4$ prior to including μ_3 is 0.8939, the dissonance of $\mu_1 \oplus \mu_3 \oplus \mu_4$ prior to including μ_2 is 1.0443; and the dissonance of $\mu_2 \oplus \mu_3 \oplus \mu_4$ prior to μ_1 is 0.7053. It appears that μ_4 contributes most conflict to the combined belief function. Note that if this Belief is retracted, the conclusion from the other three beliefs is the same, but the Beliefs are actually higher. For example, ***Bel***({c, n}) becomes 0.9612 instead of 0.9393. Given all four items of evidence, the most plausible individual outcome is a conventional missile (***Pl***({c})=0.8734); if the final item of evidence is discarded, the same outcome remains the most plausible (***Pl***({c})=0.8937), with less uncertainty due to conflict. Alternatively, discounting this belief by a factor of $a = 0.5$ reduces dissonance to 0.6007 and leads to a plausibility of a conventional missile attack of ***Pl***({c})=0.8878.

If μ_4 is retracted, and the residual dissonance of 0.5627 (0.2814 after normalization) is still not considered acceptable, the procedure may be repeated to identify a second Belief for retraction (or discounting). In general, this procedure may be used iteratively until the level of residual conflict (however measured) is considered acceptable.

It may occasionally happen that there is more than one belief that could be retracted, each leaving the same residual conflict. Even without this problem, consideration of information and uncertainty alone may not be sufficient in practical applications, and consideration of associated costs may be necessary. The costs of evidence gathering can presumably be discarded (since the evidence has already been collected whether or not it is retracted). The decisions based on different subsets of the evidence, however, may have vastly different costs. Starting a nuclear war when a telephone call to the commanding officer of a joy-riding pilot would have sufficed would clearly be tragic; losing a nuclear war without firing a shot might be considered even more of a calamity. These are issues, both moral and decision-theoretic, beyond the scope of the present paper.

In practical applications, repeating extensive computations in different sequences is not realistic. Fortunately, each individual belief function can be retracted from a combined set individually in a simple way using an alternative representation of belief functions (commonalities) not discussed in this paper (see, for example, Shafer [13]).

It is also possible that there are applications in which the principle of minimum uncertainty might be applied to nonspecificity rather than conflict; clearly, the application to Aggregate Uncertainty is also straight-forward.

4. Conclusions and Further Work

The main arguments of this paper are that the belief function formalism gives rise to new concepts of conflict and nonspecificity that are more important than conflict in the case of probability theory; that assessing this conflict is important in the strategic choices of whether to seek additional evidence or to retract (or discount) existing evidence, and which Beliefs to retract; and that it is important to consider not just the external conflict between Beliefs, but the internal conflict within belief functions arising from masses assigned to non-intersecting focal elements. The paper considers six measures of conflict: two that apply only to separable belief functions, and that require the canonical decomposition to be found, and four based on extension of the entropy concept. Detailed computations are exhibited for a number of examples. Suitable axioms for conflict are given, and it is argued that dissonance is the conflict measure that fits them most closely. Finally, a method is given for using conflict to decide which of a set of Beliefs to retract (or discount).

Potential future research in this area includes further investigation of subadditive measures of conflict that still satisfy the other axioms, the development of guidance on the relationship between different levels of conflict and strategic choices as to gathering further evidence or retracting evidence, and empirical studies of the use of such methods in practice.

References

[1] A. D. Akresh, J. K. Loebbecke and W. R. Scott (1988). Audit Approaches and Techniques. In *Research Opportunities and Auditing: The Second Decade*, ed. A. R. Abdel-khalik and I. Solomon. Sarasota, FL, American Accounting Association.

[2] G. Shafer and R. P. Srivastava (1990). The Bayesian and Belief Function Formalisms – a General Perspective for Auditing. *Auditing: A Journal of Practice & Theory* (Supplement), pp. 110-137.

[3] R. P. Srivastava, and G. R. Shafer (1990). Belief Function Formulas for Audit Risk. *The Accounting Review* (Vol. 67 No. 2), pp. 249-283.

[4] R. P. Srivastava (1993). Belief Functions and Audit Decisions. *Auditor's Report* (Vol. 17 No. 1, Fall): pp. 8-12.

[5] R. P. Srivastava (1994). A General Scheme for Aggregating Evidence in Auditing: Propagation of Beliefs in Networks. In *Artificial Intelligence in Accounting and Auditing, Vol. III*, ed. Vasarhelyi, M. A. Princeton, NJ, Markus Wiener Publishers.

[6] R. P. Srivastava (1995). The Belief Function Approach to Aggregating Audit Evidence. *International Journal of Intelligent Systems* (Vol. 10 No. 3, March).

[7] P. R. Gillett (1993). Automated Dynamic Audit Programme Tailoring: An Expert System Approach. *Auditing: A Journal of Practice & Theory* (Supplement), pp. 173-189.

[8] American Institute of Certified Public Accountants (1981). *Audit Sampling: Statement on Auditing Standards No. 39 (Section 350).*

[9] American Institute of Certified Public Accountants (1983). *Audit Risk and Materiality in Conducting an Audit: Statement on Auditing Standards No. 47 (Section 312).*

[10] R. P. Srivastava and G. R. Shafer (1994). Integrating Statistical and Non-Statistical Audit Evidence Using belief functions: A Case of Variable Sampling. *International Journal of Intelligent Systems.*

[11] P. R. Gillett (2000). Monetary unit sampling: a belief-function implementation for audit and accounting applications. *International Journal of Approximate Reasoning* (Vol. 25), pp. 43-70.

[12] P. R. Gillett and R. P. Srivastava (2000). Attribute Sampling: A Belief-Function Approach to Statistical Audit Evidence. *Auditing: A Journal of Practice and Theory* (Vol 19 No. 1), pp. 145-155.

[13] G. Shafer (1976). *A mathematical theory of evidence.* Princeton, NJ: Princeton University Press.

[14] R. R. Yager (1983). Entropy and specificity in a mathematical theory of evidence. *International Journal of General Systems* (Vol. 9 No. 4), pp. 249-60.

[15] J. Kohlas and P.-A. Monney (1995). A Mathematical Theory of Hints: An Approach to the Demspter-Shafer Theory of Evidence. Berlin: Springer.

[16] P. Smets and R. Kennes (1994). The transferable belief model. *Artificial Intelligence* (66), pp. 191-234.

[17] A. Appriou (1997). Multisensor Data Fusion in Situation Assessment Processes. In *Qualitative and Quantitative Practical Reasoning*, ed. Gabbay, D.M., R. Kruse, A. Nonnengart and H.J. Ohlbach. Berlin: Springer.

[18] P. Smets (1995). The Canonical Decomposition of a Weighted Belief. *IJCAI Montreal*, pp. 1896-1901.

[19] P. Smets (1999). Practical Uses of Belief Functions. *Uncertainty in Artificial Intelligence* (No. 15), pp. 612-621. San Fransisco, CA: Morgan Kaufman.

[20] L. Zadeh (1984). Review of Shafer's mathematical theory of evidence. *The AI Magazine* (Vol. 5 No. 3), pp. 81-83.

[21] L. Zadeh (1986). A Simple View of the Dempster-Shafer Theory of Evidence and its Implication for the Rule of Combination. *The AI Magazine* (Vol. 7 No. 2), pp. 85-90.

[22] R. R. Yager (1987). On the Dempster-Shafer framework and new combination rules. *Information Sciences*, 41, pp. 93-137.

[23] P. Smets (1988). Belief Functions. In *Non-standard Logics for Automated Reasoning*, ed. Smets, P., E. H. Mamdani, D. Dubois and H. Prade. San Diego, CA, Academic Press.

[24] C. E. Shannon (1948). The mathematical theory of communications. *The Bell System Technical Journal* (Vol. 27), pp. 379-423, 623-656.

[25] G. J. Klir (1994). Measures of uncertainty in the Dempster-Shafer theory of evidence. In *Advances in the Dempster-Shafer Theory of Evidence*, ed. R.R. Yager, M. Fedrizzi and J. Kacprzyk. New York, NY, John Wiley & Sons, Inc.

[26] U. Höhle (1982). Entropy with respect to plausibility measures. *Proc. Twelfth IEEE Symp. on Multiple-Valued Logics*. Paris, pp. 167-169.

[27] G. J. Klir and A. Ramer (1990). Uncertainty in the Dempster-Shafer theory: A critical re-examination. *International Journal of General Systems* (Vol. 18 No. 2), pp. 155-66.

[28] A. Ramer and G. J. Klir (1993). Measures of Discord in the Dempster Shafer Theory. *Information Sciences*, 67, pp. 35-50.

[29] G. J. Klir and B. Parviz (1992). A Note on the Measure of Discord. In *Proceedings of the Eighth Conference on Artificial Intelligence*. San Mateo, CA, Morgan Kaufmann.

[30] J. Vejnarova and G. J. Klir (1993). Measure of Strife in Dempster-Shafer Theory. *International Journal of General Systems* (Vol. 22), pp. 25-42.

[31] D. Dubois and H. Prade (1985). A note on measures of specificity for fuzzy sets. *International Journal of General Systems* (Vol. 10, No. 4), pp. 279-283.

[32] D. Harmanec and G. J. Klir (1994). Measuring Total Uncertainty in Dempster-Shafer Theory: A Novel Approach. *International Journal of General Systems* (Vol. 22), pp. 405-419.

[33] D. Harmanec, G. Resconi, G. J. Klir and Y. Pin (1996). On the Computation of Uncertainty Measure in Demspter-Shafer Theory. *International Journal of General Systems* (Vol. 25, No. 2), pp. 153-163.

[34] G. J. Klir and M. J. Wierman (1999). Uncertainty-Based Information. Heidleberg: Physica-Verlag.

[35] G. J. Klir and T. A. Folger (1988). Fuzzy Sets, Uncertainty and Information. Englewood Cliffs, NJ, Prentice Hall.

Belief-Function Measures of Conflict and Nonspecificity

v –	$m_1(X)$	$Bel_1(X)$	$Pl_1(X)$	E(m)	C(m)	D(m)	S(m)	N(m)	$m_2(X)$	$Bel_2(X)$	$Pl_2(X)$	E(m)	C(m)	D(m)	S(m)	N(m)	m'(X)	Bel'(X)	Pl'(X)	E(m)	C(m)	D(m)	S(m)	N(m)
{f}	0.00	0.00	0.25	0.0000	0.0000	0.0000	0.0000	0.0000	0.00	0.00	0.05	0.0000	0.0000	0.0000	0.0000	0.0000	0.0000	0.0000	0.0154	0.0000	0.0000	0.0000	0.0000	0.0000
{e}	0.00	0.00	0.25	0.0000	0.0000	0.0000	0.0000	0.0000	0.00	0.00	0.05	0.0000	0.0000	0.0000	0.0000	0.0000	0.0000	0.0000	0.0154	0.0000	0.0000	0.0000	0.0000	0.0000
{c}	0.00	0.00	0.80	0.0000	0.0000	0.0000	0.0000	0.0000	0.30	0.30	0.40	0.3966	0.5211	0.4701	0.3966	0.0000	0.2963	0.2963	0.3951	0.3970	0.5200	0.4550	0.3970	0.0000
{n}	0.00	0.00	0.80	0.0000	0.0000	0.0000	0.0000	0.0000	0.60	0.60	0.70	0.3087	0.4422	0.3897	0.3087	0.0000	0.5926	0.5926	0.6914	0.3156	0.4473	0.3799	0.3156	0.0000
{f,e}	0.20	0.20	0.25	0.4000	0.4644	0.4304	0.4000	0.2000	0.00	0.00	0.05	0.0000	0.0000	0.0000	0.0000	0.0000	0.0123	0.0123	0.0154	0.0743	0.0783	0.0762	0.0743	0.0123
{f,c}	0.00	0.00	1.00	0.0000	0.0000	0.0000	0.0000	0.0000	0.00	0.30	0.40	0.0000	0.0000	0.0000	0.0000	0.0000	0.0000	0.2963	0.4074	0.0000	0.0000	0.0000	0.0000	0.0000
{f,n}	0.00	0.00	1.00	0.0000	0.0000	0.0000	0.0000	0.0000	0.00	0.60	0.70	0.0000	0.0000	0.0000	0.0000	0.0000	0.0000	0.5926	0.7037	0.0000	0.0000	0.0000	0.0000	0.0000
{e,c}	0.00	0.00	1.00	0.0000	0.0000	0.0000	0.0000	0.0000	0.00	0.30	0.40	0.0000	0.0000	0.0000	0.0000	0.0000	0.0000	0.2963	0.4074	0.0000	0.0000	0.0000	0.0000	0.0000
{e,n}	0.00	0.00	1.00	0.0000	0.0000	0.0000	0.0000	0.0000	0.00	0.60	0.70	0.0000	0.0000	0.0000	0.0000	0.0000	0.0000	0.5926	0.7037	0.0000	0.0000	0.0000	0.0000	0.0000
{c,n}	0.75	0.75	0.80	0.2414	0.3113	0.2758	0.2414	0.7500	0.05	0.95	1.00	0.0000	0.0037	0.0018	0.0431	0.0500	0.0957	0.9846	0.9877	0.0017	0.0021	0.0019	0.0842	0.0957
{f,e,c}	0.00	0.20	1.00	0.0000	0.0000	0.0000	0.0000	0.0000	0.00	0.30	0.40	0.0000	0.0000	0.0000	0.0000	0.0000	0.0000	0.3086	0.4074	0.0000	0.0000	0.0000	0.0000	0.0000
{f,e,n}	0.00	0.20	1.00	0.0000	0.0000	0.0000	0.0000	0.0000	0.00	0.60	0.70	0.0000	0.0000	0.0000	0.0000	0.0000	0.0000	0.6049	0.7037	0.0000	0.0000	0.0000	0.0000	0.0000
{f,c,n}	0.00	0.75	1.00	0.0000	0.0000	0.0000	0.0000	0.0000	0.00	0.95	1.00	0.0000	0.0000	0.0000	0.0000	0.0000	0.0000	0.9846	1.0000	0.0000	0.0000	0.0000	0.0000	0.0000
{e,c,n}	0.00	0.75	1.00	0.0000	0.0000	0.0000	0.0000	0.0000	0.00	0.95	1.00	0.0000	0.0000	0.0000	0.0000	0.0000	0.0000	0.9846	1.0000	0.0000	0.0000	0.0000	0.0000	0.0000
{f,e,c,n}	0.05	1.00	1.00	0.0000	0.0000	0.0000	0.0465	0.1000	0.05	1.00	1.00	0.0000	0.0000	0.0000	0.0868	0.1000	0.0031	1.0000	1.0000	0.0000	0.0000	0.0000	0.0057	0.0062
κ																	0.1900							
***Con*(Bel₁, Bel₂)**																	0.2107							
E(m)				0.6414								0.7053								0.7886				
C(m)					0.7757								0.9670								1.0477			
D(m)						0.7062								0.8616								0.9131		
S(m)							0.6879								0.8353								0.8768	
N(m)								1.0500								0.1500								0.1142
Normalized				0.3207	0.3001	0.3531	0.3440	0.5250			0.3527	0.3741	0.4308	0.4176	0.0750	0.1900				0.3943	0.4053	0.4565	0.4384	0.0571

Table 1 - Panel A

Belief-Function Measures of Conflict and Nonspecificity

$X \subseteq \Theta$	m'(X)	Bel'(X)	Pl'(X)	E(m)	C(m)	D(m)	S(m)	N(m)	m_3(X)	Bel_3(X)	Pl_3(X)	E(m)	C(m)	D(m)	S(m)	N(m)	m"(X)	Bel"(X)	Pl"(X)	E(m)	C(m)	D(m)	S(m)	N(m)
{f}	0.0000	0.0000	0.0154	0.0000	0.0000	0.0000	0.0000	0.0000	0.10	0.10	0.40	0.1322	0.3322	0.2352	0.1322	0.0000	0.0039	0.0039	0.0155	0.0233	0.0311	0.0262	0.0233	0.0000
{e}	0.0000	0.0000	0.0154	0.0000	0.0000	0.0000	0.0000	0.0000	0.00	0.00	0.90	0.0000	0.0000	0.0000	0.0000	0.0000	0.0186	0.0186	0.0349	0.0901	0.1070	0.0977	0.0901	0.0000
{c}	0.2963	0.2963	0.3951	0.3970	0.5200	0.4550	0.3970	0.0000	0.00	0.00	0.90	0.0000	0.0000	0.0000	0.0000	0.0000	0.8747	0.8747	0.8937	0.1418	0.1689	0.1559	0.1418	0.0000
{n}	0.5926	0.5926	0.6914	0.3156	0.4473	0.3799	0.3156	0.0000	0.00	0.00	0.05	0.0000	0.0000	0.0000	0.0000	0.0000	0.0745	0.0745	0.0869	0.2625	0.2791	0.2706	0.2625	0.0000
{f,e}	0.0123	0.0123	0.0154	0.0743	0.0783	0.0762	0.0743	0.0123	0.00	0.10	1.00	0.0000	0.0000	0.0000	0.0000	0.0000	0.0093	0.0318	0.0388	0.0436	0.0463	0.0448	0.0494	0.0093
{f,c}	0.0000	0.2963	0.4074	0.0000	0.0000	0.0000	0.0000	0.0000	0.00	0.10	1.00	0.0000	0.0000	0.0000	0.0000	0.0000	0.0000	0.8786	0.9069	0.0000	0.0000	0.0000	0.0000	0.0000
{f,n}	0.0000	0.5926	0.7037	0.0000	0.0000	0.0000	0.0000	0.0000	0.00	0.10	0.40	0.0000	0.0000	0.0000	0.0000	0.0000	0.0000	0.0784	0.1020	0.0000	0.0000	0.0000	0.0000	0.0000
{e,c}	0.0000	0.2963	0.4074	0.0000	0.0000	0.0000	0.0000	0.0000	0.60	0.60	0.90	0.0912	0.4422	0.2022	0.0912	0.6000	0.0047	0.8980	0.9216	0.0005	0.0007	0.0006	0.0052	0.0047
{e,n}	0.0000	0.5926	0.7037	0.0000	0.0000	0.0000	0.0000	0.0000	0.00	0.00	0.90	0.0000	0.0000	0.0000	0.0000	0.0000	0.0000	0.0931	0.1214	0.0000	0.0000	0.0000	0.0000	0.0000
{c,n}	0.0957	0.9846	0.9877	0.0017	0.0021	0.0019	0.0842	0.0957	0.00	0.00	0.90	0.0000	0.0000	0.0000	0.0000	0.0000	0.0120	0.9612	0.9682	0.0006	0.0007	0.0006	0.0124	0.0120
{f,e,c}	0.0000	0.3086	0.4074	0.0000	0.0000	0.0000	0.0000	0.0000	0.25	0.95	1.00	0.0000	0.0185	0.0045	0.1119	0.3962	0.0019	0.9131	0.9255	0.0002	0.0003	0.0002	0.0032	0.0031
{f,e,n}	0.0000	0.6049	0.7037	0.0000	0.0000	0.0000	0.0000	0.0000	0.00	0.10	1.00	0.0000	0.0000	0.0000	0.0000	0.0000	0.0000	0.1063	0.1253	0.0000	0.0000	0.0000	0.0000	0.0000
{f,c,n}	0.0000	0.9846	1.0000	0.0000	0.0000	0.0000	0.0000	0.0000	0.00	0.10	1.00	0.0000	0.0000	0.0000	0.0000	0.0000	0.0000	0.9651	0.9814	0.0000	0.0000	0.0000	0.0000	0.0000
{e,c,n}	0.0000	0.9846	1.0000	0.0000	0.0000	0.0000	0.0000	0.0000	0.00	0.60	0.90	0.0000	0.0000	0.0000	0.0000	0.0000	0.0000	0.9845	0.9961	0.0000	0.0000	0.0000	0.0000	0.0000
{f,e,c,n}	0.0031	1.0000	1.0000	0.0000	0.0000	0.0000	0.0057	0.0062	0.05	1.00	1.00	0.0000	0.0000	0.0000	0.0415	0.1000	0.0004	1.0000	1.0000	0.0000	0.0000	0.0000	0.0008	0.0008
κ	(this combination)																0.6022							
κ	(cumulative)																0.6778							
Con(Bel_1, Bel_2, Bel_3)																	1.1324							
E(m)				0.7886								0.2234								0.5627				
C(m)					1.0477								0.7929								0.6340			
D(m)						0.9131								0.4420								0.5966		
S(m)							0.8768								0.3768								0.5887	
N(m)								0.1142								1.0962								0.0298
Normalized				0.3943	0.4053	0.4565	0.4384	0.0571				0.1117	0.3067	0.2210	0.1884	0.5481	0.6022			0.2814	0.2453	0.2983	0.2943	0.0149

Table 1 - Panel B

Belief-Function Measures of Conflict and Nonspecificity

v – Θ	m''(X)	Bel''(X)	Pl''(X)	E(m)	C(m)	D(m)	S(m)	N(m)	$m_4(X)$	$Bel_4(X)$	$Pl_4(X)$	E(m)	C(m)	D(m)	S(m)	N(m)	m(X)	Bel(X)	Pl(X)	E(m)	C(m)	D(m)	S(m)	N(m)
{f}	0.0039	0.0039	0.0155	0.0233	0.0311	0.0262	0.0233	0.0000	0.60	0.60	1.00	0.0000	0.4422	0.3087	0.0000	0.0000	0.0265	0.0265	0.0379	0.1253	0.1389	0.1320	0.1253	0.0000
{e}	0.0186	0.0186	0.0349	0.0901	0.1070	0.0977	0.0901	0.0000	0.00	0.00	0.40	0.0000	0.0000	0.0000	0.0000	0.0000	0.0182	0.0182	0.0341	0.0887	0.1052	0.0961	0.0887	0.0000
{c}	0.8747	0.8747	0.8937	0.1418	0.1689	0.1559	0.1418	0.0000	0.00	0.00	0.40	0.0000	0.0000	0.0000	0.0000	0.0000	0.8548	0.8548	0.8734	0.1669	0.1935	0.1807	0.1669	0.0000
{n}	0.0745	0.0745	0.0869	0.2625	0.2791	0.2706	0.2625	0.0000	0.00	0.00	0.40	0.0000	0.0000	0.0000	0.0000	0.0000	0.0728	0.0728	0.0849	0.2590	0.2751	0.2669	0.2590	0.0000
{f,e}	0.0093	0.0318	0.0388	0.0436	0.0463	0.0448	0.0494	0.0093	0.00	0.60	1.00	0.0000	0.0000	0.0000	0.0000	0.0000	0.0091	0.0538	0.0607	0.0368	0.0384	0.0375	0.0436	0.0091
{f,c}	0.0000	0.8786	0.9069	0.0000	0.0000	0.0000	0.0000	0.0000	0.00	0.60	1.00	0.0000	0.0000	0.0000	0.0000	0.0000	0.0000	0.8813	0.9090	0.0000	0.0000	0.0000	0.0000	0.0000
{f,n}	0.0000	0.0784	0.1020	0.0000	0.0000	0.0000	0.0000	0.0000	0.00	0.60	1.00	0.0000	0.0000	0.0000	0.0000	0.0000	0.0000	0.0993	0.1224	0.0000	0.0000	0.0000	0.0000	0.0000
{e,c}	0.0047	0.8980	0.9216	0.0005	0.0007	0.0006	0.0052	0.0047	0.00	0.00	0.40	0.0000	0.0000	0.0000	0.0000	0.0000	0.0045	0.8776	0.9007	0.0007	0.0009	0.0008	0.0052	0.0045
{e,n}	0.0000	0.0931	0.1214	0.0000	0.0000	0.0000	0.0000	0.0000	0.00	0.00	0.40	0.0000	0.0000	0.0000	0.0000	0.0000	0.0000	0.0910	0.1187	0.0000	0.0000	0.0000	0.0000	0.0000
{c,n}	0.0120	0.9612	0.9682	0.0006	0.0007	0.0006	0.0124	0.0120	0.00	0.00	0.40	0.0000	0.0000	0.0000	0.0000	0.0000	0.0118	0.9393	0.9462	0.0009	0.0011	0.0010	0.0125	0.0118
{f,e,c}	0.0019	0.9131	0.9255	0.0002	0.0003	0.0002	0.0032	0.0031	0.00	0.60	1.00	0.0000	0.0000	0.0000	0.0000	0.0000	0.0019	0.9151	0.9272	0.0002	0.0002	0.0002	0.0032	0.0030
{f,e,n}	0.0000	0.1063	0.1253	0.0000	0.0000	0.0000	0.0000	0.0000	0.00	0.60	1.00	0.0000	0.0000	0.0000	0.0000	0.0000	0.0000	0.1266	0.1452	0.0000	0.0000	0.0000	0.0000	0.0000
{f,c,n}	0.0000	0.9651	0.9814	0.0000	0.0000	0.0000	0.0000	0.0000	0.00	0.60	1.00	0.0000	0.0000	0.0000	0.0000	0.0000	0.0000	0.9659	0.9818	0.0000	0.0000	0.0000	0.0000	0.0000
{e,c,n}	0.0000	0.9845	0.9961	0.0000	0.0000	0.0000	0.0000	0.0000	0.00	0.00	0.40	0.0000	0.0000	0.0000	0.0000	0.0000	0.0000	0.9621	0.9735	0.0000	0.0000	0.0000	0.0000	0.0000
{f,e,c,n}	0.0004	1.0000	1.0000	0.0000	0.0000	0.0000	0.0008	0.0008	0.40	1.00	1.00	0.0000	0.0000	0.0000	0.3450	0.8000	0.0004	1.0000	1.0000	0.0000	0.0000	0.0000	0.0007	0.0008
κ	(this combination)																0.5907							
κ	(cumulative)																0.8681							
$Con(Bel_1, Bel_2, Bel_3, Bel_4)$																	2.0257							
E(m)				0.5627								0.0000								0.6785				
C(m)					0.6340								0.4422								0.7532			
D(m)						0.5966								0.3087								0.7151		
S(m)							0.5887								0.3450								0.7050	
N(m)								0.0298								0.8000								2
Normalized				0.2814	0.2453	0.2983	0.2943	0.0149			0.0000	0.1711	0.1544	0.1725	0.4000	0.5907				0.3392	0.2914	0.3576	0.3525	0.0146

Table 1 – Panel C

Belief-Function Measures of Conflict and Nonspecificity

$X \subseteq \Theta$	$m_1(X)$	$Bel_1(X)$	$Pl_1(X)$	E(m)	C(m)	D(m)	S(m)	N(m)	$m_2(X)$	$Bel_2(X)$	$Pl_2(X)$	E(m)	C(m)	D(m)	S(m)	N(m)	m'(X)	Bel'(X)	Pl'(X)	E(m)	C(m)	D(m)	S(m)	N(m)
{f}	0.00	0.00	0.25	0.0000	0.0000	0.0000	0.0000	0.0000	0.00	0.00	0.00	0.0000	0.0000	0.0000	0.0000	0.0000	0.0000	0.0000	0.0000	0.0000	0.0000	0.0000	0.0000	0.0000
{e}	0.00	0.00	0.25	0.0000	0.0000	0.0000	0.0000	0.0000	0.00	0.00	0.00	0.0000	0.0000	0.0000	0.0000	0.0000	0.0000	0.0000	0.0000	0.0000	0.0000	0.0000	0.0000	0.0000
{c}	0.00	0.00	0.80	0.0000	0.0000	0.0000	0.0000	0.0000	0.30	0.30	0.40	0.3966	0.5211	0.4544	0.3966	0.0000	0.3000	0.3000	0.4000	0.3966	0.5211	0.4544	0.3966	0.0000
{n}	0.00	0.00	0.80	0.0000	0.0000	0.0000	0.0000	0.0000	0.60	0.60	0.70	0.3087	0.4422	0.3729	0.3087	0.0000	0.6000	0.6000	0.7000	0.3087	0.4422	0.3729	0.3087	0.0000
{f,e}	0.20	0.20	0.25	0.4000	0.4644	0.4304	0.4000	0.2000	0.00	0.00	0.00	0.0000	0.0000	0.0000	0.0000	0.0000	0.0000	0.0000	0.0000	0.0000	0.0000	0.0000	0.0000	0.0000
{f,c}	0.00	0.00	1.00	0.0000	0.0000	0.0000	0.0000	0.0000	0.00	0.30	0.40	0.0000	0.0000	0.0000	0.0000	0.0000	0.0000	0.3000	0.4000	0.0000	0.0000	0.0000	0.0000	0.0000
{f,n}	0.00	0.00	1.00	0.0000	0.0000	0.0000	0.0000	0.0000	0.00	0.60	0.70	0.0000	0.0000	0.0000	0.0000	0.0000	0.0000	0.6000	0.7000	0.0000	0.0000	0.0000	0.0000	0.0000
{e,c}	0.00	0.00	1.00	0.0000	0.0000	0.0000	0.0000	0.0000	0.00	0.30	0.40	0.0000	0.0000	0.0000	0.0000	0.0000	0.0000	0.3000	0.4000	0.0000	0.0000	0.0000	0.0000	0.0000
{e,n}	0.00	0.00	1.00	0.0000	0.0000	0.0000	0.0000	0.0000	0.00	0.60	0.70	0.0000	0.0000	0.0000	0.0000	0.0000	0.0000	0.6000	0.7000	0.0000	0.0000	0.0000	0.0000	0.0000
{c,n}	0.75	0.75	0.80	0.2414	0.3113	0.2758	0.2414	0.7500	0.10	1.00	1.00	0.0000	0.0000	0.0000	0.0862	0.1000	0.1000	1.0000	1.0000	0.0000	0.0000	0.0000	0.0862	0.1000
{f,e,c}	0.00	0.20	1.00	0.0000	0.0000	0.0000	0.0000	0.0000	0.00	0.30	0.40	0.0000	0.0000	0.0000	0.0000	0.0000	0.0000	0.3000	0.4000	0.0000	0.0000	0.0000	0.0000	0.0000
{f,e,n}	0.00	0.20	1.00	0.0000	0.0000	0.0000	0.0000	0.0000	0.00	0.60	0.70	0.0000	0.0000	0.0000	0.0000	0.0000	0.0000	0.6000	0.7000	0.0000	0.0000	0.0000	0.0000	0.0000
{f,c,n}	0.00	0.75	1.00	0.0000	0.0000	0.0000	0.0000	0.0000	0.00	1.00	1.00	0.0000	0.0000	0.0000	0.0000	0.0000	0.0000	1.0000	1.0000	0.0000	0.0000	0.0000	0.0000	0.0000
{e,c,n}	0.00	0.75	1.00	0.0000	0.0000	0.0000	0.0000	0.0000	0.00	1.00	1.00	0.0000	0.0000	0.0000	0.0000	0.0000	0.0000	1.0000	1.0000	0.0000	0.0000	0.0000	0.0000	0.0000
{f,e,c,n}	0.05	1.00	1.00	0.0000	0.0000	0.0000	0.0465	0.1000	0.00	1.00	1.00	0.0000	0.0000	0.0000	0.0000	0.0000	0.0000	1.0000	1.0000	0.0000	0.0000	0.0000	0.0000	0.0000
κ																	0.2000							
Con(Bel_1, Bel_2)																	0.2231							
E(m)				0.6414								0.7053								0.7053				
C(m)					0.7757								0.9633								0.9633			
D(m)						0.7062								0.8273								0.8273		
S(m)							0.6879								0.7916								0.7916	
N(m)								1.0500								0.1000								0.1000
Normalized				0.3207	0.3001	0.3531	0.3440	0.5250			0.3527	0.3726	0.4136	0.3958	0.0500	0.2000				0.3527	0.3726	0.4136	0.3958	0.0500

Table 2 - Panel A

Belief-Function Measures of Conflict and Nonspecificity

v – Θ	m'(X)	Bel'(X)	Pl'(X)	E(m)	C(m)	D(m)	S(m)	N(m)	m_3(X)	Bel_3(X)	Pl_3(X)	E(m)	C(m)	D(m)	S(m)	N(m)	m''(X)	Bel''(X)	Pl''(X)	E(m)	C(m)	D(m)	S(m)	N(m)
{f}	0.0000	0.0000	0.0000	0.0000	0.0000	0.0000	0.0000	0.0000	0.10	0.10	0.40	0.1322	0.3322	0.2322	0.1322	0.0000	0.0000	0.0000	0.0000	0.0000	0.0000	0.0000	0.0000	0.0000
{e}	0.0000	0.0000	0.0000	0.0000	0.0000	0.0000	0.0000	0.0000	0.00	0.00	0.90	0.0000	0.0000	0.0000	0.0000	0.0000	0.0000	0.0000	0.0000	0.0000	0.0000	0.0000	0.0000	0.0000
{c}	0.3000	0.3000	0.4000	0.3966	0.5211	0.4544	0.3966	0.0000	0.00	0.00	0.90	0.0000	0.0000	0.0000	0.0000	0.0000	1.0000	1.0000	1.0000	0.0000	0.0000	0.0000	0.0000	0.0000
{n}	0.6000	0.6000	0.7000	0.3087	0.4422	0.3729	0.3087	0.0000	0.00	0.00	0.00	0.0000	0.0000	0.0000	0.0000	0.0000	0.0000	0.0000	0.0000	0.0000	0.0000	0.0000	0.0000	0.0000
{f,e}	0.0000	0.0000	0.0000	0.0000	0.0000	0.0000	0.0000	0.0000	0.00	0.10	1.00	0.0000	0.0000	0.0000	0.0000	0.0000	0.0000	0.0000	0.0000	0.0000	0.0000	0.0000	0.0000	0.0000
{f,c}	0.0000	0.3000	0.4000	0.0000	0.0000	0.0000	0.0000	0.0000	0.00	0.10	1.00	0.0000	0.0000	0.0000	0.0000	0.0000	0.0000	1.0000	1.0000	0.0000	0.0000	0.0000	0.0000	0.0000
{f,n}	0.0000	0.6000	0.7000	0.0000	0.0000	0.0000	0.0000	0.0000	0.00	0.10	0.40	0.0000	0.0000	0.0000	0.0000	0.0000	0.0000	0.0000	0.0000	0.0000	0.0000	0.0000	0.0000	0.0000
{e,c}	0.0000	0.3000	0.4000	0.0000	0.0000	0.0000	0.0000	0.0000	0.60	0.60	0.90	0.0912	0.4422	0.1932	0.0912	0.6000	0.0000	1.0000	1.0000	0.0000	0.0000	0.0000	0.0000	0.0000
{e,n}	0.0000	0.6000	0.7000	0.0000	0.0000	0.0000	0.0000	0.0000	0.00	0.00	0.90	0.0000	0.0000	0.0000	0.0000	0.0000	0.0000	0.0000	0.0000	0.0000	0.0000	0.0000	0.0000	0.0000
{c,n}	0.1000	1.0000	1.0000	0.0000	0.0000	0.0000	0.0862	0.1000	0.00	0.00	0.90	0.0000	0.0000	0.0000	0.0000	0.0000	0.0000	1.0000	1.0000	0.0000	0.0000	0.0000	0.0000	0.0000
{f,e,c}	0.0000	0.3000	0.4000	0.0000	0.0000	0.0000	0.0000	0.0000	0.30	1.00	1.00	0.0000	0.0000	0.0000	0.1342	0.4755	0.0000	1.0000	1.0000	0.0000	0.0000	0.0000	0.0000	0.0000
{f,e,n}	0.0000	0.6000	0.7000	0.0000	0.0000	0.0000	0.0000	0.0000	0.00	0.10	1.00	0.0000	0.0000	0.0000	0.0000	0.0000	0.0000	0.0000	0.0000	0.0000	0.0000	0.0000	0.0000	0.0000
{f,c,n}	0.0000	1.0000	1.0000	0.0000	0.0000	0.0000	0.0000	0.0000	0.00	0.10	1.00	0.0000	0.0000	0.0000	0.0000	0.0000	0.0000	1.0000	1.0000	0.0000	0.0000	0.0000	0.0000	0.0000
{e,c,n}	0.0000	1.0000	1.0000	0.0000	0.0000	0.0000	0.0000	0.0000	0.00	0.60	0.90	0.0000	0.0000	0.0000	0.0000	0.0000	0.0000	1.0000	1.0000	0.0000	0.0000	0.0000	0.0000	0.0000
{f,e,c,n}	0.0000	1.0000	1.0000	0.0000	0.0000	0.0000	0.0000	0.0000	0.00	1.00	1.00	0.0000	0.0000	0.0000	0.0000	0.0000	0.0000	1.0000	1.0000	0.0000	0.0000	0.0000	0.0000	0.0000
κ	(this combination)																0.6400							
κ	(cumulative)																0.7120							
Con(Bel_1, Bel_2, Bel_3)																	1.2448							
E(m)				0.7053								0.2234								0.0000				
C(m)					0.9633								0.7744								0.0000			
D(m)						0.8273								0.4253								0.0000		
S(m)							0.7916								0.3576								0.0000	
N(m)								0.1000								1.0755								0.0000
Normalized				0.3527	0.3726	0.4136	0.3958	0.0500				0.1117	0.2996	0.2127	0.1788	0.5377	0.6400			0.0000	0.0000	0.0000	0.0000	0.0000

Table 2 - Panel B

Belief-Function Measures of Conflict and Nonspecificity

∨ –	m''(X)	Bel''(X)	Pl''(X)	E(m)	C(m)	D(m)	S(m)	N(m)	m_4(X)	Bel_4(X)	Pl_4(X)	E(m)	C(m)	D(m)	S(m)	N(m)	m(X)	Bel(X)	Pl(X)	E(m)	C(m)	D(m)	S(m)	N(m)
{f}	0.0000	0.0000	0.0000	0.0000	0.0000	0.0000	0.0000	0.0000	0.60	0.60	1.00	0.0000	0.4422	0.3087	0.0000	0.0000	0.0000	0.0000	0.0000	0.0000	0.0000	0.0000	0.0000	0.0000
{e}	0.0000	0.0000	0.0000	0.0000	0.0000	0.0000	0.0000	0.0000	0.00	0.00	0.40	0.0000	0.0000	0.0000	0.0000	0.0000	0.0000	0.0000	0.0000	0.0000	0.0000	0.0000	0.0000	0.0000
{c}	1.0000	1.0000	1.0000	0.0000	0.0000	0.0000	0.0000	0.0000	0.00	0.00	0.40	0.0000	0.0000	0.0000	0.0000	0.0000	1.0000	1.0000	1.0000	0.0000	0.0000	0.0000	0.0000	0.0000
{n}	0.0000	0.0000	0.0000	0.0000	0.0000	0.0000	0.0000	0.0000	0.00	0.00	0.40	0.0000	0.0000	0.0000	0.0000	0.0000	0.0000	0.0000	0.0000	0.0000	0.0000	0.0000	0.0000	0.0000
{f,e}	0.0000	0.0000	0.0000	0.0000	0.0000	0.0000	0.0000	0.0000	0.00	0.60	1.00	0.0000	0.0000	0.0000	0.0000	0.0000	0.0000	0.0000	0.0000	0.0000	0.0000	0.0000	0.0000	0.0000
{f,c}	0.0000	1.0000	1.0000	0.0000	0.0000	0.0000	0.0000	0.0000	0.00	0.60	1.00	0.0000	0.0000	0.0000	0.0000	0.0000	0.0000	1.0000	1.0000	0.0000	0.0000	0.0000	0.0000	0.0000
{f,n}	0.0000	0.0000	0.0000	0.0000	0.0000	0.0000	0.0000	0.0000	0.00	0.60	1.00	0.0000	0.0000	0.0000	0.0000	0.0000	0.0000	0.0000	0.0000	0.0000	0.0000	0.0000	0.0000	0.0000
{e,c}	0.0000	1.0000	1.0000	0.0000	0.0000	0.0000	0.0000	0.0000	0.00	0.00	0.40	0.0000	0.0000	0.0000	0.0000	0.0000	0.0000	1.0000	1.0000	0.0000	0.0000	0.0000	0.0000	0.0000
{e,n}	0.0000	0.0000	0.0000	0.0000	0.0000	0.0000	0.0000	0.0000	0.00	0.00	0.40	0.0000	0.0000	0.0000	0.0000	0.0000	0.0000	0.0000	0.0000	0.0000	0.0000	0.0000	0.0000	0.0000
{c,n}	0.0000	1.0000	1.0000	0.0000	0.0000	0.0000	0.0000	0.0000	0.00	0.00	0.40	0.0000	0.0000	0.0000	0.0000	0.0000	0.0000	1.0000	1.0000	0.0000	0.0000	0.0000	0.0000	0.0000
{f,e,c}	0.0000	1.0000	1.0000	0.0000	0.0000	0.0000	0.0000	0.0000	0.00	0.60	1.00	0.0000	0.0000	0.0000	0.0000	0.0000	0.0000	1.0000	1.0000	0.0000	0.0000	0.0000	0.0000	0.0000
{f,e,n}	0.0000	0.0000	0.0000	0.0000	0.0000	0.0000	0.0000	0.0000	0.00	0.60	1.00	0.0000	0.0000	0.0000	0.0000	0.0000	0.0000	0.0000	0.0000	0.0000	0.0000	0.0000	0.0000	0.0000
{f,c,n}	0.0000	1.0000	1.0000	0.0000	0.0000	0.0000	0.0000	0.0000	0.00	0.60	1.00	0.0000	0.0000	0.0000	0.0000	0.0000	0.0000	1.0000	1.0000	0.0000	0.0000	0.0000	0.0000	0.0000
{e,c,n}	0.0000	1.0000	1.0000	0.0000	0.0000	0.0000	0.0000	0.0000	0.00	0.00	0.40	0.0000	0.0000	0.0000	0.0000	0.0000	0.0000	1.0000	1.0000	0.0000	0.0000	0.0000	0.0000	0.0000
{f,e,c,n}	0.0000	1.0000	1.0000	0.0000	0.0000	0.0000	0.0000	0.0000	0.40	1.00	1.00	0.0000	0.0000	0.0000	0.3450	0.8000	0.0000	1.0000	1.0000	0.0000	0.0000	0.0000	0.0000	0.0000
κ	(this combination)																0.6000							
κ	(cumulative)																0.8848							
Con(Bel_1, Bel_2, Bel_3, Bel_4)																	2.1611							
E(m)				0.0000								0.0000								0.0000				
C(m)					0.0000								0.4422								0.0000			
D(m)						0.0000								0.3087								0.0000		
S(m)							0.0000								0.3450								0.0000	
N(m)								0.0000								0.8000								0.0000
Normalized				0.0000	0.0000	0.0000	0.0000	0.0000				0.0000	0.1711	0.1544	0.1725	0.4000	0.6000			0.0000	0.0000	0.0000	0.0000	0.0000

Table 2 - Panel C

Legend

For each element of the various belief functions, the upper part of Panel A shows ***m***, ***Bel*** and ***Pl*** for μ_1, followed by the value that the element contributes to the measures of dissonance, confusion, discord and strife; similar values are then displayed for μ_2; finally, the same values are given for their combination.

The lower part of the Panel shows the computed total values of dissonance, confusion, discord and strife for μ_1, μ_2, and their combination, together with value of Shafer's measure κ of *external* conflict for the combination. In addition, the alternative measure ***Con*** defined by equation (38) is given. Normalized values of the various measures are presented in the last line of the Panel.

Panel B adds the relevant information for μ_3, and Panel C adds similar information for μ_4. These two panels show Shafer's measure κ for the most recent combination as well as the cumulative measure κ of *external* conflict for the combination.

Shafer's measure of *internal* conflict requires the canonical decomposition of the various belief functions, and is not presented in the Table.

Evaluating Mergers and Acquisitions: A Belief Function Approach

Rajendra P. Srivastava and Deepak K. Datta

School of Business, University of Kansas, 1300 Sunnyside Av, Lawrence, KS 66045-7585, rsrivastava@ukans.edu, ddatta@ukans.edu

Abstract

Studies indicate that mergers and acquisitions are characterized by a high failure rate, often attributed to an inability on the part of the acquiring firm management to effectively evaluate potential acquisition candidates. This is not surprising given the considerable uncertainties surrounding both the relationships among factors in the evaluation process and also in the assessment of evidence. This paper develops a conceptual framework for acquisition and merger decisions using evidential reasoning approach under the belief function framework. It seeks to illustrate how expert knowledge of relevant factors can be mapped and how an evidential network can be used by decision makers to incorporate uncertainties in the evidence. Also highlighted is the fact that the nature and extent of evidence that needs to be collected depends on the rules assumed to govern relationships among input variables. Implications for theory and practice are discussed.

1. Introduction

Mergers and acquisitions (M&A) represent some of the most critical strategic decisions facing top management in corporations. They are often defining moments in a company's development with significant long-term performance implications. The impact of mergers and acquisitions on the U.S. business landscape is evident when one considers the fact that in 1999 the total dollar value of acquisitions exceeded $1 trillion. Paradoxically, however, the overall track record for corporate mergers and acquisitions has not been a resounding success. Available empirical evidence suggests that acquisitions are characterized by a high failure rate; with nearly 50% of all acquisitions being categorized as failures (e.g., Lajoux & Weston [1]; Ravenscraft & Scherer [2]). In addition, a meta-analytic synthesis of the empirical literature on the wealth effects in mergers and acquisitions (Datta, Narayanan & Pinches [3]) identified that acquisitions, on average, fail to create value for the shareholders of acquiring firms. Moreover, research by Datta and Puia [4] suggests that the same is also true in the case of cross-border (international) acquisitions undertaken by U.S. based firms.

While various reasons have been advanced to explain the high failure rate among acquisitions (e.g., major dislocations in given industry sectors or broader environmental shifts), much of it can be attributed to the failure on the part of firm management to effectively evaluate acquisition opportunities. This was borne out in a study of post-merger performance involving 150 large mergers between 1990-95 by Mercer Management Consulting and *Business Week*. They found that over 50% of the mergers eroded shareholder returns, with the primary cause being inadequate due diligence by the buyer. A failure to adequately evaluate the target firm often led to lack of a compelling strategy and overly optimistic expectations of possible synergies (Lajoux and Weston [1]).

A number of evaluation frameworks have been suggested in the literature (e.g., Achtmeyer & Daniell [5]; Rappaport [6]; Reilly [7]). However, current approaches have two key limitations. First, they are often driven by *rules of thumb* in the integration of evidence. As such, they do not account for the uncertainties in the evidence used in the evaluation and decision making process. However, in reality, considerable uncertainty exists both in terms of the relationships among the factors in the evaluation model, and in the assessment of factor levels. Second, current approaches do not account for interdependencies among various factors and items of evidence. It is, however, important that decision models incorporate such interdependencies for them to be meaningful and realistic.

The primary objective of this paper is to develop a conceptual framework for acquisition and merger decisions using evidential reasoning approach under the belief function framework. Belief functions are used to represent uncertainties in the variables involved in the decision process. Following Curley and Golden [8] and Harrison [9], we believe that uncertainties associated with evidence related to factors in a decision process are more realistically expressed in terms of belief functions than in terms of probabilities. In fact, uncertainties are so prevalent in all human decisions that the managing of such uncertainties has been the focal point of considerable research in AI (Artificial Intelligence) (see, e.g., Cohen [10]; Duda et al. [11]; Lauritzen & Spiegelhalter [12]; Pearl [13]; Shenoy & Shafer [14]). The outcome of such research has made possible not only the propagation of uncertainties in complex networks through local computations but has also led to the development of several computer systems that automate propagation of uncertainties in networks (e.g., Andersen et al. [15]; Saffiotti & Umkehrer [16]; Shafer, Shenoy & Srivastava [17]; Zarley et al. [18]). Such programs are helping researchers develop "real world" applications. For example, Srivastava, Dutta and Johns [19] have analyzed the use of "Auditor's Assistant" (Shafer et al [17]) for planning and evaluation of an audit in the healthcare industry. However, applications in the context of key strategic organizational decisions have been lacking.

2. Key Factors in the Evaluation of Mergers and Acquisitions

Firms engage in acquisitions for a variety of reasons. These include quicker market entry, avoiding costs and risks associated with new product development and the acquisition of critical resources and competencies (Datta et al [3]). However, from the perspective of an acquiring firm, the primary overall objective in an acquisition is the creation of economic value (Rappaport [20]). As such, given that acquisitions typically have a significant impact on the overall profitability and financial health of a firm, they deserve the same thoughtful and thorough evaluation and planning as a major new project or the building of a new plant. Yet, many otherwise well-run organizations fail to devote the necessary time and effort required in carefully analyzing acquisition opportunities.

Effective and accurate evaluation of acquisitions is critical to the valuation of potential targets. If an organization fails to diligently and thoroughly analyze a target firm, the consequences can be rather damaging. The firm might end up overpaying for the acquisition. Roll [21] attributes overpayment to managerial hubris and inadequate rational evaluation of targets in acquisitions.

The criteria for evaluating acquisitions entail creating a benchmark against which to evaluate candidates. This includes an assessment of the (1) attractiveness of the industry or industry segment, (2) competitive strengths of the target firm, (3) potential synergistic benefits, and (4) extent of organizational fit. While the first two define the attractiveness of the target as an independent or stand-alone entity, potential synergistic benefits and integration costs relate to the benefits and costs associated with combining the acquiring and acquired firms. These are discussed in greater detail in the following paragraphs.

2.1. Economic Desirability of a Target Firm as an Independent Entity

The extensive literature in industrial organization and strategic management (e.g., Barney [22]; Markides & Williamson [23]; Porter [24]; Scherer [25]) suggests that economic attractiveness of a firm in the market place is a function of (1) the structural attractiveness of the industry, and (2) the competitive strengths of the firm within the industry. Preacquisition screening aimed at increasing the acquiring firm's knowledge of potential takeover targets should incorporate analysis along both of these dimensions.

Industry attractiveness. Research in the area of strategic management indicates that the industry environment has a direct impact on the firm's efforts to achieve strategic competitiveness and earn above-average returns. According to research conducted by Robert Spitalnic and Acquisition Horizons (Lisle & Bartlam, [26]), some of the most commonly cited reasons for failed acquisitions have to do with market factors. These include market growth of the target firm industry being lower than expected, industry margins being less than expected, and competition being tougher than expected. In most cases, the preacquisition research and evaluation was either inadequate or inaccurate.

As such, in seeking an acquisition candidate (especially in the context of corporate diversification) the potential attractiveness of the industry structure is of utmost importance. Such attractiveness depends on the economic structure of the industry (Wernerfelt & Montgomery [27]; Porter [24]). Porter's "five forces" model suggests that, in addition to demand growth, industry attractiveness depends on the industry structure. These relate to the extent of threat of new entry, the bargaining power of buyers and suppliers, the extent of rivalry in the industry and, the threat of new substitutes. Thus, an important aspect of analyzing potential target firms would be the analysis of industry forces. Other things being equal, an acquiring firm would certainly desire that the target firm be in an attractive industry. In assessing the same, evidence needs to be gathered on the factors that determine the intensity of the competitive forces and demand growth, followed by an aggregation of the evidence along the different factors. However, problems encountered in the process are twofold: (1) the uncertainty underlying the assessment along the factors that contribute to the forces needs to be accounted for, and (2) the exact nature of the relationship between factors and the forces for the purpose of evidential reasoning is unknown. Simple weighting schemes can be used -- however, such schemes do not allow the users to incorporate such subjective judgments as "I believe that the factors tell me that the industry will be attractive with 80 percent confidence but I am not sure on the remaining 20 percent -- I probably need more information."

Thus, any meaningful process needs to account for the uncertainty not only in available evidence but also in the relationships that define the aggregation process.

Competitive strengths. Along with the attractiveness of its industry, the economic desirability of a target firm depends on its competitive position within the industry. Industry experts suggest the critical importance of conducting competitive intelligence analysis that probes the competitive position of the target firm vis-à-vis it rivals (Lisle & Bartlam, [26]). Competitive intelligence can be an extraordinarily useful tool in evaluating acquisition candidates and can help in uncovering the value of potential target firms along both tangible and intangible dimensions. Research (Hitt, Hoskisson & Ireland, [28]) indicates that acquisitions are likely to be successful when target firms have complementary resources and competencies.

The competitive strengths and capabilities are typically assessed by comparing the firm to its major competitors in the industry along key industry success factors (Barney [22]; Porter [29]). When using the value chain analysis mangers seek to study a firm's resources and capabilities in relationship to key activities in the value chain. However, rating a firm's capabilities along value chain-activities poses unique challenges -- it requires judgment and is associated with a high level of uncertainty. First, there is no obviously correct model or rule available to accomplish the process. Second, the data that can be accessed for such evaluation can, at times, be unreliable and/or incomplete. Moreover, there is no mechanism to account for the uncertainty in both the assessment and also in the relationship between the factors and the overall competitive position. In addition, there are likely to be situations where the items of evidence are conflicting. Such conflicting items of evidence obviously need to be properly aggregated – something that can be effectively accomplished using the belief-function framework.

2.2. Combination Benefits

The attractiveness of industry structure, along with the competitive position determines the desirability of a particular firm as a stand-alone entity. However, the economic justification behind an acquisition often rests on synergistic benefits or economies that the acquisition may provide.

Potential synergistic benefits. Simply stated, synergy represents an acquiring firm's potential capacity to use its capabilities to improve the performance of the target firms or vice versa. As argued by Porter [30], an acquisition must pass the "better off" test – i.e., there should be opportunities for value creation through the exploitation of synergies. Literature in industrial organization and strategic management suggest that synergies associated with acquisitions emanate from three types of economies: economies of scale, economies of scope, and pecuniary or market power based economies.

An important component of synergistic benefits in acquisitions (particularly in the acquisition of a firm in a related industry) are *scale economies* (Bielinski [31]; Datta [32]; Jensen & Ruback [33]; Salter & Weinhold [34]; Singh & Montogomery [35]). In addition, acquisitions, especially related acquisitions, can result in *economies of scope* (e.g., Singh & Montgomery [35]). Benefits of economies of scope are achieved when the cost of joint production of two goods by a multiproduct firm is less than the combined costs of production of these goods by two single product firms. Economies of scope may also arise from the reuse of an input, such as the sharing of know-how or other intangible assets. Intangible resources such as brands, corporate reputation, and technology offer economies of scope primarily due to the ability to transfer them from one business to another at low marginal cost. Finally, market power or *pecuniary economies* arise in acquisitions from the ability of the combined firms to dictate prices (Scherer [25]). The gains here are from a firm's ability to extract excess profits through the exercise of increased market power over buyers and suppliers (from an acquisition).

The process of evaluating synergistic benefits in a potential acquisition involves the identification of the areas or factors that will contribute to each of the three types of synergies followed by the determination of likely benefits along each factor. Again, such an assessment involves considerable uncertainty -- not just in the determination of factors along which synergistic benefits might accrue, but also in the assessment of the synergistic benefits itself (Bielinski [31]; Sirower [36]). Sirower [36] for example, details several acquisitions where synergies were grossly overestimated by acquiring firm management. One such transaction was the acquisition of NCR by AT&T in 1991 at a 125% premium. Unfortunately, failure at systems integration resulted in failure to generate needed synergies (to justify the steep premium), contributing to the acquisition's downfall.

Organizational fit. In addition to the above, acquisition evaluation must include the consideration of significant (and, sometimes, hidden) costs associated with the post-acquisition implementation process. The assimilation and integration costs (arising out of organizational misfit), if overlooked, might even negate any available synergistic benefits (Datta [37]; Datta & Grant [38]; Jemison & Sitkin [39]; Slowinski [40]). Implementation impediments (and, hence, costs) are often associated with lack of *organizational fit* or compatibility. Existing incompatibility can be along organizational systems, prevalent organizational cultures, organizational structures, management styles etc. (Datta & Grant [38]; Datta [37]; Marks [41]). As researchers like Buono, Bowditch and Lewis [42], and Marks [41] have argued, such differences tend to destabilize the combined organization, contributing to enhanced probability of conflicts. Consequently, instead of anticipated benefits, the outcome is often a sharp decline in post-combination performance. The acquisition of MedPartners by PhyCor in 1997 provides an interesting illustration. While many analysts viewed it as a synergistic acquisition, some questioned whether the acquisition can be effectively implemented given the significant differences in their organizational cultures and operating styles (PhyCor had a slow and deliberative style of operating while MedPartners was much more aggressive). Market perception and investor concerns that integration challenges would destroy value resulted in PhyCor's stock moving lower when the acquisition was announced.

Determining ways to measure the economic impact of organizational fit (or misfit) has been a vexing problem for organizational researchers. No generally accepted procedure exists (Marks [41]) and assessments are, at best, subjective and ad-hoc. Some formal tools have been developed - these include the Merging Cultures Evaluation Index (MCEI) that analyzes several dimensions of corporate culture. However, assessment of organizational misfit is fraught with uncertainty and inexactitude. Also, given the level of uncertainty, and, the sometimes unclear relationship to acquisition performance issues of organizational fit are often excluded from the purview of acquisition analysis. As discussed later, such uncertainties can be addressed using the belief-function framework -- the relationships between the factors that determine the net synergistic benefit will be expressed using subjective judgments about the uncertainties. We believe that this approach (in comparison to the traditional narrative approach) possesses greater objectivity and should, therefore, result in greater consistency.

In sum, acquisition evaluation is characterized by the evaluation of a wide array of factors related to the target firm and the acquisition itself. These (and, the interrelationships between them) are partially depicted in the network presented in Figure 1. Moreover, it must be remembered that the decision process associated with the evaluation of acquisition candidates is characterized by (1) uncertainty in the evaluation of the candidates along the factors (the available evidence, especially on some of the key organizational and behavioral factors, is generally accompanied by a high level of uncertainty), (2) interrelationships amongst different factors and amongst various item of evidence, and (3) uncertainty pertaining to relationships between the factors. The best model is always the one that best fits the structure of evidence. At times it is a causal model and at other times it is not.

In this paper we seek to bridge the gap between work on the evaluation of mergers and acquisitions (primarily in the areas of strategic management and financial economics) and work in the area of decision making under uncertainty. A decision problem may involve multiple interrelated variables (or factors) with items of evidence that may bear on one or several variables. In other words, an M&A evaluation problem is likely to involve a network of variables, all with uncertainties associated with them.

Under the evidential reasoning approach, there are three main steps involved in the decision process. The first step is to identify all the relevant variables in the decision process. The second step is to identify the interrelationships among the variables and convert them into relational nodes under the belief-function framework. This step is quite complex because the interrelationships among variables are usually expressed in terms of 'if-then' rules. We need to convert each set of these 'if-then' rules to a relational node for propagation of beliefs in the network[1]. The third step is to build the appropriate network of variables based on the perceived interrelationships among the variables. This network is then used to combine information obtained on different variables in the network to make the final decision whether a particular company is a good candidate for acquisition or merger or not. In Appendix B we briefly discuss how logical relationships can be modeled in the belief function framework.

---

[1] An algorithm, based on Srivastava and Cogger [43], developed for this purpose is presented in Appendix A

Figure 1: A Partial Evidential Network for Acquisition Decisions*

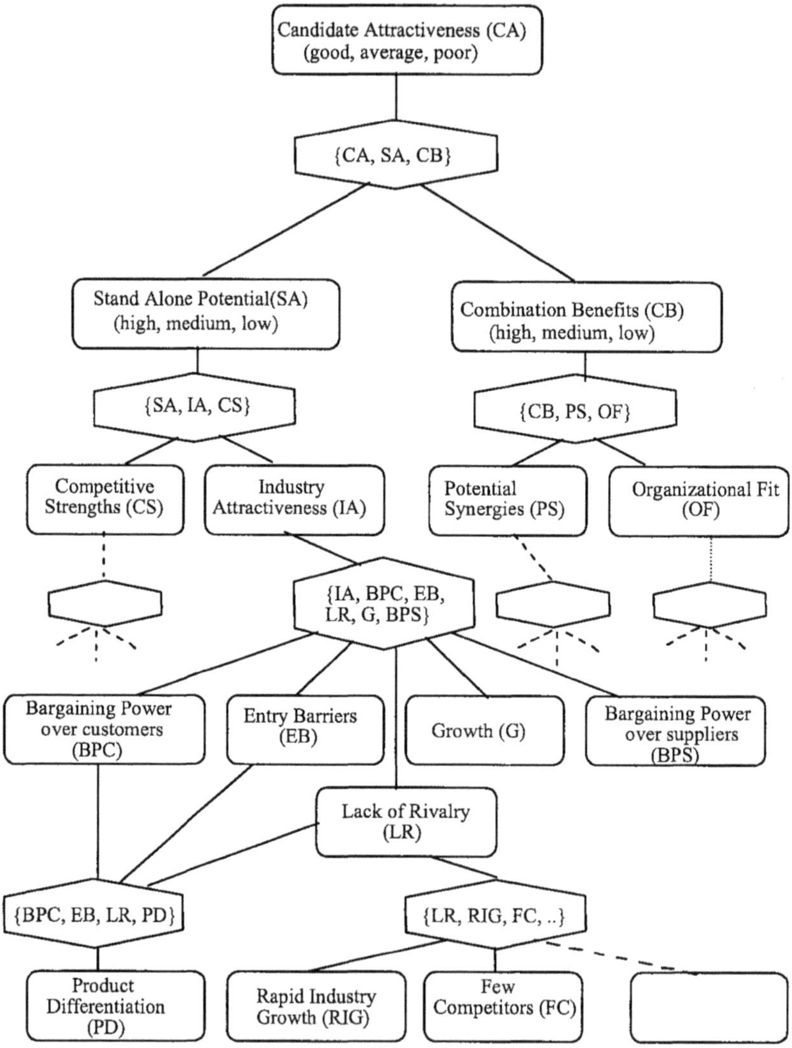

*The rectangular boxes with rounded corners represent variable nodes (factors) and the hexagonal boxes represent relational nodes.

3. Knowledge Representation in Mergers and Acquisitions Through An Evidential Network

In this section we map the expert knowledge of the relevant factors discussed in the previous section along with their interrelationships in terms of an evidential network. As seen in Figure 2, the main factor (node) 'Candidate attractiveness (CA)' depends on (i.e., is connected to) two other factors: 'Stand Alone Potential (SA),' and 'Combination Benefits (CB).' Let us assume that CA takes three possible values: good (g), average (a), or poor (p). Again, for simplicity, let's assume that the remaining variables in the network assume three possible values: high (h), medium (m), or, low (l). For example, "Stand Alone Potential (SA)" is a variable and it takes three values: high (h), medium (m), and low (l).

Figure 2: Evidential Network

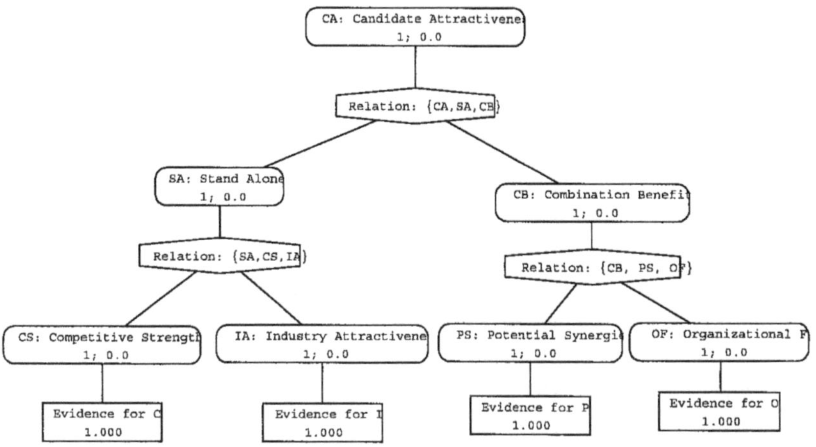

The hexagonal boxes in Figure 2 represent relationships between variables. These relationships are usually expressed in terms of 'if-then' rules, which can be determined by interviewing experts in the field. These 'if-then' rules are then converted into relational nodes using the algorithm described in Appendix A for constructing the network. As an illustration of a relational node, let us consider a specific example involving the following variables: 'Candidate Attractiveness (CA)', 'Stand Alone Potential (SA)' and 'Combination Benefits (CB).' Lets also assume that the 'if-then' rules are obtained through an interview with an expert and they are given in Table 1.

Table 1: 'If-Then' rules relating the variables 'Candidate Attractiveness (CA)', 'Stand Alone Potential (SA)' and 'Combination Benefits (CB).' h, m, and l, respectively, represent high, medium, and low level of the variable.

'If' Condition		'Then' condition's Confidence Level for Candidate Attractiveness (CA)			
SA: Stand Alone Potential	CB: Combination Benefits	Good (g)	Average (a)	Poor (p)	{g, a, p}*
h	h	1.0	0.0	0.0	0.0
h	m	0.7	0.3	0.0	0.0
h	l	0.5	0.5	0.0	0.0
m	h	0.5	0.5	0.0	0.0
m	m	0.2	0.8	0.0	0.0
m	l	0.0	0.6	0.4	0.0
l	h	0.0	0.4	0.6	0.0
l	m	0.0	0.2	0.8	0.0
l	l	0.0	0.0	1.0	0.0

*{g,a,p} represent the set of all possible values of the variable CA with the values of the corresponding beliefs provided in the last column.

Each row in Table 1 represents a part of the 'if-then' rule relating to the two variables, SA and CB with CA. For example, the first row implies that if both 'Stand Alone Potential (SA)' and 'Combination Benefits (CB)' are high (h) then the variable 'Candidate Attractiveness (CA)' would be good (g). In other words, if both SA and CB are high then the acquisition candidate is a good candidate. However, from the second row, it appears that if SA is high (h) and CB is medium (m) then Candidate Attractiveness (CA) is 'good (g)' with 0.7 level of assurance (or belief) and 'average (a)' with 0.3 level assurance (or belief). Under this condition, there is no belief that 'CA' is 'poor (p)'. Using the algorithm described in Appendix A, we obtain the following belief function representation of the rules given in Table 1:

$$\boldsymbol{m}(\{ghh, ghm, ghl, gmh, amm, aml, plh, plm, pll\}) = 0.5,$$

$$\boldsymbol{m}(\{ghh, ahm, ahl, amh, amm, pml, alh, plm, pll\}) = 0.3,$$

$$\boldsymbol{m}(\{ghh, ghm, ahl, amh, gmm, aml, alh, alm, pll\}) = 0.1,$$

$m(\{\text{ghh, ghm, ahl, amh, gmm, pml, plh, alm, pll}\}) = 0.1,$

where the symbol ***m*** stands for the ***m***-value. Each element in the argument of ***m*** represents a set of values for the three variables: 'Candidate Attractiveness (CA)', 'Stand Alone (SA)' and 'Combination Benefits (CB).' For example, an element, say 'aml' in the argument means that 'CA' is average (a), 'SA' is medium (m) and 'CB' is low (l).

As depicted in Figure 2, the variable Stand Alone (SA) depends on Competitive Strength (CS) and Industry Attractiveness (IA). The hexagonal box relating these variables represents the 'if-then' rule supposedly obtained from an expert. For the present discussion we assume the same rules as depicted in Table 1 for this relationship. From Figure 1, we see that the variable 'Combination Benefits (CB)' depends on the two variables: Potential Synergies (PS) and Organizational Fit (OF). Again, for simplicity, the relationship among these variables is assumed to be represented by 'if-then' rules as given in Table 1. As discussed in the previous section, these variables further depend on several other factors. For example, Industry Attractiveness (IA) depends on the following five factors: Bargaining power over customers (BPC), Entry barriers (EB), Lack of rivalry (LR), Growth (G), and Bargaining power over suppliers (BPS). All of these factors may further depend on another set of factors. For example, Lack of Rivalry (LR) would depend on "Rapid industry growth (RIG)", "Few competitors (FC)," "High product differentiation (PD)", "Low exit barriers (LEB)" and "High switching costs (HSC)". On the other hand, "Entry barriers (EB)" would depend on "Economies of scale", "Product differentiation (PD)", "Capital requirements", "Switching costs", "Limited access to distribution channels" and "Government policy". Figure 2 is only a partial evidential network for the decision process[2]. In the next section we show how the evidential network can help the decision maker to consider uncertainties in the evidence related to the factors relevant to the decision.

4. Sensitivity Analysis

Here we want to analyze the impact of the level of assurance for various possible values ('high', 'medium', and 'low') of the input variables: CS', 'IA', 'PS', and 'OF', on the main variable 'Candidate Attractiveness (CA)'.

[2] A complete network is beyond the scope of this paper. The objective of the present article is to show how one can develop an evidential network of relevant variables towards making merger and acquisition decisions.

4.1. Output Belief versus Input Assurance

The solid curve in Figure 3 depicts the overall belief, $Bel_{CA}(g)$, that the candidate attractiveness is good and the dotted curve depicts the overall belief, $Bel_{CA}(\{g,a\})$, that candidate attractiveness (CA) is either good or average. In this illustration, all input variables (CS, IA, PS, and OF) are assumed to be present at a 'high' level with various levels of assurance as shown on the x-axis. All the relational nodes (hexagonal boxes) in Figure 2 are assumed to be 'if-then' rules. The 'if-then' rules relating CA to SA and CB are given in Table 1 along with its belief function representation below the table in the previous section.

For simplicity (and, without the loss of generality), we assume the same structure of the 'if-then' rules relating SA to CS and IA, and CB to PS and OF as considered for relating CA to SA and CB as given in Table 1. As expected, we find the acquisition candidate to be a 'good' candidate with belief one, i.e., $Bel_{CA}(g) = 1$, when all the input variables (CS, IA, PS, and OF) are high with a level of assurance '1' on a scale of 0-1. In terms of belief masses or $\boldsymbol{m}$-values this assurance can be written as $\boldsymbol{m}_{CS}(h) = \boldsymbol{m}_{IA}(h) = \boldsymbol{m}_{S}(h) = \boldsymbol{m}_{IC}(h) = 1$. However, as the level of assurance for the input variables decreases below '1' the belief in CA that the firm will be a good candidate for acquisition decreases rapidly. For example, for 0.8 level of assurance that the input variables are 'high', the overall belief that the candidate attractiveness is good is only 0.692[3], i.e., $Bel_{CA}(g) = 0.692$, and the belief that CA is either 'good' or 'average' is 0.897, i.e., $Bel_{CA}(\{g, a\}) = 0.897$. In other words, these belief values imply that we have 0.897 level of belief on a scale of 0-1 that the candidate is either a 'good' or an 'average' acquisition candidate but we have only 0.692 level of belief that it is just a 'good' candidate.

Suppose the decision maker accepts the candidate firm for acquisition only when the overall belief that it is good is greater than a threshold value, say 0.8. The above value of 0.692 is low compared to the acceptable threshold value. The decision maker has two options in such a situation. First, he/she can decide not to acquire the firm and stop further collection of evidence relevant to the input variables. Alternatively, he/she can decide to collect further evidence to increase the level of support for a 'high' level of presence for all the input variables provided the cost of collecting evidence is reasonable[4].

---

[3] Calculated using the program 'Auditor's Assistant' developed by Shafer, Shenoy, and Srivastava [17].

[4] We are only analyzing the impact of the strength of evidence on the overall belief and ignoring the impact of cost of collecting the evidence. This aspect can easily be incorporated by considering decision making under belief functions (e.g., see Smets [44])

Figure 3

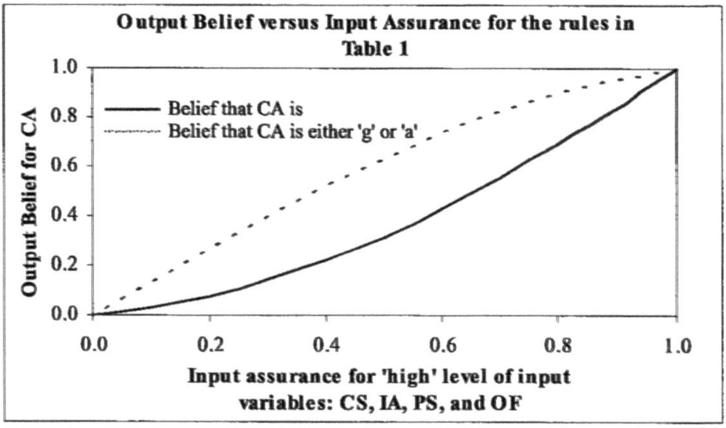

The solid curve in Figure 4 depicts the overall belief that CA is 'good' and the dotted curve depicts the overall belief that CA is either 'good' or 'average'. These beliefs are plotted as a function of input assurance for PS being 'high' with CS, IA, and OF being high at input assurance of 0.8, 0.9, and 0.7, respectively. The overall belief that CA is 'good' is relatively much higher than that depicted in Figure 3. This is due to the fact that three input variables, CS, IA, and OF, already have a high to medium level of support (0.8, 0.9, and 0.7, respectively), for them to be in "high" state. As the input assurance for Potential Synergies (PS) to be 'high" increases from 0 to 1.0, the overall belief that Candidate Attractiveness (CA) is 'good' increases from 0.423 to 0.773, and the belief that CA is either 'good' or 'average' increases from 0.843 to 0.917. This is based on the assumption that the decision maker encounters a situation where he/she has a medium to high level of support for the notion that three variables, Competitive Strength (CS), Industry Attractiveness (IA), and Organization Fit (OF), are at a 'high' level. However, the decision maker may be more uncertain about the Potential Synergies (PS) associated with the merger. A zero level of support that PS is 'high' represents a situation where there is no evidence in support of PS being 'high'. However, as the decision maker searches for more evidence and finds a greater level of support for Potential Synergies to be high, the overall belief that Candidate Attractiveness is 'good' also increases. Such an analysis would be useful in decision makers' allocation of resources for evidence collection as they pertain to individual variables/factors. In the absence of such an analysis, it is difficult to focus efforts at gathering appropriate evidence towards making the final decision on whether the merger should be pursued or not.

Figure 4

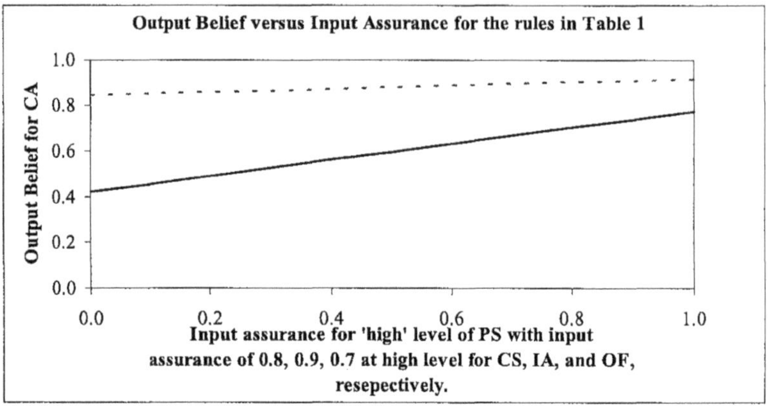

4.2. Impact of the Nature of 'If-Then' Rules on the Output Belief

In order to analyze the impact of 'if-then' rules on the output belief that Candidate Attractiveness (CA) is 'good', we consider another set of 'if-then' rules as given in Table 2. This set involves rules that are fuzzier than those presented in Table 1. For example, in Table 1, when SA is 'high' and CB is 'medium' then CA is 'high' with 0.7 level of assurance and 'medium' with 0.3 level of assurance with no ignorance. However, with the information presented in Table 2, it can be observed that, under the above condition, CA is 'high', 'medium' and 'undecided' with 0.6, 0.3 and 0.1 levels of assurance, respectively. As another illustration of fuzziness of the 'if-then' rules in Table 2, consider the situation (row three in the table) where SA is 'high' and CB is 'low'. The 'then' part of the rule suggests that CA is 'good' with 0.4 level of confidence, 'average' with 0.4, and 0.2 level of assurance is still undecided. However, in the previous case (Table 1), if SA is 'high' and CB is 'low' then CA is 'good' or 'medium' with 0.5 level of assurance each with no ignorance.

Table 2: 'If-Then' rules relating the variables 'Candidate Attractiveness (CA)', 'Stand Alone Potential (SA)' and 'Combination Benefits (CB).' h, m, and l, respectively, represent high, medium, and low level of the variable.

'If' Condition		'Then' condition's Confidence Level for Candidate Attractiveness (CA)			
SA: Stand Alone Potential	CB: Combination Benefits	Good (g)	Average (a)	Poor (p)	Undecided {g, a, p}*
h	h	1.0	0.0	0.0	0.0
h	h	0.6	0.3	0.0	0.1
h	l	0.4	0.4	0.0	0.2
m	h	0.3	0.4	0.0	0.3
m	m	0.2	0.5	0.0	0.3
m	l	0.0	0.4	0.3	0.3
l	h	0.0	0.2	0.4	0.4
l	m	0.0	0.1	0.7	0.2
l	l	0.0	0.0	1.0	0.0

Belief Function Representation using Appendix A:

$\boldsymbol{m}$({ghh, ghm, ghl, amh, amm, aml, plh, plm, pll}) = 0.4,

$\boldsymbol{m}$({ghh, ahm, ahl, gmh, gmm, amm, pmm, pml, glh, alh, plh, plm, pll }) = 0.3,

$\boldsymbol{m}$({ghh, ghm, ghl, ahl, phl, gmh, amh, pmh, gmm, gml, aml, pml, alh, glm, alm, plm, pll}) = 0.2,

$\boldsymbol{m}$({ghh, ghm, ahm, phm, ahl, gmh, amh, pmh, amm, gml, aml, pml, glh, alh, plh, alm,,pll}) = 0.1

*{g,a,p} represent the set of all possible values of the variable CA with the values of the corresponding beliefs provided in the last column.

The solid curve in Figure 5 depicts the overall belief that CA is good for the set of 'if-then' rules given in Table 2 and the dotted curve depicts the overall belief that CA is either good or average for the case where all the input variables have evidence in support of the value 'high'. Comparing Figure 3 to Figure 5, one observes that under the fuzzier 'if-then' rules given in Table 2, the two beliefs that CA is 'good' and 'good' or 'average' are much lower than the two beliefs under the 'if-then' rules given in Table 1. This has important implications for the collection of evidence. Under fuzzier rules, one would require stronger (or additional) evidence to achieve the desired level of overall belief for CA to be good. In other words, the nature and extent of evidence to be collected for a merger or acquisition decision depends on the type of 'if-then' rules assumed among the input variables.

Figure 5

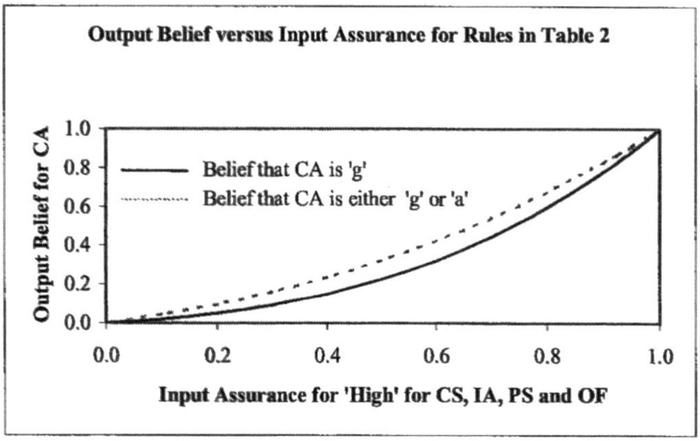

Figure 6

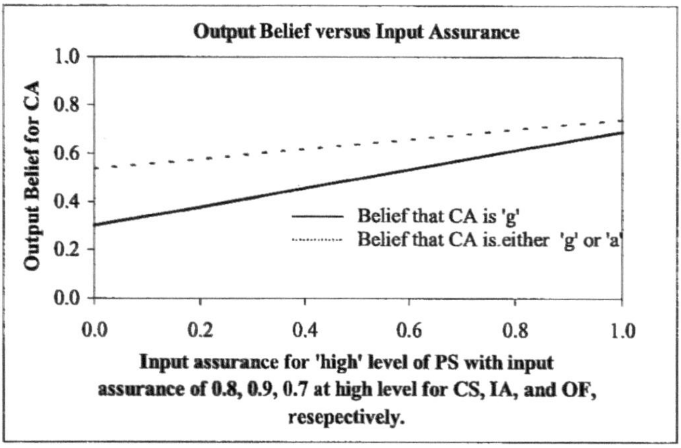

Figure 6 depicts the overall belief that CA is 'good' and CA is either 'good' or 'average' for the fuzzier rules given in Table 2. These beliefs are plotted as a function of input assurance for Potential Synergies being 'high' with input assurance of CS, IA, and OF at 'high' level being held constant at 0.8, 0.9, and 0.7 respectively. As the input assurance for Potential Synergies (PS) to be high increases from 0 to 1.0, the overall belief that Candidate Attractiveness (CA) is good also increases from 0.301 to 0.690, and the belief that CA is either 'good' or 'average' increases from 0.536 to 0.740. Comparing Figure 6 with Figure 4, it is evident that, for the same input conditions, the overall belief that Candidate Attractiveness is 'high' is much lower under the fuzzier rules than under the less fuzzy rules (Table 1). This, again, has important implications for the nature and extent of evidence that needs to be collected for decision making. In other words, when rules are fuzzy, additional and/or stronger supporting evidence needs to be collected to obtain the desired level of belief for the decision.

5. Conclusions

This paper has important theoretical and managerial implications for strategic decision making. From a theoretical perspective, the paper integrates concepts in the Dempster-Shafer theory of belief functions (Smets [45][44][46][47], Shafer [48], Yager et. al [49]) with the literature on mergers and acquisitions. The evidential reasoning approach under belief functions allows decision makers to incorporate the uncertainty judgment associated with various factors in a much more intuitive manner. The paper represents an initial effort at applying belief functions to represent uncertainties in mergers and acquisition decisions, one that results in a better understanding of how managerial decision making under uncertainty can be effectively and meaningfully addressed. In addition, we believe that the proposed framework and the approach suggested in the paper should provide the basis for future empirical studies on factors and relationships influencing acquisition performance.

Very importantly, the proposed framework should help managers in their decision making related to mergers and acquisitions. Fully developed, the suggested approach can help alleviate some of the critical shortcomings of currently used approaches – resulting in a more systematic and comprehensive evaluation of acquisition opportunities. Such evaluations are particularly critical when one considers the high failure rate among acquisitions and the considerable time and resources often expended in the pursuit of such transactions. In addition, sensitivity analysis on the relative importance of various input variables in the acquisition decision making model will help managers effectively and efficiently allocate scarce resources in the gathering of evidence (data/information) along various input factors.

In terms of its broad implications, the paper contributes to the development and building of decision making models under uncertainty in a variety of business situations. The present approach can be easily utilized in the context of other managerial decisions. For example, in recent years we have seen a surge in the number of strategic alliances between firms both in the international and domestic context. And, like mergers and acquisitions, strategic alliances are also plagued by high failure rates. Often the underlying cause is poor selection of partners. The approach developed and suggested in this paper can be easily extended (with appropriate modifications) to the evaluation of alliance partners.

References

[1] Lajoux, A.R. and J. F. Weston (1998). Do deals deliver on postmerger performance? *Mergers and Acquisitions*, 33 (2), pp. 34-37.

[2] Ravenscraft, D.J. and F.M. Scherer (1989). The profitability of mergers, *International Journal of Industrial Organization*, 7, pp. 101-116..

[3] Datta, D.K., V.K. Narayanan and G.E. Pinches (1992). Factors Influencing Wealth Creation in Mergers and Acquisitions: A Meta-analysis', *Strategic Management Journal*, 13 (1), pp. 67-84.

[4] Datta, D.K., and G. Puia (1995). Cross-border acquisitions: An examination of the influence of strategic and cultural fit on shareholder value creation in U.S. acquiring firms'. *Management International Review*, 35 (4), pp. 325-336.

[5] Achtmeyer, W.F., and M.H. Daniell (1988). How advanced planning widens acquisition rewards *Mergers and Acquisitions*, 23, pp. 37-42.

[6] Rappaport, A. (1979). Strategic analysis for more profitable acquisitions. *Harvard Business Review*, 57, pp. 99-110.

[7] Reilly, R.F. (1982). Planning for an Acquisition Strategy. *Managerial Planning*, 30 (5), pp. 36-42.

[8] Curley, S. P., and J. I. Golden (1994). Using belief functions to represent degrees of belief. *Organizational Behavior and Human Decision Processes* 58 (2), pp. 271-303.

[9] Harrison, K. (1999). Evaluation and Aggregation of Audit Evidence under Uncertainty: An Empirical Study of Belief Functions. Ph.D. Dissertation, School of Business, University of Kansas.

[10] Cohen, P. R. (1987). The control reasoning under uncertainty: A discussion of some programs, *The Knowledge Engineering Review*, Cambridge University Press.

[11] Duda, R. O., P. E. Hart, and N. J. Nilsson (1976). Subjective Bayesian Methods For Rule-Based Inference Systems, *Proceedings National Computer Conference* (AFIPS), 15.

[12] Lauritzen, S. L., and Spiegelhalter, D. J. (1988). Local Computations with Probabilities on Graphical Structures and Their Application to Expert Systems (with discussion), *Journal of the Royal Statistical Society*, series B, 50(2), pp. 157-224.

[13] Pearl, J. (1988). Bayesian and Belief-Functions Formalisms for Evidential Reasoning: A Conceptual Analysis, *Proceedings of the 5th Israeli Symposium on Artificial Intelligence*, Tele-Aviv.

[14] Shenoy, P. P. and G. Shafer (1990). Axioms for Probability and Belief-Function Propagation, in *Uncertainty in Artificial Intelligence*, Elsevier Science Publishers.

[15] Andersen, S. K., K. G. Olsen, F. V. Jensen, and F. Jensen (1989). HUGIN A Shell for Building Bayesian Belief Universes for Expert Systems, Proceedings of the Tenth *International Joint Conference on Artificial Intelligence*.

[16] Saffiotti, A, and E. Umkehrer (1991). Pulcinella: A General Tool for Propagating Uncertainty in Valuation Networks, *Proceedings of the Seventh National Conference on Artificial Intelligence*, University of California, Los Angeles, pp. 323-331.

[17] Shafer, G., P. P. Shenoy, and R. P. Srivastava (1988). AUDITOR'S ASSISTANT: A Knowledge Engineering Tool For Audit Decisions, *Proceedings of the 1988 Touche Ross University of Kansas Symposium on Auditing Problems*.

[18] Zarley, D., Y.-T. Hsia, and G. Shafer (1988). Evidential Reasoning using DELIEF, *Proceedings of the National Conference of Artificial Intelligence*.

[19] Srivastava, R.P., S.K. Dutta, and R. Johns (1996). An Expert System Approach to Audit Planning and Evaluation in the Belief-Function Framework, *International Journal of Intelligent Systems in Accounting, Finance and Management*.

[20] Rappaport, A. (1988) Calculating the value-creation potential of a deal. *Mergers and Acquisitions*, 33(1), pp. 33-44.

[21] Roll, R. (1986). The Hubris Hypothesis of Corporate Takeovers. *Journal of Business*, 59, pp. 197-216.

[22] Barney, J.B. (1995). *Gaining and Sustaining Competitive Advantage*, Reading, MA: Addison-Wesley.

[23] Markides, C. and P.J. Williamson. (1994). Related Diversification, Core Competencies and Corporate Performance, *Strategic Management Journal*, 15, pp. 149-165.

[24] Porter, M. (1980). *Competitive Strategy*. New York: Free Press.

[25] Scherer, F.M. (1980). *Industrial Market Structure and Economic performance*, Chicago: Rand McNally.

[26] Lisle, C. and J. Bartlam (1999). Can the target pass the competitive intelligence test? *Mergers & Acquisitions*, 33(4), pp. 27-32

[27] Wernerfelt, B. and C.A. Montgomery (1986). What is an attractive industry? *Management Science,* 32 (10).

[28] Hitt, M.A., R. Hoskisson and D. Ireland (1990). Mergers and Acquisitions and Managerial Commitment to Innovation in M-Form Firms, *Strategic Management Journal,* 11, pp. 29-47

[29] Porter, M.E. (1985). *Competitive Advantage: Creating and sustaining superior performance*, New York: Free Press.

[30] Porter, M.E. (1987). From competitive advantage to corporate strategy. *Harvard Business Review*, 65(3), pp. 43-59.

[31] Bielinski, D.W. (1992). Putting a realistic dollar value on acquisition synergies, Mergers and Acquisitions, November-December, pp. 9-12.

[32] Datta, D.K. (1986). *Assimilation of Acquired Organizations: An Empirical Assessment of the Impact of Selected Organizational and Behavioral Factors on Acquisition Performance,* Unpublished Doctoral Dissertation, University of Pittsburgh.

[33] Jensen, M.C. and R.S. Ruback (1983). The Market for Corporate Control: The Scientific Evidence, *Journal of Financial Economics*, 11, pp. 5-50.

[34] Salter, M.S., and W.A. Weinhold (1979). *Diversification through acquisitions: Strategies for creating economic value*, New York: The Free Press.

[35] Singh, H. and C. Montgomery (1987). Corporate acquisition strategies and economic performance, *Strategic Management Journal*, 8, pp. 377-386.

[36] Sirower, M.L. (1997). *The Synergy Trap: How Companies Lose in the Acquisition game*. New York; The Free Press.

[37] Datta, D.K. (1991). Organizational Fit and Acquisition Performance: Effects of Post-Acquisition Integration, *Strategic Management Journal*, 12(4), pp. 281-298.

[38] Datta, D.K. and J.H. Grant (1990). The relationship between type of acquisition, the autonomy given to the acquired firm and acquisitions success: An empirical analysis, *Journal of Management*, 16(1), pp. 29-44.

[39] Jemison, D.B. and S.B. Sitkin (1986). Corporate Acquisitions: A Process perspective, *Academy of Management Review*, 11 (1), pp. 145-163.

[40] Slowinski, G. (1992). The human touch in successful strategic alliances, *Mergers and Acquisitions*, 27 (1), pp. 44-47.

[41] Marks, M.L. (1999). Adding cultural fit to your diligence checklist, *Mergers and Acquisitions*, 34 (3), pp. 14-20.

[42] Buono, A.F., Bowditch, J.L., and J.W. Lewis (1985). When cultures collide: The anatomy of a merger, *Human Relations*, 38(5), pp. 477-500.

[43] Srivastava, R. P., and K. O. Cogger (1995). Algorithm for Converting Beliefs on Individual Variables from a Single Source of Evidence to m-values on the Joint Space, Working Paper, School of Business, The University of Kansas.

[44] Smets, P. (2001). Decision making in a Context where Uncertainty is Represented by Belief Functions. *Belief Functions in Business Decisions.* Edited by R. Srivastava and T. Mock. Springer-Verlag, Inc (forthcoming).

[45] Smets, P. (1990a). The Combination of Evidence in the Transferable Belief Model. *IEEE Transactions on Pattern Analysis and Machine Intelligence,* 12, 5 (May).

[46] Smets, P. (1990b). Constructing the Pignistic Probability Function in a Context of Uncertainty. *Uncertainty in Artificial Intelligence 5.* ed. by Henrion, M., Shachter, R.D., Kanal, L.N., and Lemmer, J.F. North-Holland: Elsevier Science Publishers B.V.

[47] Smets, P. (1998). The Transferable Belief Model For Quantified Belief Representation. *Quantified Representation for Uncertainty and Imprecision,* Vol. 1. Edited by P. Smets. Kluwer Academic Publishers

[48] Shafer, G. (1976). *A Mathematical Theory of Evidence*, Princeton University Press.

[49] Yager, R. R , J. Kacprzyk, and M. Fedrizzi. (1994). *Advances in the Dempster-Shafer Theory of Evidence,* John Wiley & Sons, New York, NY.

Appendix A

Algorithm for Belief Function Representation of 'If-Then' Rules

In order to propagate belief functions through a network of variables that are connected through 'if-then' rules, one must express these rules in terms of relational nodes. We will describe an algorithm to achieve this goal in this appendix and illustrate the process using a moderately complex example. Let us consider three variables A, B, and C with two possible outcomes for each variable, either the variable is true or false. Further consider the following 'if-then' rules involving A, B, and C.

Rule 1: If A is true (A = a), and B is true (B = b) then C is true (C = c) with 100% confidence.

Rule 2: If A is true (A = a) and B is false (B = ~b) then C is true (C = c) with 60% confidence and the state of C is not known whether it is true or false with 40% confidence.

Rule 3: If A is false (A = ~a) and B is true (B = b) then C is false (C = ~c) with 30% confidence, and the statc of C is not known whether it is true or false with 70% confidence.

Rule 4: If A is false (A = ~ a) and B is false (B = ~ b) then C is false (C = ~c) with 100% confidence.

These rules can represented in the form of a table as given below in Table A1.

Table A1: 'If-Then' Rules Involving Three Variables A, B, and C, with Two outcomes for Each Variable

'If' Condition		'Then' Condition's confidence level		
A	B	c	~c	$\Theta c = \{c, \sim c\}$
a	b	1.0	0.0	0.0
a	~b	0.6	0.0	0.4
~a	b	0.0	0.3	0.7
~a	~b	0.0	1.0	0.0

The Algorithm

Step 1: Prepare a table similar to Table A1 with 'If' variables in the left columns and the 'Then' variable in the right side listed in a row with all its possible values and all the possible sets consisting of these values.

Step 2: Express the 'if-then' rule with its uncertainties for each condition of the rule in the body of the table. For example, the first row in Table A1 represents the rule that if A = a, and B = b, then C = c with 100% confidence. The second row represents the condition that if A = a, and B = ~b, then C = c, with a confidence of 0.6, and C could be either c or ~c with 0.4 level of confidence.

Step 3: Select the largest confidence number in each row. These values are written inside rectangular boxes in Table A2. These values define the focal elements of the ***m***-value to be determined next.

Step 4: Select the smallest value among the set of values from each row selected in Step 3. This value represents the m-value for the set of elements consisting of the elements corresponding to the values selected in step 3.

Step 5: Subtract the minimum number obtained in Step 4 from each selected numbers in Step 3.

Step 6: Repeat Steps 3 - 4 until all cntries are zero.

Belief-Function Representation of 'If-Then' Rules

The following steps illustrate the use of the above algorithm to convert the 'if-then' rules described earlier in the appendix to a belief function representation[5].

[5] In general, there is no unique solution. There are several different belief-function representations for the same set of rules, i.e., we can obtain several different sets of m-values representing the same set of 'if-then' rules. We will investigate this issue further in a separate article. However, the overall combination of beliefs in a network of variables with 'if-then' rules where information flows from finer levels to a coarser level, which is the case in the present study, remains unaffected by the choice of the set of m-values representing the rules.

Iteration 1

Steps 1 – 3: The largest confidence number in each row is boxed in a rectangle. The lowest number among the boxed numbers is identified by an asterisk.

Table A2

'If' Condition		'Then' Condition's confidence level		
A	B	c	~c	Θc = {c,~c}
a	b	[1.0]	0.0	0.0
a	~b	[0.6*]	0.0	0.4
~a	b	0.0	0.3	[0.7]
~a	~b	0.0	[1.0]	0.0

Step 4: m({abc, a~bc, ~abc, ~ab~c, ~a~b~c}) = 0.6.

Step 5: By subtracting the lowest number identified in Step 3 from each marked numbers, one obtains the following table:

'If' Condition		'Then' Condition's confidence level		
A	B	c	~c	Θc = {c,~c}
a	b	0.4	0.0	0.0
a	~b	0.0	0.0	0.4
~a	b	0.0	0.3	0.1
~a	~b	0.0	0.4	0.0

Iteration 2

Step 3: The largest number in each row is boxed in a rectangle. The lowest number among the boxed numbers is identified by an asterisk.

'If' Condition		'Then' Condition's confidence level		
A	B	c	c	Θc = {c, ~c}
a	b	[0.4]	0.0	0.0
a	~b	0.0	0.0	[0.4]
~a	b	0.0	[0.3*]	0.1
~a	~b	0.0	[0.4]	0.0

Step 4: ***m***({abc, a~bc, a~b~c, ~ab~c, ~a~b~c}) = 0.3.

Step 5: By subtracting the lowest number identified in Step 3 from each marked numbers, one obtains the following table:

'If' Condition		'Then' Condition's confidence level		
A	B	c	~c	Θc = {c,~c}
A	b	0.1	0.0	0.0
A	~b	0.0	0.0	0.1
~a	b	0.0	0.0	0.1
~a	~b	0.0	0.1	0.0

Iteration 3

Steps 3: This step yield the following table:

'If' Condition		'Then' Condition's confidence level		
A	B	c	~c	Θc = {c,~c}
a	b	0.1	0.0	0.0
a	~b	0.1	0.0	0.0
~a	b	0.0	0.0	0.1
~a	~b	0.0	0.1	0.0

Step 4: ***m***({abc, a~bc, ~abc, ~ab~c, ~a~b~c}) = 0.1.

The Relational Node

The above process yields the relational node with the following m-values for the 'If-Then' rule defined in this appendix:

m({abc, a~bc, ~abc, ~ab~c, ~a~b~c}) = 0.6,

m({abc, a~bc, a~b~c, ~ab~c, ~a~b~c}) = 0.3,

m({abc, a~bc, ~abc, ~ab~c, ~a~b~c}) = 0.1.

Appendix B

Modeling Logical Relationships and Fuzzy 'If-Then' Rules

As mentioned earlier, in order to combine or propagate uncertainties through a network, we need to convert the interrelationships among the variables of the network into relational nodes under belief functions. In general, some of these relationships are expressed in terms of logical relationships that are categorical such as 'and', 'or', and 'exclusive or', and some relationships are expressed through 'if-then' rules. As shown below, it is much easier to model the logical relationships in belief functions than to model 'if-then' rules, especially if the rules involve uncertainties. We demonstrate the use of the algorithm described in Appendix A for converting various interrelationships among the variables in a network.

'AND' Relationship

Assume that we have three variables: A, B and C. An 'and' relationship between C, and A and B implies that C is true if and only if A and B are true ($C = A \cap B$). Such a relationship will allow only the following possible set of values[6] for the variables: {abc, a~b~c, ~ab~c, ~a~b~c}. One can express the above relationship through the following conditional probabilities:

$$P(c|ab) = 1,\ P(\sim c|ab) = 0,\ \ P(c|a\sim b) = 0,\ P(\sim c|a\sim b) = 1,$$

$$P(c|\sim ab) = 0,\ P(\sim c|\sim ab) = 1,\ \ P(c|\sim a\sim b) = 0,\ P(\sim c|\sim a\sim b) = 1.$$

In order to develop the belief function representation of the above relationship, we complete Steps 1-3 of Appendix A and obtain the following table:

'If' Condition		'Then' Condition's confidence level		
A	B	c	~c	$\Theta_c = \{c, \sim c\}$
A	b	1.0	0.0	0.0
A	~b	0.0	1.0	0.0
~a	b	0.0	1.0	0.0
~a	~b	0.0	1.0	0.0

Using Steps 4-5 of the algorithm, we obtain the following belief function representation of the 'and' relationship:

---

[6] We represent the value of a variable, say A, by the lower case letter 'a' that it is true and the value that A is not true by '~a'.

m({abc, a~b~c, ~ab~c, ~a~b~c}) = 1.

'OR' Relationship

For an 'or' relationship between C, and A and B (i.e., $C = A \cup B$), we will have the following possible values: {abc, a~bc, ~abc, ~a~b~c}. This relationship implies that C is true when either both A and B are true or when any one of them is true but it is false when both A and B are false. In terms of probabilities, we can express the above relationship as:

$$P(c|ab) = 1,\ P(\sim c|ab) = 0,\ \ P(c|a\sim b) = 1,\ P(\sim c|a\sim b) = 0,$$

$$P(c|\sim ab) = 1,\ P(\sim c|\sim ab) = 0,\ \ P(c|\sim a\sim b) = 0,\ P(\sim c|\sim a\sim b) = 1.$$

Again by completing Steps 1-3 of Appendix A we obtain the following table:

'If' Condition		'Then' Condition's confidence level		
A	B	C	~c	$\Theta_c = \{c, \sim c\}$
a	b	1.0	0.0	0.0
a	~b	1.0	0.0	0.0
~a	b	1.0	0.0	0.0
~a	~b	0.0	1.0	0.0

Using Steps 4-5 of the algorithm, we obtain the following belief-function representation of the 'or' relationship:

m({abc, a~bc, ~abc, ~a~b~c}) = 1.

Exclusive OR (EOR)

An 'exclusive or (eor)' relationship between C, and A and B implies that C is true only when either A is true or B is true but it is false when both A and B are either false or true. Such a relationship will allow only the following set of values: {ab~c, a~bc, ~abc, ~a~b~c}. The probability representation of this relationship is:

$$P(c|ab) = 0,\ P(\sim c|ab) = 1,\ \ P(c|a\sim b) = 1,\ P(\sim c|a\sim b) = 0,$$

$$P(c|\sim ab) = 1,\ P(\sim c|\sim ab) = 0,\ \ P(c|\sim a\sim b) = 0,\ P(\sim c|\sim a\sim b) = 1.$$

Again using the algorithm described in Appendix A, we obtain the following belief-function representation of the 'eor' relationship:

m({ab~c, a~bc, ~abc, ~a~b~c}) =1.

Fuzzy 'IF-Then' Relationship

Consider a simple 'if-then' rule: If A is true (A = a) then B is true (B = b) with 90% confidence but with 10% confidence B could be either true or false. Also, if A is false (A = ~a), then we do not know whether B is true or false. The following table is obtained after completing Steps 1-4 of Appendix A:

'If' Condition	'Then' Condition's confidence level		
A	b	~b	Θ_b = {b,~b}
a	0.9*	0.0	0.1
~a	0.0	0.0	1.0

And the corresponding m-value is given by:

m({ab, ~ab, ~a~b}) = 0.9.

Step 5 of the algorithm yields:

'If' Condition	'Then' Condition's confidence level		
A	b	~b	Θ_b = {b,~b}
A	0.0	0.0	0.1
~a	0.0	0.0	0.1

The second iteration of Steps 3-4 of Appendix A yields the following m-value:

m(ab, a~b, ~ab, ~a~b}) = 0.1.

Thus a belief-function representation of the above 'if-then' relationship is given by the following m-values:

m({ab, ~ab, ~a~b}) = 0.9,

m(ab, a~b, ~ab, ~a~b}) = 0.1.

Possibilistic Belief Network Constructed by Operators of Composition and its Application to Financial Analysis[1]

Radim Jiroušek, Jiřina Vejnarová, and Jozef Gemeľa

Laboratory for Intelligent Systems, University of Economics,
Prague, Czech Republic

Abstract. Bayesian networks have become one of the most popular multidimensional models for uncertain knowledge formalization. Possibilistic belief networks that are their possibilistic counterpart, though not so popular, seem to possess a couple of minor but pleasant advantages: the distributions are easier to modify to adopt expert subjective knowledge, and conditioning in possibility theory is dependent on a selected t-norm and therefore the apparatus seems to be more flexible.

The main part of this paper describes a new way of defining possibilistic belief networks as a sequence of low-dimensional distributions connected by operators of composition. To make this nonstandard technique more easily comprehensible, we introduce an extended motivation part explaining the basic notions through a simple (probabilistic) example. The paper is concluded by a lucid example: an application of the apparatus for fundamental analysis of engineering enterprises.

1 Probabilistic Motivation

One of the most popular and important probabilistic models used for knowledge representation and processing (inference) are Bayesian networks. This is a technology enabling computations with probability distributions of very high dimensions. As the possibilistic belief networks we shall deal with in the next sections of the paper represent a possibilistic counterpart of Bayesian networks, we introduce a probabilistic motivation that is determined mainly for the reader not familiar with Bayesian networks. The following simple example of a Bayesian network is used to illustrate their most important properties.

Our model will describe relationships among events influencing the fact whether Mary goes for her regular evening walk or not. All the possible situations will be described with the help of the following six variables:

[1] The research was financially supported by the grants MŠMT no. VS96008, KONTAKT ME 200/1998, and GAČR no. 201/98/1487.

W — describes whether Mary goes for her evening walk;
R — corresponds to the evening weather conditions: if it rains or not;
B — codes what a barometer read at noon;
G — describes a friend of Mary's intention to come to pay her a visit;
T — codes Mary's attitude to the evening TV programme;
D — is an "artificial" variable introduced to decrease the number of connections of the variable W in the resulting network — it corresponds to Mary's decision based on the TV programme and the visit of a friend, only.

An overview of the variables along with their possible values are summarized in Table 1.

Table 1. List of variables and their possible values

variable	brief description	no of values	possible values
B	barometer	3	*rain*, *change*, *fair*
D	preliminary decision	3	*no*, *rather no*, *rather yes*
G	guest	2	*expected to come*, *not expected to come*
R	rain	3	*heavy rain*, *drizzling*, *none*
T	TV programme	3	*uninteresting*, *not so bad*, *interesting*
W	walk	3	*long walk*, *short walk*, *none*

Relationships among variables in Bayesian networks are determined in two ways. Structural information describing the existence of a "direct" dependence of variables is given by a graph, while the quantitative information is given by conditional probability distributions. Thus, a Bayesian network is a couple: an *acyclic directed graph* and a *system of conditional probability distributions*. In our example we consider the acyclic graph from Figure 1.

1.1 Conditional Independence

From the graph in Figure 1 we can read a direct dependence between variables R and W expressing the expected fact that Mary's decision to go for a walk is based on weather. Though in this case we can imagine that rain prevents Mary from going for a walk, we would like to stress that the orientation of connections (arrows) does not necessarily have anything in common with causality. For example, the connection of nodes (variables) B and R also corresponds to common sense, but nobody expects that a barometer can cause rain.

In this model we assume that Mary's friend makes his decision about visiting Mary also upon what a barometer read at noon but we do not assume that his decision can be influenced by what is on TV. Thus, B and G

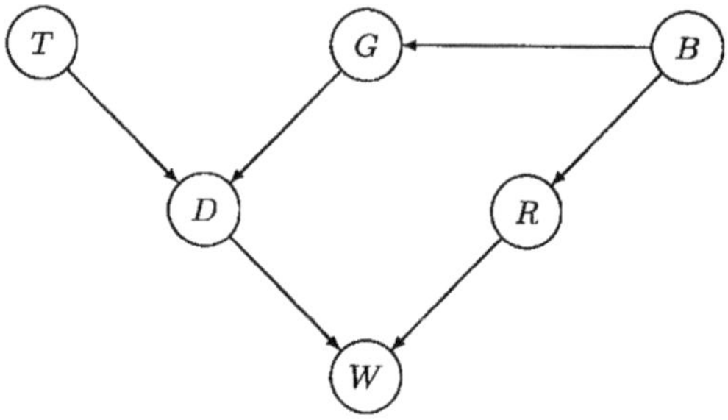

Fig. 1. Acyclic directed graph of a Bayesian network

become dependent variables whilst T and G are independent. In accordance with common sense, in our model variables T and R remain independent, expressing the TV programme's independence of weather.

As we have already said above, a Bayesian network is a couple: an acyclic directed graph (whose nodes are assigned with variables) and a system of conditional probability distributions. In this system there are as many distributions as variables, i.e. nodes of the graph. For each variable a conditional distribution is given with all *parent*[2] variables in the condition. Thus, in our example, the following system of six conditional distributions must be given (notice that for parentless nodes the conditions are empty and the distributions are in fact unconditional):

$$P_1(T), \quad P_2(B), \quad P_3(G|B),$$
$$P_4(D|T,G), P_5(R|B), P_6(W|R,D).$$

The possible values of these distributions are in Table 2. From these values the reader can see that deterministic dependences can also be modelled by Bayesian networks. In such a case, some of the probabilities are equal to 0. For example, in our situation, when a friend has announced his visit, Mary does not go for a long walk for sure.

The probability distribution defined by the introduced Bayesian network is the distribution

$$P(T,G,B,D,R,W) = P_1(T)P_2(B)P_3(G|B)P_4(D|T,G)P_5(R|B)P_6(W|R,D) \quad (1)$$

that is easy to compute for any combination of values of all the variables. However, if we want to obtain a probability only for some variables, we have to compute a marginal distribution. In our case of six variables we could easily marginalize the distribution by simple summing up over combinations of values of the omitted variables. This is, however, impossible when we consider a Bayesian network with several hundreds of variables. Therefore, one

[2] Node i is a parent of node j in a graph if there is an oriented edge leading from i to j. The set of parents of j will be denoted $pa(j)$.

Table 2. System of conditional probability distributions defining the Bayesian network

$P_1(T)$	
$T =$ *uninteresting*	.7
$T =$ *not so bad*	.2
$T =$ *interesting*	.1

$P_2(B)$	
$B =$ *rain*	.2
$B =$ *change*	.5
$B =$ *fair*	.3

$P_3(G\|B)$ B	*rain*	*change*	*fair*
$G =$ *expected*	.1	.2	.3
$G =$ *not expected*	.9	.8	.7

T	*uninterest.*		*not so bad*		*interesting*	
$P_4(D\|T,G)$ G	*exp.*	*not*	*exp.*	*not*	*exp.*	*not*
$D =$ *no*	1	0	1	0	1	.2
$D =$ *rather no*	0	0	0	.5	0	.4
$D =$ *rather yes*	0	1	0	.5	0	.4

$P_5(R\|B)$ B	*rain*	*change*	*fair*
$R =$ *heavy rain*	.2	.1	.1
$R =$ *drizzling*	.4	.3	.1
$R =$ *none*	.4	.6	.8

R	*heavy rain*			*drizzling*			*none*		
$P_6(W\|R,D)$ D	*no*	*r.no*	*r.yes*	*no*	*r.no*	*r.yes*	*no*	*r.no*	*r.yes*
$W =$ *long walk*	0	0	0	0	0	.1	0	.2	.8
$W =$ *short walk*	0	0	.1	.1	.2	.3	.3	.5	.2
$W =$ *none*	1	1	.9	.9	.8	.6	.7	.3	0

has to consider a special technique that would make computations with high-dimensional distributions represented by Bayesian networks possible. There are several such approaches; the most popular ones are based on the idea that the Bayesian network is transformed into a decomposable model representing the same probability distribution. In the case of our example we get the decomposable model whose graph is in Figure 2. As the graph consists of four cliques[3], the model is determined by the four marginal distributions $Q_1(D,T,G)$, $Q_2(G,R,B)$, $Q_3(G,R,D)$ and $Q_4(W,R,D)$ whose values are given in Table 3. Naturally, there are infinitely many 6-dimensional distributions having Q_1, Q_2, Q_3, Q_4 for their marginals but the one with the highest entropy is the distribution represented by the decomposable model and it corresponds to the original Bayesian network.

What are the advantages of decomposable models? Why are there more effective computational procedures for decomposable models than for Bayesian networks? The answers to these questions are not trivial, but roughly speak-

[3] A clique is any maximal set of nodes whose any pair is connected by an edge.

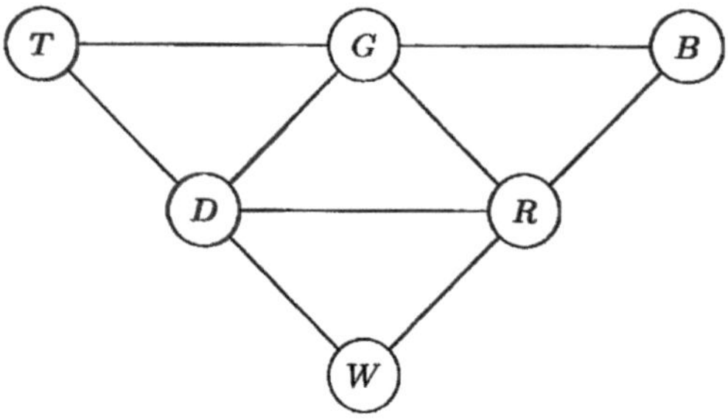

Fig. 2. Decomposable graph defining the decomposable model

Table 3. Four marginal distributions defining the decomposable model

T	*uninterest.*		*not so bad*		*interesting*	
$Q_1(D,T,G)$ G	*exp.*	*not*	*exp.*	*not*	*ann.*	*not*
$D =$ *no*	.147	0	.042	0	.021	.015
$D =$ *rather no*	0	0	0	.079	0	.032
$D =$ *rather yes*	0	.553	0	.079	0	.032

R	*heavy rain*			*drizzling*			*none*		
$Q_2(G,R,B)$ B	*rain*	*chan.*	*fair*	*rain*	*chan.*	*fair*	*rain*	*chan.*	*fair*
$G =$ *expected*	.004	.010	.009	.008	.030	.009	.008	.060	.072
$G =$ *not exp.*	.036	.040	.021	.072	.120	.021	.072	.240	.168

R	*heavy rain*			*drizzling*			*none*		
$Q_3(G,R,D)$ D	*no*	*r.no*	*r.yes*	*no*	*r.no*	*r.yes*	*no*	*r.no*	*r.yes*
$G =$ *expected*	.023	0	0	.047	0	0	.140	0	0
$G =$ *not exp.*	.002	.014	.081	.004	.030	.179	.010	.067	.403

R	*heavy rain*			*drizzling*			*none*		
$Q_4(W,R,D)$ D	*no*	*r.no*	*r.yes*	*no*	*r.no*	*r.yes*	*no*	*r.no*	*r.yes*
$W =$ *long walk*	0	0	0	0	0	.018	0	.013	.322
$W =$ *short walk*	0	0	.008	.005	.006	.054	.045	.034	.081
$W =$ *none*	.025	.014	.073	.046	.024	.107	.105	.020	0

ing, the main reason is the fact that a decomposable model is uniquely defined by its marginals. As we shall show in the sequel, a Bayesian network can also be defined by the marginals of the represented distribution. However, in order for this distribution to be defined uniquely, we also have to determine the ordering of the marginals. And the fact that for decomposable models no ordering of marginals is necessary, makes these models predominant.

The reader familiar with Bayesian networks can see that the dependence structure defined by the original Bayesian network with the graph from Figure 1 and that of the decomposable model from Figure 2 differ. From the first graph we can read some independences that are not included in the decomposable model. For example, the independence of T with G, B, R and the conditional independence of G and R given B are not represented by the decomposable model. This information was lost during the transformation. This loss of information is the price we have to pay for getting a computationally more efficient model. And yet, the conditional independence structure is what makes the models computationally efficient and enables us to represent the distribution with a relatively small number of parameters. So, we shall consider another possibility to reconstruct the probability distribution from its marginals without loosing any conditional independence.

1.2 Operators of Composition

In the sequel we shall need two special operators: operators of composition. The first one, the *operator of right composition*, when applied to two 2-dimensional distributions $R_1(X_1, X_2)$ and $R_2(X_2, X_3)$, defines a 3-dimensional distribution[4]

$$R_1 \triangleright R_2 = R_1(X_1, X_2) R_2(X_3|X_2),$$

i.e. it computes an *extension* of the first distribution, while the other operator, the *operator of left composition* computes the extension of the second distribution:

$$R_1 \triangleleft R_2 = R_2(X_2, X_3) R_1(X_1|X_2).$$

Generally and more precisely, if we consider distributions $R_1((X_i)_{i\in K_1})$ and $R_2((X_i)_{i\in K_2})$, the operator of *right composition* is defined by the formula:

$$R_1 \triangleright R_2 = \begin{cases} \frac{R_1((X_i)_{i\in K_1}) R_2((X_i)_{i\in K_2})}{R_2((X_i)_{i\in K_1\cap K_2})} & \text{if } R_1((X_i)_{i\in K_1\cap K_2}) \ll R_2((X_i)_{i\in K_1\cap K_2}), \\ \text{undefined} & \text{otherwise,} \end{cases} \tag{2}$$

where $R_1((X_i)_{i\in K_1\cap K_2}) \ll R_2((X_i)_{i\in K_1\cap K_2})$ denotes that for all combinations of values $((x_i)_{i\in K_1\cap K_2})$ of variables $((X_i)_{i\in K_1\cap K_2})$ the following implication holds:

$$R_2((X_i = x_i)_{i\in(K_1\cap K_2)}) = 0 \Longrightarrow R_1((X_i = x_i)_{i\in(K_1\cap K_2)}) = 0.$$

Taking $\frac{0.0}{0} = 0$, formula (2), when defined, defines a probability distribution of variables $(X_i)_{i\in K_1\cup K_2}$ and its marginal distribution $(R_1 \triangleright R_2)((X_i)_{i\in K_1})$ is equal to R_1. If $K_1 \cap K_2 = \emptyset$ then $R_1 \triangleright R_2$ degenerates to a simple product of R_1 and R_2.

Analogously, the operator of *left composition* is in general defined by the formula:

$$R_1 \triangleleft R_2 = \begin{cases} \frac{R_1((X_i)_{i\in K_1}) R_2((X_i)_{i\in K_2})}{R_1((X_i)_{i\in K_1\cap K_2})} & \text{if } R_2((X_i)_{i\in K_1\cap K_2}) \ll R_1((X_i)_{i\in K_1\cap K_2}), \\ \text{undefined} & \text{otherwise,} \end{cases} \tag{3}$$

[4] Here we assume that both the conditional distribution $R_2(X_3|X_2)$ and $R_1(X_1|X_2)$ are well defined.

and its marginal distribution $(R_1 \triangleleft R_2)((X_i)_{i \in K_2})$ is equal to R_2.

It is easy to show that the operators of composition are neither associative nor commutative. Therefore, let us stress that in the sequel, when the operators will be applied iteratively, we always assume their application from left to right. In fact, the possibility to omit brackets in formulae was the main reason why we introduced both the operators $\triangleleft$ and $\triangleright$.

An important notion is that of a *perfect sequence.* A sequence of (usually low-dimensional) probability distributions $R_1, R_2, \ldots, R_n$ is called *perfect* if for all $k = 2, \ldots, n$ the equality

$$R_1 \triangleright \ldots \triangleright R_k = R_1 \triangleleft \ldots \triangleleft R_k$$

holds, and all the respective expressions are defined.

In [9] it was shown that the class of Bayesian networks is equivalent to the class of perfect sequences in the following sense:

1. If $R_1, \ldots, R_n$ $(R_k((X_i)_{i \in K_k}))$ is perfect then there exists a Bayesian network representing the distribution $R_1 \triangleright \ldots \triangleright R_n$ such that for all $i \in V$ there exists $k \in \{1, \ldots, n\}$ for which $pa(i) \subset K_k$.
2. For each Bayesian network one can construct a perfect sequence $R_1, \ldots, R_n$ such that n equals the number of nodes of the Bayesian network and each distribution $R_k((X_i)_{i \in K_k})$ $(k = 1, \ldots, n)$ is defined for the set of variables whose indices K_k equal $cl(i) = \{i\} \cup pa(i)$ for some $i \in \{1, \ldots, n\}$, and $R_1 \triangleright \ldots \triangleright R_n$ equals the distribution represented by the Bayesian network.

Thus, turning back to our example, in accordance with point 2. there should exist distributions

$$R_1(T), R_2(B), R_3(G, B), R_4(D, T, G), R_5(R, B), R_6(W, R, D),$$

such that they can be ordered into a perfect sequence. The result mentioned above does not say how to find a proper permutation. In our case it can be, for example, the permutation $R_1, R_2, R_3, R_4, R_5, R_6$ and the distribution

$$R_1(T) \triangleright R_2(B) \triangleright R_3(G, B) \triangleright R_4(D, T, G) \triangleright R_5(R, B) \triangleright R_6(W, R, D) \quad (4)$$

equals the distribution represented by the original Bayesian network (i.e. formula (1)). It follows from the basic properties of perfect sequences (and it will be shown for possibilistic case in the next sections; see Theorem 2) that all the distributions R_i for $i = 1, \ldots, 6$ must be marginals of the distribution defined by formula (4). These distributions are given in Table 4. So, we see that instead of Bayesian networks we can concentrate on perfect sequences of (low-dimensional) distributions. And this is what we shall do in the next sections where we shall define possibilistic versions of operators of composition and possibilistic belief networks will be represented by perfect sequences.

Table 4. System of probability distributions forming a perfect sequence

$R_1(T)$	
$T =$ *uninteresting*	.700
$T =$ *not so bad*	.200
$T =$ *interesting*	.100

$R_2(B)$	
$B =$ *rain*	.200
$B =$ *change*	.500
$B =$ *fair*	.300

$R_3(G,B)$ B	*rain*	*chan.*	*fair*
$G =$ *expected*	.020	.100	.090
$G =$ *not expected*	.180	.400	.210

T	*uninterest.*		*not so bad*		*interesting*	
$R_4(D,T,G)$ G	*exp.*	*not*	*exp.*	*not*	*exp.*	*not*
$D =$ *no*	.147	0	.042	0	.021	.015
$D =$ *rather no*	0	0	0	.079	0	.032
$D =$ *rather yes*	0	.553	0	.079	0	.032

$R_5(R,B)$ B	*rain*	*chan.*	*fair*
$R =$ *heavy rain*	.040	.050	.030
$R =$ *drizzling*	.080	.150	.030
$R =$ *none*	.080	.300	.240

R	*heavy rain*			*drizzling*			*none*		
$R_6(W,R,D)$ D	*no*	*r.no*	*r.yes*	*no*	*r.no*	*r.yes*	*no*	*r.no*	*r.yes*
$W =$ *long walk*	0	0	0	0	0	.018	0	.013	.322
$W =$ *short walk*	0	0	.008	.005	.006	.054	.045	.034	.081
$W =$ *none*	.025	.014	.073	.046	.024	.107	.105	.020	0

2 Multidimensional Models in Possibility Theory

The additivity, which is a characteristic property of a probability measure, is often considered to be unjustifiable or too strong for applications in real situations [5]. Therefore, many other approaches have been suggested; among them we shall concentrate to possibility theory. It enables us to obtain (under substantially weaker conditions) solutions of problems that being solved in the probabilistic framework would lead to interpretational difficulties. The results thus achieved are, evidently, weaker, but their strength consists in their wider applicability.

To understand the concept of possibilistic belief networks, this and the next sections introduce the necessary mathematical background. They are written in such a way that a mathematically educated reader can find all the notions used and need not refer to other sources. The assertions introduced in the text express the basic properties of the most important notions and the proofs are included because of their simplicity and to show how to use the respective mathematical apparatus (the reader not interested can simply skip them).

The definitions of the operators of composition and their properties will be the subject of this section, but we start with the basic terminology and notation connected with possibility theory. Before introducing possibility measures and distributions, we want to recall the important notion of a t-norm. It will play the role of a product (independent composition) used in probability theory.

2.1 Triangular Norms

A *triangular norm* (or a *t-norm*) T is a binary operator on $[0,1]$ (i.e. $T : [0,1]^2 \rightarrow [0,1]$) satisfying the following three conditions:

(i) *boundary conditions:* for any $x \in [0,1]$

$$T(1,x) = x,$$
$$T(0,x) = 0;$$

(ii) *isotonicity:* for any $x_1, x_2, y_1, y_2 \in [0,1]$ such that $x_1 \leq x_2, y_1 \leq y_2$

$$T(x_1, y_1) \leq T(x_2, y_2);$$

(iii) *associativity and commutativity:* for any $x, y, z \in [0,1]$

$$T(T(x,y),z) = T(x,T(y,z)),$$
$$T(x,y) = T(y,x).$$

A t-norm T is called *continuous*, if it is a continuous function.

In the sequel we will distinguish three continuous t-norms, which will be used in all the examples:

(i) *Gödel's t-norm*: $T_G(x,y) = \min(x,y)$;
(ii) *product t-norm*: $T_p(x,y) = x \cdot y$;
(iii) *Łukasziewicz' t-norm*: $T_L(x,y) = \max(0, x+y-1)$.

It is an easy task which is left to the reader to verify that all these functions meet the conditions (i), (ii) and (iii)[5].

Let $x, y \in [0,1]$ and T be a t-norm. We will call an element $z \in [0,1]$ *T-inverse* of x w.r.t. y if $T(z,x) = T(x,z) = y$. Thus, for the product t-norm T_p-inverse of x w.r.t. y is just $\frac{y}{x}$ if $y \leq x > 0$. For $y > x$ it is undefined and T_p-inverse of 0 w.r.t. 0 is any number from $[0,1]$. Analogously, if $y < x$, T_G inverse of x w.r.t. y is y, for $x = y$ it is any number from the

[5] Not all t-norms are continuous. An example of a t-norm, which is not continuous is a *"drastic product"*: $T(x,y) = 0$ for $x, y < 1$.

interval $[y, 1]$ and if $y > x$ it remains undefined. And finally, if $y \le x$, T_L inverse of x w.r.t. y is $y - x + 1$ and for $y > x$ it is undefined.

The ambiguity of T-*inverse* of x w.r.t. y can cause serious problems in some cases, therefore we will prefer using a T-*residual* $y \triangle_T x$ of y by x which is defined as

$$y \triangle_T x = \sup\{z \in [0,1] : T(z,x) \le y\}.$$

It is well-known (see e.g. [1]) that for continuous t-norms T the *maximal* T-inverse of x w.r.t. y is equal to $y \triangle_T x$. Thus, for our famous t-norms we get

$$y \triangle_{T_G} x = \begin{cases} y & \text{if } \ x > y, \\ 1 & \text{otherwise,} \end{cases}$$

$$y \triangle_{T_p} x = \begin{cases} \frac{y}{x} & \text{if } \ 0 < x > y, \\ 1 & \text{otherwise,} \end{cases}$$

$$y \triangle_{T_L} x = \begin{cases} y - x + 1 & \text{if } \ x > y, \\ 1 & \text{otherwise.} \end{cases}$$

In the sequel we will need the following lemma concerning the properties of T-residuals.

Lemma 1. *(i) T is continuous iff for all $x, y \in [0,1]$ such that $x \ge y$ it holds that $T(y \triangle_T x, x) = y$.*

(ii) For any continuous t-norm T and any $x, y, z \in [0,1]$ such that $x, y \le z$ the equality

$$T(x \triangle_T z, y) = T(x, y \triangle_T z) \tag{5}$$

is satisfied.

Proof:

(i) is a special case of Proposition 2.2 (ii) from [1]; the reader is, therefore, referred to this paper for the proof.

(ii)

$$\begin{aligned} T(x \triangle_T z, y) &= T(x \triangle_T z, T(y \triangle_T z, z)) = T(x \triangle_T z, T(z, y \triangle_T z)) \\ &= T(T(x \triangle_T z, z), y \triangle_T z) = T(x, y \triangle_T z), \end{aligned}$$

where only (i) of this lemma and associativity and commutativity of T were used. □

2.2 Possibility Distributions

When starting to introduce notions of a possibility measure and the corresponding possibility distribution, let us stress once for ever that we deal in the paper with a finite model: we consider a finite number of finite-valued variables. Hence, we can introduce the possibilistic measure only on a finite set $\mathbf{X}$ which is supposed to contain at least two elements. A ***possibility measure*** Π on $\mathbf{X}$ is a mapping from the power set $\mathcal{P}(\mathbf{X})$ to the closed interval $[0,1]$ satisfying the following requirement: for any family $\{A_j, j \in J\}$ of elements of $\mathcal{P}(\mathbf{X})$

$$\Pi(\bigcup_{j\in J} A_j) = \max_{j\in J} \Pi(A_j).^6$$

For any $A \in \mathcal{P}(\mathbf{X})$, $\Pi(A)$ is called the ***possibility of A***. Π is called ***normal*** if $\Pi(\mathbf{X}) = 1$. Within this text we will deal only with normal possibility measures and rather than about measures we will speak about distributions.

A mapping $\pi : \mathbf{X} \to [0,1]$ such that for any $A \in \mathcal{P}(\mathbf{X})$

$$\Pi(A) = \max_{x\in A} \pi(x)$$

is called a ***distribution*** of measure Π.

Let us denote $\mathcal{G}(\mathbf{X})$ as the set of all the functions defined on $\mathbf{X}$ and taking their values in $[0,1]$, i.e.

$$\mathcal{G}(\mathbf{X}) = \{h : \mathbf{X} \longrightarrow [0,1]\}.$$

For any t-norm T and a possibility measure Π with the distribution π we define a binary relation on $\mathcal{G}(\mathbf{X})$ (see [1]): Two functions $h_1, h_2 \in \mathcal{G}(\mathbf{X})$ are said to be ***(Π,T)-equal almost everywhere*** on $\mathbf{X}$ (in symbol: $h_1 \overset{(\Pi,T)}{=} h_2$) if for all $x \in \mathbf{X}$

$$T(h_1(x), \pi(x)) = T(h_2(x), \pi(x)).$$

The importance of this notion will soon be revealed in the definition of conditional possibility distribution, which will be introduced in the next section.

Marginalization in possibility theory differs from that in probabilistic framework in using maximization instead of summation. Let us consider an arbitrary possibility measure Π defined on a Cartesian product $\mathbf{X}_1 \times \mathbf{X}_2$ and its distribution π . Its ***marginal possibility distribution*** on $\mathbf{X}_1$ is

$$\pi(x_1) = \max_{x_2\in \mathbf{X}_2} \pi(x_1, x_2) \tag{6}$$

for any $x_1 \in X_1$.

---

[6] max should be replaced by sup operator if $\mathbf{X}$ were not supposed to be finite.

2.3 Conditional Possibility Distributions

Perhaps the most important notion we have to introduce is the concept of conditioning. We follow the definition from [2] and [14] where this concept is parametrized by a t-norm. Considering a continuous t-norm T, de Cooman [2] defines the conditional possibility distribution $\pi\left(x_2|_T x_1\right)$ for each
$(x_1, x_2) \in \mathbf{X}_1 \times \mathbf{X}_2$ as *any* solution of the equation

$$\pi\left(x_1, x_2\right) = T\left(\pi\left(x_2|_T x_1\right), \pi\left(x_1\right)\right). \tag{7}$$

Since the conditional distribution defined in this way is usually ambiguous, we take for the conditional distribution the maximal (or the least specific) one. As we consider only continuous t-norms T, this solution coincides with the T-*residual* (cf. Section 2.1). Therefore we define in this paper the *conditional possibility distribution* for each $(x_1, x_2) \in \mathbf{X}_1 \times \mathbf{X}_2$ by the expression

$$\pi\left(x_2|_T x_1\right) = \pi\left(x_1, x_2\right) \Delta_T \pi\left(x_1\right). \tag{8}$$

Let us remark that in the above mentioned terminology, for each fixed $a_2 \in \mathbf{X}_2$ any solution $\pi(a_2|_T x_1)$ of the equation (7) and $\pi\left(x_1, a_2\right) \Delta_T \pi\left(x_1\right)$ (both these functions considered as functions of x_1) are (Π, T)-equal almost everywhere on $\mathbf{X}_1$[7].

Thus, for the considered three t-norms T_G, T_p and T_L the conditional distributions can be computed according to the following simple formulae

$$\pi(x_2|_{T_G} x_1) = \begin{cases} \pi(x_1, x_2) & \text{if } \pi(x_1, x_2) < \pi(x_1), \\ 1 & \text{if } \pi(x_1, x_2) = \pi(x_1). \end{cases}$$

$$\pi(x_2|_{T_p} x_1) = \begin{cases} \frac{\pi(x_1, x_2)}{\pi(x_1)} & \text{if } \pi(x_1) > 0, \\ 1 & \text{if } \pi(x_1) = 0, \end{cases}$$

$$\pi(x_2|_{T_L} x_1) = \pi(x_1, x_2) - \pi(x_1) + 1.$$

In probability theory, conditioning is closely connected with independence and analogous connection can be found also in possibility theory. Considering a two-dimensional measure Π with its distribution $\pi(x_1, x_2)$ and a t-norm T we say that the respective variables X_1 and X_2 are T-*independent*[8] if

$$\pi(x_1, x_2) = T(\pi(x_1), \pi(x_2)) \tag{9}$$

[7] Speaking about functions $\pi(a_2|_T x_1)$ and $\pi\left(x_1, a_2\right) \Delta_T \pi\left(x_1\right)$ that are (for each fixed a_2) defined on $\mathbf{X}_1$, in the symbol (Π, T) we consider in fact the marginal possibility measure of Π on $\mathbf{X}_1$, whose distribution is defined by (6).

[8] In [3] another definition of T-independence is presented but (9) is equivalent to this definition.

for all $(x_1, x_2) \in \mathbf{X}_1 \times \mathbf{X}_2$.

Regarding the definition of conditional possibility distribution $\pi(x_2|_T x_1)$ one can immediately see that variables X_1 and X_2 are T-independent *iff* $\pi(x_2|_T x_1)$ and $\pi(x_2)$ are (Π, T)-*equal almost everywhere* on $\mathbf{X}_1 \times \mathbf{X}_2$.

To avoid necessity to repeat that equations like e.g. equation (9) must hold for all values of the considered variables, we shall present them in a functional way, using variables instead of their values. Therefore, equation (9) will appear in the following form

$$\pi(X_1, X_2) = T(\pi(X_1), \pi(X_2)).$$

2.4 Operators of Composition

Eventually, using the above introduced conditional distribution, and in analogy to probabilistic case, we define the *operator of right composition* of possibilistic distributions by the expression

$$\begin{aligned}
&\pi_1\left((X_i)_{i\in K_1}\right) \triangleright_T \pi_2\left((X_i)_{i\in K_2}\right) \\
&= T\left(\pi_1\left((X_i)_{i\in K_1}\right), \pi_2\left((X_i)_{i\in K_2\setminus K_1}|_T (X_i)_{i\in K_1\cap K_2}\right)\right) \\
&= T\left(\pi_1\left((X_i)_{i\in K_1}\right), \pi_2\left((X_i)_{i\in K_2}\right) \Delta_T \pi_2\left((X_i)_{i\in K_1\cap K_2}\right)\right),
\end{aligned}$$

and analogously the *operator of left composition* by the expression

$$\begin{aligned}
&\pi_1\left((X_i)_{i\in K_1}\right) \triangleleft_T \pi_2\left((X_i)_{i\in K_2}\right) \\
&= T\left(\pi_1\left((X_i)_{i\in K_1\setminus K_2}|_T (X_i)_{i\in K_1\cap K_2}\right), \pi_2\left((X_i)_{i\in K_2}\right)\right) \\
&= T\left(\pi_1\left((X_i)_{i\in K_1}\right) \Delta_T \pi_1\left((X_i)_{i\in K_1\cap K_2}\right), \pi_2\left((X_i)_{i\in K_2}\right)\right).
\end{aligned}$$

It is evident that both $\pi_1\left((X_i)_{i\in K_1}\right) \triangleright_T \pi_2\left((X_i)_{i\in K_2}\right)$ and $\pi_1\left((X_i)_{i\in K_1}\right) \triangleleft_T \pi_2\left((X_i)_{i\in K_2}\right)$ are possibility distributions of variables $(X_i)_{i\in K_1\cup K_2}$ and we will show that (for normal possibility distributions π_1 and π_2) their marginal distributions $(\pi_1 \triangleright_T \pi_2)((X_i)_{i\in K_1})$ and $(\pi_1 \triangleleft_T \pi_2)((X_i)_{i\in K_2})$ equal to π_1 and π_2, respectively.

To prove it we need the following lemma concerning the relationship between t-norm and marginalization.

Lemma 2. *Let T be a t-norm and $\pi_1((X_i)_{i\in K_1})$ and $\pi_2((X_i)_{i\in K_2})$ be two possibility distributions such that $K_1 \cap K_2 = \emptyset$. Then the equality*

$$T(\pi_1, \pi_2)((x_i)_{i\in L}) = T(\pi_1((x_i)_{i\in K_1\cap L}), \pi_2((x_i)_{i\in K_2\cap L}))$$

is satisfied for any $(x_i)_{i\in L} \in \mathbf{X}_L, L \subseteq K_1 \cup K_2$.

Proof: For any t-norm T and K_1, K_2 satisfying the above requirements we can compute

$$T(\pi_1, \pi_2)((x_i)_{i\in L}) = \max_{x\in X_{(K_1\cup K_2)\setminus L}} T(\pi_1, \pi_2)((x_i)_{i\in L}, x)$$

$$= \max_{y \in \mathbf{X}_{K_1 \setminus L}} \max_{z \in \mathbf{X}_{K_2 \setminus L}} T(\pi_1, \pi_2)((x_i)_{i \in K_1 \cap L}, (x_i)_{i \in K_2 \cap L}, y, z)$$
$$= T(\max_{y \in \mathbf{X}_{K_1 \setminus L}} \pi_1((x_i)_{i \in K_1 \cap L}, y), \max_{z \in \mathbf{X}_{K_2 \setminus L}} \pi_2((x_i)_{i \in K_2 \cap L}, z))$$
$$= T(\pi_1((x_i)_{i \in K_1 \cap L}), \pi_2((x_i)_{i \in K_2 \cap L})),$$

due to the equality (6) and the isotonicity of a t-norm. □

Theorem 1. *Let T be a continuous t-norm and $\pi_1((X_i)_{i \in K_1})$ and $\pi_2((X_i)_{i \in K_2})$ be two possibility distributions. Then*

$$(\pi_1 \triangleright_T \pi_2)((X_i)_{i \in K_1}) = \pi_1((X_i)_{i \in K_1}),$$
$$(\pi_1 \triangleleft_T \pi_2)((X_i)_{i \in K_2}) = \pi_2((X_i)_{i \in K_2}).$$

Proof: The following equality holds for any $(x_i)_{i \in K_1} \in \mathbf{X}_{K_1}$ by definition of $\triangleright_T$ and due to Lemma 2

$$(\pi_1 \triangleright_T \pi_2)((x_i)_{i \in K_1}) = T(\pi_1((x_i)_{i \in K_1}), \pi_2((x_i)_{i \in (K_2 \setminus K_1) \cap K_1} |_T (x_i)_{i \in K_2 \cap K_1})).$$

Since $(K_2 \setminus K_1) \cap K_1 = \emptyset$, the conditional possibility distribution $\pi_2((x_i)_{i \in (K_2 \setminus K_1) \cap K_1} |_T (x_i)_{i \in K_2 \cap K_1}))$ degenerates to constant 1 and therefore

$$T(\pi_1((x_i)_{i \in K_1}), \pi_2((x_i)_{i \in (K_2 \setminus K_1) \cap K_1} |_T (x_i)_{i \in K_2 \cap K_1})) = T(\pi_1((x_i)_{i \in K_1}), 1)$$
$$= \pi_1((x_i)_{i \in K_1})$$

because of (i) from the definition of the t-norm. The proof of the second equality is completely analogous. □

Let us finish this section by presenting two examples. The first one demonstrates basic properties of introduced operators — lack of commutativity and associativity, which fully corresponds to the properties of these operators in the probabilistic framework. The aim of the second one is to demonstrate the dependence of the resulting multidimensional model on the choice of a t-norm.

2.5 Noncommutativity and Nonassociativity of $\triangleright_T$

Consider $\mathbf{X}_1 = \mathbf{X}_2 = \{0, 1\}$ and four possibility distributions from Table 5. These distributions possess values 0 and 1 only; for such distributions all t-norms yield the same results.

Evidently, the marginal distribution of π_2 on $\mathbf{X}_1$ is $\pi_2(X_1) \equiv 1$ and therefore $\pi_2(X_2 |_T X_1) \equiv \pi_2(X_1, X_2)$ (for any choice of t-norm). Thus we get

$$(\pi_1 \triangleright_T \pi_2)(0,0) = T(0,0) = 0,$$
$$(\pi_1 \triangleright_T \pi_2)(0,1) = T(0,1) = 0,$$
$$(\pi_1 \triangleright_T \pi_2)(1,0) = T(1,1) = 1,$$
$$(\pi_1 \triangleright_T \pi_2)(1,1) = T(1,1) = 1,$$

Table 5. Four possibility distributions

$\pi_1(X_1)$		
$X_1 = 0$	0	
$X_1 = 1$	1	
$\pi_2(X_1, X_2)$ X_2	0	1
$X_1 = 0$	0	1
$X_1 = 1$	1	1

$\pi_3(X_2)$		
$X_2 = 0$	0	
$X_2 = 1$	1	
$\pi_4(X_1, X_2)$ X_2	0	1
$X_1 = 0$	1	1
$X_1 = 1$	1	0

which differs from $(\pi_2 \rhd_T \pi_1) = \pi_2$. Therefore,

$$(\pi_1 \rhd_T \pi_2) \neq (\pi_2 \rhd_T \pi_1).$$

Let us now consider $((\pi_1 \rhd_T \pi_3) \rhd_T \pi_4) = \pi_1 \rhd_T \pi_3 \rhd_T \pi_4 = \pi_1 \rhd_T \pi_3$. (The last equality holds due to Theorem 1.) Thus, this 2-dimensional distribution can be computed

$$\begin{aligned}(\pi_1 \rhd_T \pi_3)(0,0) &= T(0,0) = 0,\\ (\pi_1 \rhd_T \pi_3)(0,1) &= T(0,1) = 0,\\ (\pi_1 \rhd_T \pi_3)(1,0) &= T(1,0) = 0,\\ (\pi_1 \rhd_T \pi_3)(1,1) &= T(1,1) = 1.\end{aligned}$$

Considering, now, the expression $(\pi_1 \rhd_T (\pi_3 \rhd_T \pi_4))$ we have to compute first

$$\begin{aligned}\pi_3(X_2) \rhd_T \pi_4(X_1, X_2) &= T(\pi_3(X_2), \pi_4(X_1|_T X_2))\\ &= T(\pi_3(X_2), \pi_4(X_1, X_2)\Delta_T \pi_4(X_2)).\end{aligned}$$

Since $\pi_4(X_2) \equiv 1$ we get $\pi_4(X_1|_T X_2) \equiv \pi_4(X_1, X_2)$ and therefore

$$\begin{aligned}(\pi_3 \rhd_T \pi_4)(0,0) &= T(0,1) = 0,\\ (\pi_3 \rhd_T \pi_4)(0,1) &= T(1,1) = 1,\\ (\pi_3 \rhd_T \pi_4)(1,0) &= T(0,1) = 0,\\ (\pi_3 \rhd_T \pi_4)(1,1) &= T(1,0) = 0.\end{aligned}$$

Regarding the definition

$$(\pi_3 \rhd \pi_4)(X_2|_T X_1) = (\pi_3 \rhd \pi_4)(X_1, X_2)\Delta_T(\pi_3 \rhd \pi_4)(X_1)$$

we get

$$\begin{aligned}&(\pi_3 \rhd_T \pi_4)(X_2 = 0|X_1 = 0)\\ &= (\pi_3 \rhd_T \pi_4)(X_1 = 0, X_2 = 0)\Delta_T(\pi_3 \rhd_T \pi_4)(X_1 = 0) = 0\Delta_T 1 = 0,\\ &(\pi_3 \rhd_T \pi_4)(X_2 = 1|X_1 = 0)\\ &= (\pi_3 \rhd_T \pi_4)(X_1 = 0, X_2 = 1)\Delta_T(\pi_3 \rhd_T \pi_4)(X_1 = 0) = 1\Delta_T 1 = 1,\end{aligned}$$

$$(\pi_3 \rhd_T \pi_4)(X_2 = 0|X_1 = 1)$$
$$= (\pi_3 \rhd_T \pi_4)(X_1 = 1, X_2 = 0)\Delta_T(\pi_3 \rhd_T \pi_4)(X_1 = 1) = 0\Delta_T 0 = 1,$$
$$(\pi_3 \rhd_T \pi_4)(X_2 = 1|X_1 = 1)$$
$$= (\pi_3 \rhd_T \pi_4)(X_1 = 1, X_2 = 1)\Delta_T(\pi_3 \rhd_T \pi_4)(X_1 = 1) = 0\Delta_T 0 = 1,$$

and finally we obtain

$$(\pi_1 \rhd_T (\pi_2 \rhd_T \pi_3))(X_1 = 0, X_2 = 0) = T(0,0) = 0,$$
$$(\pi_1 \rhd_T (\pi_2 \rhd_T \pi_3))(X_1 = 0, X_2 = 1) = T(0,1) = 0,$$
$$(\pi_1 \rhd_T (\pi_2 \rhd_T \pi_3))(X_1 = 1, X_2 = 0) = T(1,1) = 1,$$
$$(\pi_1 \rhd_T (\pi_2 \rhd_T \pi_3))(X_1 = 1, X_2 = 1) = T(1,1) = 1.$$

Thus, in the considered case

$$((\pi_1 \rhd_T \pi_2) \rhd_T \pi_3) \neq (\pi_1 \rhd_T (\pi_2 \rhd_T \pi_3)).$$

2.6 Influence of t-norm on Decision-making

Let us present a simple example showing that, using different t-norms, we can obtain different multidimensional models yielding different decision rules. For this, consider $\mathbf{X}_1 = \mathbf{X}_2 = \{0, 1\}$ and $\mathbf{X}_3 = \{0, 1, 2\}$ and two possibility distributions from Table 6.

Table 6. Two possibility distributions

$\pi_1(X_1, X_3)$	X_3	0	1	2
$X_1 = 0$		1	1	1
$X_1 = 1$		.5	.7	.9

$\pi_2(X_2, X_3)$	X_3	0	1	2
$X_2 = 0$		1	1	1
$X_2 = 1$		.5	.4	.3

Our aim is to construct 3-dimensional possibility distributions on $\mathbf{X}_1 \times \mathbf{X}_2 \times \mathbf{X}_3$ and to use them for decision-making. Using operators $\rhd_T$ for three distinguished t-norms mentioned in Section 2.1 (Gödel's, product and Łukasziewicz's one) we will obtain the three possibility distributions summarized in Table 7[9].

Now, let us use these 3-dimensional possibility distributions for a decision-making problem: knowing values of X_1 and X_2 we have to choose the "most possible" value of X_3. In this example, the most interesting case is for $X_1 = X_2 = 1$. In this case, the model based on Gödel's t-norm chooses $X_3 = 0$, while the model based on product t-norm $X_3 = 1$ and that based on Łukasziewicz' t-norm $X_3 = 2$; see Table 8, where the respective conditional possibilities are summarized.

[9] Let us mention at this moment that the marginal of π_2 on X_3 equals identically to 1 and therefore (for any continuous t-norm) conditional possibility distribution $\pi_2(X_2|X_3)$ coincide with the joint one $\pi_2(X_2, X_3)$.

Table 7. Three 3-dimensional possibility distributions

X_1	X_2	X_3	$\pi_1 \rhd_T \pi_2(X_1, X_2, X_3)$		
			G	p	L
0	0	0	1	1	1
0	0	1	1	1	1
0	0	2	1	1	1
0	1	0	.5	.5	.5
0	1	1	.4	.4	.4
0	1	2	.3	.3	.3
1	0	0	.5	.5	.5
1	0	1	.7	.7	.7
1	0	2	.9	.9	.9
1	1	0	.5	.25	0
1	1	1	.4	.28	.1
1	1	2	.3	.27	.2

Table 8. Conditional possibilities

X_3	$\pi_1 \rhd_T \pi_2(X_3 \mid X_1 = 1, X_2 = 1)$		
	G	p	L
0	1	25/28	.8
1	.4	1	.9
2	.3	27/28	1

3 Perfect Sequences and their Application

Iterative application of operators of composition to a sequence $\pi_1, \pi_2, \ldots, \pi_n$ of low-dimensional possibility distributions gives rise to a multidimensional possibility distribution that can serve as a model incorporating all the knowledge contained in all π_i's.

Naturally, not all the sequences are equally convenient for the purpose. Not all the sequences can be effectively used for inference. As we mentioned at the beginning of the paper, suitable sequences are those that correspond to possibilistic belief networks. In our terminology we call these sequences perfect.

Analogous to the probabilistic framework, an ordered sequence of possibility distributions $\pi_1, \pi_2, \ldots, \pi_n$ is said to be *perfect* if

$$\pi_1 \rhd_T \pi_2 = \pi_1 \lhd_T \pi_2,$$

$$\pi_1 \rhd_T \pi_2 \rhd_T \pi_3 = \pi_1 \lhd_T \pi_2 \lhd_T \pi_3,$$

$$\vdots$$

$$\pi_1 \rhd_T \cdots \rhd_T \pi_n = \pi_1 \lhd_T \cdots \lhd_T \pi_n.$$

As the reader can see, the concept of perfectness is dependent on t-norm T used in the definition of the operators. Thus, sequences perfect with respect to one t-norm need not be perfect with respect to another t-norm. Therefore, to avoid a cumbersome terminology we will consider one fixed continuous t-norm T in this section. The first important result we are going to present is the fact that perfect sequences compose multidimensional distributions that are extensions of all the distributions from which the joint distribution is composed. To prove this we will need the following two simple assertions. Both of them concern the following concept of projectivity. We call two distributions $\pi_1((X_i)_{i\in K_1})$ and $\pi_2((X_i)_{i\in K_2})$ *projective* if

$$\pi_1((X_i)_{i\in K_1\cap K_2}) = \pi_2((X_i)_{i\in K_1\cap K_2}).$$

Lemma 3. *Let T be a continuous t-norm. Two distributions $\pi_1((X_i)_{i\in K_1})$ and $\pi_2((X_i)_{i\in K_2})$ are projective iff*

$$\pi_1 \triangleright_T \pi_2 = \pi_1 \triangleleft_T \pi_2. \tag{10}$$

Proof: Using commutativity of T and Lemma 1 we obtain

$$\begin{aligned}
\pi_1 \triangleright_T \pi_2((x_i)_{i\in K_1\cup K_2}) &= T(\pi_1((x_i)_{i\in K_1}), \pi_2((x_i)_{i\in K_2\setminus K_1}|_T (x_i)_{i\in K_1\cap K_2}))\\
&= T(\pi_1((x_i)_{i\in K_1}), \pi_2((x_i)_{i\in K_2}) \Delta_T \pi_2((x_i)_{i\in K_1\cap K_2}))\\
&= T(\pi_1((x_i)_{i\in K_1}) \Delta_T \pi_2((x_i)_{i\in K_1\cap K_2}), \pi_2((x_i)_{i\in K_2}))\\
&= T(\pi_1((x_i)_{i\in K_1}) \Delta_T \pi_1((x_i)_{i\in K_1\cap K_2}), \pi_2((x_i)_{i\in K_2}))\\
&= T(\pi_1((x_i)_{i\in K_1\setminus K_2}|_T (x_i)_{i\in K_1\cap K_2}), \pi_2((x_i)_{i\in K_2}))\\
&= \pi_1 \triangleleft_T \pi_2((x_i)_{i\in K_1\cup K_2}),
\end{aligned}$$

where the fourth equality holds iff π_1 and π_2 are projective. □

An inductive application of the preceding lemma immediately proves the following assertion.

Corollary 1. *The sequence $\pi_1, \pi_2, \ldots, \pi_n$ is perfect, iff for all $m = 2, 3, \ldots, n$ the pairs of distributions $(\pi_1 \triangleright_T \cdots \triangleright_T \pi_{m-1})$ and π_m are projective.*

Corollary 2. *If the sequence $\pi_1, \pi_2, \ldots, \pi_n$ is perfect then for all $m = 1, 2, \ldots, n$ the distributions $(\pi_1 \triangleright_T \cdots \triangleright_T \pi_m)$ are marginal to the distribution $(\pi_1 \triangleright_T \cdots \triangleright_T \pi_n)$.*

The reader can prove the preceding corollary just by an inductive application of Theorem 1.

The following, most important theorem suggests that perfectness is, in a sense, a generalization of projectivity.

Theorem 2. *Let $\pi_1((X_i)_{i\in K_1}), \pi_2((X_i)_{i\in K_2}), \ldots, \pi_n((X_i)_{i\in K_n})$ be a sequence of possibility distributions. $\pi_1, \pi_2, \ldots, \pi_n$ is perfect iff for all $i = 1, \ldots, n$ π_i are marginal distributions of $\pi_1 \triangleright_T \cdots \triangleright_T \pi_n$.*

Proof: Let $\pi_1((X_i)_{i\in K_1}), \pi_2((X_i)_{i\in K_2}), \ldots, \pi_n((X_i)_{i\in K_n})$ be a perfect sequence of possibility distributions. Let us consider arbitrary $m \in \{1, \ldots, n-1\}$ and denote $\rho = \pi_1 \triangleright_T \cdots \triangleright_T \pi_m$. Since, due to the perfectness of $\pi_1, \ldots, \pi_m$,

$$\rho = \pi_1 \triangleleft_T \cdots \triangleleft_T \pi_m,$$

it is evident that ρ is an extension of π_m on $\mathbf{X}_{K_1\cup\cdots\cup K_m}$. From this fact and from Corollary 2 we will immediately obtain that $\pi_1 \triangleright_T \cdots \triangleright_T \pi_n$ is an extension of π_m, too.

Let for all $i = 1, \ldots, n$, π_i be marginal distributions of $\pi_1 \triangleright_T \cdots \triangleright_T \pi_n$. Let us consider an arbitrary $i \in \{1, \ldots, n\}$. Projectivity must hold for π_i and $\pi_1 \triangleright_T \cdots \triangleright_T \pi_{i-1}$ as the latter distribution is also a marginal of $\pi_1 \triangleright_T \cdots \triangleright_T \pi_n$. Therefore, from Corollary 1 we immediately obtain that the sequence $\pi_1, \ldots, \pi_n$ of possibility distributions is perfect, which completes the proof. $\square$

An application of Corollary 1 yields the following assertion which will be used in the next section. It expresses the fact that any sequence of distributions can be easily transformed into a perfect sequence.

Lemma 4. *Let $\pi_1, \ldots, \pi_n$ be a sequence of possibility measures. Then the sequence $\rho_1, \ldots, \rho_n$ computed by the following process*

$$\begin{aligned}
\rho_1((X_i)_{i\in K_1}) &= \pi_1((X_i)_{i\in K_1}),\\
\rho_2((X_i)_{i\in K_2}) &= \rho_1((X_i)_{i\in K_1\cap K_2}) \triangleright_T \pi_2((X_i)_{i\in K_2}),\\
\rho_3((X_i)_{i\in K_3}) &= (\rho_1 \triangleright_T \rho_2)((X_i)_{i\in (K_1\cup K_2)\cap K_3}) \triangleright_T \pi_3((X_i)_{i\in K_3}),\\
&\vdots\\
\rho_n((X_i)_{i\in K_n}) &= (\rho_1 \triangleright_T \cdots \triangleright_T \rho_{n-1})((X_i)_{i\in (K_1\cup\cdots\cup K_{n-1})\cap K_n}) \triangleright_T \pi_n((X_i)_{i\in K_n})
\end{aligned}$$

is perfect and

$$\pi_1 \triangleright_T \cdots \triangleright_T \pi_n = \rho_1 \triangleright_T \cdots \triangleright_T \rho_n.$$

This corollary means that any sequence of possibilistic distributions can be transformed into a perfect sequence in such a way that the composed multidimensional distribution is identical for both the original and the transformed sequences.

3.1 Reconstruction of a Possibilistic Belief Network from a Perfect Sequence

The process of reconstruction of a possibilistic belief network from a perfect sequence must consist of a definition of a graph and a computation of conditional distributions.

Having a perfect sequence $\rho_1, \rho_2, \ldots, \rho_n$ ($\rho_k((X_i)_{i\in K_k})$), we first order (in an arbitrary way) all the variables for which at least one of the distributions ρ_k is defined, i.e.

$$\{X_1, X_2, X_3, \ldots, X_m\} = \{X_i\}_{i\in K_1\cup\ldots\cup K_n}.$$

Then we get a graph of the constructed Bayesian network in the following way:

1. the nodes are all the variables $X_1, X_2, X_3, \ldots, X_m$;
2. there is an edge $(X_i \to X_j)$ if there exists a distribution ρ_k such that both $i, j \in K_k$, $j \notin K_1 \cup \ldots \cup K_{k-1}$ and either $i \in K_1 \cup \ldots \cup K_{k-1}$ or $i < j$.

For each j the requirement $j \in K_k$, $j \notin K_1 \cup \ldots \cup K_{k-1}$ is met exactly for one $k \in \{1, \ldots, n\}$. It means that all the parents of node X_j must be from the respective set $\{X_i\}_{i\in K_k}$ and therefore the necessary conditional distribution $\pi_j(X_j|(X_i)_{i\in pa(j)})$ can be easily computed from distribution ρ_k.

Let us illustrate this simple procedure for reconstruction of a possibilistic belief network from the perfect sequence of distributions

$$\rho_3(G,B), \rho_1(T), \rho_2(B), \rho_4(D,T,G), \rho_5(R,B), \rho_6(W,R,D)$$

that are given in Table 9[10].

Regarding the described process we have to start by ordering the variables. Let us consider, for example, the ordering

$$T, G, B, D, R, W.$$

Node T first appears among the variables of ρ_1. As this distribution is defined only for this single variable there is no edge leading to this node. The second variable G appears first in distribution $\rho_3(G,B)$. The arrow $(B \to G)$ would be inserted into the graph if either B would be before variable G in the selected ordering, or, if it were among the variables for which some of the preceding distributions would be defined. None of these conditions is met and therefore the edge $(B \to G)$ is not included into the graph. The third variable B appears again among the variables for which ρ_3 is defined. This time, however, G precedes B in the chosen ordering of the variables, and therefore edge $(G \to B)$ is included into the graph.

Variable D appears first among the arguments of ρ_4. Both the remaining variables T, G are among the arguments of the preceding distributions (ρ_3 and ρ_1, respectively) and therefore we have to define both the edges $(T \to D)$

[10] Verification, which is simple but time consuming, that the sequence $\rho_3, \rho_1, \rho_2, \rho_4, \rho_5, \rho_6$ is perfect (regarding Gödel's t-norm), as well as that (for example) the sequence $\rho_6, \rho_1, \rho_2, \rho_3, \rho_4, \rho_5$ is not perfect, is left to the reader.

Table 9. System of possibility distributions forming a perfect sequence

$\rho_1(T)$	
$T =$ *uninteresting*	1
$T =$ *not so bad*	.5
$T =$ *interesting*	.2

$\rho_2(B)$	
$B =$ *rain*	.4
$B =$ *change*	1
$B =$ *fair*	.6

$\rho_3(G, B)$ B	*rain*	*chan.*	*fair*
$G =$ *expected*	.1	.3	.2
$G =$ *not expected*	.4	1	.6

T	*uninterest.*		*not so bad*		*interesting*	
$\rho_4(D, T, G)$ G	*exp.*	*not*	*exp.*	*not*	*exp.*	*not*
$D =$ *no*	.3	0	.3	0	.2	.1
$D =$ *rather no*	0	0	0	.5	0	.2
$D =$ *rather yes*	0	1	0	.5	0	.2

$\rho_5(R, B)$ B	*rain*	*chan.*	*fair*
$R =$ *heavy rain*	.2	.2	.1
$R =$ *drizzling*	.4	.5	.1
$R =$ *none*	.4	1	.6

R	*heavy rain*			*drizzling*			*none*		
$\rho_6(W, R, D)$ D	*no*	*r.no*	*r.yes*	*no*	*r.no*	*r.yes*	*no*	*r.no*	*r.yes*
$W =$ *long walk*	0	0	0	0	0	.1	0	.1	1
$W =$ *short walk*	0	0	.1	.1	.1	.3	.3	.5	.7
$W =$ *none*	.2	.2	.2	.3	.5	.5	.3	.2	0

and $(G \rightarrow D)$. Similarly, we have to include edges $(B \rightarrow R)$ (B is among the variables for which ρ_3 is defined) and $(D \rightarrow W)$ and $(R \rightarrow W)$ (D and R are among the arguments of ρ_4 and ρ_5, respectively). The resulting graph is in Figure 3.

This graph differs from that in Figure 1 only in the orientation of the edge connecting nodes G and B. This is because of the selected ordering of variables. If we chose (for example) the alphabetic ordering B, D, G, R, T, W, then the resulting graph would coincide with that from Figure 1. Nevertheless, let us stress that both the possibilistic belief networks constructed in this way define the same 6-dimensional possibility distribution.

4 Application

In this chapter we present a small example of an application of the approach introduced in the previous sections to financial analysis. Naturally, for the purpose of this paper we have to concentrate only on one part of the problem.

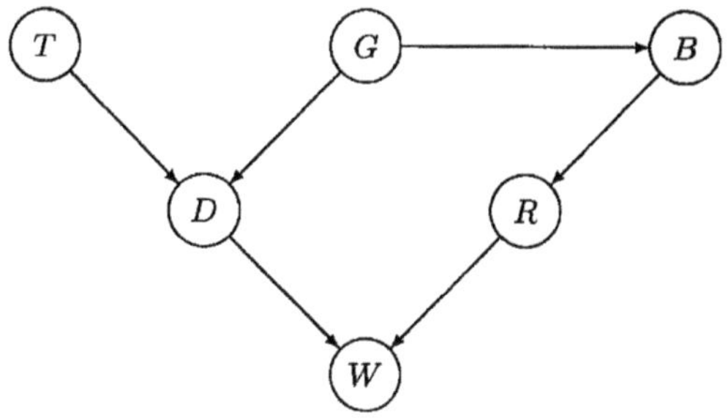

Fig. 3. Acyclic directed graph of a possibilistic belief network reconstructed from a perfect sequence $\rho_3, \rho_1, \rho_2, \rho_4, \rho_5, \rho_6$

We selected fundamental analysis of enterprises. The object of the fundamental analysis is to analyse an enterprise economic situation using data collected inside of the enterprise. This is the main difference between the fundamental and technical financial analysis; the latter analyses the enterprise position using statistical data obtained at financial markets such as stock markets, bond markets, options markets etc.

As we have mentioned above, the fundamental financial analysis [4] uses the financial data having their source inside of the enterprises. These data summarize the structure of the enterprise's assets and give an overview of the enterprise's basic economic activities. The data are systematically summarized in accounting ledgers and regularly published in annual reports. On the basis of these reports financial analysts compute various financial indices which give the basic characteristics of the enterprise's economic situation. It is not surprising that the computed financial characteristics usually vary with the respective economic sector. For example metallurgy, energy industry and chemistry are characterized by high measure of investments. On the other hand, trade and research require low investments but high labour expenditures. Therefore, if we want to analyse a particular enterprise we have to compare its financial characteristics with the given sector or subsector characteristics rather than with the economic averages. Comparing financial characteristics of the enterprise one can discover threats and opportunities of its current economic position.

4.1 Objectives of the Application

In this paper we shall concentrate on the analysis of the financial indices of one economic sector: engineering. Our choice ensued from the fact that we have at our disposal a rather large number of annual reports. We have collected about 4400 reports of engineering enterprises from the years 1993-

1997 from which we selected the following 6 basic financial indices which are typically used by bank analysts to judge an enterprise application for a loan:

- *Debt Ratio* measures the risk of the possibility that the company will become insolvent before all creditor's claims are met. Desired levels of this ratio usually vary with the stability of company income. Generally, the more stable the historical income, the greater the likelihood that investors and creditors will tolerate increased debt.
- *Liquidity* compares current assets to current liabilities. It is an indicator of a company's ability to meet its short-term obligations with current assets.
- *Return on Sales* is one of the profitability ratios. This ratio indicates the return a company receives for each dollar of sales.
- *Inventory Turnover*. Turnover is the relationship between the amount of an asset and some measure of its use. Inventory Turnover is the number of days the inventory is turning in the production process.
- *Accounts Receivable Turnover* provides an indication of how quickly the average amount of receivables are being collected.
- *Accounts Payable Turnover*, apart from Accounts Receivable, is the number of days the average amount of payables are being settled.

The list of these indices (including the proposed discretization of their values) is given in Table 10. We use ratio indices mainly because they are probably the most widely used financial analysis technique as it investigates relationships between two or more line items on the financial statements. Generally, financial ratios are calculated for the purpose of evaluating four aspects of a company's operations: liquidity, activity or turnover of assets, leverage and profitability.

4.2 Constructing Possibilistic Model

As mentioned above, in our application we used data from Czech engineering enterprises. Since the Czech economy is under transformation from "centrally directed" to "free market", it seems to be rather reasonable, when making decision about future, not to rely too much on the formerly collected data. This is one of the reasons, why we prefer possibilistic framework to probabilistic one and why we used data source only as a support (or hint) for the experts in the field and not to get estimates of probabilities.

The task of assembling a perfect sequence of possibility distributions splits naturally into two subproblems:

- For which groups of variables should the distributions be defined? (This is in fact the question of how to get a *structure* of the model.)
- How to get values of the respective distributions?

Table 10. List of indices

Index	Definition	Values
Debt Ratio	Debt/Assets	0.00 – 0.25
		0.25 – 0.50
DR		0.50 – 0.75
		0.75 – 1.00
Liquidity	Current assets/Current liabilities	0.0 – 0.5
		0.5 – 1.0
		1.0 – 1.5
L		1.5 – 2.0
		over 2.0
Return on Sales	Net income/net sales	under -0.05
		-0.05 – 0.00
		0.00 – 0.05
RS		0.05 – 1.00
		over 1.00
Inventory Turnover	365· Average inventory/	0 – 30 days
	Cost of goods sold	30 – 90
		90 – 180
IT		180 – 360
		over 360
Accounts Receivable	365· Average net Accounts Receivable/	0 – 30 days
Turnover	Cost of goods sold	30 – 90
		90 – 180
RT		180 – 360
		over 360
Accounts Payable	365· Average net Accounts Payable/	0 – 30 days
Turnover	Cost of goods sold	30 – 90
		90 – 180
PT		180 – 360
		over 360

In our experiment, we left the first problem to algorithms for the construction of probabilistic Bayesian networks or probabilistic decomposable models using MDL (minimum description length) principle [11].

Nevertheless, we were also given several dependences which were supposed to hold by expert analysts. As we wanted to meet these experts' requirements, the algorithm was made to prefer those networks which obeyed the expert knowledge.

Having a data file we had to solve the second mentioned problem: how to use the information contained in the data to get reasonable estimates of possibility distributions and how to combine this type of information with the experts' subjective beliefs.

We came to the conclusion that the first rule the constructed possibility distribution π_D should meet is that $\pi_D(x) = 0$ for each logically impossible value x[11]. For the other logically possible values we would prefer experts to estimate values of the respective possibilities. This was, however, beyond their capability because of the number of the necessary possibilities and also because for some of the combinations of values they did not have a slightest intuition how to assign the necessary possibilities. Therefore, to help the experts we proposed positive possibilities in a proportional way with the relative frequencies of the respective values. These possibilities have been afterwards adapted by experts to express their subjective beliefs. The advantage of possibility distributions is that the experts can change the values (almost) arbitrarily and no final normalization is necessary. Changing one value in a distribution need not influence other values.

In collaboration with the experts we constructed possibility distributions that are normalized but need not be pairwise projective (which is, according to Theorem 2, a necessary condition for a perfect sequence of distributions). Therefore, we do not have a chance to get a perfect sequence from the constructed distributions directly. To get a perfect sequence we had to take advantage of Lemma 4 that proposes a way how to make a sequence perfect from an arbitrary sequence of distributions.

4.3 Achieved Results

In this section we shall comment on the results achieved by the perfect sequence

$$\pi_1(IT, RT, PT, L), \pi_2(RS, IT, L), \pi_3(PT, L, DR),$$

values of which were received in the way that was described at the end of the previous section.

The application concerned the financial analysis process, more exactly the evaluation of the financial position of a particular engineering company.

A financial expert, when evaluating a financial position of a particular company, should compare the financial characteristics of this company with the characteristics of the respective economic sector, i.e. averages received for a group of similar companies. An example of these sector characteristics for Liquidity, Inventory Turnover, Accounts Receivable Turnover and Accounts Payable Turnover is in Table 11, which summarizes unconditional possibility distributions of these four financial indices. Values in columns headed by p, G and L are marginals of the respective variables computed from the perfect sequences in which the operators of composition was based on the product, Gödel's and Łukasziewicz' t-norms, respectively. The reader can see that in this case these possibilistic distributions do not depend on the t-norm selected.

What else can we read from the values in this table?

[11] Considering that π_D is usually *several*-dimensional distribution, x is in fact a combination of values of several variables and we are in fact speaking about impossible combination of values of individual variables.

Table 11. Sector characteristics

Index	Value	p	G	L
Liquidity	0.0 - 0.25	.5	.5	.5
	0.5 - 1.0	1	1	1
	1.0 - 1.5	1	1	1
	1.5 - 2.0	.75	.75	.75
	over 2.0	1	1	1
Inventory Turnover	0 - 30 days	.75	.75	.75
	30 - 90	1	1	1
	90 - 180	.75	.75	.75
	180 - 360	.5	.5	.5
	over 360	.5	.5	.5
Accounts Receivable Turnover	0 - 30 days	.5	.5	.5
	30 - 90	1	1	1
	90 - 180	.75	.75	.75
	180 - 360	.5	.5	.5
	over 360	.5	.5	.5
Accounts Payable Turnover	0 - 30 days	1	1	1
	30 - 90	1	1	1
	90 - 180	1	1	1
	180 - 360	.5	.5	.5
	over 360	.5	.5	.5

- *Liquidity.* If the Liquidity index of a company falls into 0.0- 0.25 it should be regarded as too small and alternatively, values between 0.5 and 1.5 and over 2 will be considered "normal".
- *Inventory Turnover* and *Accounts Receivable Turnover.* The values of these indices will have the maximum possibility if they are in the interval 30-90 days. The possibility decreases if values divert from this "normal" interval.
- *Accounts Payable Turnover.* Analogously, we can find out that values of Accounts Payable Turnover are "good" in the interval 0-180 days and "bad" over 180 days.

Now, let us focus our attention to the Liquidity index which is, in a way, the most interesting. We can observe, that the index is not homogeneous in the sense that the "normal" values are those in the interval 0.5-1.5 and over 2.0. As the possibility of the interval 1.5-2.0 is 0.75 we do not consider these values to be "normal". The existence of this "gap in normality" could be explained by a hypothesis that there are different subsectors in the engineering sector whose values of the Liquidity index differ. For a given company having Liquidity in the interval 1.5-2.0, an expert can conclude that this value in not desirable but cannot say whether the value is too high or too small. Thus, it seems necessary to perform more detailed analysis of the particular subsector of the engineering sector. Financial experts did it and observed that companies which have similar production programmes have similar Debt

Ratio and Return on Sales indices. While Debt Ratio is strongly influenced by the production technology used by the company, the Return on Sales index is given by the market position of the given company. Therefore, fixing both these indices we can identify some subsectors of the engineering sector which have similar production programmes (e.g. car production, production of agricultural machines etc.).

On the other hand, the remaining three indices seem to be quite homogeneous. We can see the intervals where the indices achieve the maximum possibility and the possibility decreases out of these intervals. Moreover, let us note that in the case of Inventory Turnover and Accounts Receivable Turnover the possibility decreases according to the distance from the interval of "normality".

Let us consider three subsectors A, B and C identified by various instances of the Debt Ratio and Return on Sales indices as suggested in Table 12.

Table 12. Subsectors identification

Subsector	Debt Ratio	Ret. on Sales
A	0.00-0.25	0-0.05
B	0.25-0.50	0-0.05
C	0.50-0.75	0-0.05

Table 13 contains conditional possibility distributions of the four indices within these subsectors (i.e. given the respective values of Debt Ratio and Return on Sales). This table gives us deeper insight into the engineering sector:

- *Liquidity.* For the subsector A "normal" Liquidity values are those over 2.0. However, for companies in subsector B the values with maximum possibility are in the interval 1.0-1.5 and for companies in subsector C they are in the interval 0.5-1.5.
- *Inventory Turnover* and *Accounts Receivable Turnover.* We can consider these two indices as to be stable throughout the engineering sector. The nature of these indices does not change over particular engineering subsectors.
- *Accounts Payable Turnover.* The presented subsector analysis discovered that the engineering sector is not homogeneous in terms of the Accounts Payable Turnover index as it seemed from the previous sector analysis (cf. Table 11). Conditional possibilities of this index significantly vary over particular subsectors as can be seen from Table 13.

The presented sector and subsector analyses offer the following conclusion: An expert evaluating the current financial position of a particular company

Table 13. Subsector characteristics

	Subs. A			Subs. B			Subs. C		
Index	p	G	L	p	G	L	p	G	L
Liquidity	.5	.5	.5	.5	.5	.5	.67	.5	.75
	.5	.5	.5	.75	.75	.75	1	1	1
	.5	.5	.5	1	1	1	1	1	1
	.5	.5	.5	.75	.75	.75	.67	.5	.75
	1	1	1	.75	.75	.75	.67	.5	.75
Inventory Turnover	.5	.5	.5	.75	.75	.75	.75	1	.75
	1	1	1	1	1	1	1	1	1
	.75	.75	.75	.75	.75	.75	.75	1	.75
	.5	.5	.5	.5	.5	.5	.67	.5	.75
	.5	.5	.5	.5	.5	.5	.67	.5	.75
Accounts Receivable Turnover	.5	.5	.5	.5	.5	.5	.67	.5	.75
	1	1	1	1	1	1	1	1	1
	.75	.75	.75	.75	.75	.75	.67	.5	.75
	.5	.5	.5	.5	.5	.5	.67	.5	.75
	.5	.5	.5	.5	.5	.5	.67	.5	.75
Accounts Payable Turnover	1	1	1	.75	.75	.75	.67	.5	.75
	.75	.75	.75	1	1	1	1	1	1
	.5	.5	.5	.75	.75	.75	1	1	1
	.5	.5	.5	.5	.5	.5	.67	.5	.75
	.5	.5	.5	.5	.5	.5	.67	.5	.75

should take into account the insufficient sensitivity of sector financial characteristics in comparison with the subsector ones. The possibilistic belief network, as applied to the financial analysis in this section, seems to be a useful tool for the decision-maker since it enables quantitative modelling of various economic subsectors and thus more accurate and confident evaluation.

5 Conclusions

The presented approach builds a multidimensional model from low-dimensional distributions in the same way as a jigsaw puzzle picture is assembled from a large number of small pieces. In the puzzle, each piece bearing an item of local information contributes to the resulting picture when inserted into its proper position. Analogously, the local information encoded into a low-dimensional distribution is fully employed when the distribution is placed into its proper position in a perfect sequence. Thus, perfect sequences, describing global knowledge about the area of interest through a multidimensional distribution, are assembled from low-dimensional distributions. These are comparably easy to obtain by taking advantage of both the information contained in data files and expert knowledge.

In the paper, we described the necessary amount of theory to understand how the multidimensional distributions are constructed. We did not discuss how to use these distributions for inference. This is not so simple, but fortunately, one can take advantage of computational procedures based on Shafer-Shenoy architecture [13]. We do not deny, however, that there are still some open problems connected with application of this new technique for multidimensional model construction. One of the most important is the question how to select a t-norm that is involved in defining the operator of composition. As shown in Section 2.6, the results achieved can vary with different t-norms and therefore future research must concentrate on the problem of its selection. In the case studied in Section 4 we were suggested by the anonymous referee that the suitable one is the product t-norm, due to the character of the possibility distributions. Nevertheless, in general case the problem remains open.

References

[1] de Cooman, G. (1997) Possibility theory I: The measure- and integral-theoretic groundwork. Int. J. of General Systems **25**, 291-323.

[2] de Cooman, G. (1997) Possibility theory II: Conditional possibility. Int. J. of General Systems **25**, 325-351.

[3] de Cooman, G. (1997) Possibility theory III: Possibilistic independence. Int. J. of General Systems, **25**, 353-371.

[4] Danos, P., Imhoff, E. A. (1992) Introduction to Financial Accounting. Irwin 1992.

[5] Dubois, D., Prade, H. (1988) *Possibility theory*. Plenum Press, New York, 1988.

[6] Gemeła, J. (2000) Financial Analysis Using Bayesian Networks. To appear in: *Applied Stochastic Models in Business and Industry.*

[7] Hájek, P., Havránek, T., Jiroušek, R. (1992) Uncertain Information Processing in Expert Systems. CRC Press, Inc., Boca Raton.

[8] Jensen, F. V. (1996) Introduction to Bayesian Network. UCL Press, London.

[9] Jiroušek, R. (1997) Composition of probability measures on finite spaces. In Proc. of the 13th Con. Uncertainty in Artificial Intelligence UAI'97, Providence, RI, August 1997 (D. Geiger, P. P. Shenoy, eds.). Morgan Kaufmann Publ. San Francisco, California, 274-281.

[10] Jiroušek, R. (1998) Graph Modelling without Graphs. In Proc. of the 7th Conf. on Information Processing and Management of Uncertainty IPMU'98, Paris, France, July 1998 (B. Bouchon-Meunier, R. R. Yager, eds.). E.D.K., Paris, 809-816.

[11] Lam, W., Bacchus, F. (1994) Learning Bayesian Belief Networks: An Approach Based on the MDL Principle. Computational Intelligence **10**, 269-293.

[12] Lauritzen, S. L., Spiegelhalter, D. (1988) Local computations with probabilities on graphical structures and their applications to expert systems. J. Roy. Stat. Soc. Ser. B. **50**, 157-189.

[13] Shafer, G. (1996) Probabilistic Expert Systems. SIAM, Philadelphia.

[14] Vejnarová, J. (1998) Composition of possibility measures on finite spaces: preliminary results. In Proc. of the 7th Conf. on Information Processing and Management of Uncertainty IPMU'98, Paris, France, July 1998 (B. Bouchon-Meunier, R. R. Yager, eds.). E.D.K., Paris, 25-30.

Using Belief Functions to Forecast Demand for Mobile Satellite Services

Peter McBurney and Simon Parsons

Intelligent Systems Applications Group,
Department of Electronic Engineering,
Queen Mary & Westfield College,
University of London,
London E1 4NS, UK
{p.j.mcburney,s.d.parsons}@elec.qmw.ac.uk

Abstract. This paper outlines an application of belief functions to forecasting the demand for a new service in a new category, based on new technology. Forecasting demand for a new product or service is always difficult. It is more so when the product category itself is new, and so unfamiliar to potential consumers, and the quality of service of the product is dependent upon a new technology whose actual performance quality is not known in advance. In such a situation, market research is often unreliable, and so the beliefs of key stakeholders regarding the true values of underlying variables typically vary considerably. Belief functions provide a means of representing and combining these varied beliefs which is more expressive than traditional point probability estimates.

1 Introduction

This paper is concerned with forecasting demand for a new telecommunications service—global mobile satellite services (GMSS). Companies intending to provide these services will be offering services in a new market category to new groups of customers [5,44,54]. As will be seen, forecasting demand for new technologies and services in new categories such as this presents both methodological and practical issues. Our contention is that approaches which make use of belief functions have the potential to assist in the resolution of some of these issues, because of their allowance for imprecision of knowledge, and their ability to coherently combine disparate sources of information. We support this contention by giving a detailed example of the use of belief functions in the area of demand forecasting for GMSS, from the perspective of the second GMSS operator to enter the market.

Belief functions were first introduced by Shafer [80], who himself built on the work of Dempster [16], and was subsequently developed by a number of authors. This development has led to a wide body of work on what has often been called Dempster-Shafer theory. At the time of writing, there are three main schools of thought within this body of work—these are the upper and lower probability model [30], the probability of provability model [73], and Smet's transferable belief model [89]. This paper applies Smets' transferable belief model (TBM), and we adopted this because it seems to us to be the most appealing, as well as the most developed, version of the theory. Since our aim in this article is to concentrate on the application of belief functions rather than the detail of the belief fucntions themselves, we have assumed that the reader is familiar with the transferable belief model. Those readers who do not know the model are encouraged to consult [83,87,89,90]. Descriptions of other approaches to belief functions and Dempster-Shafer Theory can be found in [42,28], while general introductions can be found in many papers and textbooks, for example [67,79].

The various belief function approaches have been widely applied. Indeed, they have been applied to auditing [19,82,91,92,94,104]; to climatology and water resources management [9,10,55]; to nuclear power plant control [18]; to information retrieval [48,74,88]; to call hand-off in a mobile telecommunications network [103]; to discriminant analysis and pattern recognition [17,88]; to systems reliability and fault diagnosis [84,86,88,111]; and to inspection of defects in manufacturing processes [108]. To our knowledge, no work has been published which applies the theory to forecasting demand for a new product or service. In addition, although the forecasting model structure outlined below in Section 4 is typical of those adopted by start-up telecommunications companies, we have not seen it described in print before.

This article is structured as follows: Section 2 presents a brief introduction to the Global Mobile Satellite Services industry. Section 3 discusses some of the methodological and practical issues involved in forecasting demand for a new telecommunications service. Section 4 outlines the structure of a forecasting model developed for forecasting GMSS demand, and this model is used as the basis for the application of belief functions presented in Section 5. Finally, Section 6 looks at further work and concludes. The work described in this article has been motivated by consultancy undertaken by the authors for two intending satellite network operators. Forecasting model structures have been vastly simplified here for presentational purposes, and both structures and parameter values have been disguised in order to protect the identities and the commercial information of our clients. We do not believe this necessary simplification and camouflage detracts from the value of the approach demonstrated here.

2 Global Mobile Satellite Services

Global Mobile Satellite Services (GMSS) businesses are a new telecommunications service aiming to provide voice and data communications to customers with hand-held mobile devices anywhere on the planet. These services are provided by radio links between the devices and a network of satellites, typically in low-earth (less than 1,500 kilometers above earth) or intermediate orbits (greater than 10,000 km). These orbits contrast with the original communications satellites, introduced in 1965, which operate from geostationary orbits (35,786 km) [57].[1]

2.1 The GMSS Market

To an observer standing on earth, a geostationary satellite appears not to move, and so service can be provided to customers within a footprint from one satellite. Thus, a network of geostationary satellites could be launched incrementally, with service progressively switched on in successive world regions. Non-geostationary satellites, however, require multiple, apparently-moving, satellites to provide services to a fixed customer. This means that it is generally not possible to launch commercial services with such satellites until all or most of the satellites in the network have been deployed [6]. Thus, unlike most telecommunications businesses, the vast majority of investment costs—for construction and deployment of the satellites and the ground network—are incurred before the first dollar of revenue can be earnt. This capital investment is of the order of US$3–5 billion [32,33,77,110], which means there are few serious intending operators; for this and other reasons, each comprises a consortium of companies and organizations.

The three main companies providing or intending to provide GMSS voice services are listed here in their expected order of entry to the marketplace:

- Iridium (`http://www.iridium.com`), of Washington, DC, USA, a consortium led by US communications equipment vendor, Motorola, which launched commercial service in November 1998 [34,35].
- Globalstar (`http://www.globalstar.com`), of San Jose, CA, USA, a consortium comprising primarily of terrestrial mobile communications operators, and including British-American cellular company Vodafone-AirTouch and US equipment manufacturer, Qualcomm. Globalstar is expected to launch commercial service in the first quarter of 2000.
- ICO Global (`http://www.ico.com`), of London, UK, a consortium of fixed and mobile telecommunications operators from around the world, and including Inmarsat, the International Maritime Satellite organization, and US equipment manufacturer, Hughes Aerospace. ICO is due to launch service in the last quarter of 2000.

The three companies have adopted different technological solutions to the design and implementation problems they each face, and have different business models and commercial structures. For example, ICO has elected to deploy satellites in a medium-earth orbit, while both Iridium and Globalstar have opted for low-earth orbit constellations. The lower the orbit of the

[1] Satellites are not placed between 1,500 and 10,000 km, in order to avoid the major radiation belts. Descriptions of various proposals for GMSS systems can be found in [6,20,23,71,96], although some of this information is now dated.

satellites, the less the delay callers will experience in speaking on a satellite-enabled call ("propagation delays") [6]. On the other hand, the lower the orbit, the faster the satellite will disappear over the horizon (or be obscured by trees or buildings), and so the greater the likelihood of inadvertent call termination ("dropout") [71,75].

As a second example of design differences, Iridium, unlike either Globalstar or ICO, uses inter–satellite links (so that Iridium's satellites require telecommunications switching capabilities) to transmit calls from the calling party to the earth station nearest the destination party. Globalstar will instead bring calls to earth as quickly as possible and transmit them via the world's public telecommunications networks. ICO will also bring calls to earth as quickly as possible but then transmit them via its own private global network constructed of leased lines [107]. As a consequence of these different approaches to transmission, users of the different networks may experience very different grades of service.

In another example of differences, Globalstar has selected a technological and commercial structure which means that its network is more closely integrated with the various terrestrial cellular networks of its investors and distribution partners than is the case with either Iridium or ICO [23]. This structure provides Globalstar's partners with more control over the nature and deployment of the GMSS service in their territory, but at the expense of the overall consortium being able to offer globally-seamless services, such as uniform prompts for voicemail.

As suggested, these technical and commercial differences impact the levels and nature of service quality experienced by end–users of each service. To a customer of GMSS, the telephone handset—called a user terminal—looks and feels very similar to a terrestrial mobile handset, although both the antenna and the phone itself are larger and heavier in early-generation MSS models than for current terrestrial mobile services. Service will be available, local conditions permitting, almost anywhere on earth.[2] Despite this wide availability, levels of service quality are likely to be very different from terrestrial cellular. Service will not typically be available indoors, or in the downtowns of major cities (due to satellite invisibility) [33]. As with terrestrial wireless services [7], weather conditions such as rain and snow will impact service availability and quality. Network congestion, call dropout and propagation delay may be noticeable on particular networks or at particular times [71].

2.2 GMSS Services

The main voice application markets identified by GMSS operators are as follows [6,32,39]:

[2] ICO's service will not be available at the poles, and Globalstar's service will not be available in the middle of the oceans.

Enhancements to terrestrial mobile services. Because GMSS provides services to a handheld terminal, an obvious application is the provision of mobile–like services in areas outside mobile coverage. Customers for these services may be both people living outside terrestrial coverage areas and people inside terrestrial coverage areas with a need to travel outside. Even travellers between areas under terrestrial mobile coverage are a potential customer segment for GMSS because of the proliferation of incompatible cellular and personal communications services technology standards around the world.

Fixed–network extension. Large numbers of the world's population live outside the areas covered by terrestrial fixed telecommunications networks, or face long delays in obtaining connection to a fixed network. GMSS provides the opportunity to provide services quickly and relatively easily to such customers. While the vast majority of people living outside the footprint of fixed network services would be unable to afford GMSS services, GMSS operators believe that significant market potential exists in such regions. Examples include the provision of services in developing countries to remote minerals-extraction operations and community-owned payphones to rural villages.

Specialized or niche applications. These include user terminals installed in aircraft, on-board ships or in road and rail transport vehicles, along with remote data sensing devices installed, for example, to monitor pressures and flows on oil pipelines or in remote rivers. Such applications may be aimed at the general public (such as satellite–enabled payphones on trains or in aeroplanes) or at particular business customers (such as terminals installed in freight trucks).

Many of the fixed–network extension and specialized applications may require only limited or no mobility in the user terminal. Accordingly, such applications are commonly referred to as semi-fixed.

GMSS operators will be able to offer both voice and data communications services, but their primary focus to date has been on providing voice services. Several other companies are also preparing to deploy satellite networks but with the key application being data communications. One such company is Teledesic (`http://www.teledesic.com`), sponsored by Bill Gates, Craig McCaw and the Boeing Corporation, who plan a 288-satellite network for an estimated total capital investment of US$9–15 billion [6,96]. In addition to these global MSS operators, a number of companies are providing or are preparing to provide services only on a regional basis, for instance in South-East Asia or the Middle East. In North America, one such company already in service is American Mobile Satellite Corporation (AMSC) (`http://www.ammobile.com`), whose investors include AT&T. For simplicity of presentation, only the three major GMSS operators are considered further in this article, although all deployed and intending operators need to be considered as competitors in any comprehensive demand forecasting model.

3 Forecasting Demand for a New Telecoms Service

Planning a new telecommunications business, as with planning any new high-technology business, requires a large number of technical and commercial decisions to be made in advance of launch of service. Many of these decisions depend crucially upon knowing the numbers of customers (what we refer to as "demand") and the patterns of usage of those customers. In the absence of live, operating data, these decisions can only be made on the basis of forecasts of demand and usage.

In a new GMSS operator, market forecasts are used to guide decisions and actions across all areas of the business, to the point where they become, in the words of a former colleague, "the veins of the organization". Three broad groups of "stakeholders" require demand forecasts: engineering design and implementation teams; marketing and commercial development teams; and external entities, such as potential investors, government and security industry regulators, equipment and applications suppliers, and service distribution partners. In another paper [59], we present and contrast the forecasting requirements of these users, and relate their differing needs to the business life-stages of a new telecommunications company.

3.1 The Challenges of Forecasting Demand

Traditional methods of forecasting demand—such as time series analysis and econometric modeling, for example [45,51,98]—require historical data on the market concerned or on a closely-related one. Such data is clearly not available for innovative products such as GMSS which, in the language of marketing, define a new market category [5,44]. In fact, even when historical data is available, it isn't necessarily a good thing to use it since in turbulent markets, which do not behave exactly as they have in the past, it can inhibit the identification of new opportunities, changes in trends, market discontinuities, and so on [27], actually degrading the quality of the forecast.[3]

The terrestrial mobile communications industry provides a good example of the difficulty of forecasting demand for a new category in a turbulent environment. Public mobile communications services based on cellular technologies were introduced from the early 1980s, starting in Scandinavia and Japan. Services were then launched in North America and elsewhere in Western Europe from the middle of the 1980s and have since been introduced in most countries around the world. The services were completely new to customers, to operators and their distribution channel partners, to equipment vendors and suppliers, and to Government regulators. In addition, the last

[3] Traditional methods of forecasting have been likened to "looking forward through a rear-view mirror" [43]. Walsham [105], developing 30-year demand forecasts for telecommunications services, regarded the model as "a forum for debate rather than a forecasting tool".

fifteen years have been a period of great change in the telecommunications industry, due to technological innovations, privatization and corporatization of state-owned enterprises, the entry of new competitors to the market and changing customer preferences. As a consequence, forecasting of demand has been a difficult task. The head of forecasting and analysis for the International Telecommunications Union has stated *"the mobile communications market has proved to be one of the most dynamic, but also one of the most difficult to forecast, of all the parts of the telecommunications sector. The forecasts produced by equipment suppliers, network operators and by specialist consultancies have consistently underestimated the actual market potential"* [41]. Even by 1995, when forecasters had a decade's experience of the rapid growth of demand and the category was no longer new to customers or to operators, forecasts from credible forecasters for world-wide terrestrial mobile customers in the year 2000—just five years ahead—ranged from 200 million to 350 million customers [41]. Yet even the largest of these may have been under-estimates. In early 1999, a mobile industry technology association forecast that the world-wide demand would 426 million customers by the year 2000 [99].

Since Lancaster [49,50], marketers have viewed a product or service as a bundle of features or attributes. It is these attributes which together form the basis of customer preferences for the product. For telecommunications services, the feature set may include basic technical characteristics of the service (such as propagation delays; likely congestion levels; data communications capacities; and so on); value-added or enhanced features (such as voicemail; call diversion capabilities; conference calling; and so on) and commercial elements (for example purchase and activation arrangements; pricing structures and levels; billing and payment arrangements; and after-sales customer service). Experience within the marketing community has been that demand will often depend crucially on the particular set of features offered, and different customers may exhibit very different preferences for different bundles [38]. In other words, the utility which each customer derives from the product or service is a function of its specific attributes, and can change dramatically as those attributes change.

As mentioned in Section 2, the specific features of MSS services will depend upon design decisions made by each intending operator. Such different feature-bundles are likely to appeal to different customer segments to different degrees, and thus have an impact on the market demand for each company's offering. A key task of marketing strategy and implementation in the pre-launch period is to design product features so as to achieve the company's objectives in the marketplace [38,44,100]. At the early stages of business planning for a new product, considerable latitude exists for each company in the choice of product and service attributes, and consequently there is considerable variability in the likely levels of possible demand for the product. In the case of GMSS, where lead times between project inception and commercial launch are so long—a lead time of eight or more years seems to be typical [110]—customer expectations and preferences may well change considerably through the planning period, adding to the uncertainty in any forecasting activity.

However, as mentioned earlier, forecasts of demand are needed by the company and its various stakeholders in order to plan the business. In addition, many of the issues involved are complex and inter-related [32], and can only be solved knowing the results of the others. Because this is impossible, interim solutions are typically adopted, with periodic revisions through a process of iteration, in a manner very analogous to a blackboard architecture for complex decision-making [64,68]. Some decisions, such as the choice of satellite orbit (which influences the nature of satellites to be manufactured) need to be made early in the design process and can only be revised with prohibitive financial costs and delays. Others, such as the type of retail outlets to be used, may be postponed until much closer to the launch date of commercial service and even revised subsequent to launch, if found necessary. In this situation, any useful demand forecasting activity must be iterative, with successive forecasts being adopted by the company as its current official forecasts.

3.2 Primary Market Research

The large financial stakes at risk by GMSS companies mean that the case for undertaking primary market research—in other words interviews with prospective customers [1,26]—as a basis for market demand forecasts is compelling. However, primary market research in this situation is not necessarily reliable, for a number of reasons [59].

Firstly, as mentioned above, demand may depend crucially on specific service and quality features, and these are not known at the outset of the planning activity, when forecasts of demand are first needed. Indeed, one purpose of primary market research is to gather information relevant to their specification [100]. Likewise, actual demand will depend also on what alternatives, complementary and substitute services are available to customers at the time of their purchase decision.[4]

Secondly, even if interview respondents were to know and appreciate the exact features of a new service and of competing services, respondents are not necessarily accurate predictors of their own future behavior. Market research surveys of purchase intentions typically ask prospective customers to rate their likelihood of purchase using a qualitative linguistic scale such as: *Very likely; Likely; Unsure; Unlikely; Very unlikely* [44]. Even though such

[4] A market research technique known as conjoint analysis is often used to simulate and model such multi-attribute purchase decisions [25,100,109]. Even advice to prospective customers from others—what marketers refer to as "word-of-mouth"—can be simulated and its impact calibrated, as in [101,102].

a scale permits some uncertainty about future intentions to be represented, respondents may act differently when placed in an actual purchase situation. This is especially likely to be the case with a new product category, such as GMSS, where early market research surveys have been conducted several years in advance of the service launch.

Finally, primary research is unreliable because estimating demand for a global service requires market research to be conducted across the globe. However, different cultures accord different status and meanings to a market research interview and to the questions within it [97], and statistical market research techniques do not always transfer readily across cultures (see, for example, [11,47,95,61]).

In addition to unreliability, another challenge for primary market research of GMSS demand is the fact of sparse target populations. Although the global market for GMS services may total thirty million or more customers by 2005 [77], the numbers of terrestrial mobile customers at this time may exceed 500 million. Indeed, one industry group recently predicted 1.7 billion terrestrial mobile customers globally by 2010 [99]. Hence, GMSS demand will be a small percentage of the total terrestrial mobile demand. If potential GMSS customers comprise, say, 2% of existing mobile users then we will need to interview an average of 50 terrestrial mobile users to locate just one potential GMSS customer. In order to make statistically-valid comparisons between potential GMSS customers (for instance, according to their country of origin or their frequency of usage) we may require a realized sample size of several hundred GMSS respondents [1,26]. To achieve 300 potential GMSS users would require interviews with 15,000 cellular customers, a sample size that would be prohibitively expensive.

As a result of the great uncertainty regarding the true levels of demand in the pre-launch situation, a situation arises which may be termed opinion proliferation. The combination of an absence of comparable historical data and the unreliability of primary market research mean there is generally no one single prevailing viewpoint regarding demand levels within an intending GMSS operator and among its stakeholders. Everyone has an opinion on the size of the market and its dynamics, and there is often no agreed or objective way to arbitrate between these opinions. Primary market research findings might conceivably provide a resolution, were they not subject to so many challenges of reliability and validity. In such circumstances, interval rather than point estimates of unknown parameters provide greater robustness, firstly because more people can typically support any selected interval than any selected point, and because they can provide an indication of the uncertainty associated with the parameter being estimated.

3.3 The Relevance of Belief Functions

There are several reasons for thinking that use of belief functions may be appropriate to the forecasting problems faced by intending GMSS operators.

Firstly, because of the unresolved technological, marketing and business issues associated with planning a new high-technology business in a new market category, the situation facing the management of an intending GMSS operator as they undertake pre-launch planning is one of great uncertainty. In one typology of business uncertainty, [15], this environment would be Level 3 ("A Range of Futures") or Level 4 ("True Ambiguity") on a 4-level scale. Caselton and Luo [10,55] have termed a similar situation, in the field of water resources management, decision-making under conditions of "near-ignorance".[5]

Belief functions, because they permit the assignment of degrees of belief to sets of outcomes of unknown parameters without requiring further assignment to the specific point-values contained in those sets, provides a means to represent what little is known in such a situation. In our experience, telecommunications managers faced with decision-making under uncertainty, feel much more comfortable with statements such as: *"I believe demand is likely to be in the range x to y."* than with statements such as: *"I believe demand is likely to be exactly z."* or even: *"I believe demand is likely to be close to z"*. As Srivastava [93] has argued, belief functions provide a better framework for representation of uncertainty than does probability in such circumstances.

A second reason for believing belief functions are applicable in this situation arises from the blackboard-like process mentioned above which new telecommunications companies go through in order to resolve the many interconnected issues they face. Such a process results in a need for the company to adopt a series of forecasts, each the official company forecast until revised. These may need to be in point-form because of the nature of downstream models which use them (such as the financial forecast models, or the network sizing models) and for readiness of communication to stakeholders, such as investors and regulators. However, with any point forecast there is a danger of unjustified precision: because the forecast is expressed as a point and not an interval, stakeholders (both internal and external) can come to believe it to be more accurate than it really is. When there are so many consequences of the forecast, and so much resting on it, problems can arise with such misperceptions of accuracy, both at the time and later, for example when the forecast is revised.

Because belief functions enable degrees of belief to be assigned to intervals rather than to points, it provides the opportunity to present a point forecast as a representative point-value from an interval chosen to facilitate planning issue resolution in the current iteration. The company's beliefs about the future can be embodied in the interval, not the representative point, and this has, we believe, tremendous value. In particular, those stakeholders drawing conclusions from or making decisions on the basis of the forecasts are made aware of the degree of imprecision they embody. As is noted by Caselton and Luo [9], making decisions with weaker information is likely to lead to

[5] Here, just as in Caselton and Luo, this term is not used pejoratively.

more equivocal views of the decision alternatives. This is particularly important for business decisions being made in a context of rapid change, where stakeholders need to keep as many options open as long as possible [15].

Finally, belief functions are relevant here because they also provide a coherent mechanism for combining disparate evidence about uncertain events. Because of the long timescales associated with implementing a GMSS business, the market environment of the intending GMSS operator has undergone significant changes in the time between project conception and launch of service. To give just one example, before 1992 most forecasts for terrestrial mobile demand for 2000 were typically under 100 million customers worldwide [41]. As mentioned earlier, a recent telecommunications industry association forecast now projects this figure to be 426 million [99]. In such a turbulent environment, evidence of future demand may be very different from different sources. Belief functions provide a means to combine these coherently.

Now, to some extent these needs could be met by a number of different formalisms, including interval [8] and fuzzy [114] probability models. Even if the decision is taken to adopt a belief function approach the question remains as to which of the three variations on the belief function theme, mentioned in Section 1, should be adopted. When faced with this choice, we chose to use the transferable belief model. We did this partly because we find it the most intuitively appealing variant, partly because of the solid foundations provided by Smets' axiomisation of credal level beliefs [85], and partly because of the separation it maintains between the credal level, which is what we are mainly dealing with here, and the pignistic level [89].

In Section 5, we build a model using the TBM, and demonstrate how it may be used to incorporate evidence obtained from the entry of the first operator into the market into forecast models developed for a later entrant.

4 GMSS Forecasting Model Structure

In this section, we outline the structure of a forecasting model for estimating demand for GMSS. The model approach adopted is a hierarchical one, centered on end-user application segments, and is a typical market forecasting model in new telecommunications ventures. We begin by dividing the total global market into distinct geographic territories (such as countries) and then, within each territory, we divide demand into three components, according to the different application segments for GMSS described in Section 2 above: Mobile Enhancement; Fixed Extension; and Niche Applications. Total global demand is obtained by summing demand in all distinct geographic territories. Total demand in a specific territory is obtained by summing demand across these three application segments in that territory, and so we assume here that demand for each can be calculated separately.[6]

[6] Note that we are here assuming that demand in one segment is independent of that in another, which will not be true in reality. For example, customers living

We now describe the forecasting model structure for just the Mobile Enhancement component. Demand in this segment will arise both from people who are existing customers terrestrial mobile network and those who are not. We assume the latter all live outside terrestrial mobile coverage areas, as those inside who desire GMSS but are not at that time customers of terrestrial mobile networks can be directed to become terrestrial mobile customers in order to obtain GMSS services.[7]

Of all those people who are customers of terrestrial mobile networks, we assume some percentage, say θ, will become customers of a GMSS network by, say, the end of the year 2008. This date is selected because it is ten years after the launch of the first GMSS operator, Iridium; for the purposes of forecast modelling, the total number of customers by this time can represent the long-run potential of the GMSS market, called the market saturation level. We refer to θ as the longrun market penetration level for demand for Mobile Enhancement GMS Services.[8]

Our next step is to forecast the market demand for each year within this ten-year period.[9] The yearly forecasts, expressed as percentages of the total number of terrestrial mobile customers, begin at zero and rise to the market saturation level θ over the course of the ten-year period. Uptake of new products or services in this way is typically modeled by marketers with an S-shaped diffusion curve [2,4,22,54,56,62], this is a curve which grows slowly at the beginning, accelerates quickly through some middle period, and then flattens off to an asymptotic point toward the end of the period of forecasting, as market saturation is reached. As well as having been validated empirically [78], such diffusion models are appropriate because they potentially reflect, for instance, the following: the differential growth through time in sales and distribution capabilities of companies serving a target market; the differential growth through time in the awareness and education of prospective customers

outside fixed and mobile network coverage may opt for either or both of Mobile Enhancement and Fixed Extension services. This particular example reflects a potential distribution channel conflict, which would require a marketing strategy decision to resolve.

7 Again, the appropriate treatment of this anomaly in the forecasting model will ultimately depend upon marketing strategy decisions taken by the company using the model.

8 In reality, demand will most likely depend heavily on pricing structures and levels. However, price will be one feature among many in the bundle of attributes upon which prospective customers make their purchase decisions. At the early stages of new GMSS business planning, price levels—like most everything else in the decision mix of the operator—are very uncertain. We therefore ignore price as an issue, in the same way we are ignoring attributes such as distribution reach, both of which are typical approaches at the outset of market modeling.

9 In practice, certain stakeholders, such as financial and security industry regulators, often require more granular forecasts, especially for the early years of commercial operation.

about the products or services in the market category; the entry of new suppliers to the market category; and the product life cycles to which marketers believe all products and services are subject [53,63,100].

Forecasting the uptake of GMSS services in our hierarchical model is thus equivalent to distributing the percentage θ across the ten year forecasting period according to some S-curve model. One can use primary market research to forecast demand across years in this manner, although this is not commonly done because long-run purchase intentions are likely to be even less reliable than are short-run intentions. Alternatively, assuming the same dynamics exist in this market as in some other market (although possibly from a different base level) allows us to use an historical diffusion curve, such as in this case that for the growth in penetration of terrestrial cellular services, as a benchmark. This results in a yearly-forecast of GMSS demand for the entire market—that is, a forecast for the demand that will be experienced by all operators combined.

Any one GMSS operator will also need to know its own forecast subscriber numbers, for example, for network sizing and financial modelling. Such market shares can be calibrated by means of primary market research using a conjoint model once information on the likely feature-attribute sets of the various competitors in the marketplace is known. Before such primary information is available, appropriate assumptions about the distribution of market share between the respective operators can be made. In the description of the model presented here, we assume only the three global voice operators mentioned in Section 2, although in reality the existence of regional MSS competitors and data-only GMSS competitors should be incorporated into the model.

We therefore have an hierarchical forecasting model for the Mobile Enhancement segment in any territory which begins with the total number of terrestrial mobile customers in a specific territory and results in forecast GMSS demand for each operator for each year to 2008. In the way this model has been constructed, the parameter θ can vary by territory, which is likely to be the case once GMSS services are launched. Allowing the parameter to vary by territory also provides the means to forecast overall demand when service is not offered in particular territories, either due to failure to achieve necessary regulatory permissions or for reasons of business strategy: in such cases the parameter can be set to zero in the model. However, in the initial period of forecasting, when ignorance is greatest, there is likely to be insufficient information on which to assign differential values to θ in different territories. At such times, a constant value, across all territories can be assumed or estimated. For simplicity, this is the approach adopted here. Likewise, benchmark uptake data and market shares may also be varied by territory.

The other two application segments can be treated in a similar fashion, with, of course, appropriate modifications, for example, to the historical benchmark data used for estimating uptake. In the case of the Fixed Extension segment, for instance, the penetration of residential satellite television or microwave ovens may be a more appropriate benchmark than mobile telephones. The niche application segment would need to be further sub-divided into the different types of applications, such as: marine applications; aeronautical applications; land transport applications; etc. Further subdivision is appropriate here, as each of these sub-segments contains a variety of different user types and segments.

The authors are familiar with the forecasting model structures used by two intending satellite network operators, and they are very complex. Complexity arises because of the variety of services being planned for offer to customers, the diversity of target customer segments, their likely needs and patterns of usage, and the complex, global nature of the GMSS business.[10] Although the model presented here is a simplification of the actual model structures adopted by these MSS operators, it is sufficiently realistic to represent the main features of the application domain, and to demonstrate the applicability of the TBM.

5 Applying the Transferable Belief Model

In this section, we present an example of the TBM applied to the forecasting model described above. In order to do this, we begin by assuming that forecasting is initially being undertaken before any of the three operators has launched commercial services, that is before November 1998, when Iridium began offering public services. Moreover, in forecasting GMSS demand, we do so from the perspective of a late entrant to the market (i.e. not Iridium). Publicly-available information about Iridium's launch will then be used to revise the forecast, using Dempster's rule of combination.

5.1 Preliminaries

Until Iridium's commercial launch of service, none of the three intending operators knew if either of the other two would enter the market. Now that Iridium has launched, none of the three operators knows if one or both the

[10] For example, it is common in terrestrial mobile and fixed telecommunications networks to assume an average usage per customer, often measured as Minutes Of Use (MOU) per month [38]. In these networks, the MOU measure is often disaggregated by customer segment or by hour of the week, so as to estimate peak network utilizations [52,113]. With GMSS, customers with mobile terminals may travel anywhere across the globe and make and receive calls wherever they are. In order, then, to accurately estimate network utilization at any time requires aggregating usage by customers from one country currently in a second country calling or receiving calls from someone in a third country, across all time periods and all possible combinations of countries.

two late entrants will succeed in achieving commercial launch. In other words, none of the three GMSS operators knows if 1, 2 or 3 operators will enter the market, and, of course, none knows if all those who enter the market will survive in the long term.[11] Because the principles are identical for each application segment, our example is confined to the Mobile Enhancement segment. In this section, therefore, mention of demand, market, capacity, and so on refers only to the Mobile Enhancement segment.

For any given level of demand, we assume the number of operators offering GMSS services has an impact on the profitability of those in the market: it is better for the operators concerned to divide a given market size by one or two than by three [3]. For simplicity of modelling, we also assume that the saturation level of demand is not affected by the number of operators, although economic theory would suggest that more competitors would lead to lower prices which would in turn lead to greater demand [3,46].[12] In the early days of business planning, when commercial launch is still some years away, no operator has any information on the likely market shares they will each achieve once all are in the market. In these circumstances, it is usual to assume equal shares, possibly modified to give an advantage in the early years to the early market entrants. We will assume equal shares in this example, noting that when the service features of each intending operator are better understood, it is possible, as was mentioned earlier, to undertake market research using conjoint analysis to better calibrate market shares. Thus our analysis here can be considered as a first attempt at prediction, an attempt which would later be refined.

In addition to assuming that all operators have equal market share, we assume that each operator has the same, fixed level of network capacity, as measured by numbers of customers. This is not true in reality because of the different system designs adopted by each and the possibly very different usage profiles of the customers each operator will attract. However, since no operator knows the capacity of its competitors, assuming a constant capacity is a reasonable first approximation prior to launch of service. For the purposes of this example, we assume that each operator has total capacity of 2 million customers.[13]

---

[11] As an example of the kind of event that can affect market entry, Globalstar's plans received a major setback in September 1998 with the explosion soon after launch of the rocket carrying its first 12 satellites, which resulted in their failure to achieve their designated orbiting positions [21,77]. The fact that the construction of a GMSS network is a long and risky process means that right up until the launch date there is considerable uncertainty about whether or not a company will survive long enough to see any revenue.

[12] The impact of additional competitors is often approximated in forecasting models in practice by assuming a faster uptake rather than a higher saturation level.

[13] In fact, GMSS operators may have difficulty in arriving at a single figure for their own network capacities, because of the non-uniform nature of the frequencies they have generally been assigned in different countries around the world, and the fact

Likewise, assume each operator has a level of demand at which the business breaks-even.[14] Again this is likely to differ—and markedly—for the three companies in question, but no operator knows the true level for the other two, and, in the early stages of planning, is likely to have only a very uncertain view of its own breakeven point and the associated financial sensitivities. Hence, we again assume each has the same break-even level, and, for the purposes of this example, that this common level is 1 million customers. Thus, if total market demand was under 3 million customers and all three operators enter the market, none would break even.[15] If only two operators enter the market, the market need only be 2 million in total for break-even to be achieved.

These considerations have defined two threshold values in the level of demand—the two break-even points of 2 million and 3 million total customers —which have major consequences for the investors in the GMSS operators undertaking the forecasting. We will now use these and similar considerations at the other end of the forecast spectrum to construct a set of intervals for the level of demand. These intervals will be defined in terms of their decision consequences to the operator undertaking the forecasting.

Recall that in Section 3 we mentioned that GMSS satellite networks will last between 5-10 years before needing to be replaced. Replacement of the initial networks by so-called second-generation satellite networks will enable each operator to take advantage of advances in satellite and launch technology, and in telecommunications generally, as well as providing new services not capable with the first generation of satellites. Accordingly, operators will need to expend time and effort on designing and implementing their second generation networks, and may even need to commit to proceeding with them before the initial commercial launch of service, due to the long-lead times involved in satellite manufacture and launch [110].

In this regard, the more positive is the market forecast, the greater is the argument for advancing development of the second generation. If market demand exceeds the total capacities of all operators, then it goes unmet.[16] The excess is revenue, and hence profit, which no one (under the assumptions of equal shares and capacities) obtains.[17] Therefore, if demand were believed

that because low-earth and medium-earth orbit satellites are moving relative to a fixed point on the earth, the extent of network availability to a customer at any such point will be different at different times, even without network congestion.

[14] Break-even is the point at which all costs—which may include both interest on borrowed funds and taxes due—are covered, but there is no profit. According to press reports, Iridium requires 500,000 customers to reach this point [24].

[15] Recall that we are assuming equal market shares.

[16] Globalstar reportedly estimates the total potential MSS market demand at 30 million customers and is aiming for 10% of this by 2002 [77] They believe the three companies combined would serve only 50% of the total demand.

[17] Because telecommunications services are perishable resources—unsold network minutes at any one time cannot be offered for sale at a later time—it behooves

by an operator to be likely to exceed, say, 1.5 times capacity levels, then a good case could be made to advance the deployment of the second generation system. If demand were believed to exceed total capacity by, say, three times, then, one could argue, such demand levels would be likely to attract additional entrants, and a case could be made for a first-generation system with significantly greater capacity than currently envisaged. As the reader probably understands, these decisions have associated with them significant financial consequences and risks.

Putting these considerations together, we can therefore envisage five intervals for the forecast for saturation demand. In ascending order of number of customers, these are:

1. Market demand believed to be less than 2 million customers, at which point two operators each break even. In this case, the operator undertaking the forecasts would not proceed with entry to the market.
2. Market demand believed to be between 2 and 3 million customers, at which point three operators each break even. In this case, the operator undertaking the forecasts would again not proceed with entry to the market if it was believed that all three operators would enter the market.
3. Market demand believed to be between 3 million and 9 million customers ($1.5 \times 3 \times 2$): continue with current plans for first-generation system and do nothing about second-generation system.
4. Market demand believed to be between 9 million and 18 million customers ($3 \times 2 \times 3$): advance plans for second-generation system.
5. Market demand believed to be above 18 million customers ($3 \times 2 \times 3$): plan for enhanced first-generation system.

It is important to realize that, from the perspective of the corporate management involved, these intervals are not arbitrary. As the description given for the way in which they were derived indicates, each interval represents different sets of consequences for the company and different sets of feasible strategic options. Of course it is possible to derive different intervals based on different sets of assumptions about the number of customers required for an operator to break even and so, but the point is that it is possible to come up with meaningful intervals of which these are a suitable example.

It is also important to realize that the use of the transferable belief model is not restricted to problems in which the frame of discernment is divided into a finite set of non-overlapping intervals like those given here. See [84] for details on how to handle cases where the value of θ ranges over any subset of the $[0,1]$ interval. Here the point is that the transferable belief model is capable to handling whatever set of intervals are decided upon.

---

the operators to adopt so-called yield management techniques [106], which seek to optimize profits by judicious design and adoption of feature bundles targeted at different customer segments.

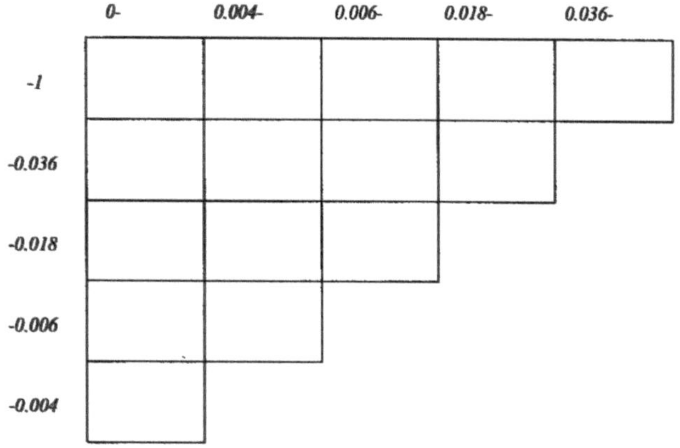

Fig. 1. The frame of possible subsets for parameter θ. The labels along the top of the cells are the lower bounds on θ, and those down the left hand side are the upper bounds. The range of values indicated by a given cell is the combination of its lower column bound and its upper row bound. Thus the top left hand cell corresponds to $0 \leq \theta \leq 1$, and the cell in the second column of the third row corresponds to $0.004 \leq \theta \leq 0.018$.

We are here assuming that GMSS demand consists only of the one application segment: Mobile Enhancement. If we assume that there will be 500 million terrestrial cellular customers worldwide in 2008, then the customer ranges listed here can be converted to intervals for θ, the saturation proportion of terrestrial mobile customers who are also GMSS customers:[18]

$$\begin{aligned} 0 &\leq \theta < 0.004 \\ 0.004 &\leq \theta < 0.006 \\ 0.006 &\leq \theta < 0.018 \\ 0.018 &\leq \theta < 0.036 \\ 0.036 &\leq \theta \leq \ \ 1 \end{aligned}$$

We next examine basic belief assignments (BBAs) across the possible unions of these five sets. As with the applications discussed by Caselton and Luo [9,55], only unions of contiguous sets have meaning in the market demand context, and so we are able to represent the frame of possible subsets in a two-dimensional diagram, as shown in Figure 1. For ease of labelling, the cells in this figure are represented as the intersections of the events denoted by the respective column and row labels. Thus, the cell which is third from the left in the second row is the event $\{0.006 \leq \theta < 0.036\}$, which is formed from the intersection of the event denoted by the column label $\{0.006 \leq \theta\}$ and that

[18] Such a division of the universe of discourse into meaningful intervals could also form the basis for semi-qualitative order-of-magnitude reasoning using interval algebras [65], regarding possible competitor strategies and counter-strategies.

	0-	*0.004-*	*0.006-*	*0.018-*	*0.036-*
-1			**0.60**	**0.15**	**0.05**
-0.036				**0.10**	
-0.018					
-0.006	**0.05**				
-0.004	**0.05**				

Fig. 2. BBA1: Initial Subjective Judgment. The labels along the top of the cells are the lower bounds on θ, and those down the left hand side are the upper bounds. The range of values indicated by a given cell is the combination of its lower column bound and its upper row bound. Thus the top left hand cell corresponds to $0 \leq \theta \leq 1$, and the cell in the second column of the third row corresponds to $0.004 \leq \theta \leq 0.018$.

denoted by the row label $\{\theta < 0.036\}$. The respective row and column labels therefore give the end-points of the interval represented by that particular cell.

5.2 Initial Subjective Judgment

We begin by assigning basic belief masses to the 15 events represented by the diagram. One can imagine these being assigned as a result of discussions with the internal company managers involved.[19] In our experience, most people readily understand the idea of allocating a fixed total quantity of belief to different propositions, and consensus ageement among managers of the one company is also quite feasible. It is important to note that this assignment may be subjective, arising from discussions and compromise between different people with different perspectives and interests. We let the function $m_1(\cdot)$ denote this first Basic Belief Assignment (BBA).

- Of the total belief, 5% is assigned to the proposition that the market is too small for 3 players, i.e. $m_1(0 \leq \theta < 0.006) = 0.05$.
- Of the total belief, 5% is assigned to the proposition that the market is too small even for 2 players, i.e. $m_1(0 \leq \theta < 0.004) = 0.05$.
- Of the total belief, 15% is assigned to the proposition that the market is bigger than we are currently planning for, i.e. $m_1(0.018 \leq \theta) = 0.15$.

[19] The assessment of basic mass assignments is discussed by Smets and Kennes [86,89].

- Of the total belief, 10% is assigned to the proposition that we will need to advance the development of the second generation, i.e. $m_1(0.018 \leq \theta < 0.036) = 0.10$.
- Of the total belief, 5% is assigned to the proposition that we will need to redesign the first generation system, i.e. $m_1(0.036 \leq \theta) = 0.05$.
- Of the total belief, 60% is assigned to the proposition that the market is large enough for all three players, i.e. $m_1(0.006 \leq \theta) = 0.60$.
- The belief allocated to all other subsets of the frame is zero.

Figure 2 shows this BBA, which we call BBA1, diagrammatically. Note that elicitation of such beliefs does not require managers to make explicit their assumptions as to causal influences on the outcomes, nor the relationships between such influences, which would be required, for example, to undertake Structured Scenario Analysis [27]. Belief functions are thus more appropriate in this uncertain domain.

5.3 Market Research Results

We assume next that a second BBA arises from the collection of primary market research data, subsequently to the initial subjective estimation of BBA1. This may take the form of a global market research survey of current terrestrial cellular users who are prospective customers of MSS services. If an MSS service with broadly-defined features, functionality and price is described to respondents and they are asked what is the likelihood that they would purchase such a service at any time in the future, the following responses could be obtained (with the percentage figure being the proportion of respondents agreeing with the verbal description of their likelihood of purchase):

Very Likely:	2%
Likely:	5%
Unsure:	20%
Unlikely:	45%
Very Unlikely:	28%

To produce a single forecast of uptake, it is common in market research to weight these percentages and then sum them. In doing so, the weights correspond to the proportion of respondents who are believed to be going to act according to their stated intentions in the reference time period. It is assumed that between 50% and 100% of the respondents answering *"Very Likely"* will purchase at some time in the future; that between 30% and 70% of the respondents answering *"Likely"* will purchase; and that none of the respondents answering *"Unsure"*, *"Unlikely"* or *"Very Unlikely"* will purchase. Applying these weights results in the estimated penetration level varying between 0.025 and 0.055. Thus the primary market research has provided evidence for a saturation penetration parameter value of $\theta \geq 0.018$,

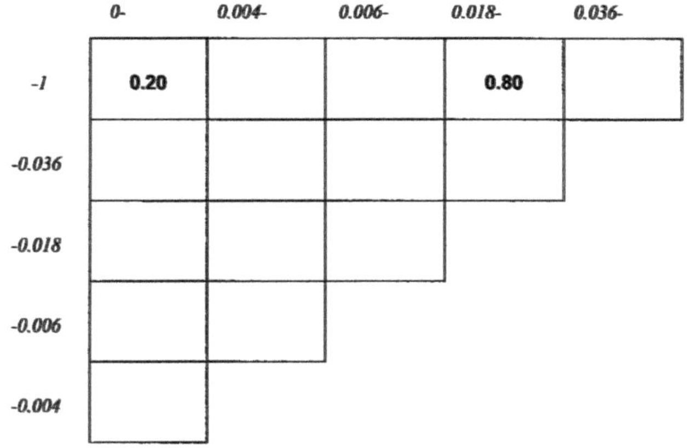

Fig. 3. BBA2: Market Research Results. The labels along the top of the cells are the lower bounds on θ, and those down the left hand side are the upper bounds. The range of values indicated by a given cell is the combination of its lower column bound and its upper row bound. Thus the top left hand cell corresponds to $0 \leq \theta \leq 1$, and the cell in the second column of the third row corresponds to $0.004 \leq \theta \leq 0.018$.

as this is the subset of the frame frame of discernment which includes the interval suggested by the market research.

However, for the reasons outlined in Section 3 above, it is assumed that we are not fully confident in the reliability of the market research results. Accordingly, we can imagine that the market research agency undertaking the project is asked to provide their belief, based on their long experience of primary data gathering, that the true parameter is within the interval indicated by the research. Suppose that their subjective belief (independent of the subjective estimates of the GMSS company managers used for BBA1) is allocated in the proportions of 80% to the proposition that the research is correct, and 20% to the proposition that the true value of θ is anywhere between zero and one. In other words, if we denote this second BBA by the function m_2, then we have the following values:

- $m_2(0.018 \leq \theta \leq 1) = 0.80$
- $m_2(0 \leq \theta \leq 1) = 0.20$

The resulting BBA, called BBA2, is shown in Figure 3. For very many purposes, a point estimate of demand is required, not a range. Commonly, specific weights are assumed for the proportions of intenders who eventually purchase, for instance 80% of those responding *"Very Likely"* and 50% of those responding *"Likely"*, which would yield an estimate for θ of 0.041. This value is in fact close to the mid-point, 0.040, of the range identified by the market research.

5.4 First Combination

We have now two independent assignments of belief to the frame. These can be combined using the normalised version of Dempster's rule of combination, with the resulting BBA denoted by the function m_3, as follows:

$$m_3(C) = \frac{1}{1-k} \sum_{A \cap B = C} m_1(A).m_2(B)$$

where

$$k = \sum_{A \cap B = \emptyset} m_1(A).m_2(B).$$

The resulting BBA (called BBA3) is shown in Figure 4. As an example, we calculate $m_3(0 \leq \theta < 0.004)$. Considering only non-zero values, the numerator of the combination formula is equal to:

$$\begin{aligned} m_3(0 \leq \theta < 0.004) &= m_1(0 \leq \theta < 0.004).m_2(0 \leq \theta \leq 1) \\ &= 0.05 \times 0.20 \\ &= 0.01 \end{aligned}$$

Calculation shows that the normalizing constant $k = 0.08$, and so applying the combination formula gives:

$$\begin{aligned} m_3(0 \leq \theta < 0.004) &= 1.087 \times 0.01 \\ &= 0.011 \end{aligned}$$

to three decimal places. The use of the normalized version of Dempster's rule implies the adoption of the closed world assumption about the frame of discernment. In our particular case, this is natural since it is logically impossible for θ to take a value outside the range $0 \leq \theta \leq 1$.

The calculation can be interpreted as follows. The market research provided strong evidence that θ was above 0.018, and as a result the balance of the belief assignment moves from the interval $[0.006, 1.0]$ to the interval $[0.018, 1.0]$. However, there are still beliefs assigned to values of θ outside this range—a total of 15.2% is so assigned. The use of a single estimate or the most likely range as a result of the market research may create a false impression of precision. The use of belief functions here has ensured we have not overlooked the uncertainty inherent in the estimates. In addition, for simplicity of presentation of this example, we only update the forecast once here with market research findings. However, with a project of the timescales of GMSS ventures, market research is undertaken repeatedly and forecasts will be updated accordingly. This can, of course, be captured in the belief function model by repeated combinations.

It should also be noted that we are only operating at the credal level at this point. Indeed, we are only dealing with mass assignments and their

	0-	0.004-	0.006-	0.018-	0.036-
-1			0.13	0.685	0.054
-0.036				0.109	
-0.018					
-0.006	0.011				
-0.004	0.011				

Fig. 4. BBA3: Combination of Subjective Judgment with Market Research. The labels along the top of the cells are the lower bounds on θ, and those down the left hand side are the upper bounds. The range of values indicated by a given cell is the combination of its lower column bound and its upper row bound. Thus the top left hand cell corresponds to $0 \leq \theta \leq 1$, and the cell in the second column of the third row corresponds to $0.004 \leq \theta \leq 0.018$.

combinations. We can, of course, use these mass assignments to calculate beliefs. In particular, we can calculate the belief that θ takes a value between 0 and 0.006. The general formula for establishing belief in a subset of the frame of discernment, A, is:

$$Bel(A) = \sum_{B \subseteq A} m_3(B)$$

which gives us, for instance:

$$\begin{aligned} Bel(0 \leq \theta \leq 0.006) &= m_3(0 \leq \theta \leq 0.004) + m_3(0 \leq \theta \leq 0.006) \\ &= 0.011 + 0.011 \\ &= 0.22 \end{aligned}$$

If we want to use these beliefs to make a decision about what to do, and we want to employ decision analysis [76] to do this, we need to convert the masses into probabilities. This can be done using Smets' pignistic transformation [89], which gives:

$$\Pr(B) = \sum_{A} m(A) \frac{|B \cap A|}{|A|}$$

Essentially this takes the mass assigned to a set A and distributes this equally over all the members of A. Note that because our underlying sets A, B, etc are real intervals and not finite sets, we interpret the weighting fraction which is

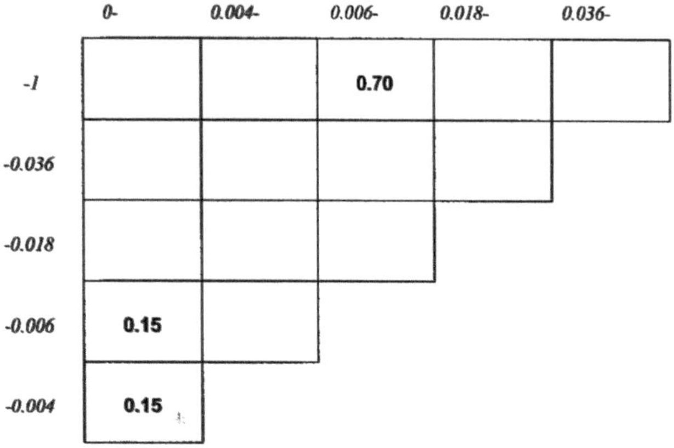

Fig. 5. BBA4O: Optimistic Analysis of Iridium Experience. The labels along the top of the cells are the lower bounds on θ, and those down the left hand side are the upper bounds. The range of values indicated by a given cell is the combination of its lower column bound and its upper row bound. Thus the top left hand cell corresponds to $0 \leq \theta \leq 1$, and the cell in the second column of the third row corresponds to $0.004 \leq \theta \leq 0.018$.

multiplied by each $m(A)$ as the ratio of the lengths of the respective intervals, $B \cap A$ and A. The result is the pignistic probability for B, the probability which should be used when making decisions as opposed to the belief mass which should be used when reasoning about beliefs. In our example, for instance, we can calculate the pignistic probability of $(0.036 \leq \theta \leq 1)$ as:

$$\begin{aligned} \Pr(B) &= \frac{0.054}{1} + 0.685\frac{1-0.036}{1-0.018} + 0.13\frac{1-0.036}{1-0.006} \\ &= 0.853 \end{aligned}$$

Similar calculations can be carried out for other possible values of θ.

5.5 Iridium Launch

As mentioned, Iridium launched their commercial service, the world's first public Global Mobile Satellite Service, in the last quarter of 1998. The launch was originally scheduled for 23 September 1998 [34] and then postponed to 1 November due to technical problems [35]. By 31 May 1999, the company reportedly had signed up just 10,300 customers compared with the 27,000 they were aiming for by this date [110], and the target of 500,000 to 600,000 customers by the end of 1999 [36]. By August 1999, they had an estimated 20,000 customers [13].

This failure is dramatic, and resulted in the departure in the first few months of 1999 of the company's Chief Executive Officer, its Chief Financial Officer and its head of Marketing [31,75]. The company's key sponsor,

Motorola, warned in official filings in May 1999 that Iridium may have to declare bankruptcy [24], and in August, the company filed for so-called Chapter 11 protection from its creditors as part of bankruptcy proceedings [13].[20] A number of reasons have been publicly proposed for this lack of marketplace success, including: technical performance problems [75,110]; the mis-timing of pre-launch marketing communications and advertising campaigns [31]; slow production and distribution of user terminals [37]; poor sales efforts by the company's distribution partners [14,31,37,110]; difficulties with training sales staff [37]; difficulties in responding to sales leads and reaching potential customers [14,36]; and the company's "complex and expensive call pricing plan" [14,110].

These possible causes for failure to achieve sales targets are primarily ones of execution, especially marketing and commercial execution.[21] In other words, Iridium's failure to achieve its sales targets is not, in itself, necessarily evidence that market demand for MSS is smaller than anticipated. Accordingly, opinions may vary as to whether Iridium's apparent market failure is due primarily to poor marketing and sales execution or due to there being insufficient demand for GMSS. Both views have been proposed in the published accounts of Iridium's progression toward bankruptcy [14]. Recall that we are undertaking this forecasting exercise from the perspective of a potential competitor to Iridium. In order to ensure distinctness of belief assignments and to ensure that internal biases (i.e. internal to the company doing the forecasting) do not color the mass assignment, one could imagine seeking the opinions of external GMSS experts as to the true market size in the light of Iridium's post-launch experiences. If undertaken in a systematic way, such a sounding of outside experts (for example, trade journalists, investment analysts, regulators, etc) is known as a Delphi study [40], and is a common market research technique [58,60,99]. For this work we suppose that a Delphi study is undertaken, and that the opinions of the experts polled regarding the size of the GMSS market coalesce around two views. These views depend upon which attribution for Iridium's apparent failure is most strongly believed by the experts.

Those experts believing the cause of Iridium's problems lie with the company itself remain optimistic about the size of the GMSS market, although they do assign a non-zero belief mass to the events that the market is too small for viability. This mass assignment is shown in Figure 5 (BBA4O). On the other hand, those experts who believe that Iridium's apparent failure is due to the size of the GMSS market being much smaller in reality than fore-

[20] Two weeks after Iridium's filing, ICO also sought Chapter 11 protection from its creditors. ICO had failed to raise the additional cash needed to execute its original plans, a failure caused in part by investor nervousness following Iridium's marketplace failure [12].

[21] They are in fact not uncommon with the launch of new mobile telecommunications services [29,38].

	0-	0.004-	0.006-	0.018-	0.036-
-1			0.05		
-0.036					
-0.018					
-0.006	0.25				
-0.004	0.70				

Fig. 6. BBA4P: Pessimistic Analysis of Iridium Experience. The labels along the top of the cells are the lower bounds on θ, and those down the left hand side are the upper bounds. The range of values indicated by a given cell is the combination of its lower column bound and its upper row bound. Thus the top left hand cell corresponds to $0 \leq \theta \leq 1$, and the cell in the second column of the third row corresponds to $0.004 \leq \theta \leq 0.018$.

cast assign far greater belief mass to the events that the market is too small for viability, as shown in Figure 6 (BBA4P).

5.6 Second Combinations

Similarly to the first combination, we then combine the previous combined belief assignment, BBA3, with the both the optimistic and the pessimistic expert opinions of the market size following Iridium's launch, BBA4O and BBA4P. The resulting second combinations, BBA5O and BBA5P, are shown in Figures 7 and 8, respectively.

In the optimistic scenario, the balance of belief mass following the Iridium launch is again on θ being above 0.006, and so the weight of the combined BBA is to the right-hand end of the diagram. In this case, just under 1% of the the mass is assigned to the proposition that the market size is insufficient for viability for 2 or 3 operators. In the pessimistic scenario, by contrast, greater mass is assigned to the opposite end of the diagram, with almost 30% being assigned to the proposition of non-viability.

Which of these two scenarios is believed will depend upon the opinions of the management of the company undertaking the forecasting, and upon the specific purposes for which the forecasting activity is being undertaken. Depending on such purposes, either an optimistic or a pessimistic forecast may be appropriate. Indeed, both may be appropriate simultaneously, for example when best-case vs. worst-case planning is being undertaken. If a single mass assignment were to be required which incorporated both the optimistic and

	0 -	*0.004 -*	*0.006 -*	*0.018 -*	*0.036 -*
- 1			**0.132**	**0.694**	**0.055**
- 0.036				**0.11**	
- 0.018					
- 0.006	**0.002**				
- 0.004	**0.007**				

Fig. 7. BBA5O: Optimistic Second Combination. The labels along the top of the cells are the lower bounds on θ, and those down the left hand side are the upper bounds. The range of values indicated by a given cell is the combination of its lower column bound and its upper row bound. Thus the top left hand cell corresponds to $0 \leq \theta \leq 1$, and the cell in the second column of the third row corresponds to $0.004 \leq \theta \leq 0.018$.

the pessimistic views of GMSS market demand, then Dempster's rule of combination could be used again with BBA5O and BBA5P, possibly weighted by the relative proportions of Delphi experts supporting the two scenarios.

5.7 Refinements of the Model

The model developed in previous sections is, from the perspective of the TBM itself, quite a simple model. That is not to say that such a model is not useful for demand forecasting, but it does mean that the theory can be used to build much richer models. Two such refinements are particularly worth considering.

The first refinement, which was hinted at above, is that of weighting the various pieces of evidence. The model we presented took the expert opinion and market research results at face value—if market research indicated that there was a 5% chance that the market is too small for three players, the fact *"market is too small for 3 players"* was given a mass of 5%. It is easy to develop models in which these opinions are weighted, so that, for instance, it is possible to represent the fact that we, the model builders, only believe that the market research results have a 75% chance of being correct. Indeed, it is possible to build models which not only take such information into account, but also update these weights based on the degree to which past information agreed with what actually happened. Such a model, in a rather different context, is discussed in [69].

	0-	0.004-	0.006-	0.018-	0.036-
-1			**0.09**	**0.49**	**0.04**
-0.036				**0.08**	
-0.018					
-0.006	**0.04**				
-0.004	**0.26**				

Fig. 8. BBA5P: Pessimistic Second Combination. The labels along the top of the cells are the lower bounds on θ, and those down the left hand side are the upper bounds. The range of values indicated by a given cell is the combination of its lower column bound and its upper row bound. Thus the top left hand cell corresponds to $0 \leq \theta \leq 1$, and the cell in the second column of the third row corresponds to $0.004 \leq \theta \leq 0.018$.

The second refinement is that of dealing with the dependencies between the pieces of evidence. One of the restrictions of Dempster's rule of combination for updating beliefs is that it assumes the the sources of the mass distributions being combined are *distinct.* Within the transferable belief model [87] this means, broadly speaking, that the mass distributions do not use any common information. This has led to many people being under the impression that belief functions can *only* be deployed in situations in which the various mass distributions are distinct, and therefore ruling out the possibility of using belief functions to model situations where there are known dependencies between the various sources of evidence (the kind of situations which are neatly handled by Bayesian networks [72]). However, this is not true. It is perfectly possible to build models using belief functions which deal with non-distinct mass distributions, provided one takes the non-distinctness into account in the appropriate way. One particularly attractive way of doing this is suggested by Xu and Smets [112], who introduce an approach which has much in common with Bayesian networks. Methods based on the Shenoy-Shafer hypertree computation approach [81] can also be used to deal with the problem.

6 Conclusions

This article has described an application of belief functions to forecasting demand for a new telecommunications service, Global Mobile Satellite Services.

Although the model presented here has been simplified, and disguised rather than real numbers have been used, we believe the example has demonstrated the power of the TBM for demand forecasting in uncertain environments. Demand estimation for a new high-technology product or service category is often a situation of "near ignorance", both for intending operators and for their prospective customers. In such circumstances, belief functions enable uncertainty to be represented appropriately and prevent an unwarranted precision being inserted into or perceived in market forecasts.

In addition, the theory provides a coherent mechanism for combining new evidence with existing forecasts, on an on-going basis, essential in an environment with the long lead times between project commencement and the launch of commercial service seen in the MSS industry. It has benefits over alternative approaches to demand forecasting which require information on a past which may be non-existent or irrelevant (as is the case with time series analysis and econometric methods) or which require explicit and agreed knowledge of a very uncertain future (as is the case with Structured Scenario Analysis).

Moreover, the transferable belief model permits the assignment of a portion of the total belief mass to values of the forecast parameters which are considered highly unlikely but are still believed possible. In this way it ensures that the uncertainty inherent in any forecaster's view of the future is represented, and is not supressed through quantification and summarization. Indeed, as this example has demonstrated, the TBM even permits the formal representation of doubt in a view of the future which is otherwise predominantly optmistic or predominantly pessimistic. For the reasons presented here, then, we believe that belief functions have considerable potential for application in highly-uncertain business domains, such as in the forecasting of demand for new products and services.

This application demonstrated the assignment of belief values to intervals of an unknown parameter. At the earliest stages of planning of new products or services, however, uncertainty regarding market potential may be so great as to preclude the assignment of numeric values to unknown parameters, even when expressed as intervals. Stakeholders in such circumstances may only be comfortable assigning linguistic or qualitative labels to such intervals. One area worthy of further investigation, then, is the application of qualitative and linguistic belief function approaches to demand forecasting. Some of the theory for such an approach has already been developed [66,67,70], and is a topic of further exploration by the authors.

Acknowledgments

The work reported herein was motivated by consultancy projects undertaken by the authors for two intending global satellite network operators, and we wish to thank our anonymous clients for the opportunities we have had to work with them. This work has been partly supported by the British Engineering and Physical Sciences Research Council (EPSRC), under grant GR/L84117 and a PhD studentship, and this support is also appreciated. We are also grateful to Philippe Smets for detailed comments on an earlier draft of this paper.

References

1. D. A. Aaker, V. Kumar, and G. S. Day. *Marketing Research*. John Wiley and Sons, New York City, NY, USA, 1995.
2. K. Altinkemer, W. T. Yue, and L. Yu. Adoption of Low Earth Orbit satellite system: a diffusion model under competition. In *Proceedings of the 7th International Conference on Telecommunications Systems Modeling and Analysis*, pages 339–355, Nashville, TN, USA, 1999. American Telecommunications Systems Management Association.
3. Austel. Public Mobile Telecommunications Services. Report to the Minister of Transport and Communications, Australian Telecommunications Authority, Commonwealth of Australia, Melbourne, Australia, 1990.
4. F. M. Bass. A new product growth model for consumer durables. *Management Science*, 15:215–227, 1969.
5. Booz, Allen and Hamilton. New Product Management for the 1980s. Report, Booz, Allen and Hamilton, New York City, NY, USA, 1982.
6. I. Brodsky. *Wireless: The Revolution in Personal Telecommunications*. Artech House Publishers, Boston, MA, USA, 1995.
7. G. Calhoun. *Digital Cellular Radio*. Artech House, Norwood, MA, USA, 1988.
8. J. Cano, S. Moral, and J. F. Verdegay López. Combination of lower and upper probabilities. In *Proceedings of the 7th Conference on Uncertainty in AI, Los Angeles.*, 1991.
9. W. F. Caselton and W. Luo. Decision making with imprecise probabilities: Dempster-Shafer Theory and application. *Water Resources Research*, 28 (12):3071–3083, 1992.
10. W. F. Caselton and W. Luo. Inference and decision under near ignorance conditions. In L. Duckstein and E. Parent, editors, *Engineering Risk in Natural Resources Management*, pages 291–304. Kluwer Academic (NATO Advanced Study Institute Series), 1994.
11. D. Casley and D. A. Lury. *Data Collection in Developing Countries*. Oxford University Press, Oxford UK, 1981.
12. L. Cauley. ICO Global satellite-phone venture, affiliates, seek bankruptcy protection. *Wall Street Journal*, 30 August 1999.
13. L. Cauley. Iridium seeks bankruptcy protection after bondholders submit petition. *Wall Street Journal*, 16 August 1999.
14. L. Cauley. Iridium's phone marketing took a back seat to science. *Wall Street Journal*, page 1, 18 August 1999.
15. H. Courtney, J. Kirkland, and P. Viguerie. Strategy under uncertainty. *Harvard Business Review*, 75 (6):66–79, 1997.
16. A. P. Dempster. Upper and lower probabilities induced by a multi-valued mapping. *Annals of Mathematical Statistics*, 38:325–339, 1967.

17. T. Denoeux. A k-nearest neighbour classification rule based on Dempster-Shafer theory. *IEEE Transactions on Systems, Man, and Cybernetics*, 25:804–813, 1995.
18. A. F. Dragoni and P. Giorgini. Sensor data validation for nuclear power plants through Bayesian conditioning and Dempster's rule of combination. *Computers and Artificial Intelligence*, 17:151–168, 1998.
19. R. Dusenbury, J. L. Reimers, and S. Wheeler. An empirical study of belief-based and probability-based specifications of audit risk. *Auditing: A Journal of Practice and Theory*, 15 (2):12–28, 1996.
20. A. L. Evans, J. S. Rose, and R. Venkataraman. The future of satellite communicating. *The McKinsey Quarterly*, 2:7–17, 1998.
21. D. Fost. Globalstar stock crashes with rocket. *San Francisco Chronicle*, 11 September, 1998.
22. B. Frank. Internationale Entwicklungsmuster zellularen Mobilfunks. In J. Kruse, editor, *Zellularer Mobilfunk: Neue Märkte mit neuen Netzen für das Funktelefon*, pages 271–281. R. v. Decker's Verlag, G. Schenk, Heidelberg, Germany, 1992.
23. J. Gardiner. The role of satellites in PCS. In J. Gardiner and B. West, editors, *Personal Communications Systems and Technologies*, pages 145–167. Artech House Publishers, Boston, MA, UK, 1995.
24. T. Goren. Will Iridium losses sink Motorola? *Dow Jones Newswires*, 25 May 1999.
25. P. E. Green and A. M. Krieger. Conjoint analysis with product-positioning applications. In J. Eliashberg and G. L. Lilien, editors, *Handbooks in Operations Research and Management Science, Volume 5: Marketing*, pages 467–516. North-Holland, Amsterdam, The Netherlands, 1993.
26. P. E. Green, D. S. Tull, and G. Albaum. *Research for Marketing Decisions, Fifth Edition*. Prentice-Hall, Englewood Cliffs, NJ, USA, 1988.
27. M. Gruszecki and R. N. Andries. Some new concepts in demand and traffic forecasting and planning of future telecommunic tions services. *Computer Networks and ISDN Systems*, 20 (1-5):65–74, 1990.
28. J. W. Guan and D. A. Bell. *Evidence theory and its applications*. North Holland, Amsterdam, The Netherlands, 1991.
29. A. D. Hadden. *Personal Communications Networks: Practical Implementation*. Artech House Publishers, Boston, MA, USA, 1995.
30. J.Y. Halpern and R. Fagin. Two views of belief: belief as generalized probability and belief as evidence. *Artificial Intelligence*, 54:275–317, 1992.
31. D. P. Hamilton. Iridium LLC's Chief Executive quits abruptly. *Wall Street Journal*, page B8, 23 April 1999.
32. Q. Hardy. How a wife's question led Motorola to chase global cell-phone plan. *Wall Street Journal*, page 1, 16 December 1996.
33. Q. Hardy. Iridium creates new plan for global cellular service. *Wall Street Journal*, 18 August 1997.
34. Q. Hardy. Iridium delays commercial phone links. *Wall Street Journal*, page A3, 9 September 1998.
35. Q. Hardy. Iridium is set to launch call service but concerns mount over performance. *Wall Street Journal*, page B8, 28 October 1998.
36. Q. Hardy. Global-minded Iridium has down-to-earth need: Profit. *Wall Street Journal*, page B4, 26 January 1999.

37. Q. Hardy. Iridium says it expects to miss targets for subscribers, revenue in 1st Quarter. *Wall Street Journal*, page B6, 1 March 1999.
38. P. Hemming, D. P. Shuker, and P. J. McBurney. *Innovative PCS Marketing: How to Build and Execute a Winning Marketing Plan.* Redwing Consulting Ltd, Dallas, TX, USA, 1996.
39. ICO. *ICO Facts.* ICO Global Communications Ltd, Hammersmith, London, UK, March 1999.
40. M. A. Jolson and G. L. Rossow. The Delphi approach in marketing decision making. *Journal of Marketing Research*, 8:443–448, 1971.
41. T. Kelly. Forecasting the mobile communications market: A finger in the airwaves? Paper presented at Conference on Market Forecasting in the Telecoms Industry, Hong Kong, International Telecommunications Union, Geneva, Switzerland, March 1996.
42. J. Kohlas and P. A. Monney. *A Mathematical Theory of Hints: An Approach to Dempster Shafer Theory of Evidence.* Springer Verlag (Lecture Notes in Economics and Mathematical Systems), Berlin, Germany, 1995.
43. S. Koreisha and R. Stobaugh. Limits to models. In R. Stobaugh and D. Yergin, editors, *Energy Future: Report of the Energy Project of the Harvard Business School*, pages 234–265. Random House, New York City, NY, USA, 1979.
44. P. Kotler. *Marketing Management: Analysis, Planning, Implementation and Control.* Prentice-Hall, Englewood Cliffs, NJ, USA, 1991.
45. D. J. Kridel and D. R. Dolk. Modeling telecommunications demand analysis. *Interfaces*, 23 (2):3–13, 1993.
46. J. Kruse. *Lizenzierung und Wettbewerb im Mobilfunk.* Springer Verlag, Berlin, Germany, 1993.
47. J. M. Kushner. Market research in a non-Western context: The Asian example. *Journal of the Market Research Society*, 24:116–122, 1982.
48. M. Lalmas. Information retrieval and Dempster-Shafer's theory of evidence. In A. Hunter and S. Parsons, editors, *Applications of Uncertainty Formalisms*, pages 157–176. Springer Verlag (LNAI 1455), Berlin, Germany, 1998.
49. K. J. Lancaster. A new approach to consumer theory. *Journal of Political Economy*, 74:132–157, 1966.
50. K. J. Lancaster. *Consumer Demand: A New Approach.* Columbia University Press, New York City, NY, USA, 1971.
51. J. C. Lee. Nested Rotterdam Model: Applications to marketing research with special reference to telecommunications demand. *International Journal of Forecasting*, 4:193–206, 1988.
52. W. C. Y. Lee. *Mobile Cellular Telecommunications Systems.* McGraw-Hill, New York City, NY, USA, 1989.
53. T. Levitt. Exploit the Product Life Cycle. *Harvard Business Review*, 43 (6):81–94, 1965.
54. G. L. Lilien, P. Kotler, and K. S. Moorthy. *Marketing Models.* Prentice-Hall, Englewood Cliffs, NJ, USA, 1992.
55. W. B. Luo and B. Caselton. Using Dempster-Shafer Theory to represent climate change. *Journal of Environmental Management*, 49:73–93, 1997.
56. V. Mahajan, E. Muller, and F. M. Bass. New-product diffusion models. In J. Eliashberg and G. L. Lilien, editors, *Handbooks in Operations Research and Management Science, Volume 5: Marketing*, pages 349–408. North-Holland, Amsterdam, The Netherlands, 1993.

57. G. Maral and M. Bousquet. *Satellite Communications Systems: Systems, Techniques and Technology, Third Edition.* John Wiley and Sons, Chichester, UK, 1998.
58. P. McBurney and M. Dobbin. Prospects for Australian Participation in L-Band Mobile Satellite Communications: A Report for the Australian Department of Industry, Technology and Commerce (DITAC). Consultancy report, BIS Shrapnel Pty. Ltd., Sydney, Australia, 1989.
59. P. McBurney, J. Green, and S. Parsons. Forecasting demand for new telecommunications services: an introduction. Technical report, Department of Electronic Engineering, Queen Mary and Westfield College, University of London, Mile End, London, UK, 1999.
60. P. McBurney and D. Shuker. The World Avionics Market: A Report for the Australian Department of Industry, Technology and Commerce (DITAC). Consultancy report, BIS Shrapnel Pty. Ltd., Sydney, Australia, 1990.
61. P. J. McBurney. On transferring statistical techniques across cultures: The Kish Grid. *Current Anthropology*, 29 (2):323–325, 1988.
62. D. F. Midgley. *Innovation and New Product Marketing.* Croom Helm, London, UK, 1977.
63. G. A. Moore. *Crossing the Chasm: Marketing and Selling High-Tech Products to Mainstream Consumers.* HarperCollins, New York City, NY, USA, 1991.
64. H. P. Nii. Blackboard systems (part one): the blackboard model of problem solving and the evolution of blackboard architectures. *The AI Magazine*, Summer:38–53, 1986.
65. S. Parsons. Using interval algebras to model order of magnitude reasoning. *Artificial Intelligence in Engineering*, 8 (2):87–98, 1993.
66. S. Parsons. Some qualitative approaches to applying the Dempster-Shafer theory. *Information and Decision Technologies*, 19:321–337, 1994.
67. S. Parsons. *Qualitative Approaches to Reasoning Under Uncertainty.* MIT Press (to appear), Cambridge, MA, USA, 1999.
68. S. Parsons, T. Brown, S. King, and E. H. Mamdani. A blackboard system for active decision support in configuring telecommunications services. In *Proceedings of the 13th International Conference on Artificial Intelligence, Expert Systems and Natural Language*, Avignon, France, 1993.
69. S. Parsons and P. Giorgini. An approach to using degrees of belief in BDI agents. In B. Bouchon-Meunier, R. R. Yager, and L. A. Zadeh, editors, *Information, Uncertainty, Fusion.* Kluwer, Dordrecht, 1999.
70. S. Parsons and E. H. Mamdani. Qualitative Dempster-Shafer Theory. In *Proceedings of the Third EMACS International Workshop on Qualitative Reasoning and Decision Technologies*, Barcelona, Spain, 1993.
71. B. Pattan. *Satellite-Based Global Cellular Communications.* McGraw-Hill, New York City, NY, USA, 1998.
72. J. Pearl. *Probabilistic Reasoning in Intelligent Systems: Networks of Plausible Inference.* Morgan Kaufmann, Palo Alto, CA, 1988.
73. J. Pearl. Reasoning with belief functions: an analysis of compatibility. *International Journal of Approximate Reasoning*, 4:363–389, 1990.
74. J. Picard. Two applications of probabilistic argumentation systems to information retrieval. In *Proceedings of the Workshop on Logical and Uncertainty Models for Information Systems.* European Conference on Symbolic and Quantitative Approaches to Reasoning and Uncertainty, London, 1999.

75. H. Pope and Q. Hardy. Glitches surface as Iridium phones go to war. *Wall Street Journal*, page B1, 27 April 1999.
76. H. Raiffa. *Decision Analysis: Introductory Lectures on Choices under Uncertainty.* Addison-Wesley, Reading, MA, 1970.
77. S. Rhinds. Globalstar expects break-even results in first full year. *Wall Street Journal*, page B5B, 26 February 1999.
78. E. M. Rogers. *Diffusion of Innovations, Third Edition.* The Free Press, New York City, NY, USA, 1983.
79. A. Saffiotti, S. Parsons, and E. Umkehrer. A case study in comparing uncertainty management techniques. *Microcomputers in Civil Engineering: Special Issue on Uncertainty in Expert Systems*, 9:367–380, 1994.
80. G. Shafer. *A Mathematical Theory of Evidence.* Princeton University Press, Princeton, NJ, USA, 1976.
81. G. Shafer, P. P. Shenoy, and K. Mellouli. Propagating belief functions in qualitative Markov trees. *International Journal of Approximate Reasoning*, 1:349–400, 1987.
82. G. Shafer and R. P. Srivastava. The Bayesian and Belief-Function formalisms—a general approach for auditing. *Auditing—A Journal of Practice and Theory*, 9:110–137, 1990.
83. P. Smets. Belief functions. In P. Smets, A. Mamdani, D. Dubois, and H. Prade, editors, *Non-Standard Logics for Automated Reasoning*, pages 253–286. Academic Press, London, UK, 1988.
84. P. Smets. The transferable belief model for expert judgments and reliability problems. *Reliability Engineering and System Safety*, 38:59–66, 1992.
85. P. Smets. Quantifying beliefs by belief functions: an axiomatic justification. In *Proceedings of the 13th International Joint Conference on Artificial Intelligence*, pages 598–603, San Mateo, CA, 1993. Morgan Kaufmann.
86. P. Smets. Application of the transferable belief model to diagnostic problems. *International Journal of Intelligent Systems*, 13:127–157, 1998.
87. P. Smets. The transferable belief model for quantified belief representation. In D. M. Gabbay and P. Smets, editors, *Handbook of Defeasible Reasoning and Uncertainty Management Systems, Vol. 1*, pages 267–301. Kluwer, Doordrecht, The Netherlands, 1998.
88. P. Smets. Practical uses of belief functions. In *Proceedings of the 14th Conference on Uncertainty in Artificial Intelligence, Stockholm, Sweden*, 1999.
89. P. Smets and R. Kennes. The transferable belief model. *Artificial Intelligence*, 66:191–234, 1994.
90. P. Smets and R. Kruse. The transferable belief model for quantified belief representation. In A. Motro and P. Smets, editors, *Uncertainty in Information Systems: From Needs to Solutions*, pages 343–368. Kluwer, Boston, MA, 1997.
91. R. P. Srivastava. The Belief-Function approach to aggregating audit evidence. *International Journal of Intelligent Systems*, 10:329–356, 1995.
92. R. P. Srivastava. Audit decisions using belief functions: a review. *Control and Cybernetics*, 26 (2):135–160, 1997.
93. R. P. Srivastava. Decision making under ambiguity: a belief function perspective. *Archives of Control Sciences*, 6 (1-2):5–27, 1997.
94. R. P. Srivastava and G. Shafer. Integrating statistical and non-statistical audit evidence using belief functions: a case of variable sampling. *International Journal of Intelligent Systems*, 9:519–539, 1994.

95. J. L. Stanton, R. Chandran, and S. A. Hernandez. Marketing research problems in Latin America. *Journal of the Market Research Society*, 24:124–139, 1982.
96. P. L. Stepankowsky. Teledesic looks to avoid problems that hurt other satellite providers. *Wall Street Journal*, 3 September 1999.
97. A. Stepick and C. D. Stepick. People in the shadows: survey research among Haitians in Miami. *Human Organization*, 49 (1):64–77, 1990.
98. L. D. Taylor. *Telecommunications Demand: A Survey and Critique*. Ballinger Publishing, Cambridge, MA, USA, 1980.
99. UMTS Forum. The Future Mobile Market: Global trends and developments with a focus on Western Europe. Report 8, Universal Mobile Telecommunications Services Forum, London, UK, 1999.
100. G. L. Urban and J. R. Hauser. *Design and Marketing of New Products*. Prentice-Hall, Englewood Cliffs, NJ, USA, 1993.
101. G. L. Urban, J. R. Hauser, and J. H. Roberts. Prelaunch forecasting of new automobiles. *Management Science*, 36 (4):401–421, 1990.
102. G. L. Urban, B. D. Weinberg, and J. R. Hauser. Premarket forecasting really new products. *Journal of Marketing*, 60 (1):47–60, 1996.
103. K. van Dam. Using uncertainty techniques in radio communications systems. In A. Hunter and S. Parsons, editors, *Applications of Uncertainty Formalisms*, pages 76–87. Springer Verlag (LNAI 1455), Berlin, Germany, 1998.
104. C. Van den Acker and J. Vanthienen. Integrating statistical audit evidence with belief function theory. In *Proceedings of the First International Conference on Formal and Applied Reasoning*, pages 1–14, 1996.
105. G. Walsham. A model of future telecommunications demand. *Journal of the Operational Research Society*, 33:A34, 1982.
106. I. R. Weatherford and S. E. Bodily. A taxonomy and research overview of perishable-asset revenue management: Yield management, pricing, and overbooking. *Operations Research*, 40:831–844, 1992.
107. R. Wetenhall. Propagation delay – an MSS red herring. *Mobile Communications International*, page 25, June 1998.
108. D. Wilson, A. Grieg, J. Gilbey, and R. Smith. Some problems in trying to implement uncertainty techniques in automated inspection. In A. Hunter and S. Parsons, editors, *Applications of Uncertainty Formalisms*, pages 225–241. Springer Verlag (LNAI 1455), Berlin, Germany, 1998.
109. D. R. Wittink and P. Cattin. Commercial use of conjoint analysis: An update. *Journal of Marketing*, 53:91–96, 1989.
110. WSJ. Iridium reaches debt waiver as it struggles to win customers. *Wall Street Journal*, 1 June 1999.
111. H. Xu, Y. T. Hsia, and P. Smets. Transferable Belief Model for decision making in valuation-based systems. *IEEE Transactions on Systems, Man, and Cybernetics*, 26A:698–707, 1996.
112. H. Xu and P. Smets. Evidential reasoning with conditional belief functions. In *Proceedings of the 10th Conference on Uncertainty in Artificial Intelligence*, pages 598–605, San Francisco, CA, 1994. Morgan Kaufmann.
113. M. D. Yacoub. Cell design principles. In J. D. Gibson, editor, *The Mobile Communications Handbook, Second Edition*, chapter 21. CRC Press and Springer Verlag, Boca Raton, FL, USA, 1999.
114. L. A. Zadeh. Fuzzy probabilities. *Information Processing & Management*, 3:363–372, 1984.

MODELING FINANCIAL PORTFOLIOS USING BELIEF FUNCTIONS

Catherine Shenoy and Prakash P. Shenoy

University of Kansas, School of Business, 1300 Sunnyside Av, Lawrence, KS 66045-7585 USA

cshenoy@ku.edu • pshenoy@ku.edu

1. Introduction

The main goal of this paper is to demonstrate how the theory of belief functions [Dempster 1967, Shafer 1976, Kohlas and Monney 1995, Smets 1998] can be used to model financial portfolios. In particular, we are interested in modeling how a portfolio return distribution changes as we learn new information about the different factors that impact the portfolio.

In [Shenoy and Shenoy 2000], we describe how Bayes nets can be used to model financial portfolios. Here we build on the Bayes net framework, but we use belief functions instead to model the dependence of factors of a portfolio model. The theory of belief functions offers an alternative technique for modeling the dependence between the various factors that determine the return distribution of a portfolio. In particular, we use the semantics of 'distinct evidence' to model prior distribution and new evidence about factors that will change portfolio return and risk predictions.

We divide our modeling and analysis into two parts. The first part focuses on the historical, quantitative relationships between economic variables. In financial theory, this part is well described by the capital asset pricing model, the arbitrage pricing theory, and other asset pricing models that have been built on these foundations. The goal of these analyses is to predict the value of a variable as a function of others—an input-output analysis. There is no attempt to understand or explain the process by which the inputs are transformed to outputs. Our goal here is to attempt to model the process by which different factors are related to the variable of interest in a little more detail than those provided by financial theories. In [Shenoy and Shenoy 2000], we used the theory of Bayesian networks to describe the dependencies between a collection of variables. In this paper, we focus on the use of belief functions to model such dependencies.

The second part of a financial analysis is to study how changes in current economic events change historical relationships between the variables. We are unaware of any formal models in financial theory that do this. Both steps are necessary for good predictions, but historically more attention has been devoted to the first step. The theory of belief functions provides a natural method for modeling evidence. And incorporating evidence into our prior model entails modeling evidence as a belief function and ensuring that there is no double-counting of uncertain evidence with our prior belief function so one can use Dempster's rule of combination to arrive at inferences based on the combined knowledge.

We use a portfolio of three gold stocks to illustrate our belief function model. Each stock is affected by three factors—the overall stock market, the gold market, and firm specific effects. Changes in any of these factors may affect the price, return, and/or risk of the stock. The output of the network is a marginal belief function for the portfolio and stock variables. Changes in the inputs affect the output distribution so that changes in risk and return can be assessed. A belief function can be summarized by a probability mass function and from this summary probability distribution, value-at-risk can be calculated.

This paper is organized as follows. In section two, we present a brief overview of belief functions. In section three, we construct the belief function portfolio model. This section includes the graphical model, a description of how belief functions can be generated, and how basic probability assignment functions are constructed. In section four, we illustrate how new evidence can be added to the model and the impact of the new evidence on the portfolio risk and return distribution. In section five, we conclude with a summary and some concluding remarks.

2. Basics of the Theory of Belief Functions

In this section, we sketch briefly the basics of the Dempster-Shafer theory of belief functions.

There are several equivalent ways to represent knowledge and/or evidence in the theory of belief functions. One can use either basic probability assignment (bpa) functions, or belief functions, or plausibility functions. We start by describing bpa functions. But first we set out our notation.

Notation. We use upper-case Roman alphabets to describe *variables*. Each variable X is associated with a finite set of its possible values denoted by Ω_X. We call the elements of Ω_X *states* of X, and denote them by bold-faced alphabets such as $\mathbf{x}_1$, $\mathbf{x}_2$, etc. We use lower-case alphabets to denote sets of variables. Suppose *s* is a subset of variables. The state space of s, denoted by Ω_s, is the Cartesian product of the state space of X for $X \in s$, i.e., $\Omega_s = \times\{\Omega_X \mid X \in s\}$. 2^{Ω_s} denotes the set of all subsets of Ω_s, and elements of 2^{Ω_s} (subsets of Ω_s) are denoted by lower-case bold-faced letter in Chicago font, a, b, c, etc.

Basic probability assignment functions. A bpa function for s is a function μ: $2^{\Omega_s} \rightarrow [0, 1]$ such that $\mu(\varnothing) = 0$, and

$$\Sigma\{\mu(\mathsf{a}) \mid \mathsf{a} \in 2^{\Omega_s}\} = 1 \tag{1.1}$$

$\mu(\mathsf{a})$ can be interpreted as the proportion of belief that is assigned to proposition a exactly and nothing else. Propositions a such that $\mu(\mathsf{a}) > 0$ are called *focal elements* of μ. We will describe bpa functions by listing only the values of the bpa function for the focal elements.

Suppose we have evidence, which if reliable, supports proposition a, and which if unreliable, supports Ω_s. Also suppose that the probability of reliability of the evidence is p. In this case, we can model the evidence by a bpa function μ_e such that $\mu_e(\mathsf{a}) = p$, and $\mu_e(\Omega_s) = 1-p$. A bpa function for s that represents complete ignorance is $\mu_v(\Omega_s) = 1$, it is referred to as the *vacuous* bpa function.

Belief functions. Related to each bpa function μ are functions called belief β and plausibility π. A *belief function* for s, β: $2^{\Omega_s} \rightarrow [0, 1]$ can be defined in terms of a bpa function μ for s as follows:

$$\beta(\mathsf{a}) = \Sigma\{\mu(\mathsf{b}) \mid \mathsf{b} \subseteq \mathsf{a}\} \tag{1.2}$$

for each a in 2^{Ω_s}. $\beta(\mathsf{a})$ can be interpreted as a conservative measure of belief in proposition a. Since proposition b logically entails all propositions a such that b $\subseteq$ a, this explains the definition of β in terms of μ in (1.2). Notice that as a consequence of (1.2) and the definition of μ is that $\beta(\varnothing) = 0$, and $\beta(\Omega_s) = 1$. Also notice that unlike a probability function, $\beta(\mathsf{a}) \geq \Sigma\{\beta(\{\mathbf{x}\}) \mid \mathbf{x} \in \mathsf{a}\}$. If all focal elements of μ are singleton subsets, then in this case, we do have $\beta(\mathsf{a}) = \Sigma\{\beta(\{\mathbf{x}\}) \mid \mathbf{x} \in \mathsf{a}\}$ for all $\mathsf{a} \in 2^{\Omega_s}$.

Plausibility functions. A *plausibility function* π for s corresponding to a bpa function μ for s is a function π: $2^{\Omega_s} \rightarrow [0, 1]$ such that

$$\pi(\mathsf{a}) = \Sigma\{\mu(\mathsf{b}) \mid \mathsf{b} \cap \mathsf{a} \neq \varnothing\} \tag{1.3}$$

for each a in 2^{Ω_s}. It follows from (1.2) and (1.3) that $\pi(\mathrm{a}) \geq \beta(\mathrm{a})$, and $\pi(\mathrm{a}) = 1 - \beta(\mathrm{a}^c)$, where $\mathrm{a}^c = \Omega_s - \mathrm{a}$ is the complement of a in Ω_s. Thus, a plausibility function is not as conservative as the corresponding belief function. If all focal elements of μ are singleton subsets, then, $\pi(\mathrm{a}) = \beta(\mathrm{a}) = \Sigma\{\beta(\{\mathbf{x}\}) \mid \mathbf{x} \in \mathrm{a}\}$ for all $\mathrm{a} \in 2^{\Omega_s}$.

Discounting bpa functions. Suppose μ is a bpa function for s. Often we would like to discount bpa functions by some weight w where $0 \leq \mathrm{w} \leq 1$. Let $(1-\mathrm{w})\mu$ denote the discounted bpa function. $(1-\mathrm{w})\mu$ is defined as follows: $((1-\mathrm{w})\mu)(\mathrm{a}) = (1-\mathrm{w})\ \mu(\mathrm{a})$ for all $\mathrm{a} \in 2^{\Omega_s} - \{\Omega_s\}$, and $((1-\mathrm{w})\mu)(\Omega_s) = (1-\mathrm{w})\ \mu(\Omega_s) + \mathrm{w}$. Intuitively, to discount a bpa function by w means to move a total of mass w from the focal elements of μ to the state space of the domain of μ. Thus, if $\mathrm{w} = 0$ (0% discounting), then $1\mu = \mu$, and if $\mathrm{w} = 1$ (100% discounting), then $0\mu = \mu_V$, where μ_V is the vacuous bpa function for s.

Dempster's rule of combination. The rule for updating bpa functions in light of new evidence is called *Dempster's rule of combination* [Dempster 1967]. Suppose μ_0 is our prior bpa function for s and suppose we get evidence for t that is represented by bpa function μ_1 for t. The combination of μ_0 and μ_1, denoted by $\mu_0 \oplus \mu_1$, is the bpa function for $s \cup t$ defined as follows: $(\mu_0 \oplus \mu_1)(\varnothing) = 0$, and

$$(\mu_0 \oplus \mu_1)(\mathrm{c}) = \mathrm{K}^{-1} \Sigma\{\mu_0(\mathrm{a})\mu_1(\mathrm{b}) \mid (\mathrm{a} \times \Omega_{t-s}) \cap (\mathrm{b} \times \Omega_{s-t}) = \mathrm{c}\} \tag{1.4}$$

for all non-empty $\mathrm{c} \in 2^{\Omega_{s \cup t}}$, where $\mathrm{K} = \Sigma\{\mu_0(\mathrm{a})\mu_1(\mathrm{b}) \mid (\mathrm{a} \times \Omega_{t-s}) \cap (\mathrm{b} \times \Omega_{s-t}) \neq \varnothing\}$ is the normalization constant. If the pieces of evidence on which μ_0 and μ_1 are based are "distinct," then $\mu_0 \oplus \mu_1$ is the bpa representation of the aggregate of such evidence. In general, $\mu \oplus \mu \neq \mu$. Therefore, it is important to ensure that there is no double counting of evidence.

Marginalization. Finally, we will define marginalization for bpa functions. Suppose μ is a bpa function for s, and suppose $t \subset s$. The marginal of μ for t, denoted by $\mu^{\downarrow t}$, is the bpa function for t defined as follows:

$$\mu^{\downarrow t}(\mathrm{a}) = \Sigma\{\mu(\mathrm{b}) \mid \mathrm{b}^{\downarrow t} = \mathrm{a}\} \tag{1.5}$$

for each $\mathrm{a} \in \Omega_t$, where $\mathrm{b}^{\downarrow t}$ denotes the subset of Ω_t obtained by projecting each element of b to t.

Summarizing bpa functions by probability mass functions. Often, we would like to summarize a bpa function μ for s by a corresponding probability mass function for s, Pr: $\Omega_s \rightarrow [0, 1]$. There are a couple of ways of doing this. One way is called the *pignistic transformation* [Smets 1990]. The pignistic transformation is defined as follows:

$$\Pr(\mathbf{x}) = \Sigma\{\mu(\mathsf{a})/|\mathsf{a}| \mid \mathsf{a} \in 2^{\Omega_s} \text{ such that } \mathbf{x} \in \mathsf{a}\} \tag{1.6}$$

for each $\mathbf{x} \in \Omega_s$. It's easy to verify that Pr as defined above is a probability mass function.

Another way to transform a bpa function to a probability mass function is to use plausibilities of singleton subsets suitably normalized. Suppose μ is a bpa function for s. A *plausibility transformation* is a probability mass function Pr: $\Omega_s \rightarrow [0, 1]$ defined as follows:

$$\Pr(\mathbf{x}) = K^{-1}\pi(\{\mathbf{x}\}) \tag{1.7}$$

for each $\mathbf{x} \in \Omega_s$, where π is the plausibility function for s corresponding to bpa function μ, and $K = \Sigma\{\pi(\{\mathbf{x}\} \mid \mathbf{x} \in \Omega_s\}$. If μ_V is the vacuous bpa function for s, then both the pignistic and the plausibility transformations of μ_V result in the equally-likely probability mass function for s, $\Pr(\mathbf{x}) = 1/|\Omega_s|$ for each $\mathbf{x} \in \Omega_s$. However, in general, the two transformations lead to different probability mass functions. In this paper, we will use the plausibility transformation to summarize a bpa function.

3. A Simple Portfolio Model

We construct a simple portfolio model constituting of three stocks. Each of the stocks is a gold-mining stock. Each stock can be affected by changes in the stock market, the gold price, or other unspecified factors. This example is small enough to illustrate the computations, yet it includes the features of a large class of portfolios. It builds on the traditional framework of finance models such as the capital asset pricing model and multi-factor models. In a multi-factor model the return on a stock is:

$$r_i = \alpha + \beta_1 f_1 + \beta_2 f_2 + \ldots + \beta_k f_k + \varepsilon_i \tag{2.1}$$

where r_i is the return on stock i, f_k is the return on factor k, β_k is the responsive of the stock to factor k, and ε_i is a random component of the return due to firm specific effects. Some of the assumptions of this model that can be relaxed in our more general belief function model are:

the factors f_1 to f_k are assumed to be uncorrelated;

the expected value of the firm specific component, $E(\varepsilon_i)$, is equal to zero;

there is no correlation between ε_i and any factor, $f_1, \ldots, f_k$; and

the correlation between the firm specific effects for any firms i and j is equal to zero, $\rho(\varepsilon_i,\varepsilon_j) = 0$.

The model in (2.1) is a conditional probability model, where the distribution of the stock return is conditioned on the factor distributions and the firm specific effect distributions. In [Shenoy and Shenoy 2000], we show how an equivalent Bayes net models can be constructed. In this paper, however, we will describe a "knowledge-based" model in which we use knowledge to describe the relations between the variables. Also, we will use belief functions instead of probability distributions to model the uncertainty in the relationship among the variables.

3.1. The Graphical Structure of the Model

Our portfolio consists of three gold-mining stocks—Stock 1 (S_1), Stock 2 (S_2), and Stock 3 (S_3). Each stock is influenced by three factors: the stock market (M), the price of gold (G), and other firm specific factors. We denote the firm specific factors for the three firms as FS_1, FS_2, and FS_3, respectively. The firm specific factors are variables that include anything that will affect the firm that is not already included in the factors. Finally, we are interested in the return distribution of the portfolio (P).

The graphical structure of the portfolio is shown in Figure 1 as a valuation network. There are two types of nodes in a valuation network. The elliptical nodes represent variables, and the rectangular nodes represent bpa functions. A valuation network is a bi-partite graph in which there are edges only between variable nodes and bpa function nodes. The edges between a rectangular node and elliptical nodes denote the domain of the bpa function. Thus, for example, the domain of μ_1 is $\{G, M, FS_1, S_1\}$, and it represents how the return of Stock 1 is related to the values of gold, market, and FS_1. The bpa function μ_P denotes how the portfolio return is related to the individual stock returns and is a deterministic function of the number of stocks of each firm in the portfolio. A fundamental assumption of a valuation network model is that all bpa functions in the model are based on distinct pieces of evidence and knowledge, i.e., there is no double counting of uncertain knowledge/evidence.

Figure 1

The Graphical Structure of the Portfolio Model.

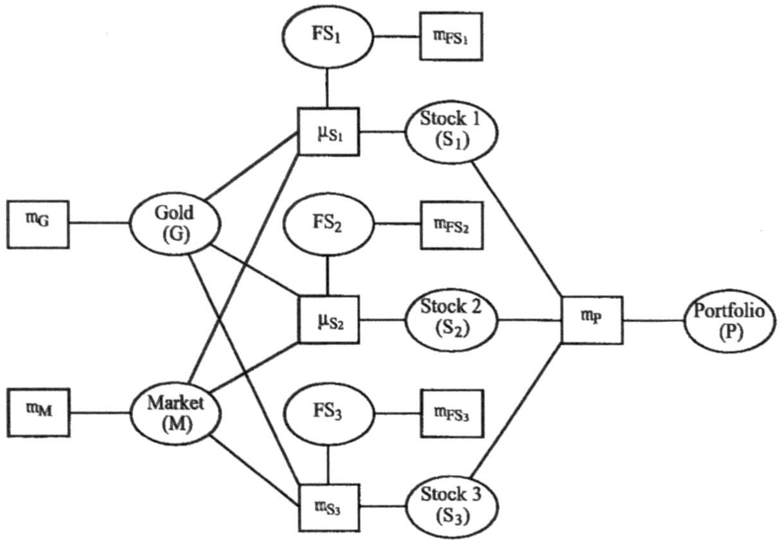

This portfolio structure is similar to traditional asset pricing models. For example, the capital asset pricing model describes individual stock returns as a conditional expectation of the market return and a residual term. Here we have the market level and the price of gold as factors affecting gold stocks. However, we will describe a knowledge-based model to describe the relationship between the variables.

Once we have specified the model completely by defining all bpa functions, we can evaluate the model by combining all bpa functions using Dempster's rule of combination to yield a joint bpa function. Then we compute the marginal of the joint bpa function for any variable of interest. In our portfolio model, we are interested in computing the marginal of the joint bpa function for the portfolio variable P and for each individual stock variables, S_1, S_2, and S_3.

The output of the evaluation is bpa functions $\mu^{\downarrow P}$ for P, $\mu^{\downarrow S_1}$ for S_1, $\mu^{\downarrow S_2}$ for S_2, and $\mu^{\downarrow S_3}$ for S_3, where $\mu = \mu_G \oplus \mu_M \oplus \mu_{S_1} \oplus \mu_{S_2} \oplus \mu_{S_3} \oplus \mu_{FS_1} \oplus \mu_{FS_2} \oplus \mu_{FS_2} \oplus \mu_P$ is the *joint* bpa function. Since probability distributions are more familiar and easier to interpret than bpa functions, we summarize the output bpa functions $\mu^{\downarrow P}$, $\mu^{\downarrow S_1}$, $\mu^{\downarrow S_2}$, and $\mu^{\downarrow S_3}$ by probability mass functions using the plausibility transformation.

3.2. Defining Basic Probability Assignment Functions

In this section, we describe the details of the bpa functions in the graphical model. First, we determine the state space of each of the variables. Next, we describe our knowledge and represent it by bpa functions. In our example, we define three states for each of the stocks, the market, gold, and the portfolio variables[1]: low (l), average (a), and high (h). To identify the states with the corresponding variables, we will subscript the states with the variable name. Thus, for example, $\Omega_G = \{l_G, a_G, h_G\}$, $\Omega_M = \{l_M, a_M, h_M\}$, etc. For the firm specific factors, we define two states: favorable (f) and unfavorable (u). Thus, $\Omega_{FS_1} = \{f_{FS_1}, u_{FS_1}\}$, etc.

The variables can be measured as returns or prices. For example, the 'low' state might be a "buy" price, the 'high' state might be a "sell" price, and 'average' might be a "hold" price. We can also define these states using historical returns over a specified period. For example, 'low,' may be defined as below the 12.5 percentile; high, above the 87.5 percentile; and 'average', between the 12.5 and 87.5 percentiles. The exact specification depends on the type of decision that the model will be used to support. A short-term day trading model may be more useful with prices, and a longer-term evaluation of the portfolio would likely use returns.

Returns and prices are typically described by continuous state spaces. But here we will restrict ourselves to the discrete case. However, the number of states can be expanded as needed. Smith [1993] describes procedures for discretizing continuous state spaces in order to use these variables in a decision problem.

First we define the bpa functions μ_G, μ_M, μ_{FS_1}, μ_{FS_2}, and μ_{FS_3}. Each of these bpa functions has a single variable in its domain. Their role is similar to the prior distributions in a Bayesian probability model. If we don't have any information

---

[1] It may be more natural to describe the state space as a continuous space. However, the computational theory of belief function is well developed only for the discrete case. Since without computational aids, a model becomes just an academic exercise, we will restrict our model to the case of discrete state spaces for all variables.

regarding these variables, we can always use the vacuous bpa function for this situation.

We illustrate the construction of a gold BPA with an example. One kind of information that frequently affects gold prices is news that a central bank is selling gold. Suppose that we have observed in the past that one of three circumstances occurs when central bank information is released. Many times the news will not change the gold price from its average state because the sale is relatively small. This state occurs 55% of the time. On occasion, because the sale is large or because the news is unexpected, the news will decrease the gold price. The amount of decrease is unknown. If the decrease is slight, the price remains in the average category. If the decrease is severe, the price dips to the low category. We assume that from past data, 15% of the time the price of gold has decreased. The remaining 30% of the time announcements of gold sale were made, there is no record of what happened to the price of gold. Therefore we assign this mass to the entire state space. Table 1 summarizes the Gold evidence from a central bank announcement.

Table 1: Bpa function μ_G for gold

$a \in 2^{\Omega_G}$	$\mu_G(a)$
$\{a_G\}$	0.55
$\{l_G, a_G\}$	0.15
Ω_G	0.30

The bpa function μ_M is shown in Table 2. It is derived from evidence similar to μ_G.

Table 2: Bpa function for market

$a \in 2^{\Omega_M}$	$\mu_M(a)$
$\{a_M\}$	0.45
$\{a_M, h_M\}$	0.40
Ω_M	0.15

For now, we will assume that the bpa functions μ_{FS_1}, μ_{FS_2}, and μ_{FS_3} are vacuous. When we receive evidence about these firm specific factors, we can update these bpa functions.

Next we define the bpa functions μ_{S_1}, μ_{S_2}, and μ_{S_3}, which describe how each of the three gold stocks are related to the gold, market and the corresponding firm specific factor. Like the noisy-OR model in Bayes nets, we assume that the bpa function μ_{S_1} decomposes into three separate distinct bpa functions—one that has $\{M, S_1\}$ for its domain, one that has $\{G, S_1\}$ in its domain, and one that has $\{FS_1, S_1\}$ in its domain. This implicitly assumes that there are no interactions between the three causes of stock 1. Furthermore, we assume that μ_{S_1} is a "weighted average" of these three bpa functions.

Table 3 shows the details of the bpa function $\mu_{G\text{-}S_1}$ that describes the relationship between gold and stock 1 assuming gold is the only factor that influences stock 1. There are two focal elements. In the first, stock 1 tracks gold exactly. The probability assigned to this focal element is 0.7. In the second, we assume that the gold has a 'lag' effect on stock 1. The probability assigned to this element is 0.1. The remaining 0.2 probability mass is uncommitted.

Table 3: Bpa function $\mu_{G\text{-}S_1}$

$a \in 2^{\Omega_{\{G, S1\}}}$	$\mu_{G\text{-}S_1}(a)$
$\{(l_G, l_{S_1}), (a_G, a_{S_1}), (h_G, h_{S_1})\}$	0.70
$\{(l_G, l_{S_1}), (a_G, a_{S_1}), (h_G, h_{S_1}), (h_G, a_{S_1}), (a_G, l_{S_1})\}$	0.10
$\Omega_{\{G, S_1\}}$	0.20

Tables 4 and 5 show a similar relationship between market and stock 1, and between FS_1 and stock 1. For $\mu_{G\text{-}S_1}$ and $\mu_{M\text{-}S_1}$ we have uncommitted masses of 0.20. This means that our knowledge is based on fair amount of knowledge. If the uncommitted mass is high, then this means we have little evidence about the relationship between the variables.

Table 4: Bpa function $\mu_{M\text{-}S_1}$

$a \in 2^{\Omega_{\{M, S1\}}}$	$\mu_{M\text{-}S_1}(a)$
$\{(l_M, l_{S_1}), (a_M, a_{S_1}), (h_M, h_{S_1})\}$	0.40
$\{(l_M, l_{S_1}), (a_M, a_{S_1}), (h_M, h_{S_1}), (h_M, a_{S_1}), (a_M, l_{S_1})\}$	0.40
$\Omega_{\{M, S_1\}}$	0.20

Table 5: Bpa function $\mu_{FS_1\text{-}S_1}$

$a \in 2^{\Omega_{\{FS1, S1\}}}$	$\mu_{FS_1\text{-}S_1}(a)$
$\{(f_{FS_1}, h_{S_1}), (u_{FS_1}, l_{S_1})\}$	0.80
$\{(f_{FS_1}, h_{S_1}), (u_{FS_1}, l_{S_1}), (f_{FS_1}, a_{S_1})\}$	0.10
$\Omega_{\{FS_1, S_1\}}$	0.10

We assume that μ_{S_1} is the "weighted average" of the three bpa functions $\mu_{G\text{-}S_1}$, $\mu_{M\text{-}S_1}$, and $\mu_{FS_1\text{-}S_1}$. By weighted average, we mean we first discount[2] each bpa function by some weight $1-w_i$ and then we combine the discounted bpa function using Dempster's rule. If the weights used are w_G. w_M, and w_{FS_1} where $w_G + w_M + w_{FS_1} = 1$, then $\mu_{S_1} = w_G\mu_{G\text{-}S_1} \oplus w_M\mu_{M\text{-}S_1} \oplus w_{FS_1}\mu_{FS_1\text{-}S_1}$. To determine the weights to be used, we could either assess these subjectively from an expert or we could use an objective measure. We choose to do the latter, and we base the weights computed from a linear regression model using historical data as follows. The regression model of the stock i return (r_i) given the return on the market (r_M) and the return on gold (r_G) is given by: $r_i = \alpha + \beta_G r_G + \beta_M r_M + \varepsilon_i$ where ε_i is the residual. Let SS_G, SS_M, SS_{error}, and SS_{total} denote the sum of squares due to market, gold, error, and total, respectively. Then we define $w_G = SS_G/SS_{total}$, $w_M = SS_M/SS_{total}$, and $w_{FS_i} = SS_{error}/SS_{total}$. Table 6 shows the weights that we used in our example to combine the basic probability assignments for each stock. We assume that $\mu_{G\text{-}S_2}$ and $\mu_{G\text{-}S_3}$ are similar to $\mu_{G\text{-}S_1}$; $\mu_{M\text{-}S_2}$ and $\mu_{M\text{-}S_3}$ are similar to

[2] The process of discounting bpa functions is explained in Section 2.

$\mu_{M\text{-}S_1}$; and $\mu_{FS_2\text{-}S_2}$ and $\mu_{FS_3\text{-}S_3}$ are similar to $\mu_{FS_1\text{-}S_1}$. The differences in the three stocks are captured in our model by the weights shown in Table 6.

Table 6: Bpa combination weights for each stock

Stock 1	w_i	Stock 2	w_i	Stock 3	w_i
$G\text{-}S_1$	0.60	$G\text{-}S_2$	0.45	$G\text{-}S_3$	0.50
$M\text{-}S_1$	0.10	$M\text{-}S_2$	0.15	$M\text{-}S_3$	0.05
$FS_1\text{-}S_1$	0.30	$FS_2\text{-}S_2$	0.40	$FS_3\text{-}S_3$	0.45

Finally, we describe the bpa function μ_P that describes the relationship between the three stocks and the portfolio. This relationship is a deterministic one depending on the number of stocks of each type that constitutes the portfolio. Assuming that we have equal number of funds in each stock, this deterministic relationship is defined by the bpa function shown in Table 7. This bpa function has only one focal element with value (that is necessarily) 1. Such bpa functions (with a single focal element) are called *deterministic*.

This completes our description of the belief function portfolio model. In the next section, we discuss making inferences from this model.

Table 7: Bpa function μ_P

$A \in 2^{\Omega_{\{S_1, S_2, S_3, P\}}}$	$\mu_P(a)$
$\{(l_{S_1}, l_{S_2}, l_{S_3}, l_P), (l_{S_1}, l_{S_2}, a_{S_3}, l_P), (l_{S_1}, l_{S_2}, h_{S_3}, a_P),$ $(l_{S_1}, a_{S_2}, l_{S_3}, l_P), \{(l_{S_1}, a_{S_2}, a_{S_3}, a_P), (l_{S_1}, a_{S_2}, h_{S_3}, a_P),$ $(l_{S_1}, h_{S_2}, l_{S_3}, a_P), (l_{S_1}, h_{S_2}, a_{S_3}, a_P), (l_{S_1}, h_{S_2}, h_{S_3}, a_P),$ $(a_{S_1}, l_{S_2}, l_{S_3}, l_P), (a_{S_1}, l_{S_2}, a_{S_3}, a_P), (a_{S_1}, l_{S_2}, h_{S_3}, a_P),$ $(a_{S_1}, a_{S_2}, l_{S_3}, a_P), (a_{S_1}, a_{S_2}, a_{S_3}, a_P), (a_{S_1}, a_{S_2}, h_{S_3}, a_P),$ $(a_{S_1}, h_{S_2}, l_{S_3}, a_P), (a_{S_1}, h_{S_2}, a_{S_3}, a_P), (a_{S_1}, h_{S_2}, h_{S_3}, h_P),$ $(h_{S_1}, l_{S_2}, l_{S_3}, a_P), (h_{S_1}, l_{S_2}, a_{S_3}, a_P), (h_{S_1}, l_{S_2}, h_{S_3}, a_P),$ $(h_{S_1}, a_{S_2}, l_{S_3}, a_P), (h_{S_1}, a_{S_2}, a_{S_3}, a_P), (h_{S_1}, a_{S_2}, h_{S_3}, h_P),$ $(h_{S_1}, h_{S_2}, l_{S_3}, a_P), (h_{S_1}, h_{S_2}, a_{S_3}, h_P), (h_{S_1}, h_{S_2}, h_{S_3}, h_P)\}$	1

3.3. Inferences from the Portfolio Model

The belief function model is evaluated by first combining all of the basic probability assignments using Dempster's rule, and then computing the marginal of the joint for the variables of interest. When there are a large number of variables, it may be computationally intractable to compute the joint bpa function. Nevertheless, one can compute the marginal of the joint bpa function without explicitly computing the joint bpa function using so-called local computation [Shenoy and Shafer 1990, Shenoy 1994]. We use a software implementation of belief functions called MacEvidence [Hsia and Shenoy 1989, Shafer *et al.* 1988] to compute the marginals of the joint bpa function.

Table 8 describes the marginal bpa function for the portfolio variable. As we said earlier, bpa functions are difficult to interpret. We can compute the corresponding belief function $\beta^{\downarrow P}$ or corresponding plausibility function $\pi^{\downarrow P}$. These are shown in Table 8. Alternatively, we can summarize the bpa function by a probability mass function using the plausibility transformation. The first step is to find plausibilities for each state. For example $\pi^{\downarrow P}(l_P) = 0.009 + 0.014 + 0.143 + 0.714 = 0.880$. Table 9 summarizes the plausibilities of each of the states of P and the corresponding probability mass function. We emphasize that when we summarize a bpa function by a probability mass function, some information is necessarily lost.

Table 8: Marginal bpa function $\mu^{\downarrow P}$, belief function $\beta^{\downarrow P}$, and plausibility function $\pi^{\downarrow P}$

$a \in 2^{\Omega_P}$	$\mu^{\downarrow P}(a)$	$\beta^{\downarrow P}(a)$	$\pi^{\downarrow P}(a)$
$\{l_P\}$	0.009	0.009	0.880
$\{a_P\}$	0.102	0.102	0.976
$\{h_P\}$	0.001	0.001	0.746
$\{l_P, h_P\}$	0.014	0.024	0.898
$\{l_P, a_P\}$	0.143	0.254	0.999
$\{a_P, h_P\}$	0.017	0.120	0.991
Ω_P	0.714	1.000	1.000

Table 9: Plausibilities of singleton subsets of P

Ω_P	$\pi^{\downarrow P}$	Pr(P)
l_P	0.880	0.338
a_P	0.976	0.375
h_P	0.746	0.287
Total	2.601	1.000

In a similar manner, we first compute the marginal bpa functions for S_1, S_2, and S_3, and then the summary probability mass functions using the plausibility transformations. These are shown in Table 10.

Table 10: Probabilities mass functions for the three stock variables

Ω	$Pr(S_1)$	$Pr(S_2)$	$Pr(S_3)$
low	0.356	0.368	0.377
average	0.338	0.302	0.289
high	0.306	0.331	0.335

4. Entering Evidence

Belief functions can be used to represent conflicting evidence from different sources. For example, consider a report that Asian jewelry makers are entering the gold market to stockpile inventory. There is a small (10%) chance that this report is just idle speculation on the part of some analyst. If the report is genuine, it is not certain from the report just how much inventory the Asian jewelry makers will stockpile. Based on previous knowledge, there is a 15% chance that the report is genuine and that they will stockpile a significant amount leading to high gold returns. There is a 75% chance that the report is genuine and that they will stockpile enough gold to result in either average or high gold returns. This second piece of evidence can be represented by a bpa function μ_{G_2} as shown in Table 11. To avoid double counting of uncertain knowledge, μ_{G_2} is based on the evidence alone (disregarding all other evidence).

Table 11: Additional evidence assessment for gold

$a \in 2^{\Omega_G}$	$\mu_{G_2}(a)$
$\{h_G\}$	0.15
$\{a_G, h_G\}$	0.75
Ω_G	0.10

If we include this piece of evidence, and re-compute the marginals for the three stock variables and the portfolio variable, the results summarized as probability distributions are shown in Table 12 below.

Table 12: Revised probability mass functions for stock and portfolio variables

Ω	$Pr(S_1)$	$Pr(S_2)$	$Pr(S_3)$	Pr(P)
low	0.292	0.323	0.326	0.279
average	0.364	0.318	0.307	0.398
high	0.344	0.359	0.367	0.323

As expected, comparing with the prior distributions (as seen in Table 10), the probability of the portfolio being in the low state decreases, and the probability of being in the average or high state increases. The same is also true for each of the stock variables.

5. Summary and Conclusion

In this paper, we demonstrate how the theory of belief functions may be used to model financial portfolios. In particular, we show how to model portfolio changes as we learn new information about different factors that influence individual stocks or a portfolio. Financial theory focuses primarily on describing historical relationship between financial variables, and they do this using regression models. Regression models do not attempt to either understand or explain how the inputs are converted to outputs—they simply attempt to predict the outputs from the inputs using data. Our goal in this paper is to describe a knowledge-based model that describes the dependencies between all variables based on knowledge of relationships between variables. We use the theory of belief functions to describe the relationships and make inferences from the model. We also show how new information or evidence can be modeled as independent belief functions and then be used to update the predictions.

Acknowledgements

This paper has benefited from comments and discussions with Philippe Smets, Jürg Kohlas, Rajendra Srivastava, and one anonymous reviewer.

References

Dempster, A. P. (1967), "Upper and lower probabilities induced by a multivalued mapping." *Annals of Mathematical Statistics*, **38**, 325–339.

Hsia, Y. T. and P. P. Shenoy (1989), "An evidential language for expert systems," in Z. W. Ras (ed.), *Methodologies for Intelligent Systems*, **4**, 9–16, North-Holland, Amsterdam.

Kohlas, J. and P.-A. Monney (1995), *A Mathematical Theory of Hints: An Approach to Dempster-Shafer Theory of Evidence*, Lecture Notes in Economics and Mathematical Systems, **425**, Spring-Verlag, Berlin.

Shafer, G. (1976), *A Mathematical Theory of Evidence*, Princeton University Press, Princeton, NJ.

Shafer, G., P. P. Shenoy, and R. P. Srivastava (1988), "AUDITOR'S ASSISTANT: A knowledge engineering tool for audit decisions," in R. P. Srivastava and J. E. Rebele (eds.), *Auditing Symposium IX*, 61–84, School of Business, University of Kansas, Lawrence, KS.

Shenoy, P. P. (1994), "Using Dempster-Shafer's belief-function theory in expert systems," in R. R. Yager, M. Fedrizzi and J. Kacprzyk (eds.), *Advances in the Dempster-Shafer Theory of Evidence*, 395–414, Wiley, New York.

Shenoy, P. P. and G. Shafer (1990), "Axioms for probability and belief-function propagation," in Shachter, R. D., T. S. Levitt, J. F. Lemmer and L. N. Kanal (eds.), *Uncertainty in Artificial Intelligence*, **4**, 169–198, North-Holland, Amsterdam. Reprinted in: Shafer, G. and J. Pearl (eds.), *Readings in Uncertain Reasoning*, 575–610, 1990, Morgan Kaufmann, San Mateo, CA.

Shenoy, C. and P. P. Shenoy (2000), "Bayesian Network Models of Portfolio Risk and Return," in Y. S. Abu-Mostafa, B. LeBaron, A. W. Lo, and A. S. Weigend (eds.), *Computational Finance 1999*, 87–106, MIT Press.

Smets, P. (1990), "Constructing the pignistic probability function in a context of uncertainty," in Henrion, M., R. D. Shachter, L. N. Kanal, and J. F. Lemmer (eds.), Uncertainty in Artificial Intelligence, **5**, 29–40, North-Holland, Amsterdam.

Smets, P. (1998), "The transferable belief model for quantified belief representation," in P. Smets (ed.), *Handbook of Defeasible Reasoning and Uncertainty Management Systems: Quantified Representation of Uncertainty and Imprecision,* **1**, 267–301, Kluwer, Netherlands.

Smith, J. E. (1993), "Moment methods for decision analysis," *Management Science*, **39**, 340–358.

Futures Hedging under Prospect Utility and Knightian Uncertainty[1]

Donald Lien

Department of Economics, University of Kansas, Lawrence, Kansas 66045

Abstract

This paper introduces Knightian uncertainty and loss aversion into the hedging decision framework. Knightian uncertainty allows for imprecision in the joint density function of spot and futures prices. Loss aversion dictates that an individual is more sensitive to losses (compared to a reference point) than to gains. The optimal futures position is characterized. It is found that inertia prevails. That is, there is a wide range of parameter configurations under which the conventional one-to-one hedge strategy is optimal. Moreover, loss aversion acts to reduce any deviation from this conventional strategy.

1. Introduction

Risk management has become an important component of business operations. Firms frequently engage in derivative trading to reduce risk exposure. More generally, financing cost, tax structure, and managerial risk aversion help determine a firm's decision to trade in derivative markets. Whatever the structural factors may be, they result in a concave utility function over the firm's profit. Consequently, derivative hedging leads to a higher expected utility for the firm.

To determine the optimal position in a derivative, say, a futures contract, one assumes a known joint density function for the spot and futures prices in the future and proceeds with expected utility maximization. Under certain (reasonable) assumptions, Lence (1995) demonstrated that the optimal futures position is proportional to the spot position regardless of the functional form of utility. Lien (1999a) introduced Knightian uncertainty into the production and hedging

[1] The author is grateful to Raj Srivastava for his encouragement to pursue the current research. Elizabeth Asiedu, Raymond Leuthold, and Joseph Sicilian provided helpful comments and suggestions on earlier related work. Of course, the author is fully responsible for any omissions and commissions.

framework. Herein Kinghtian uncertainty allows for imprecision of the joint density function. While the optimal futures position is a continuous function of the current spot and futures prices in Lence (1995), Knightian uncertainty leads to inertia. That is, within a band surrounding the condition prescribed in Lence (1995), the optimal futures position remains unchanged. Traditionally, the inertia was explained by the presence of transaction cost; for an example, see Lence (1996). Given that the transaction cost is rather small, Knightian uncertain provides a better alternative.

Both Lence (1995) and Lien (1999a) adopted a von Neumann – Morgenstern (vN-M) utility function. Recent experimental evidence, however, suggested violations of vN-M axioms by subjects and lent support for the prospect theory. In particular, Kahneman, Knetsch, and Thaler (1990), Benartzi and Thaler (1995), and Thaler, Tversky, Kahneman, and Schwartz (1997) all concluded the importance of "loss aversion" in human decision-making. Loss aversion implies that an individual is more sensitive to losses (to a reference point) than to gains. Consequently, the utility function contains a kink at the reference point. Lien (1999b) examined the effect of loss aversion on the optimal futures position when there is no ambiguity for the joint probability function of spot and futures prices.

This paper incorporates both prospect utility theory and Knightian uncertainty into the futures hedging framework. In the next section, the hedging decision-making framework is described. Section 3 introduces Kinghtian uncertainty and the ε-contamination method. The relationship between the method and the belief function approach is discussed. Section 4 considers prospect utility theory and loss aversion. The hedging decision problem in the presence of Knightian uncertainty and loss aversion is formulated in Section 5. Sections 6 and 7 describe the solution procedure. The optimal futures position is provided in Section 8. The effects of Knightian uncertainty and loss aversion on the optimal futures position are discussed. Finally, Section 9 concludes the paper.

2. The Basic Framework

Consider a one-period model from $t = 0$ to $t = 1$. At $t = 0$, a firm purchases a given amount of input to be used at $t = 1$ through forward contracting at the price of p_0 per unit. Without loss of generality, the amount of input is normalized to one. Thus, the firm writes a contract with a supplier at $t = 0$. The contract specifies that, at $t = 1$, the firm will pay its supplier p_0 to receive a unit of input. Let p_1 denote the spot price of the input at $t = 1$. If p_1 is larger than p_0, the firm gains from forward contracting as it purchases the input at a cheaper price. On the other hand, if p_1 is smaller than p_0, the firm incurs a loss from forward contracting. Specifically, it purchases the input at a higher price than available at the market.

In accepting the forward contract, the firm may speculate that the input price will increase from $t = 0$ to $t = 1$. Alternatively, the firm may simply wish to ensure the input supply at $t = 1$. In this case, the forward contract incurs risk and the firm may look for risk management instruments.

Suppose that there is a futures market for the input. Let f_0 denote the price of a futures contract (with a given maturity) at $t = 0$ and let f_1 denote the price of the contract at $t = 1$. A futures contract promises the delivery of a unit of input at a specified maturity. While forward contracts are usually written between two private parties, futures contracts are traded in organized exchanges. Assume the firm sells x (≥ 0) futures contracts at $t = 0$. The firm's futures position is then x. At time $t = 1$, it will buy x futures contracts from the exchange, offsetting the original futures position. The gains or losses from futures trading are $(f_0 - f_1)x$. If f_1 is larger than f_0, the firm gains from futures trading. On the other hand, when f_1 is smaller than f_0, the firm incurs losses.

Note that, the firm gains $(p_1 - p_0)$ from the forward contract and $(f_0 - f_1)x$ from futures trading. In general, the futures price movement tends to parallel the spot price movement. When p_1 is large (or small), f_1 is also likely to be large (or small). As a result, $(p_1 - p_0)$ and $(f_0 - f_1)x$ tends to have opposite signs, effectively reducing the firm's risk exposure in the forward contract. That is, the futures contract serves as a useful risk management instrument. The remaining problem is to find the "optimal" futures position, i.e., the optimal number of futures contracts to be sold.

Let π_p denote the firm's profit from production taking place from $t = 0$ to $t = 1$. At $t = 1$, the firm's total profit is

$$\pi = \pi_p + (p_1 - p_0) + (f_0 - f_1)x.$$

Conventional approach assumes the firm has a von Neumann – Morgenstern utility function u(.). Also, the joint probability density function of p_1 and f_1 is known. Let E(.) denote the expectation operator under the given joint density. The optimal futures position is the solution to the maximization problem with the objective function $Eu(\pi)$. Under certain assumptions, Lence (1995) showed that the optimal futures position is $x^* = \mathrm{cov}(p_1, f_1) / \mathrm{var}(f_1)$, the ratio of the covariance between p_1 and f_1 to the variance of f_1, regardless of the functional form of u(.).

3. Knightian Uncertainty and Belief Functions

Lien (1999a) incorporated the production decision into the above hedging framework. More importantly, Knightian uncertainty was considered.

Specifically, it was assumed that the probability density function is not exactly known. Instead, with a given probability the density function is completely specified. Otherwise, there is no information about the density except the support; see Dow and Werlang (1992). For example, the probability density function of p_2 is specified as follows. With probability ε ($0 \le \varepsilon \le 1$), the density function of p_2 is a completely specified function g(.) and with probability ($1 - \varepsilon$) the density function of p_2 is unknown except that its support is the same as g(.). In the presence of imprecision on the density function, the decision rule calls for considerations of the worst-case scenario. Following this decision rule, Lien (1999a) showed that, Knightian uncertainty strengthens the result of Lence (1995).

The approach adopted in Lien (1999a) is the so-called "ε-contamination method." Rigotti (1998) assumed that, under Knightian uncertainty, there are several candidate density functions with allocated weights. Epstein and Wang (1994) considered a more general approach including the ε-contamination method and the belief function (see Dempster (1967) and Shafer (1976)) as special cases. In fact, the former is a special case of the latter. To demonstrate this property, I follow the analysis of Wasserman (1990).

Let Y be a Polish space with Borel σ-algebra B(Y) and let X be a convex, compact, metrizable subset of a locally convex topological space with Borel σ-algebra B(X). In addition, μ is a probability measure on (X, B(X)) and F(.) is a mapping from a point in X to nonempty, closed subsets of Y. For each $A \subset Y$, define the following:

$$A_* = \{x \in X \mid F(x) \subset A\} \text{ and } A^* = \{x \in X \mid F(x) \cap A \neq \phi\}.$$

The belief function and the plausibility function are defined as follows:

$$\mathrm{Bel}(A) = \mu(A_*) \text{ and } \mathrm{Pl}(A) = \mu(A^*).$$ Clearly, $\mathrm{Bel}(A) \le \mathrm{Pl}(A)$.

Let P be a probability measure such that $\mathrm{Bel}(A) \le P(A) \le \mathrm{Pl}(A)$ whenever $A \in B(Y)$. The collection of all these probability measures is denoted by Π. Then the belief function is the lower bound of Π:

$$\mathrm{Bel}(A) = \inf\{P(A): P \in \Pi\}.$$

Associated with the belief function, the lower expectation is defined as:

$$E_*(k) = \inf\{E_P(k): P \in \Pi\},$$

where k is a given function and $E_P(.)$ denotes the expectation with the probability measure P. Thus, the lower expectation considers the worst-case scenario. The resemblance of the ε-contamination method to the belief function approach is apparent.

Consider the following: $X = Y \cup \{x_0\}$, $B(X) = B(Y) \times \{x_0\}$. Let $\mu = \varepsilon g' + (1 - \varepsilon)\delta$, where g' is a probability measure on X that gives zero probability to x_0 and is identical to g on $X - \{x_0\}$ and δ is a point mass on x_0. Then the resulting Π is exactly the family specified by the ε-contamination method. By considering the worst-case scenario, the ε-contamination method adopts a decision rule on the basis of lower expectation supported by the belief function with a specific configuration.

While the ε-contamination method is a special case of the belief function approach (also, a specific method to deal with Knightian uncertainty), it has an advantage in providing an explicit form for further analysis. The method is adopted in this paper.

4. Prospect Utility and Loss Aversion

Kahneman and Tversky (1979) and Tversky and Kahneman (1992) advocated prospect utility theory and suggested certain properties for u(.). In comparing outcomes, the individual has a reference point and is only concerned with gains or losses from the reference point. In our case, the status quo for the firm is π_p when there is no forward or futures trading. The prospect theory then suggests that the utility function has $(p_1 - p_0) + (f_0 - f_1)x$ as its argument. The reference point is $(p_1 - p_0) + (f_0 - f_1)x = 0$.

Moreover, experiment results from Kahneman, Knetsch, and Thaler (1990), Benartzi and Thaler (1995), and Thaler, Tversky, Kahneman, and Schwartz (1997) indicate the prevalence of loss aversion. That is, individuals are more sensitive to losses than to gains. Let u(.) denote a vN-M (concave) utility function such that $u(0) = 0$ and let R denote the reference point. Lien (1999b) suggested the following utility function to account for loss aversion:

$$v(z) = u(z - R) \text{ if } z \geq R \text{ and } v(z) = \beta\, u(z - R) \text{ otherwise,}$$

where $\beta \geq 1$. Note that β measures the sensitivity to losses. A larger β corresponds to a greater loss aversion.

Assume that the individual has a constant absolute risk aversion utility (CARA) function and assume that spot and futures prices are jointly normally distributed. Lien (1999b) characterized the effects of loss aversion on futures hedging. In this paper, Knightian uncertainty is incorporated into the above framework.

5. A Perfect Futures Market

From the above descriptions, the firm's futures hedging problem can be written mathematically as follows:

$$\underset{x}{\text{Maximize}}\ \underset{m \in \Pi}{\text{Minimize}}\ \varepsilon\, E_g\{v(\Delta p - x\, \Delta f)\} + (1 - \varepsilon)\, E_m\{v(\Delta p - x\, \Delta f)\}$$

where $\Delta p = p_1 - p_0$ and $\Delta f = f_1 - f_0$; $E_g(.)$ and $E_m(.)$ are expectation operators when the joint density function of p_1 and f_1 is $g(.,.)$ and $m(.,.)$, respectively; $g(.,.)$ is completely specified with a given support $[p_b, p_u]$; Π is the collection of all density functions with support $[p_b, p_u]$. Also, $v(z) = u(z)$ if $z > 0$ and $v(z) = \beta\, u(z)$, $\beta > 1$, otherwise; where u(.) is a von Neumann – Morgenstern (concave) utility function. Note that the minimization corresponds to the lower expectation of the belief function approach.

Consider a "perfect" futures market, that is, a futures market that exactly matches the hedger's demand. Within the current framework, a perfect futures market provides a futures contract the price of which is based on the firm's input with maturity date $t = 1$. Consequently, $p_1 = f_1$. Therefore,

$$\Delta p - x\, \Delta f = (1 - x)p_1 - (p_0 - x\, f_0).$$

To solve the firm's problem, I distinguish two cases, $x \leq 1$ (i.e., underhedge) and $x \geq 1$ (i.e., overhedge) .

6. The Underhedge Case

When $x \leq 1$, the worst-case scenario occurs when m assumes a mass point at p_b. Thus, the firm's hedging problem becomes:

$$\text{Maximize}\ \varepsilon\, E_g\{v((1 - x)p_1 - (p_0 - x\, f_0))\} + (1 - \varepsilon)\, v((1 - x)p_b - (p_0 - x\, f_0))$$

over the feasible set $\{x: x \leq 1\}$.

Note that

$$(1 - x)p_b - (p_0 - x\, f_0) = (1 - x)(p_b - f_0) - (p_0 - f_0).$$

As p_b is the lower bound of $p_1 = f_1$, it is reasonable to assume that $p_b \leq f_0$. Consequently, when $p_0 \geq f_0$, $(1-x)p_b - (p_0 - x f_0) \leq 0$ and $v((1-x)p_b - (p_0 - x f_0)) = \beta u((1-x)p_b - (p_0 - x f_0))$. The firm's objective function is:

$$L = \varepsilon[\int_{k(x)}^{p_u} u(h(x,p_1))g(p_1)dp_1 + \beta \int_{p_b}^{k(x)} u(h(x,p_1))g(p_1)dp_1] + (1-\varepsilon)\beta u(h(x,p_b)),$$

where $k(x) = (p_0 - x f_0)/(1-x)$, $h(x, p_1) = (1-x)p_1 - (p_0 - x f_0)$ and $h(x, p_b) = (1-x)p_b - (p_0 - x f_0)$. Upon taking partial derivative with respect to x,

$$\frac{\partial L}{\partial x} = \varepsilon[\int_{k(x)}^{p_u} u'(h(x,p_1))(f_0 - p_1)g(p_1)dp_1 + \beta \int_{p_b}^{k(x)} u'(h(x,p_1))(f_0 - p_1)g(p_1)dp_1]$$

$$+(1-\varepsilon)\beta u'(h(x,p_b))(f_0 - p_b),$$

where $u'(.)$ denotes the first derivative of $u(.)$. When evaluated at $x = 1$,

$$\left.\frac{\partial L}{\partial x}\right|_{x=1} = \beta u'(f_0 - p_0)[\varepsilon E_g(f_0 - p_1) + (1-\varepsilon)(f_0 - p_b)].$$

Thus, $x = 1$ dominates other feasible solution within the set $\{x: x \leq 1\}$ when

$$\varepsilon E_g(f_0 - p_1) + (1 - \varepsilon)(f_0 - p_b) \geq 0.$$

Otherwise, $x = 1$ is dominated by some other feasible points. These results can be summarized as follows.

Theorem 1: Let x^* denote the optimal futures position and let $p_* = \varepsilon E_g(p_1) + (1 - \varepsilon)p_b$. Then $x^* \geq 1$ when $p_0 > f_0 \geq p_*$ and $x^* < 1$ when $f_0 < \min(p_0, p_*)$.

In case that $x^* < 1$, then it must satisfy $\partial L/\partial x = 0$. Note that $f_0 - k(x) = (f_0 - p_0)/(1 - x) < 0$. Therefore, $f_0 - p_1 < 0$ whenever $p_1 \geq k(x)$. The first term of $\partial L/\partial x$ is negative. As a result, $\partial^2 L/\partial x \partial \beta > 0$ whereas $\partial^2 L/\partial x^2 < 0$ by the second order condition. By comparative static analysis, the following theorem is established.

Theorem 2: When $f_0 < \min(p_0, p_*)$, x^* is an increasing function of β. That is, if the firm is more sensitive to losses, then a larger futures position (although it remains smaller than one) will be undertaken.

When $p_0 \le f_0$, there will be two cases: (I) $v((1-x)p_b - (p_0 - x f_0)) = u((1-x)p_b - (p_0 - x f_0))$ if $0 \le 1 - x \le (f_0 - p_0)/(f_0 - p_b)$ and (II) $v((1-x)p_b - (p_0 - x f_0)) = \beta u((1-x)p_b - (p_0 - x f_0))$, otherwise.

For case (I), $(1-x)(p_b - f_0) - (p_0 - f_0) \ge 0$, and henceforth $(1-x)(p_1 - f_0) - (p_0 - f_0) \ge 0$.

The firm's objective function becomes

$L = \varepsilon E_g u(h(x, p_1)) + (1 - \varepsilon)u(x, p_b)$.

The first partial derivative with respect to x is:

$$\frac{\partial L}{\partial x} = \varepsilon E_g[u'(h(x,p_1))(f_0 - p_1)] + (1-\varepsilon)u'(h(x,p_b))(f_0 - p_b).$$

When evaluated at $x = 1$,

$$\left.\frac{\partial L}{\partial x}\right|_{x=1} = u'(f_0 - p_0)[\varepsilon E_g(f_0 - p_1) + (1-\varepsilon)(f_0 - p_b)].$$

Once again, $x = 1$ dominates other feasible solution within the set $\{x: x \le 1\}$ when

$\varepsilon E_g(f_0 - p_1) + (1 - \varepsilon)(f_0 - p_b) \ge 0$.

Otherwise, $x = 1$ is dominated by some other feasible points. Theorem 3 follows.

Theorem 3: Let x^* denote the optimal futures position. Then $x^* \ge 1$ when $f_0 > \max(p_0, p_*)$ and $x^* < 1$ when $p_0 < f_0 < p_*$.

The remaining case, Case (II) restricts x^* to be smaller than $1 - (f_0 - p_0)/(f_0 - p_b)$ which is in turn smaller than one. It may prevail only when $p_0 < f_0 < p_*$. Hereby the objective function and the first order condition are the same as those held when $p_0 > f_0$. Because the second and third terms of $\partial L/\partial x$ are both positive, again $\partial x^*/\partial \beta$ is positive.

Theorem 4: Suppose that $p_0 < f_0 < p_*$. There will be two possibilities: (a) $x^* < 1 - (f_0 - p_0)/(f_0 - p_b)$; (b) $1 - (f_0 - p_0)/(f_0 - p_b) < x^* < 1$. When (a) prevails, x^* is an increasing function of β. If (b) holds, then β has no effect on x^*.

7. The Overhedge Case

The above section characterizes the optimal futures position when $x \le 1$. Now I turn to the case $x \ge 1$. Herein the worst-case scenario occurs when m(.) assumes a mass point at p_u. The firm's objective function becomes

Maximize $\varepsilon\, E_g\{v((1-x)p_1 - (p_0 - x\, f_0))\} + (1-\varepsilon)\, v((1-x)p_u - (p_0 - x\, f_0))$

over the feasible set $\{x: x \ge 1\}$.

Note that

$$(1-x)p_u - (p_0 - x\, f_0) = (1-x)(p_u - f_0) - (p_0 - f_0).$$

As p_u is the upper bound of $p_1 = f_1$, it is reasonable to assume that $p_u \ge f_0$. Consequently, when $p_0 \ge f_0$, $(1-x)p_b - (p_0 - x\, f_0) \le 0$ and $v((1-x)p_b - (p_0 - x\, f_0)) = \beta\, u((1-x)p_b - (p_0 - x\, f_0))$. The firm's objective function is:

$$L = \varepsilon[\beta \int_{k(x)}^{p_u} u(h(x,p_1))g(p_1)dp_1 + \int_{p_b}^{k(x)} u(h(x,p_1))g(p_1)dp_1] + (1-\varepsilon)\beta u(h(x,p_u)),$$

where k(.) and h(.,.) are defined in the previous section. Upon taking the partial derivative with respect to x,

$$\frac{\partial L}{\partial x} = \varepsilon[\beta \int_{k(x)}^{p_u} u'(h(x,p_1))(f_0 - p_1)g(p_1)dp_1 + \int_{p_b}^{k(x)} u'(h(x,p_1))(f_0 - p_1)g(p_1)dp_1]$$

$$+(1-\varepsilon)\beta u'(h(x,p_u))(f_0 - p_u).$$

When evaluated at $x = 1$,

$$\left.\frac{\partial L}{\partial x}\right|_{x=1} = \beta u'(f_0 - p_0)[\varepsilon E_g(f_0 - p_1) + (1-\varepsilon)(f_0 - p_u)].$$

Consequently, $x = 1$ is a dominant solution over the set $\{x: x \ge 1\}$ if

$\varepsilon\, E_g(f_0 - p_1) + (1-\varepsilon)(f_0 - p_u) \le 0.$

Otherwise, the solution is established at a point smaller than one. These results can be summarized as follows.

Theorem 5: Let x^* denote the optimal futures position and let $p^* = \varepsilon E_g(p_1) + (1 - \varepsilon)p_u$. Then $x^* \leq 1$ when $f_0 < \min(p_0, p^*)$ and $x^* > 1$ when $p_0 > f_0 \geq p^*$.

Note that $f_0 - k(x)$ is positive. Thus, the second term in the $\partial L/\partial x$ expression is positive. By comparative static analysis, Theorem 6 can be established.

Theorem 6: When $p_0 > f_0 \geq p^*$, x^* is a decreasing function of β. That is, if the firm is more sensitive to losses, then a smaller futures position (although it remains larger than one) will be undertaken.

Now, I turn to the case $p_0 \leq f_0$. Herein, (I) $v((1 - x)p_b - (p_0 - x f_0)) = u((1 - x)p_b - (p_0 - x f_0))$ if $0 \geq 1 - x \geq (f_0 - p_0)/(f_0 - p_u)$ and (II) $v((1 - x)p_b - (p_0 - x f_0)) = \beta u((1 - x)p_b - (p_0 - x f_0))$, otherwise. For case (I), $(1 - x)(p_u - f_0) - (p_0 - f_0) \geq 0$, and henceforth $(1 - x)(p_1 - f_0) - (p_0 - f_0) \geq 0$. The firm's objective function becomes

$$L = \varepsilon E_g u(h(x, p_1)) + (1 - \varepsilon)u(x, p_u).$$

The first partial derivative with respect to x is:

$$\frac{\partial L}{\partial x} = \varepsilon E_g[u'(h(x,p_1))(f_0 - p_1)] + (1-\varepsilon)u'(h(x,p_b))(f_0 - p_u).$$

When evaluated at $x = 1$,

$$\left.\frac{\partial L}{\partial x}\right|_{x=1} = u'(f_0 - p_0)[\varepsilon E_g(f_0 - p_1) + (1-\varepsilon)(f_0 - p_u)].$$

Once again, $x = 1$ is a dominant solution within the set $\{x: x \geq 1\}$ when

$$\varepsilon E_g(f_0 - p_1) + (1 - \varepsilon)(f_0 - p_u) \leq 0.$$

Following similar analyses to the previous section, Theorems 7 and 8 can be derived.

Theorem 7: Let x^* denote the optimal futures position. Then $x^* \leq 1$ when $p_0 < f_0 < p^*$ and $x^* > 1$ when $f_0 > \max(p_0, p^*)$.

Theorem 8: Suppose that $f_0 > \max(p_0, p^*)$. There will be two possibilities: (a) $1 < x^* < 1 - (f_0 - p_0)/(f_0 - p_u)$; (b) $1 - (f_0 - p_0)/(f_0 - p_u) < x^*$. When (b) prevails, x^* is a decreasing function of β. If (a) holds, then β has no effect on x^*.

8. Optimal Futures Position

Upon combining the results from the above two sections, the optimal futures position can be derived. This is described in the following theorem.

Theorem 9: Let $p_* = \varepsilon\, E(p_1) + (1 - \varepsilon)\, p_b$ and let $p^* = \varepsilon\, E(p_1) + (1 - \varepsilon)\, p_u$ such that $p_* < p^*$. The optimal futures position depends upon the parameter configuration:

If $p_0 < f_0 < p_* < p^*$, then $x^* < 1$; (2) If $f_0 < p_0 < p_* < p^*$, then $x^* < 1$;

If $p_0 < p_* < f_0 < p^*$, then $x^* = 1$; (4) If $f_0 < p_* < p_0 < p^*$, then $x^* < 1$;

If $p_* < p_0 < f_0 < p^*$, then $x^* = 1$; (6) If $p_* < f_0 < p_0 < p^*$, then $x^* = 1$;

If $p_0 < p_* < p^* < f_0$, then $x^* > 1$; (8) If $f_0 < p_* < p^* < p_0$, then $x^* < 1$;

If $p_* < p_0 < p^* < f_0$, then $x^* > 1$; (10) If $p_* < f_0 < p^* < p_0$, then $x^* = 1$;

(11) If $p_* < p^* < f_0 < p_0$, then $x^* > 1$; (12) If $p_* < p^* < p_0 < f_0$, then $x^* > 1$.

Moreover, when $x^* > 1$, an increase in β leads to a decrease in x^*. If $x^* < 1$, then an increase in β causes x^* to increase.

The above theorem indicates that inertia prevails in the firm's hedging decision. That is, there is a wide range of parameter configurations within which the firm will adopt the conventional hedging strategy: sell the same amount of futures contract as committed in the forward market. In absence of Knightian uncertainty, the conventional strategy is almost always sub-optimal. Considerations of Knightian uncertainty support the widespread adoption of such strategy.

Loss aversion has no effect on the prevalence of the inertia. However, when the optimal strategy is underhedge or overhedge, loss aversion causes the firm not to deviate too far from the conventional strategy. The sensitivity to losses induce the firm not to undertake great risk and, therefore, to abide by the conventional strategy as close as possible.

9. Conclusions and Extensions

This paper considers the futures hedging problem under Knightian uncertainty and loss aversion. Assuming a perfect futures market, the optimal futures position is characterized. It is found that inertia prevails: there is a wide range of parameter configurations under which the conventional one-to-one hedge strategy is optimal. In case the optimal strategy deviates from the conventional one, loss aversion acts to reduce the deviation. A firm more sensitive to losses will not adopt a strategy far from the conventional one.

In general, the futures market is not perfect. There is basis risk (i.e., $p_1 \neq f_1$) due to mismatches in timing or input grades. The hedging problem becomes much more complicated as a joint density for spot and futures prices needs to be introduced. Lien (1999a) considers Knightian uncertainty in the conditional density function. Following this approach, it is found that the conclusions derived under a perfect futures market assumption remain valid qualitatively in the presence of basis risk.

References

Benartzi, S. and Thaler, R. H. (1995): "Myopic Loss Aversion and the Equity Premium Puzzle," *Quarterly Journal of Economics*, 110: 75-92.

Dempster, A. P. (1967): "Upper and Lower Probabilities Induced by a Multivariate Mapping," *Annals of Mathematical Statistics*, 38: 325 – 339.

Dow, J. and Werlang, S. (1992): "Uncertainty Aversion, Risk Aversion, and the Optimal Choice of Portfolio," *Econometrica*, 60: 197 – 204.

Epstein, L. G. and Wang, T. (1994): "Intertemporal Asset Pricing under Knightian Uncertainty," *Econometrica*, 62: 283 – 322.

Kahneman, D., Knetsch, J. and Thaler, R. (1990): "Experimental Tests of the Endowment Effect and the Coase Theorem," *Journal of Political Economy*, 98: 1325-1348.

Lence, S. G. (1995): "On the Optimal Hedge under Unbiased Futures Prices," *Economics Letters*, 47: 385 – 388.

Lien, D. (1999a): "Production and Hedging under Knightian Uncertainty," *Journal of Futures Markets*, forthcoming.

Lien, D. (1999b): Loss Aversion and Futures Hedging. Mimeo. University of Kansas.

Rigotti, L. (1998): Imprecise Beliefs in a Principal-Agent Model. CentER D.P. 98128, Tilburg University.

Shafer, G. (1976): A Mathematical Theory of Evidence. Princeton University Press, Priceton, New Jersey.

Thaler, R., Tversky, A., Kahneman, D., and Schwartz, A. (1997): The Effect of Myopia and Loss Aversion on Risk Taking: An Experimental Test," *Quarterly Journal of Economics*, 112: 647-661.

Tversky, A. and Kahneman, D. (1992): "Advances in Prospect Theory: Cumulative Representation of Uncertainty," *Journal of Risk and Uncertainty*, 5: 297-323.

Wasserman, L. A. (1990): "Prior Envelopes Based on Belief Functions," *Annals of Statistics*, 18: 454 – 464.

www.ingramcontent.com/pod-product-compliance
Ingram Content Group UK Ltd.
Pitfield, Milton Keynes, MK11 3LW, UK
UKHW020346220926
15297UKWH00021BA/147
* 9 7 8 3 6 6 2 0 0 3 3 0 5 *